Automating Instructional Design

Concepts and Issues

Automating Instructional Design
Concepts and Issues

EDITORS

J. Michael Spector
Armstrong Laboratory, Human Resources Directorate
Brooks AFB, Texas

Martha C. Polson
Institute of Cognitive Science, University of Colorado
Boulder, Colorado

Daniel J. Muraida
Armstrong Laboratory, Human Resources Directorate
Brooks AFB, Texas

Educational Technology Publications
Englewood Cliffs, New Jersey 07632

Library of Congress Cataloging-in-Publication Data

Automating insructional design : concepts and issues / editors, J.
Michael Spector, Martha C. Polson, Daniel J. Muraida.
    p.   cm.
    Includes bibliographical references and index.
    ISBN 0-87778-259-8
    1. Instructional systems—Design—Data processing.   2. Computer-
assisted instruction.   I. Spector, J. Michael.   II. Polson, Martha
C. (Martha Campbell)   III. Muraida, Daniel J.
    LB1028.38.A94   1993   92-46057
    371.3'078—dc20   CIP

Printed in the United States of America.

Library of Congress Catalog Card Number:
92-46057.

International Standard Book Number:
0-87778-259-8.

First Printing: April 1993.

Preface

Devising intellectual tasks that explore the limits of computer capabilities has come to be an endeavor of enduring and widespread effort. Recognition of the possibilities of inventions of this sort intrigues and challenges many kinds of people—investigators of cognitive psychology and artificial intelligence, computer scientists, designers of practical systems that do intellectual work. Computer-based operations have been applied in a variety of fields, covering a broad spectrum of human undertakings from chess playing to astronomical prediction, and from simple arithmetic computation to medical diagnosis. It is difficult to imagine the ultimate attainments of trends such as these.

The writings in this book express the thoughts of a number of people who are giving consideration to a computerized basis for the intellectual task of designing instruction. The focus of interest here is instruction on the maintenance of aircraft and their installed systems—mechanical, electrical, electronic. In contrast to the frequent practice in manufacturing and service industries of the civilian sector, instructional designers in the Air Force are not highly trained in this specialty. Comparatively, they are "novices," although usually they are experienced in the subject matter of aircraft maintenance. The strategies of instructional design must therefore be taught with the assumption of scanty prerequisite skills and little background knowledge of learning processes.

Designed to address this problem was Project AIDA (Advanced Instructional Design Advisor), originally proposed in conceptual form by Dr. Michael Spector while on a research grant at the Air Force Armstrong Laboratory (Human Resources Directorate) with Dr. Scott Newcomb's Instructional Design Branch. The problem of courseware authoring was identified as a source of difficulty and expense in designing materials for courses in a variety of instructional settings of the Air Force. A computer-based tool was proposed to assist in the instructional design process, with the objective of producing consistently effective instructional materials with reduced course development time. AIDA would incorporate prescriptive advice about lesson and course authoring, based upon the findings and theories of knowledge, learning, and instruction.

As development of the AIDA concept proceeded, it was thought desirable to contemplate a variety of tools, rather than a single one. Some would automate processes that were established and well understood. Others would provide advice to authors engaged in designing effective instructional materials for a variety of media. Tools might be content-free, and thus capable of application to a number of different kinds of learning tasks, while others would be special-purpose tools, using a shared database of course and content information. In its early stage of development, the AIDA concept had to plan for a good deal of flexibility. This quality was found to be of continuing value throughout the life of the project, contributing to the formulation of multiple research approaches to the automation of instructional design.

In line with this thinking, the beginning period of operation of the project was devoted to explorations of systematic knowledge in the fields of epistemology, cognitive psychology, artificial intelligence, computer systems, and instructional design. This was done by assembling a team of experts in these fields, seven in all: Henry Halff, David Merrill, Harry O'Neil, Martha Polson, Charles Reigeluth, Bob Tennyson, and myself. These were people with a number of different viewpoints about learning and instruction, which made for lively discussions when we were assembled. Other contributors to the formulation of the AIDA concept were a number of military advisors representing the three services. Management of the project was undertaken by Mei Associates of Lexington, Massachusetts, with Al Hickey as the principal investigator.

Meetings of consultants and advisors were set in motion by concept papers contributed by each of the consultant members. Discussions ranged broadly over a host of issues relevant to the design and delivery of automated systems for instructional design, and systems for delivering advice and guidance to such a process. The range of system features considered in these discussions is broad: the nature of task analysis, the description and classification of learning objectives, the development of instructional strategies and a taxonomy of strategies, the means of presenting instruction, including text, graphics, and simulations. In conducting these discussions, the primary aim was not to propose new technologies, but rather to assure that suitable consideration would be given to current advances and innovations.

The papers and discussions that have emanated from the early months of project AIDA are set forth in this volume. Some ideas stick out as being truly novel, and therefore worthy of further exploration in research. Others can be seen as having had their corners knocked off, and consequently as becoming more rounded and centrist. Over time, as the project progresses, these ideas will form a solid basis for the development of effective technology for systems of instruction.

Robert M. Gagné

Introduction

J. Michael Spector

Background

The primary purpose of the instructional design process is to structure the environment so as to provide a learner with conditions which will support learning processes (Gagné, Briggs, Wager, 1988). When learning goals are simple and delivery media are restricted to lecture and blackboard, this process is easily manageable. However, as learning goals grow in complexity and media choices proliferate, the complexity of the instructional design process generates a number of difficult problems.

The process of instructional systems development (ISD) is intended to respond to such problems. ISD has been described by a number of authors (e.g., Dick & Carey, 1990; Tennyson, 1991). The description typically takes place at the task level in terms of identifying learner characteristics, analyzing task and instructional requirements, developing learning objectives and test items, specifying instructional strategies, producing and delivering the instruction, conducting formative and summative evaluations, and maintaining the instructional materials.

Several models of this ISD process exist (Andrews & Goodson, 1980; Tennyson, 1991). Most ISD models typically divide the process into five phases: analysis, design, production (development), implementation (delivery), and maintenance. Some authors group the process into three phases: front-end analysis, design/development/delivery, and rear-end analysis (Spector, 1990). Many instructional scientists maintain that however the phases are listed or specified they should be regarded as interrelated and cyclic (cf. Van Merriënboer et al., 1991; Tennyson, 1991). Few, if any, working ISD models successfully integrate all of these activities. Few, if any, provide specific planning and guidance for optimal use of new interactive technologies. One aim of this book is to begin to correct this situation.

As the number of students receiving computer-based instruction increases, the importance of being systematic in the development process becomes more evident. As the delivery of the instruction is automated, following a sound and systematic development process becomes crucial to success. Computers are not nearly as adept as human instructors in compensating for poorly conceived lessons.

This book is concerned primarily with the process of designing instruction for computer-based settings. Our emphasis is mainly on the middle phases of the ISD process, especially as they pertain to the design of effective computer-based instructional materials. We devote some attention in Part III to the first and last phases of the process, since we agree that all phases should be integrated if the process is to be truly useful in fostering learning.

Traditional instructional design is being challenged by constructivism (the entire May 1991 issue of *Educational Technology* is devoted to this challenge). Perkins (1991) represents the constructivist view as follows:

> In particular, learners do not just take in and store up information. They make tentative interpretations of experience and go on to elaborate and test those interpretations. Even when the learning process appears to be relatively straightforward, say a matter of learning a new friend's name or a term in a foreign language, constructive processes operate: Candidate mental structures are formed, elaborated, and tested, until a satisfactory structure emerges.
>
> If learning has this constructive character inherently, it follows that teaching practices need to be supportive of the construction that must occur. The constructivist critique of much conventional educational practice is that it is not especially supportive of the work of construction that needs to be done in the minds of the learners.

Perkins goes on to claim that nearly all contemporary educators and psychologists are constructivists in some sense, however weak. The reader of this volume will certainly find some support for the general notion of constructivism, most noticeably in the chapters by Kintsch and Polson.

One of our general assumptions is consistent with the above constructivist critique: To be effective, CBI should be designed to actively involve learners. In addition, we believe that advanced interactive technologies (such as digitized video and audio) offer new kinds of opportunities for learner involvement, but that optimal use of these technologies awaits R&D of the kind proposed in this volume.

We have chosen to focus on instructional design for computer-based settings for two reasons: 1) there already exists a significant amount of literature and research on instructional design for instructor-based settings; and 2) since there aren't many experts in this area, computer-based instruction (CBI) is often poorly designed and ineffective.

Our specific focus is on the automation of instructional design, development, and delivery. Once there is a commitment to deliver instruction by means of a computer, it is natural for much of the course development (production) to involve the computer. Then there occurs the natural inclination to wonder just how much of the entire ISD process can be automated. Specifically, can instructional design be automated? How? What issues arise? This book can be considered an attempt to provide substantive answers to these questions.

We construe CBI in the largest and most generic sense. We use the term CBI interchangeably with CBT (computer-based training), CAI (computer-assisted instruction), and CAL (computer-assisted learning), whereas other writers take pains to make these distinctions (Carter, 1990). We consider all to have an important common element: the use of a computer to deliver instruction. When this is the case, there are significant consequences for the design of the instruction to be delivered. What works well in a lecture setting may not work well in a computer-based setting; for example, provocative questions and open-ended responses are not easily managed by a computer program. Likewise, what works well in a computer setting may be difficult or impossible to replicate in a lecture; for example, an interactive simulation is not easily set up in the classroom.

As Professor Gagné indicates in the Preface, the Air Force has recognized the design of effective CBI as a problem area. The Air Training Command has called on the Air Force research community to devote effort and attention to the problem of developing guidelines for the authoring of effective courseware (instructional materials to be delivered by a computer). Most of the papers collected in this volume were originally written in response to this need. We believe, however, that the implications for education and training go well beyond military settings.

As a consequence, we have taken those initial papers, asked the authors to make appropriate changes, and added papers by Muraida/Spector/O'Neil/Marlino and Reigeluth to complete our exploration of the issues involved in automating the process of instructional design. Because this is a collection of papers, there are occasional differences in terminology (e.g., Halff and Tennyson use 'advisory system' quite differently). These differences are rare and should cause no difficulty in making coherent sense of these papers.

Automating Instructional Design

There are a number of reasons for automating a process. Some of the more obvious reasons include those in the following three groups:

Group I:

1. The process is tedious.
2. The process is time-consuming.
3. The process is repetitive.

Group II:

4. Human intervention in the process affects its integrity.
5. The process is simple and potentially dehumanizing.
6. The cost of a human processor is prohibitive.
7. The quality of a machine processor is necessary.

Group III:

8. The process is difficult for humans.
9. The process requires difficult-to-acquire expertise.
10. Human processors introduce unacceptable errors.

What, then, is the motivation for automating the process of designing and developing instruction intended for delivery by computer-based systems? The first group of three reasons may apply in many cases: Courseware design and development are time-consuming, tedious, and somewhat repetitive. There are lesson plans to develop, lesson flowcharts to draw, and storyboards to create. Such tasks could serve as adequate justification for automation. However, a tool developed in response to those three needs alone would not necessarily improve courseware; it might serve to make courseware production more cost-effective, however. Several such automated instructional design toolsets have been built. We do not explore them in this volume.

The second group of four reasons do not apply to courseware design and development. Human intervention in some form is most likely necessary in instructional design. Perhaps selecting test questions may be an area in which human intervention introduces an unacceptable bias, and machine generated test items might be an improvement. In general, however, maintaining the integrity of the process is not the central issue. Instructional design is certainly not a simple process, so we need not be concerned with the dehumanizing effect of routine activity. Human designers and developers may be expensive, but educational specialists are rarely paid prohibitive salaries. Because the automation of instructional design and development is not a tried and proven enterprise, there is no guarantee that machine processors will improve the quality of courseware. Although there is that hope, we are not in a position to argue that the quality of automated instructional design and development will offer an improvement.

Let's consider the three remaining motives for automation: The process is difficult for humans; the process requires special expertise; human designers and developers commit too many unacceptable errors. An automated tool developed with these three motives in mind would look very different from one that merely shifted the bureaucratic burdens of the process from humans to machines. Such a tool would probably need to contain some form of intelligence or expertise. It would address the more serious issues involved with designing and developing courseware, and not merely the more tedious tasks. For example, such a system might advise courseware developers what type of graphic might be effective in a particular setting, or how to make use of a computer-based simulation, or when to provide learner control. It is this sort of instructional design tool that forms the subject matter for this volume.

Is there a need for such a tool? If so, could an intelligent courseware design advisor be built and how would it work? The essays collected in this volume proceed on these two assumptions: 1) there is a need for a tool which automates the design and development of courseware; and 2) the need is to incorporate instructional design expertise with regard to the selection, sequencing, and presentation of materials in support of various lesson objectives and subject-matter domains.

It is not especially difficult to defend the claim that there is a need to automate instructional design and development expertise due to a lack of human experts. Expert CBI designers are scarce. There are few human experts in the area of computer-based instructional design science for two reasons: 1) computer-aided instruction is relatively new; and 2) learning theory has only recently been re-born as a result of contributions from cognitive science. Perhaps of greater significance is the invaluable knowledge about learning and instruction that results when theories are forced into the detailed articulation required by the process of computer implementation (Glaser, 1990).

Another way to indicate the need for an automated instructional design advisor is to review the available courseware authoring tools, environments, and languages. The March/April 1991 issue of *Instruction Delivery Systems* contains a summary of 89 authoring systems. What is noticeably absent from this impressive collection of tools is an intelligent tool which can present instructional design expertise relevant to specific instructional settings and users. IDE (Pirolli & Russell, 1991) approaches this aim, but it is not commercially available and requires a great deal of instructional design expertise on the part of the user. The essays included in this volume describe the concept of such a tool along with the issues and obstacles that stand in the way of its construction.

Principles of Instructional Theory*

In order to establish a common starting point and foundation, we mention here a basic and well-established distinction from cognitive learning theory along with twelve instructional principles that are widely known and accepted. These principles are not specific to the design of CBI. Rather, they serve as a point of departure for elaborating more specific principles appropriate to the automation of instructional design for computer-based settings. [These principles were originally part of a paper written by Professor Gagné as part of the Air Force Armstrong Laboratory's Advanced Instructional Design Advisor project.]

An important basic distinction from cognitive science is that between declarative and procedural knowledge (Anderson, 1983; Shiffrin & Dumais, 1981). This distinction is basic because it involves different cognitive structures with implications for learning and instruction. For example, Anderson (1983) postulates that declarative knowledge is stored in human memory in the form of a semantic associative network, whereas procedural knowledge is stored in the form of compiled production rules. Issues concerning the attainment of automaticity arise with regard to procedural learning tasks. We believe that many learning tasks involve both types of knowledge. However, procedural learning tasks pose particular problems for CBI design, especially in the area of creating effective computer-based simulations. As a consequence, Part III emphasizes issues related to automating the design of CBI which supports procedural knowledge.

The principles listed below are intended to be those concerning which there is much agreement and virtually no disagreement among writers who have put forward theories or models of instruction. The theories represented here can be found in C. M. Reigeluth's, *Instructional-Design Theories and Models: An Overview of Their Current Status* (1983).

*This section was contributed by Prof. Robert M. Gagné.

The theories from which common principles of instructional design are to be drawn are as follows, identified by the name or phrase by which they are commonly known:

a. Gagné-Briggs Theory—R. M. Gagné & L. J. Briggs
b. Behavioral Approach—G. L. Gropper
c. Algo-Heuristic Theory—L. N. Landa
d. Structural Learning Theory—J. M. Scandura
e. Inquiry Teaching—A. Collins & A. L. Stevens
f. Component Display Theory—M. D. Merrill
g. Elaboration Theory—C. M. Reigeluth
h. Motivational Theory—J. M. Keller

Some Differences

The task of finding common principles of instruction has to be done against a framework of features that make the theories incoordinate in several respects. Prominent differences are these:

(1) *Single versus multiple learning outcomes.* Some of the theories focus exclusively on a single kind of outcome. Some deal with the learning of verbal information (*declarative knowledge*), or solely with the learning of procedures. Others aim for a number of different kinds of learning objectives.

(2) *Micro-strategies versus macro-strategies.* Some theories are oriented to the organization of large units of instruction, such as courses or course segments. These macro-strategies contrast with micro-strategies, focusing on relatively small units such as lessons and lesson components, and aimed at single objectives such as a concept or a procedure. Most of these theories deal with micro-strategies.

(3) *Discovery learning versus expository teaching.* One of these theories exclusively uses instruction that requires the learner to arrive at the proposition to be learned by "putting together" in a novel fashion items of knowledge already possessed in memory. Most theories allow for the occurrence of such discovery learning at some points during instruction. With greater or lesser degrees of emphasis, they employ questioning techniques designed to facilitate the discovery of what is to be learned.

Design Principles

According to design theories, these are the principles that will yield optimal learning:

1. DIFFERENT LEARNING OBJECTIVES REQUIRE DIFFERENT INSTRUCTIONAL STRATEGIES. Instruction for removing insu-

lation from the end of a wire is different from instruction for knowing the names and functions of the components of an electronic circuit. Instruction on the origins of the American Revolution is different from instruction on analyzing cases in business law. Instruction aimed at reducing the use of harmful drugs is different from instruction on diagnosing illness.

2. FIVE DIFFERENT TYPES OF LEARNING OBJECTIVES ARE THE FOLLOWING (Particular instructional strategies that are most distinctive for each type of objective are listed):

a. *Verbal knowledge* (declarative knowledge). Relate to organized knowledge already known. Use spaced review.

b. *Concepts*. Provide definition, examples and non-examples, and practice in identifying new examples.

c. *Procedural rules*. Assure that component parts of a procedure are mastered before the total skill is tried.

d. *Motor skills*. Practice with reinforcement.

e. *Attitudes*. Demonstrate using human models.

3. BEGIN WITH AN EVENT THAT AROUSES AND SUSTAINS LEARNER INTEREST. This may be any attention-getting stimulus. Often, it is an introductory message or demonstration that "grabs" the learner's conscious attention.

4. COMMUNICATE CLEARLY WHAT THE LEARNER MUST LEARN TO DO. This communication may be a statement, a demonstration, or both. It should include an indication of the usefulness of the learned performance to the learner.

5. STIMULATE RECOLLECTION OF PREVIOUSLY LEARNED RELEVANT KNOWLEDGE. If the learning objective is procedural, this may be components or prerequisites. If the objective is declarative, previously learned knowledge may be more general, related or analogous. If the learning objective involves a motor skill, previously learned knowledge may be part-skills. This principle is an example of the requirement for different learning strategies, in accordance with principle number one.

6. MAKE THE STIMULUS ASPECT OF THE TASK READILY PERCEPTIBLE. Avoid uncertainties and ambiguities in what is displayed, visually or aurally. If the display tends to be obscure or fuzzy, make its main features prominent by enhancement or distortion that is gradually removed.

7. STATEMENT OF RULE-THEN-EXAMPLE OR EXAMPLE-THEN-RULE FOLLOWED BY LEARNER PERFORMANCE. BOTH RULE AND EXAMPLE SHOULD BE PRESENTED, BUT THEIR ORDER IS NOT CRITICAL. Note that this principle applies only to the learning of concepts and rules, not to verbal knowledge. A general rule (or defined concept) is communicated to the learner, and followed by a concrete instance as an example. The learner is asked to respond to the example,

thus applying the rule or definition. When discovery learning is employed, the order of presentation of rule-then-example is reversed to example-then-rule. Learner performance should follow in either case.

8. GUIDE THE LEARNING THROUGH ELABORATIONS. Mainly, elaboration means extending the meaning of what is presented by relating it to prior knowledge. Sometimes, this is done by means of pictures or diagrams; sometimes, by suggesting analogies; sometimes, by reminding the learner of highly familiar bodies of knowledge. Questioning techniques are particularly good illustrations of learning guidance by the use of elaborations.

9. VERIFY INITIAL LEARNING BY LEARNER PERFORMANCE. Arrange one or two "trials" in which learner performance is called for in the absence of prompting or tutelage. Before extensive practice is continued, there should be an occasion in which the learner "shows what he can do."

10. PROVIDE VARIED PRACTICE WITH CORRECTIVE FEEDBACK. Virtually all theories agree that some amount of additional practice should be provided following the initial "trial." To allow for the action of reinforcement, practice trials should include knowledge of results and corrections when appropriate. Varied practice implies the use of examples that are varied in content; also, it means embedding the examples in varied contexts.

11. COMMUNICATE THE RELATION BETWEEN WHAT IS BEING LEARNED AND HOW IT WILL BE USED. A part of what is to be learned and stored is a scenario that connects learner performance in the learning situation with projected performance on the job. As theories usually recognize, such knowledge can be a major factor in the transfer of learning to whatever situation requires the use of what has been learned.

12. ARRANGE OCCASIONS THAT REQUIRE RETRIEVAL. Retention of what has been learned demands several additional periods of practice, spaced over time, and in varied situational contexts.

Organization of This Volume

This book is divided into three parts: 1) Cognitive Learning Theory & Instructional Design, 2) Approaches to Instructional Design, and 3) R&D Issues in Automating Instructional Design. Each part is briefly described below.

Part I

The purpose of Part I is to provide theoretical foundations for the automation of instructional design. These theoretical foundations in large part come from cognitive science. There have been significant advances in our understanding of the mind and learning as a result of progress in cognitive science. Most theorists accept the distinctions between declarative, procedural, and causal (or contextual) knowledge already mentioned. Polson and Kintsch agree that the organization of knowledge in memory determines its accessibility and the depth of understanding. As a consequence, instruction should be systematically designed to link new knowledge structures to existing knowledge structures and to provide multiple pathways for access and retrieval.

Polson provides a preliminary model of cognition as a starting point. She argues that our knowledge of cognition is incomplete, and, as a result, there is no unified and complete theory of cognition that can be used to provide a solid foundation for instructional design. The best that we can hope to do is to incorporate the most well-established theoretical foundations into instructional science. Two such sources are Anderson's ACT* Theory and W. Kintsch's Theory of Discourse Comprehension. Anderson's theory is directed at procedural knowledge, whereas Kintsch's theory is aimed primarily at declarative knowledge. Both theories have led to efforts to build intelligent and non-intelligent tutors; in short, both have been used to guide instructional design efforts. Although our knowledge of cognitive science is incomplete, Polson agrees with Glaser that constructing automated instructional design advisors will provide an important source for experimental data to help advance our understanding of human learning.

Reigeluth provides an up-to-date summary of instructional design theories and models. His review of cognitively oriented instructional design theories suggests a number of approaches to automating instructional design, thereby providing a nice transition to Part II.

Part II

The purpose of Part II is to provide a variety of approaches to the automation of instructional design. Halff provides a clear distinction between two kinds of approaches: advisory and generative. Advisory approaches devise new instructional strategies based on input gathered from users. Generative approaches automate existing strategies. Halff argues that only generative approaches can be automated with any expectation of success, and generative systems will involve tradeoffs and limitations.

Three specific generative approaches are then discussed in detail: 1) Gagné's system for providing design guidance, 2) Merrill's expert system built around transaction shells, and 3) Tennyson's intelligent tutoring system for instructional design. Other approaches have been described in the literature (e.g., a critiquing system, Duchastel, 1990; a planning system,

Brecht, McCalla, Greer, & Jones, 1989; an expert toolset, Pirolli & Russell, 1991).

The three systems described here, however, represent the full range of possibilities. Gagné's system is probably the least complex and most easily implemented (Ford Aerospace's TIPS approximates an early version of what Gagné has in mind). Merrill's system claims to be the most revolutionary, being based on a second generation of instructional design and explicitly incorporating the latest object-oriented design techniques from computer science. Tennyson's system is clearly the most ambitious in that his proposal includes an intelligent tutoring system (ITS) for the domain of instructional design. While there has been some success with ITS technology for more well-defined domains, it is not clear that we know enough about instructional design to build an intelligent instructional design tutor.

Much of the discussion in Part III is directed at the issues that arise when an attempt is made to implement Merrill's kind of system. Most of these problems also arise with a system like Tennyson's. Some of the problems do not arise in Gagné's system, nor would they arise in Duchastel's critiquing system (Duchastel, 1990), IDE (Pirolli & Russell, 1991), or Expert CML (Jones & Wipond, 1990), since these place greater decision-making responsibilities on the users (instructional designers).

Part III

The purpose of Part III is to review the research and development issues that arise when one attempts to implement one or more of the approaches introduced in Part II. It is here that task analysis and evaluation issues arise. Polson proposes a cognitively-based task analysis that could provide input to any of the systems discussed in Part II. Muraida, Spector, O'Neil, & Marlino discuss evaluation issues that are likely to arise with regard to such systems. The evaluation techniques that were actually applied to Merrill's transaction shells are also discussed. These techniques are significant in their own right because they involve a process for cognitive modeling of expert human activity when there are a limited number of subjects (i.e., there are not very many CBI design experts).

The issue of selecting mental models to support instruction runs throughout Part III. This is an area which separates the kinds of systems introduced in Part II. If the conclusion of subsequent R&D efforts is that providing advice concerning mental model selection in particular instructional settings is too difficult for automation, then this area should be left in control of the human decision-maker/designer; the best that could be offered would be general reminders, examples, and rules-of-thumb (i.e., Gagné's kind of guidance).

Friedman makes this point extremely well with regard to advice concerning types of graphics to use in support of particular instructional content. We are far from knowing enough to construct an automated graphics advisor for instructional design.

Reading Guidance

The following chapters can be read alone and viewed as isolated treatments of particular concepts and issues involved with automating CBI design and development. However, their real value is that they present a full range of views concerning the possibilities and problems in automating instructional design and development. The reader should be left with the discomforting feeling that we cannot automate the instructional design process and expect to make CBI more effective until we learn more about the details of various cognitive learning mechanisms in a wide variety of settings. However, it is unlikely that we will learn what we need to know about human learning in CBI settings without building and evaluating several different kinds of automated instructional design advisors, most especially those which attempt to automate as much of the design process as possible.

References

Anderson, J. R. (1983). *The architecture of cognition*. Cambridge, MA: Harvard University Press.

Andrews, D. H., & Goodson, L. A. (1980). A comparative analysis of models of instructional design. *Journal of Instructional Development, 3*(4), 2–16.

Brecht (Wasson), B., McCalla, G., Greer, J., & Jones, M. (1989). Planning the contents of instruction. *Proceedings of the 4th International Conference on AI and Education*, 32–41, Amsterdam.

Carter, J. (1990). *The interactive courseware decision handbook*. (Contract No. F4168989D0252). Randolph AFB, TX: HQ Air Training Command.

Dick, W., & Carey, L. M. (1990). *The systematic design of instruction*. Glenview, IL: Scott Foresman.

Duchastel, P. C. (1990). Cognitive designs for instructional design. *Instructional Science, 19*(6), 437–444.

Gagné, R. M., Briggs, L., & Wager, W. (1988). *Principles of instructional design* (3rd ed.) New York: Holt, Rinehart, and Winston.

Glaser, R. (1990). The reemergence of learning theory in instructional technology. *American Psychologist, 45*, 29–39.

Jones, M., & Wipond, K. (1990). Curriculum and knowledge representation in a knowledge-based system for curriculum development. *Educational Technology, 30*(5), 7–14.

Perkins, D. N. (1991). Technology meets constructivism: Do they make a marriage? *Educational Technology, 31*(5), 18–23.

Pirolli, P., & Russell, D. M. (1991). Instructional design environment: Technology to support design problem solving. *Instructional Science, 19*(2), 121–144.

Reigeluth, C. M. (1983). *Instructional design theories and models: An overview of their current status*. Hillsdale, NJ: Lawrence Erlbaum Associates.

Shiffrin, R. M., & Dumais, S. T. (1981). The development of automatism. In J. R. Anderson (Ed.), *Cognitive skills and their acquisition*. Hillsdale, NJ: Lawrence Erlbaum Associates.

Spector, J. M. (1990). *Designing and developing an advanced instructional design advisor* (AFHRL-TP-90-52). Brooks AFB, TX: Armstrong Laboratory.

Tennyson, R. D. (1991). Framework specifications document for an instructional systems development expert system. In R. M. Gagné, R. D. Tennyson, & D. J. Gettman, *Designing an advanced instructional design advisor: Conceptual frameworks (vol. 5 of 6)* (AL-TP-1991-0017-Vol-5). Brooks AFB, TX: Armstrong Laboratory.

van Merriënboer, J. J. G., Jelsma, O., & Paas, F. G. W. C. (1991). Training for reflective expertise: A four-part component instructional design model for complex cognitive skills. Paper presented at the annual meeting of the American Educational Research Association, Chicago, IL.

About the Authors

EDITORS

J. Michael Spector, Ph.D., is Senior Scientist, Instructional Design Branch, Armstrong Laboratory (Human Resources Directorate).

Martha C. Polson, Ph.D., is Assistant Director, Institute of Cognitive Science, University of Colorado.

Daniel J. Muraida, Ph.D., is AIDA Project Manager, Technical Training R&D Division, Armstrong Laboratory (Human Resources Directorate).

PREFACE

Professor Robert M. Gagné, Ph.D., is Senior Research Fellow, Armstrong Laboratory (Human Resources Directorate).

CONTRIBUTORS

Alinda Friedman, Ph.D., is with the department of Psychology, University of Alberta, Edmonton, Alberta, Canada.

Robert M. Gagné, Ph.D., is Senior Research Fellow, Armstrong Laboratory (Human Resources Directorate), Brooks AFB, Texas.

Henry M. Halff, Ph.D., is Chief Scientist, Halff Resources, Inc., Arlington, Virginia.

Eileen Kintsch, Ph.D., is Research Associate, Institute of Cognitive Science, University of Colorado, Boulder.

Mary R. Marlino, Ph.D., is Director of Educational Technology, United States Air Force Academy.

M. David Merrill, Ph.D., is Professor of Instructional Technology, Utah State University, Logan.

Daniel J. Muraida, Ph.D., is Research Psychologist, AL/HRTC, Brooks AFB, Texas.

Martha C. Polson, Ph.D., is Assistant Director, Institute of Cognitive Science, University of Colorado, Boulder.

Harold F. O'Neil, Jr., Ph.D., is Professor of Educational Psychology, University of Southern California, Los Angeles.

Charles M. Reigeluth, is Professor, Indiana University, Bloomington.

J. Michael Spector, Ph.D., is Senior Scientist, AL/HRTC, Brooks AFB, Texas.

Robert D. Tennyson, Ph.D., is Professor of Educational Psychology, University of Minnesota, Minneapolis.

Contents

Automating Instructional Design

Concepts and Issues

Part I

An Overview

Introductory Remarks

Martha C. Polson

As pointed out in the general introduction to this volume, this section is intended to provide, from the fields of cognitive science and instructional design, the necessary background and overview knowledge for understanding the later chapters. The first chapter, *Cognitive Theory as a Basis for Instructional Design*, was written in response to a request from the development team for a "general theory of knowledge" which could serve as the theoretical motivation for an Advanced Instructional Design Advisor (AIDA). As the chapter makes clear, no such theory exists, and if it did exist, it would take several volumes to describe. Given that limitation, in responding to the request I chose to emphasize the relative narrow area of knowledge representation and how concepts concerning the representation of knowledge impact upon our theories of how people acquire knowledge and ways to facilitate that acquisition. In later chapters as the other authors talk about networks, frames, schemas, transactions, mental models, etc., it becomes apparent why theories about how knowledge is represented are central to building a computer-based instructional design aid.

The second chapter, *Principles of Instruction from Research on Human Cognition*, by Eileen Kintsch, was also generated at the request of the development team. It began as a list of ten principles of instructional theory with a short discussion of each and was later elaborated into a chapter. The purpose of the original list was to provide specific educational principles which could guide the development of an AIDA. The current chapter consists of two sections. The first part is an overview of the learning process from the constructivist perspective and some general instructional implications drawn from that viewpoint. The second section offers specific suggestions for the design of instruction to support the learning process outlined in section one.

The third chapter, *Functions of an Automated Instructional Design System*, by Charles Reigeluth, was solicited after the decision was made to turn the collection of papers generated in the design process into a book. While the first and second chapters served as background material for the reader unfamiliar with modern cognitive theory, there was not equivalent material for the person coming from a cognitive science background who was unfamiliar with the instructional design area.

Chapters Two and Three differ quite markedly in perspective, a difference which can be characterized by their location on the " constructivist " continuum. This is particularly true when taken in conjunction with the principles provided by Gagné listed in the introduction (see page xiv) and first generation instructional design discussed by Merrill in Part II of this volume.

Kintsch's statement given below essentially captures the constructivist viewpoint.

> Perhaps the most important influence of cognitive science research on instruction has been to change our concept of the learner from one whose learning is primarily determined by the form in which the new knowledge is imparted to a person who actively participates in the learning process. Specifically, we now view learning from spoken or written text as the interaction between an individual learner and a particular content during which the learner actively creates his or her own meaning.

If one takes the constructivist approach as the embodiment of the principles which can be derived from the cognitive science perspective, then an interesting exercise to keep in mind as one reads these chapters is determining how the material in the following chapters map onto that continuum and at the same time assigning a rating as to how difficult a given principle or bit of information would be to implement in a computer-based advisor.

Chapter One

Cognitive Theory as a Basis for Instructional Design

Martha C. Polson

Introduction

Within the last 10 years the field of cognitive science has increasingly focused on educational issues. My goal in this chapter is to summarize from the field what I consider to be the work most relevant to instructional design. The particular goal is to abstract a relevant "theory of knowledge." The consensus in the area of cognitive science is that intelligent action is produced by processes that operate on complex knowledge structures. Key issues are how these knowledge structures are acquired and the nature of the representation. The task as an instructional designer is to understand the knowledge necessary to perform relevant skills and then to ask how such knowledge structures might best be acquired.

Unfortunately, there is not a single unified theory of cognition that I can draw on for these relevant theoretical implications. Two investigators have the announced intent of formulating a unified theory of cognition, John Anderson (Anderson, 1983) with his ACT* theory and Allen Newell with his SOAR system (Laird, Newell, & Rosenbloom, 1987; Newell, 1987,1990). Of these two, Anderson has made a serious effort to delineate the educational implications of his theoretical approach, particularly with respect to how procedural knowledge (i.e., knowledge of how to perform a task) is acquired.

Newell has concentrated more on developing a theory which accounts for performance of cognitive and motor tasks than on understanding the acquisition of knowledge necessary to perform the tasks. From an educational standpoint, however, both of these theories have serious gaps in coverage and are in disagreement on certain issues. For instance, neither theory seriously addresses the issue of how facts (declarative knowledge) are acquired. Also the educational role of regulation or control of knowledge and the awareness of the contents of one's knowledge (metacognition) are not well developed in these theories. These less well developed aspects must be drawn from other theories or approaches which are less comprehensive than those of Anderson and Newell, but cover more thoroughly these particular aspects of cognition (Palincsar & Brown, 1984; van Dijk & Kintsch, 1983; Kintsch, 1988, 1989). The account presented here will be of necessity a synthesis of various approaches.

The major current theories of cognition and knowledge arise from the cognitive science perspective. Many of the major concepts and assumptions, both implicit and explicit, which underlie the approach are directly relevant to instructional design and differ radically from earlier approaches. Only a brief discussion of these issues, for the purpose of orienting the reader, will be given here. For those interested in a more through discussion, an excellent and very readable account of the history of the field of cognitive science and a delineation of its major assumptions can be found in Gardner (1985). Phye and Andre (1986), Estes (1988), and Glaser and Bassok (1989) also provide an excellent overview of why the current approaches are more relevant to everyday human learning and performance and how they differ from the earlier behaviorist approaches that dominated the field of learning prior to 1950. Two edited volumes which respectively honor two pioneers in the field, Herbert Simon and Robert Glaser, are also excellent sources for work which highlight the aspect of current knowledge theory that is relevant to instructional design (Klahr & Kotovsky, 1989; Resnick, 1989).

The view of human cognition that dominates the last 30 years of theory development and research draws heavily on the concept of information processing. This view is articulated by Card, Moran, and Newell (1983):

> A computer engineer describing an information-processing system at the system level (as opposed, for instance, to the component level) would talk in terms of memories and processors, their parameters and interconnections. The human mind can also be described as an information-processing system and a description of the same spirit can be given for it (p. 24).

In the information processing approach, the processing of information during learning, cognition, and performance is viewed as an active, not a passive, process that occurs in stages. Some processes occur in parallel and others occur serially. Each stage of information processing is thought of as having its own memories, processors, and types of representation. The two units of this information processing system that are most pertinent to this discussion are working memory and long term memory. Working memory, the active subset of memory, is limited in capacity and requires active processing to maintain information. The fact that working memory has a limited capacity and the nature of this limit play an important role in instructional design. (See Friedman, this volume, for a discussion of the role in graphics design.) Long term memory, which is our store of previously acquired knowledge, can be thought of as being of unlimited capacity and does not require active processing to maintain its knowledge.

One goal of the theories using the information processing approach is to explain how information acquired at one point is transformed and organized within this information processing system, such that it can be retrieved at a later point for use. Equally important is an understanding of why information fails to be encoded, or if encoded fails to be retrieved or is not retrieved in a usable form. For the theories to be relevant to instructional design they have to provide guidance on how to design instruction to foster the encoding of the information in a manner that facilitates its retrieval in a form useful in the context of performing a given task.

That purposive human behavior is rational and goal oriented is another key concept in current theories of cognition. This viewpoint is expressed by the rationality principle of the principles of operation for the Model Human Processor outlined by Card, Moran, and Newell (1983):

> Rationality Principle. People act so as to attain their goals through rational action, given the structure of the task and their inputs of information and bounded by limitations on their knowledge and processing abilities:
>
> goals + task + operators + inputs + knowledge + processing limits Æ behavior (p. 27).

This emphasis on goal directed behavior is particularly apparent in the accounts of the acquisition and use of procedural knowledge (Anderson, 1983; Newell, 1990) and cognitive task analysis (Kieras, 1988), but also plays an important role in the acquisition of declarative knowledge and the comprehension of verbal information, as well as the use of that information (Kintsch, 1974, 1988, 1989).

The emphasis on the active, strategic nature of the information processing approach is another concept that has primary importance for instructional design. This aspect of the approach is in particular contrast to the earlier behaviorist views of learning where the active participation of the learner in the event was not considered important. From the information processing approach, learning is a matter of using strategic processing to encode and organize information so that it can be retrieved at the appropriate time for use. How the information is encoded or represented during that processing to form one's knowledge base is of prime importance in understanding the implications for instruction.

Representational Systems

A theory of knowledge must be based on how knowledge is represented. Issues of representation of knowledge play a key role in all theories of memory and cognition. Details of how knowledge is stored, retrieved, and used are involved in nearly every aspect of memory and cognition. The educational implications of the theories of cognition that I will discuss follow directly from their view of how knowledge is represented. Gardner (1985) states the importance of mental representations as follows:

> To my mind, the major accomplishment of cognitive science has been the clear demonstration of the validity of positing a level of mental representation: a set of constructs that can be invoked for the explanation of cognitive phenomena, ranging from visual perception to story comprehension. Where forty years ago, at the height of the behaviorist era, a few scientists dared to speak of schemas, images, rules, transformations, and other mental structures and operations, these representational assumptions are now taken for granted and permeate the cognitive sciences (p. 383).

A large number of the educational implications of a given theory follow directly from its view of how knowledge is represented. An excellent review of memory representation is given in Rumelhart and Norman (1988).[1] Representational systems in a theory of cognition or knowledge need to capture the most salient psychological aspects of human knowledge. Rumelhart and Norman summarize these as follows:

- The associative nature of knowledge.
- The notion of knowledge units or packages, so that knowledge about a single concept or event is organized together in one functional unit.
- The detailed structure of knowledge about any single concept or event.
- The everyday reasoning of people, in which default values seem to be substituted for information that is not known explicitly, in which information known for one concept is applied to other concepts, and in which inconsistent knowledge can exist.

[1]A large part of this discussion of representational issues is based on this paper.

- The consideration [of] different levels of knowledge, each level playing a different organizational role, with higher order units adding structure to lower order ones (adapted from Rumelhart & Norman, 1988, p. 523).

The major types of representational systems with known educational implications will be described briefly. Most theories of cognition and knowledge are hybrids using more than one type of representation.

Definition of Representational Systems

A representational system maps the events in a *represented world* to a *representing world* in such a manner that the representation mirrors *some* aspects of the world which is being represented. For instance, a representation of the heights of individuals using the set of symbols ($<$, $>$, $=$) to signal less than, greater than, and equal could tell us which of two individuals was the tallest, but not the absolute difference in their heights. If height were represented by either line lengths or numbers, then absolute differences would be available. A representational system includes not only the representation itself, but also processes for interpreting the representations. These processes are as important as the representations themselves. If height is to be represented by lines or numbers, then there must be some process comparing the lengths of the lines or interpreting the numbers accordingly to arrive at the height comparisons.

Types of knowledge represented

A number of different ways to classify the knowledge types in long term memory have been proposed. A traditional approach has been to classify knowledge as *declarative*, knowing what; *procedural*, knowing how; *causal*, knowing why, and *contextual*, knowing when or in what context to apply the knowledge. The current theories of cognition that are candidates for comprising a unified theory of cognitions do not always divide the contents of memory into exactly these categories. The distinctions among these types of knowledge may be made either on the basis of the way the knowledge is represented or on the basis of the processes that operate on the representations.

Anderson (1983) postulates two distinctive memory types in long term memory, declarative memory and production memory. Declarative memory is represented as associative nets in the form of a *tangled hierarchy*. The nodes or cognitive units of that hierarchy are propositions, spatial images in analogical representation, and temporal strings. Procedural knowledge is represented as productions in production memory. Declarative and production memory interact through processes that operate on the contents of working memory. The distinction between these two types of long term memory and their interaction in working memory is the key to his ACT*

theory. His prescriptions on instructional methods and his intelligent tutoring systems are all based on this representational system (Anderson, Boyle, Farrell, & Reiser, 1984).

A description of knowledge that cuts across representational types is the concept of *mental model* or *situation model*. In this terminology, to learn about something, to come to understand it, is to construct a mental model. Mental models may have as elements structures which are in any of the representational types. Gentner and Stevens (1983) and Johnson-Laird (1983) are good sources for descriptions of much of the work in this field. From the mental model approach, learning is viewed as successively transforming a naive mental model of a given situation into a series of increasingly more conceptually complete models that are adequate for larger sets of problems.

An instructional program developed by White and Frederiksen (1987; in press) to teach ⁺rouble shooting uses the increasing complex mental models approach. White and Frederiksen emphasize *qualitative models* that teach causal knowledge. Each model incorporates declarative knowledge as well as procedural knowledge and control structures that determine how the knowledge is used. Glaser and Bassok (1989) provide a discussion of the educational principles underlying this approach. In the educational field, the elaboration theory of Reigeluth follows a similar principle.

Types of representations

Meaning: Propositional Representation.[2] A proposition represents a single idea or cognitive unit (van Dijk & Kintsch, 1983; Anderson, 1983). Each *proposition* contains a predicate followed by its *arguments*. A predicate asserts a relationship among its arguments. For instance the predicate *visit* would have the arguments of agent and object. A predicate can be represented as a *frame* which includes a set of *slots* for its arguments. The frame for the predicate visit would be visit [agent, object]. The propositional representation of the previous sentence, *Mike visited the Alamo*, would be: visit [mike, alamo]. The argument for a predicate can be another proposition. The sentence, *Mike visited the Alamo in San Antonio*, would have the predicate frame visit [agent, object, location] with the argument location being another proposition:

[2]The term proposition and propositional representation as these investigators use it does not have exactly the same meaning as a proposition in philosophy. The various propositional representations used by psychologists and AI researchers differ somewhat in terminology and structure, but the underlying differences are relatively minor and generally not of theoretical importance. I will use the terminology and framework of Kintsch and his colleagues to illustrate this type of representation (Kintsch & van Dijk, 1983; 1978; Turner, 1987).

P1: visit[mike, alamo, P2]
P2: location:in[San Antonio].

The meaning of the concepts which fill the argument slots can be represented in either a propositional form themselves or in an associative net, which better captures some of the psychological aspects of the concepts. Kintsch's theory of discourse comprehension (van Dijk & Kintsch, 1983; Kintsch, 1988) has several layers of propositional representations which are connected in associative or semantic nets in memory.

Semantic nets, scripts, and schemata. Although it is widely agreed that propositions represent the units of meaningful knowledge, they are not useful notations to describe larger highly organized knowledge structures that are employed to represent complex concepts, routine sequences of events and actions, and plans. Other types of representations have been developed for representing these types of knowledge structures.

A semantic net represents knowledge as a series of interconnected nodes with the connections having directed, labeled values (which are in some respects equivalent to the predicates in the propositional approach just discussed). The nets may be represented as graphs (Quillian, 1968; Kintsch, 1988) or may be presented in outline form (Rumelhart & Norman, 1988). In the simplest of the associative nets, the nodes are concepts with the connections being relations. The nodes are directed because the associations may not be of equal strength in both directions. For instance, the word *river* is more likely to elicit the association *bank*, than the word *bank* is to elicit the association *river*. Links may have negative values as well as positive values. A negative link indicates that the activiation of one node will inhibit the other. Illustrated in Figure 1.1 is a semantic net for the various meaning of the word *bank* (Kintsch, 1988, p. 165).

In some current theories of cognition (Kintsch, 1988; Anderson, 1983) the cognitive units of an associative or semantic net can themselves be other representational types, such as the propositions just discussed or other higher order structures.

One of the major advantages of the semantic net representation is the ease of representing hierarchies such as those that characterize category information. Figure 1.2 shows the semantic net representation of parts of the concepts animal, bird, and person. (Adapted from Norman & Rumelhart, 1988. Figure 8.7, p. 525.)

These hierarchies allow for default type reasoning and classification and the inheritance of features as well as the existence of contradictions. If a feature is specified in a superordinate concept and there is not a contradictory relationship in the concept of interest, then the feature is assumed by default to apply to the concept. The fact that, in general, birds can fly but ostriches don't is easily represented as can be seen in Figure 1.2.

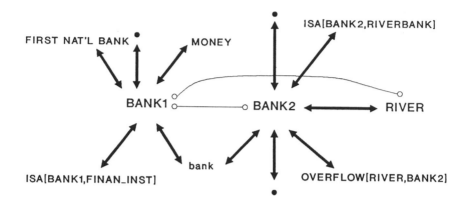

Figure 1.1. Semantic Net for 'Bank.'

Schemata, frames, scripts, plans. The associative nets account for the associative nature of knowledge, the default inheritance of features, and the structured nature of concept knowledge and the propositional representations capture the meaning of single ideas. Higher order representational systems such as schemata (Rumelhart & Ortony, 1977; Rumelhart & Norman, 1977) and scripts and plans (Schank & Abelson, 1977) were developed to account for higher levels of structure in human knowledge.

Schemata, scripts, etc., can be used to represent individual concepts, such as the concept animal, or more complicated knowledge, such as our knowledge about the order and type of events that take place when we go to a restaurant or to a grocery store. Schemata, frames, scripts, etc., like propositions, can be thought of as frames with slots for variables. Schemata will be described as examples of this type of representational system. A given schema frame contains fixed parts and and variable parts. Thus a fixed part of the schema for horse would be *Has-Four-Legs*. Fixed parts for bird would be *Has-Feathers*. For both concepts, color would be a variable. Schemata, like propositions, can embed within one another to provide very complicated structures which represent large bodies of interrelated knowledge.

The evaluations of schemata in the processing of knowledge is an active process in which incoming information is evaluated for fit, variables are bound, etc. If there is an appropriate fit to the schemata then that schema is activated. The data that a schema (singular of schemata) evaluates is both

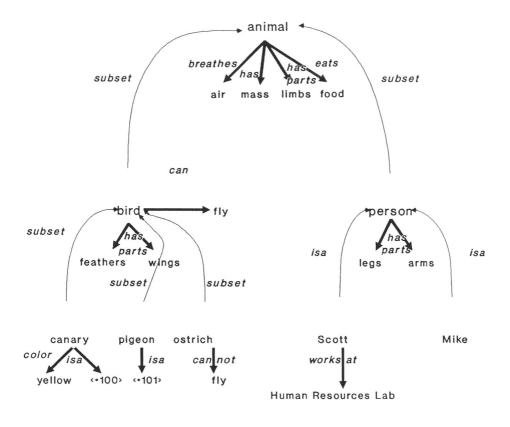

Figure 1.2. Semantic Net for 'Animal.'

top-down, in that superordinate schemata give input as to the degree to which their information is relevant, and *bottom-up,* in that information from subschemata input information about how well they account for the information being evaluated. Having representational structures with higher levels of structure and organization accounts for the structured nature of human knowledge in which higher level structures and lower level structures both play a role in the knowledge evaluation and construction that is going on in any one point.

Procedural representation. In a procedural representation, knowledge is represented as a set of actions. Motor acts and skills, such as how to ride a bike, are the most obvious behaviors to be represented in a procedural representation, although cognitive skills, such as how to code a LISP function are equally amenable to being represented as procedures (Anderson, Boyle, Farrell, & Reiser, 1984). One major difference between declarative and procedural knowledge, which must be captured in the representational systems, is that the conscious access which we seem to have to declarative knowledge does not appear to be available for procedural knowledge. We can explain why banks are related to rivers or money, but we cannot tell someone how to ride a bicycle or what motor actions are involved in pronouncing the word *representation*.

Production systems. Production systems are the most prevalent form of procedural representation used in psychology and are a form of pattern directed system. A thorough coverage of production and other pattern directed systems can be found in Waterman and Hayes-Roth (1978). Newell is primarily responsible for their introduction into modern psychology and artificial intelligence. His theory of cognition (SOAR) uses productions as the primary representational system (Laird, Newell, & Rosenbloom, 1987; Newell, 1987, 1990). Anderson (1983) makes production systems the core of his theory of skill acquisition in his ACT* theory. A production is a recognize-act or condition-action cycle. It can also be thought of as an if-then statement.

Productions can be conceived of as compiled representations of knowledge which are not accessible to introspection. When new "macro" productions are learned, which compile several previous productions involved into an action in one single production, all the intermediate steps are lost. In contrast, the structure of our knowledge represented in the propositional or semantic network representations is open to inspection. This is the basis of our metacognitive knowledge. In fact, to a large degree our acquisition of knowledge is governed by inspecting, comparing, modifying, adding to, and subtracting from these knowledge structures. In contrast to the unlabeled connections in a production system, the nature of the connections plays a key role in our use of the other types of knowledge structures.

Control structures and processes

In an information processing approach there exist control processes and structures which guide the processing of information. Included in this category is *metacognitive knowledge*. Awareness of one's own cognitive processing governs the modification of the knowledge base in expert knowledge acquisition. Self-regulatory processes, such as monitoring the processing of knowledge and progress toward a solution of a problem, the comprehension of written material, etc. are examples of *metacognitive control* processes. The educational impliations are furthur discussed in Kintsch (Chapter Two of this volume, principle 6).

Expert-novice differences in knowledge structures

In the past 25 years, the focus of cognitive research has been on the analysis of complex skills, rather than how they are acquired. Cognitive task analysis of complex skills has probably been one of the most important contributions of cognitive science to instructional design. After analyzing cognitive research in three areas for their relevance to learning: 1) the acquisitions of proceduralized skill, 2) self-regulatory skills and performance control strategies in expert performance, and 3) the acquisition of organized structures of knowledge, Glaser and Bassok conclude that ". . . it is apparent that the single most important contribution to date of the knowledge and methodology of cognitive science to instructional psychology has been the analysis of complex human performance" (Glaser & Bassok, 1989, p.662).

One important aspect of the analysis of complex skills for instructional design has been the exploration of the differences between the knowledge structures of experts and those of novices (e.g., Chase & Simon, 1973; Simon & Simon, 1978; Ericsson & Staszewski, 1989). Glaser & Bassok (1989) give a very succinct account of the implications of these differences for instructional design.

With increasing expertise, the knowledge structures in long term memory become more interconnected and organized into larger integrated chunks of information rather than isolated fragments. This allows not only larger chunks of information to be retrieved from memory and held active in working memory to be processed, but also larger amounts of information can be stored in long term memory from working memory in a given amount of time. From an educational standpoint, for a given amount of information, this reduces the load on working memory, thereby freeing up resources to process other new information. The goal of instruction should be to promote coherent, interrelated, well structured knowledge units which are highly accessible. For any given field of instruction, in order that the instructional goals can be aimed at promoting the correct knowledge structures, the first task must be an analysis of the knowledge structures necessary for achieving the task. This includes not only the final expert knowledge structures, but also intervening intermediate structures.

However, it should be noted that the learner has to play an active role in the building and interconnecting of his knowledge base. They cannot be passively imparted (Ericsson & Staszewski, 1989; Resnick, 1989). Reigeluth (this volume) and Kintsch (this volume) discuss this issue further.

Elements of a Unified Theory of Cognition

In the following sections, I will briefly review two well developed theories of cognition, the construction-integration model of discourse comprehension of Kintsch and colleagues (Kintsch, 1974; Kintsch & van Dijk, 1978; Kintsch, 1988; Mannes & Kintsch, in press) and the ACT* theory of Anderson (Anderson, 1983), which are based on the knowledge structures and processes that I have just outlined. Both emphasize their educational application. They are complementary in that the Kintsch model is primarily aimed at how declarative knowledge structures are acquired and used in discourse comprehension (including reading comprehension), problem solving, planning, etc.) and the Anderson theory has been primarily used to model the acquisition of procedural knowledge. When the elements and the emphasis of the two are combined they contain much of the information that would make a strong start toward a complete theory of knowledge. Each is committed to developing computer based training systems that are based on the principles of their theory of knowledge. Anderson advocates the use of intelligent tutoring systems and has already built several tutors. Kintsch promotes the use of "nonintelligent" training systems that leave the control of learning to the student, but provide scaffolding to support inexpert processing.

Kintsch's Model of Discourse Comprehension

In adults, much of our knowledge is acquired through discourse either from written text or spoken dialogue such as lectures, etc. The fact that knowledge has been acquired from a discourse is demonstrated through some use of that knowledge, providing answers to questions, providing summaries or paraphrases, solving problems which require the use of that knowledge, etc. The comprehension and acquisition of knowledge from these situations is referred to as discourse comprehension.

Discourse comprehension, according to the theoretical model of Kintsch and van Dijk (1978), consists of a hierarchy of strategic processes which operate on successively more complex units of the text. The outcome of each strategic operation is a mental representation in memory. Thus, local-level *microprocesses* operate on surface features of the text, deriving the meaning from graphemes, words, syntactic patterns, and organizing it into a list of propositions. Middle-level *coherence processes* are gap-filling inferences that complete the meaning of the propositional microstructure, for example, by connecting pronouns to their referents, establishing the identity of coreferents, and filling in unstated relationships within and between propositions.

Macroprocesses are higher-order processes that operate on the filled-in microstructure, forming a generalized representation of the meaning at different levels of importance. Other inferential processes may further elaborate the content and serve to integrate it into the reader's own knowledge background. These interpretive processes result in a memory representation of the situation described by the text which is termed the *situation model* in van Dijk and Kintsch (1983). Successful reading comprehension thus results in a hierarchical network of macropropositions that represents the gist of the content, and the reader's conceptual understanding of that content. The theoretical educational implications of this approach are based on the use of the situation model to mediate between a representation based on written information and a representation that is adequate to produce the desired performance.

While this theory was originally developed to understand the comprehension of discourse, it has recently been extended to understanding how comprehension failures play a role in the application of the knowledge, particularly problem solving. One example is children's simple word arithmetic problems. These problems are very difficult for children to solve even if they know the mathematical procedures involved (Kintsch & Greeno, 1985). The work of Kintsch and colleagues shows that many of the difficulties in solving word arithmetic problems are comprehension problems that result from the construction of an inadequate knowledge representation. There is a mismatch between the model of the problem produced in the process of forming the textbase, the *problem model*, and the known mathematical procedures. From this Kintsch has concluded that the instructional strategy which should underlie tutoring word problems should be focused on using the situation model as mediator between the representation of the text meaning and the representation of the problem space (Kintsch, 1989).

Under development is a computer-based tutoring system for word algebra problem solving, ANIMATE, that is based on an extension of the discourse computer model (Kintsch & Greeno, 1985; Kintsch, 1988, 1989). This tutoring system is aimed at aiding the student in developing a representation or situation model of the problem which goes beyond the textual information which may not be adequate for problem solution without additional inferences. This tutor is not intelligent in that it has no model of the specific problem being addressed nor does it have a specific model of the knowledge the student has. The idea behind this "nonintelligent" approach is to provide support or scaffolding of learning rather than planning and monitoring the student's progress. With this tutor students can construct a graphical problem model which drives a computer simulation of the situation. Students can compare the resulting animation to their internal situation model in order to evaluate and alter the problem model. It has been argued that systems which let the student do the planning and monitoring, rather than doing it for them, promote the development of self regulatory skills which characterize expert performance (Bereiter & Scardama-lia, 1989; Collins, Brown, & Newman, 1989; Brown & Palincsar, 1989).

Anderson's ACT* Theory: Acquisition of Proceduralized Skills

Anderson (1983, 1987) has the broadest theory of cognition in which there has been a serious attempt to relate the theoretical principles to acquisition of proceduralized skills. This application of his ACT* theory is very nicely elucidated in his annual review paper (Anderson, 1987).

Productions are the key element of Anderson's view of skill acquisition. Cognitive skills are modeled by a set of productions which are hierarchically arranged. Productions form both the cognitive units and specify the hierarchical goal structure that organize the problem solving. Working memory contains the active knowledge that is available at the time. When a new goal, such as "solve this algebra problem," is established by some external event, then this goal becomes active in working memory. If this goal is the condition part of an established "macro" production for solving that type of problem which exists in production memory, then that production will be applied and a solution generated to the problem. However, if a known solution does not exist, then a search must begin for a solution. The assumption is made that people solve novel problems by applying weak-problem solving to the declarative memory that they have about this domain. This weak-problem solving solution includes analogy, means-ends analysis, working backward, hill climbing, and forward search (Newell & Simon, 1972).

Using these weak problem solving rules, which are not specific to any domain, a solution to the problem is generated. Which weak method will be used is determined by what declarative knowledge exists about the domain. As the problem is solved by successively searching through declarative memory for the necessary conditions, a trace of the hierarchically organized productions is produced. The learning mechanism is a compilation process that creates efficient domain specific productions from this trace. Proceduralization is the first aspect of this compilation process. As the production trace is generated in the production memory, it is now no longer necessary to search declarative memory for the conditions, therefore they no longer have to be held in working memory, thereby reducing the processing load. The next stage is compilation. The series of productions are compiled into a single production which accomplishes the same task. Compilation speeds up performance considerably. This compiled production is now available to produce solutions to future problems of this nature.

Anderson has developed intelligent tutoring systems for LISP and Geometry that are based on this account of learning (Anderson, Boyle, Farrell, & Reiser, 1984). These tutors have been very successful. In fact, the LISP tutor is one of the few tutors which evaluation has shown to be successful. These tutors do have the drawback of needing a problem domain which is closed and formal or highly constrained in some way.

Conclusion

The two theories outlined here embody the characteristics of knowledge representation outlined in this paper. For each, attempts have been made to derive instructional principles and apply them in a computer-based training program. However, this is only a small step towards having a unified or even synthesized theory of knowledge and other cognitive processes that can be directly applied to instructional design. Glaser and Bassok (1989), after reviewing three classes of studies and educational approaches that were purportedly based on cognitive principles, concluded:

> The design of instruction in the studies we have reviewed relies more on models of competent performances in specified areas of knowledge and skill than on models of how this performance is acquired. Anderson's work is the most rigorous in explicitly attempting to use instruction to test a theory of learning. But, in general, assumptions about learning, not well-specified theory, are loosely connected to instructional principles. (Glaser & Bassok, 1989, p.662)

While this conclusion does not bode well for the immediate development of a complete theory of cognition that can be applied to the development of instructions, Glaser and Bassok were not entirely pessimistic.

> An evolution of instructional theory and the learning theory that underlies it will come about by investigations of questions that emerge from work of the kind we have described here. Progress in an area is often made on the basis of instrumentation that facilitates scientific work, and, at the present time, a significant tool is the design of instructional interventions that operationalize theory in the form of environments, techniques, materials, and equipment that can be carefully studied. These investigations can be testing ground for new theories of learning and instruction that will benefit both the practice of education and the advance of science. (Glaser & Bassok, 1989, p.662)

References

Anderson, J. R. (1983). *The architecture of cognition*. Cambridge, MA: Harvard University Press.

Anderson, J. R. (1987). Skill acquisition: Compilation of weak–method problem solutions. *Psychological Review, 94*(2), 192–210.

Anderson, J. R., Boyle, C. F., Farrell, R., & Reiser, B. J. (1984). Cognitive principles in the design of computer tutors. In *Sixth Annual Conference of the Cognitive Science Society Program* (pp. 2–16).

Anderson, J.R., Boyle, C. F., Corbet, A. T., & Lewis, M. (1990). Cognitive modeling and intelligent tutoring. *Artificial Intelligence,42,7–49.*

Bereiter, C., & Scardamalia, M. (1989). Intentional learning as a goal of instruction. In L.B. Resnick (Ed.), *Knowing, learning, and instruction: Essays in honor of Robert Glaser.* Hillsdale, NJ: Lawrence Erlbaum Associates.

Brown, A. L., & Palincsar, A. S. (1989). Guided, cooperative learning and individual knowledge acquisition. In L. B. Resnick (Ed.), *Knowing, learning, and instruction: Essays in honor of Robert Glaser.* Hillsdale, NJ: Lawrence Erlbaum Associates.

Card, S. K., Moran, T., & Newell, A. (1983). *The psychology of human computer interaction.* Hillsdale NJ: Lawrence Erlbaum Associates.

Chase, W. G., & Simon, H. A. (1973). Perception in chess. *Cognitive Psychology, 4,* 55–81.

Collins, A., Brown, J. S., & Newman, S. E. (1989). Cognitive apprenticeship: Teaching the crafts of reading, writing, and mathematics. In L. B. Resnick (Ed.), *Knowing, learning, and instruction: Essays in honor of Robert Glaser.* Hillsdale, NJ: Lawrence Erlbaum Associates.

van Dijk, T. A., & Kintsch, W. (1983). *Strategies of discourse comprehension.* New York: Academic Press.

Ericsson, K. A., & Staszewski, J. J. (1989). Skilled memory and expertise: Mechanisms of exceptional performance? In D. Klahr & K. Kotovsky (Eds.), *Complex information processing: The impact of Herbert A. Simon.* Hillsdale, NJ: Lawrence Erlbaum Associates.

Estes, W. K. (1988). Human learning and memory. In R.C. Atkinson, R. J. Herrnstein, G. Lindzey, & R. D. Luce (Eds.), *Stevens' handbook of experimental psychology, Second Edition, Vol. 2: Learning and cognition* (pp. 351–415). New York: Wiley.

Gardner, H. (1985). *The mind's new science: A history of the cognitive revolution.* New York: Basic Books.

Gentner, D., & Stevens, A. (Eds.) (1983). *Mental models.* Hillsdale, NJ: Lawrence Erlbaum Associates.

Glaser, R., & Bassok, M. (1989). Learning theory and the study of instruction. In M. R. Rosenzweig & L. W. Porter (Eds.), *Annual Review of Psychology* (Vol. 40 pp. 631–666). Palo Alto, CA: Annual Reviews, Inc.

Johnson–Laird, P. N. (1983). *Mental models.* Cambridge, MA: Harvard University Press.

Kieras, D. E. (1988). What mental model should be taught? Choosing instructional content for complex engineered systems. In J. Psotka, L. D. Massey, & S. A. Mutter (Eds.), *Intelligent tutoring systems: Lessons learned* (pp. 85–111). Hillsdale, NJ: Lawrence Erlbaum Associates.

Kintsch, W. (1974). *The representation of meaning in memory.* Hillsdale, NJ: Lawrence Erlbaum Associates.

Kintsch, W. (1988). The role of knowledge in discourse comprehension: A construction–integration model. *Psychological Review, 95,* 163–182.

Kintsch, W. (1989). *A theory of discourse comprehension: Implications for a tutor of word algebra problems.* Paper presented at meetings of the European Association for Research in Learning and Instruction, Madrid.

Kintsch, W., & van Dijk, T. A. (1978). Toward a model of text comprehension and production. *Psychological Review, 85,* 363–394.

Kintsch, W., & Greeno, J. (1985). Understanding and solving word arithmetic problems. *Psychological Review, 92,* 109–129.

Klahr, D., & Kotovsky, K. (Eds.) (1989). *Complex information processing: The impact of Herbert A. Simon.* Hillsdale, NJ: Lawrence Erlbaum Associates.

Laird, J. E., Newell, A., & Rosenbloom, P. S. (1987). SOAR: An architecture for general intelligence. *Artificial Intelligence, 33*(1), 1–64.

Mannes, S.M., & Kintsch, W. (in press). Routine computing tasks: Planning as understanding. *Cognitive Science.*

Nathan, M., Kintsch, W., & Lewis, C. (1988). *Tutoring algebra word problems.* (Technical Report number 88–12). University of Colorado at Boulder, Institute of Cognitive Science.

Newell, A. (1987). *Unified theories of cognition. The William James Lectures.* Harvard University, Spring 1987. (Available in videocassette, Psychology Department, Harvard.)

Newell, A. (1989). Putting it all together. In D. Klahr & K. Kotovsky (Eds.), *Complex information processing: The impact of Herbert A. Simon.* Hillsdale, NJ: Lawrence Erlbaum Associates.

Newell, A. (1990). *Unified theories of cognition.* Cambridge MA: Harvard University Press.

Newell, A., & Simon, H. A. (1972). *Human problem solving.* Englewood Cliffs, NJ: Prentice–Hall.

Palincsar, A. S., & Brown, A. L. (1984). Reciprocal teaching of comprehension fostering and comprehension monitoring activities. *Cognition & Instruction, 1,* 117–175.

Perfetti, C. A. (1985). *Reading ability.* New York: Oxford University Press.

Phye, G. B., & Andre, T. (1986). *Cognitive classroom education: Understanding, thinking, and problem solving.* New York: Academic Press.

Quillian, M. R. (1968). Semantic memory. In M. Minsky (Ed.), *Semantic information processing* (pp. 227–270). Cambridge, MA: MIT Press.

Reigeluth, C. M. (1983). *Instructional design theories and models; An overview of their current status.* Hillsdale, NJ: Lawrence Erlbaum Associates.

Resnick, L. B. (1989). Introduction. In L. B. Resnick (Ed.), *Knowing, learning, and instruction: Essays in honor of Robert Glaser.* Hillsdale, NJ: Lawrence Erlbaum Associates.

Rumelhart, D. E., & Norman, D. A. (1978). Accretion, tuning, and restructuring: Three modes of learning. In J. W. Cotton & R. L. Klatzky (Eds.), *Semantic factors in cognition* (pp. 37–53). Hillsdale, NJ: Lawrence Erlbaum Associates.

Rumelhart, D. E., & Norman, D. (1988). Representation in memory. In R. C. Atkinson, R. J. Herrnstein, G. Lindzey, & R. D. Luce, (Eds.), *Stevens' handbook of experimental psychology, Second Editon, Vol. 2: Learning and cognition.* New York: Wiley.

Rumelhart, D. E., & Ortony, A. (1977). The representation of knowledge in memory. In R. C. Anderson, R. J. Spiro, & W. E. Montague (Eds.), *Schooling and the acquisition of knowledge* (pp. 99–135). Hillsdale, NJ: Lawrence Erlbaum Associates.

Schank, R. C., & Abelson, R. (1977). *Scripts, plans, goals, and understanding.* Hillsdale, NJ: Lawrence Erlbaum Associates.

Simon, D. P., & Simon, H.A. (1978). Individual differences in solving physics problems. In R. S. Siegler (Ed.), *Children's thinking: What develops?* (pp. 325–48). Hillsdale, NJ: Lawrence Erlbaum Associates.

Turner, A. A. (1987). *The propositional analysis system, Version 1.0.* (Technical Report number 87–2). University of Colorado at Boulder, Institute of Cognitive Science.

Waterman, D. A., & Hayes–Roth, F. (Eds.) (1978). *Pattern–directed inference systems.* New York: Academic Press.

White, B. Y., & Frederiksen, J. R. (1987). Qualatative models and intelligent learning environments. In R. Lawler and M. Yazdani (Eds.), *AI and Education.* Norword, NJ: Ablex.

White, B. Y., & Frederiksen, J. R. (in press). Causal model progressions as a foundation for intelligent learning enviroments. *Artificial Intellligence.*

Chapter Two

Principles of Instruction from Research on Human Cognition

Eileen Kintsch

The past two decades of research in cognitive science on human information processing have provided detailed accounts of both expert and novice performance on various kinds of tasks in different domains, but as yet no general theory of how expertise is acquired. Even though we still lack a unified theory of learning, this body of research has provided tools for the analysis of complex behavior which now make it possible to focus our attention on the inexpert learner and on the processes by which new knowledge and new skills are learned. As a result, some agreement regarding instructional principles is beginning to emerge, though there are differences in where the emphasis is placed among several recent instructional programs which attempt to train cognitive processes. To some extent these differences are dictated by the particular aspect of competence that is the focus of instruction.

Cognitive research generally distinguishes three types of knowledge that enter into expert performance: knowledge of the subject domain, usually referred to as declarative knowledge; a set of automated subprocesses or procedures for operating with the knowledge; and knowledge about the conditions of knowledge use, which acts as an executive control structure. (See Polson, Chapter One, for a more extensive discussion of knowledge types and theories about how knowledge is represented in memory.) In most cases, the complex tasks studied by cognitive researchers involve an interaction of different kinds of knowledge with different demands on the information processing system. The focus of this chapter is on how a learner acquires factual or declarative knowledge from spoken or written discourse. However, my concern is not merely with the ability to remember textual material, but with the acquisition of knowledge in such a way that it can be readily accessed later and used in different situations.

The instructional principles discussed here represent a distillation from several recent reviews of cognitive research on learning, most notably the following. Resnick's (1989) edited volume provides a general introduction to the theoretical framework and methodological tools used in cognitive research on learning in a number of different domains. Glaser and Bassok (1989) have critically evaluated several individual instructional programs for cognitive skill development, which are based on current theoretical assumptions about the learning process. From a somewhat different perspective, Reusser (1992) discusses a related set of principles, derived from pedagogical theory and cognitive research, to serve as the basis for designing educational software. The common assumption underlying the effort to draw educational implications from this body of research is that effective instruction must consider more than the body of information that is to be conveyed. Instead, a more differentiated view of learning is necessary that reflects a detailed explication of the knowledge and processes required to perform a particular learning task and that takes into account the characteristics of individual learners, their strategies, knowledge, and goals.

Perhaps the most important influence of cognitive science research on instruction has been to change our concept of the learner from one whose learning is primarily determined by the form in which the new knowledge is imparted to a person who actively participates in the learning process. Specifically, we now view learning from spoken or written text as the interaction between an individual learner and a particular content during which the learner actively creates his or her own meaning. As a result, the goal of instruction is no longer defined simply in terms of knowledge acquisition, as such, but rather in terms of how new information modifies and extends the knowledge that the learner already possesses. Hence, the focus in cognitive research and instructional applications alike has shifted from a concern with how content knowledge is best transmitted, to understanding and supporting the processes by which the learner acquires expert reasoning and problem solving skills in a new domain (Resnick, 1989). The learner's attempts to comprehend, remember, and solve problems are described with respect to the strategic operations engaged in and how these function within the constraints of the human processing system. The principles of instruction which are outlined in this chapter derive from this perspective.

The following discussion is organized into two sections: First, an overview is provided of the learning process, which is described as a process of meaning construction, and some general instructional implications are drawn from this viewpoint. The second section offers some more specific suggestions for how instruction can be designed to support the learning process. However, as will become obvious to the reader, the attempt to map particular instructional implications onto each of the topics discussed is somewhat artificial. In fact, there is a great deal of overlap in the instructional suggestions that are made, which results from their common goal of fostering the learner's own effort to construct meaning.

The Constructivist View of Learning and General Implications for Instruction

Contemporary discourse processing theories (e.g., van Dijk & Kintsch, 1983; Just & Carpenter, 1987; Kintsch, 1988; Perfetti, 1989) view comprehension and learning as an active process of meaning construction in which the learner creates a personal interpretation of the information in a text or discourse. According to van Dijk and Kintsch, in order to understand a text the reader constructs not only a coherent mental representation of the content—termed the textbase—but also of the situation it describes—the situation model. While the former representation closely resembles the original input in form and content, the situation model includes elements from both the text and from the reader or listener's own knowledge base. Successful learning in this view depends on the adequacy of the situation model representation that is constructed. To the extent that it captures the relevant aspects of the situation, or events, or scientific domain evoked by the text and is well connected with the learner's own knowledge, the learner's ability to retrieve and use that knowledge is enhanced.

New knowledge becomes integrated with prior knowledge through higher-level inferences by which relationships are constructed between individual pieces of information, or which serve to elaborate it with extensions from the store of personal knowledge. For learners with little domain knowledge, these inferences are not generated automatically. Instead, true conceptual understanding is the result of conscious, problem-solving operations. For example, in order to understand difficult text on a unfamiliar topic, skilled readers resort to a variety of higher-level strategies, such as, selective rereading portions of the text, formulating summaries of main points, paraphrasing the text in their own words, self questioning and self explanation. Through such activities the active learner strives to construct a mental model of a problem situation, of an event, or of the principles that relate individual facts and ideas. Such activities also help the learner to identify gaps in his or her knowledge, or discrepancies between prior knowledge and the new information.

The product of learning is, ultimately (and ideally), the ability to construct a mental model in a particular situation to use as the basis for reasoning and solving problems. Expertise in a domain is thus defined not in terms of having a structured body of knowledge in one's memory, but rather, in being able to rapidly access a large amount of related knowledge in the memory base to relate to incoming information, and to organize the new information during comprehension in a form that makes it readily available for later use (Kintsch, 1988; Ericsson & Kintsch, 1991).

Instruction. In contrast to traditional theories of instruction, the goal of instruction, according to constructivist theories of comprehension, is no longer primarily to impart new knowledge in a readily accessible form, but to facilitate the individual's own attempts to construct meaning. Rather than fostering reproductive skills, instructional design should find ways to encourage and support the learner's independent attempts to interpret, restructure, and use new knowledge. Brown and Palincsar (1989, p. 395), for example, advocate "learning environments that encourage questioning, evaluating, criticizing, and generally worrying knowledge, taking it as an object of thought."

Growth of Knowledge and Expertise

Learning occurs by extending existing knowledge; however, this can happen in several ways.

Knowledge accumulates by adding new facts and ideas to the network of associatively linked concepts and propositions in memory. New knowledge is also acquired by elaborating and modifying existing knowledge. Domain knowledge is updated by adding details, by generalizing information, and by creating new relationships between concepts that extend the network downwards and outwards to other concepts in memory. Occasionally, large-scale restructuring occurs which links elements of knowledge in novel ways so as to encompass larger amounts of related information or so as to resolve conflicts between new and existing knowledge. Thus, as knowledge in a subject area expands, a kind of chunking takes place that allows larger, functional units of knowledge to be retrieved from memory and which results in increased processing efficiency. This is referred to as a process of knowledge transformation.

Rapid access to information stored in memory also depends on automatizing low level routines and procedures through extensive practice and experience. Rapid identification of word meanings and syntactic parsing are examples of automatic processes which are essential to the construction of higher-level meaning during reading. Although skilled readers develop general reading strategies that are relatively independent of specific domain knowledge (Perfetti, 1989), expertise in a domain largely depends on rapid and direct access to knowledge and solution procedures that can be applied in particular comprehension or problem solving situations. The kind of automatic retrieval of specialized knowledge exhibited during problem solving by experts in physics, geometry, and chess, for example, is highly domain specific and is acquired over a long period of time. Ericsson and Kintsch (1991) provide a detailed discussion of how these memory processes operate during text comprehension and problem solving.

Instruction. In designing instruction one needs to be aware both of where students are in the acquisition of new skills and of what particular kinds of knowledge are needed in a given instructional situation. Most instructional settings involve complex interactions of various types of knowledge, both factual and strategic; however, instruction and learning activities should reflect clearly defined goals. At the most basic level, it would be important to decide whether reflective, interpretive thinking is to be emphasized or the rapid execution of routinized procedures. Although procedural skills are primarily learned through extensive, error-free practice (Anderson, 1987), cognitive research strongly suggests that achieving conceptual understanding in a new domain is fostered by activities which engage the learner in construction and restructuring of knowledge—much more than has been the case in traditional instruction—because these kinds of operations richly connect new content to elements in the personal knowledge base. Hence, the kinds of learning activities that involve working with new knowledge, rather than merely rehearsing it, are more likely to result in long term retention and the ability to use it in novel contexts.

Knowledge Organization and Knowledge Use

How knowledge is organized as it is encoded affects its accessibility and the depth of understanding that is achieved. Building organizing structures that relate incoming information to existing concepts and propositions in memory provides cues that facilitate rapid information retrieval. Among some cognitive researchers, memory is conceived as a network of associately linked concepts and propositions, rather than organized in terms of hierarchical knowledge structures. For example, the construction-integration model of Kintsch (1988) assumes a broadly reaching and nonselective process of knowledge activation which is triggered by the concepts encountered in a text. As information enters into the short-term buffer, a great deal of associated knowledge in memory becomes activated during the initial construction phase of comprehension, much of which is irrelevant or even contradictory. During the second, integration phase, the activation level of irrelevant pieces of knowledge quickly diminishes, leaving only those elements that fit into a coherent interpretation of the content. In this model, knowledge is constructed and organized on the spot, in response to a particular situation. Thus, it offers a much more dynamic and flexible account of how prior knowledge is used during reading than models that assume preorganized memory structures, such as schemata and frames, which govern comprehension in a top-down manner. These issues are treated in more depth in Kintsch (1988) and Kintsch, Britton, Fletcher, Kintsch, Mannes, and Nathan (in prep.).

Instructional text that is written in a well organized and coherent form is easier to understand and to remember because it facilitates the activation of related knowledge in the reader's knowledge base. However, the constructivist position strongly rejects the traditional method of presenting information in preorganized, decontextualized components to be learned from the bottom up (Resnick, 1989). Cognitive research has shown that such knowledge is not maintained well over long periods, nor does it transfer as readily to other contexts. Indeed, several recent studies even suggest that it may not always be desirable to minimize the learner's workload by providing highly coherent, easy-to-read instructional text. When understanding takes place too rapidly and automatically, fewer knowledge building inferences may be generated than when understanding is difficult or problematic. For example, in a study of summarization skills, college students' summaries of a poorly organized informational text contained more higher-order, meaning construction inferences than their summaries of a well ordered text (E. Kintsch, 1990). Similarly, Mannes and Kintsch (1987) observed better recall among students who read well structured materials, yet students who had to find a new way of organizing the content were better able to apply the information to a later problem-solving task.

Such qualitative differences in learning can be related to the distinction made in the van Dijk and Kintsch (1983) model between two levels of meaning representation that are constructed during comprehension: the textbase and the situation model. The textbase representation, which closely mirrors the original text content, provides a foundation for reproductive learning tasks. In contrast, the mental model of the situation depicted by the text includes more elements from the reader's own knowledge base. Hence it may differ widely from the original input and may not serve reproductive needs as well. Mannes and Kintsch (1987) argue that even though more accurate recall results when the reader constructs a well formed textbase representation, a deeper, situational understanding occurs when the reader engages in more inferential processing. This kind of memory representation provides a better foundation for further actions, such as using new knowledge to solve problems or to evaluate ideas.

Instruction. What this implies for design of instruction and assessment alike is a need to be clear about which kind of learning is to be promoted in a given learning situation and how the new knowledge is to be used later. Tasks such as recognition, recall, and summarization require reproductive capability, which depends on an accurate and coherent representation of the textual content. Such learning can be facilitated by coherent, well organized learning materials and presentations. However, building a conceptual model of a domain requires, in addition, activities that provide multiple ways to tie new information to existing knowledge. The construction of mental models is encouraged by offering learners numerous opportunities to work with new knowledge, to construct and reconstruct it in different ways, so as to create numerous, inferential links between pieces of knowledge in the memory system. An example of such tasks are those that elicit different organizational schemes, that require another perspective to be taken, or that apply the material to a new context or to a different subject area.

Reading text about an unfamiliar topic is in itself a difficult challenge, and it is a difficult problem for an instructor, or textbook writer, to decide when or how far to go in simplifying presentation of new information, how much background information to supply, how much can be left for the reader to infer. On the one hand, the information has to be accessible to the learner: there must be many points of contact between the new content and the learner's prior knowledge, and the construction of a coherent textbase is obviously facilitated by well-structured, coherent content (Britton & Gulgoz, 1990). On the other hand, the instructor sometimes might want to exploit a difficult reading situation as an occasion for deeper inferential processing and problem solving, as the Mannes and Kintsch (1987) study suggests. Yet, this is only possible in so far as the learner's knowledge gaps are not too great to be bridged, or in so far as procedural supports can be provided that allow this kind of effortful reading to be successful, as described in the second part of this chapter.

Transfer of Knowledge

The ability to access and use relevant knowledge in a variety of situations depends on whether multiple links can be constructed between concepts in the memory network. Expertise is a function of how broadly and efficiently these retrieval pathways can be established so that a large body of related knowledge can be brought to bear on a particular comprehension or problem solving situation (Ericsson & Kintsch, 1991).

Instruction. Transfer of knowledge and skills to other applications occurs more readily when instruction emphasizes the meaningfulness of the information beyond the specific situation in which it is initially introduced. For many learners knowledge becomes compartmentalized into sets of procedures whose applicability is perceived only with respect to a specific situation. For example, countless numbers of algebra students fail to realize that overtake and collision scenarios are variants of the same problem type. Cognitive research suggests that such knowledge compartmentalization can be avoided by applying new content across different contexts and by extending it to different domains, provided that the learner is allowed to discover common themes or underlying principles that relate different subject areas. Resnick (1989, p. 9) emphasizes the active role of the learner in this process: "... the observed generality and transfer to learning comes from intentional efforts to find links among elements of knowledge, to develop explanations and justifications, and to raise questions."

It follows that learning is greatly enhanced when knowledge is learned in a specific context, in the service of a problem that needs to be solved, or in order to attain a specific cognitive goal, rather than as a decontextualized and abstract body of knowledge. That is, one learns by doing, by manipulating knowledge, by evaluating ideas, and by understanding the purpose of what one is learning, both in relation to an overall goal and to the particular task at hand. Therefore, new content should be taught in a meaningful context so that its relation to a particular cognitive goal is apparent, not as a sequence of skills or facts learned in isolation. Further, it is helpful if students are allowed to choose their own goals, to formulate their own plans for accomplishing them, and to mark their own progress through a sequence of subgoals in pursuit of a higher-level learning goal.

Learning as a Strategic Process

Comprehension, writing, problem solving, and learning in general are strategic, rather than rule governed processes. Strategies are an effective, though approximate means of accomplishing some goal within given time and resource limitations, but unlike rules they do not guarantee a correct outcome. Strategies are flexible—they can be applied in varying contexts, they may be more or less optimal, more or less powerful, and they vary as well in terms of the cognitive effort they require (van Dijk & Kintsch, 1983). Numerous studies have shown that qualitative differences in strategy use are an important differentiator between skilled and less skilled learners and between persons with much or little experience and knowledge of a particular domain.

In general, novices in a domain tend to process new information in a straightforward, linear fashion, while experts process more recursively. They make repeated passes through the material, selectively focusing on certain types of information. Novices generate fewer inferences than experts, who enrich the incoming information with extensions from their own knowledge base. Novices generally attend more to the surface features of a problem or situation, while experts readily grasp the underlying principles or structure of a problem, or the important points or overall significance of a discourse. Such differences in expertise have been consistently found across a wide variety of text processing and problem-solving contexts. However, the existence of general learning strategies is a controversial issue. To what extent there are such strategies that are independent of domain knowledge and whether these could be effectively taught to less skilled learners is still unresolved. Nevertheless, attempts to teach certain kinds of strategic knowledge, generally to school-age children, have shown some promise and make it possible to offer suggestions for designing instruction. These are discussed in the next section.

Instruction. A likely starting point for strategy instruction might be metacognitive awareness: Metacognition, the ability to monitor one's own comprehension and to control strategic processing, is an important component of skilled learning that extends beyond expertise in a specific domain. The use of cognitive control strategies to monitor on-going comprehension or progress in solving a problem, to plan future processing, to redirect attention to problematic areas, and to deploy the appropriate remedial strategies has been singled out as a major distinguisher between the learning styles of younger and older students, between successful and less successful learners, and between those who have or who lack expertise in a given domain (Glaser & Bassok, 1989). Much of the research on metacognition has dealt with individual and age related differences in reading comprehension in school-age populations. Notable success has been documented by several programs designed to train metacognitive skills in children, most notably the reciprocal teaching method of Palincsar and Brown (1984; Brown & Palincsar, 1989). Some related programs, known as cognitive apprenticeship (summarized in Collins, J. S. Brown, & Newman, 1989), attempt to adapt methods that are effective in traditional apprenticeship settings to classroom instruction.

Although most of the metacognitive research and strategy training studies have been carried out with younger students, there are indications that deficiencies in metacognitive control over knowledge processing are also characteristic of older students who are poor learners. As yet, little research has been directly concerned with this question, though it seems plausible that older students would similarly benefit from learning environments designed around principles which have been found to maximize use of strategies for self directed, independent learning in a younger population. The programs mentioned above are flexible enough to be adapted to a broad range of abilities and content areas.

Supporting the Learning Process

The strategy based view of information processing which governs cognitive research today necessarily entails a shift from the content-product orientation of traditional instruction to process oriented instruction. Of course, content knowledge, as always, remains an important component of expertise in a domain; however, the shift in focus concerns *how* that knowledge is acquired in a form that makes it accessible and usable for novel tasks and in different situations. Can we use what we know about expert processes to upgrade those of less skilled learners? The following section summarizes some specific instructional principles, derived from cognitive and pedagogical research. These principles have been incorporated into both teacher directed and computer assisted tutoring programs currently being developed and tested.

Making Hidden Cognitive Processes Explicit

Expert strategies, including, to some degree, metacognitive ones, are inextricably bound to specific and detailed knowledge of the domain. It is well elaborated knowledge, knowledge that is broadly linked to other related knowledge in memory, that empowers inferential thinking and that enables the learner to detect and deal with breakdowns in comprehension and problem solving. Hence, it is not very surprising that attempts to explicitly teach "expert strategies" in isolation have had mixed success. In contrast, modeling of expert strategy use in a particular situation has been more promising, especially when it is combined with explicit instruction in strategy use (e.g., Bereiter & Bird, 1985). What modeling does is to bring into the open the hidden mental processes that enable an expert to surmount a comprehension or writing impasse, for example, or to debug a faulty solution to a complicated problem. That is, students are allowed to see how experts reason through difficult, problematic situations, rather than simply observing a smooth progression down to the correct solution path. Modeling also contextualizes the use of both domain-specific strategies and metacognitive control strategies, showing how experts can exert conscious control over their thinking processes in order to attain particular, meaningful goals.

Modeling is most effective when learners are also allowed multiple opportunities to practice cognitive strategies under the guidance of a skilled teacher, as in reciprocal teaching (Brown & Palincsar, 1989; Palincsar and Brown, 1984). According to these authors (see also Reusser, 1992), by making both thinking processes and goals explicit, by actively constructing one's knowledge in the open, these processes become themselves available for contemplation, comment, and ultimately control.

An important consideration for instructional design in any setting is to determine what kinds of strategic knowledge the learner needs to have. What kinds of mental activities should be modeled, explicitly described, and practiced? Cognitive task analysis, a detailed specification of the conceptual knowledge and processes required to perform a complex task, is a valuable tool for putting expert-instructors, with their superior and largely internalized skills, in the shoes of the learner. Essentially, cognitive analysis involves decomposing a task into its individual components, i.e., in terms of the mental operations, skills, as well as the knowledge representations required to accomplish each subtask. An application of this method, called a "cognitive walk through," has been used, for example, to anticipate and remedy problems arising from human interaction with complex technological tools, such as a multi-access telephone system (Polson, Lewis, Reiman, & Wharton, in press). In essence, this is what an instructor's modeling of his or her own thinking processes aloud also does, because in so doing the instructor becomes aware of precisely what it is that the learner needs to know and do in a given situation.

Procedural Facilitation

The theoretical construct of "procedural facilitation," or "expert scaffolding," mainly originates from developmental research, especially that of Vygotsky (1978), that describes the instructional role played by parents in guiding a child's learning. This idea has been further elaborated and incorporated into classroom training studies by Brown and Palincsar (1989) and by Scardamalia, Bereiter, McLean, Swallow, and Woodruff (1989). Essentially the term refers to providing supports that enable learners to use higher-level skills to work on more complex tasks that they would be unable to perform unaided, just as a parent supports and shapes a child's early attempts at linguistic expression. In Brown and Palincsar's reciprocal teaching program the supports are embedded in an interactive teaching method designed to instruct and practice four comprehension monitoring strategies that are characteristic of skilled reading and that maximize the reader's involvement in the content: summarizing content to check comprehension, clarifying any problems, formulating questions, especially inferential ones that go beyond the information presented in the text, and predicting forthcoming content. As the term implies, teachers and students take turns modeling the strategies as they read aloud, guiding and shaping each others' responses, with the teacher's role diminishing as the students become able to use the strategies on their own. Thus, as Brown and Palincsar point out, these procedural supports are temporary and are flexibly tailored to the learner's level of competence and domain knowledge: They are gradually phased out as the learner becomes increasingly competent in the skill.

Prompts and cues. Procedural supports may take widely differing forms. They may be delivered by the teacher or by a tutoring system, but in all instances, the function of these supports is to alleviate working memory load so that the student can concentrate on some of the critical aspects of the task without being overwhelmed by the demands of the overall task. For example, in Scardamalia, Bereiter, and Steinbach (1984), procedural facilitation consists of a list of verbal hints or cues that prompt inexpert writers for the various kinds of information needed to develop and elaborate ideas in essay writing. The cues are fairly successful in promoting use of more expert-like strategies, such as planning, organizing, and deep level revisions, among middle school students. These ideas have been further elaborated in a computer assisted learning environment (CSILE) currently being tested by Scardamalia *et al.* (1989). In this training program computers provide various kinds of supports for manipulating and keeping track of information (e.g., record keeping, graphics, animations, organizational and retrieval aids, and so on). The focus of this program is broadly conceived as a knowledge building environment in which the classroom functions as a "community of learners," with each learner contributing to and drawing from a jointly constructed pool of knowledge.

Educational microworlds. Thus, the concept of procedural facilitation or scaffolding can be used to create an educational microworld in the sense of Burton, J. S. Brown, and Fischer (1984, p. 139), whose purpose is "to provide the student with a task that he can perform successfully using a simplified version of the final skill that is the goal." Burton *et al.* use the analogy of learning to ski with short skis, which make it quite easy to execute parallel turns. The novice skier then progresses to the more complex demands of skiing with longer skis as competence (and the desire for greater speed and steeper terrain) grows. Rauenbusch and Bereiter (1991, pp. 182-183) further specify the conception of an educational microworld, as one that is artificially constrained in order to direct the learner's attention toward certain critical aspects of the final skill. However, they also make the point that learning a simplified version of a skill does not entail decomposing a complex skill or knowledge into discrete subcomponents. Instead, the goal of a microworld is to permit the learner to focus on and practice particular subskills in the context of the complete task. Rauenbusch and Bereiter have implemented these ideas in a novel kind of educational microworld, in which school age readers are required to decode passages of degraded text (texts with every third letter missing). In so doing, comprehension based strategies are elicited, explicitly discussed, and practiced much more than would be the case in a normal reading situation.

Representational aids. Various kinds of symbolic representations can also provide procedural facilitation for understanding abstract concepts, for the reasoning processes needed to solve a problem, or for learning a set of complex procedures. Representational tools, such as graphs, tree diagrams, tables, conceptual networks, and the like can serve to focus attention on the critical features of a problem, for example, that are relevant to its solution. However, as Reusser (1992) points out, their value as pedagogical tools depends on a number of considerations. These include not only whether a representation faithfully renders important characteristics of the entity it purports to represent, but also whether the student actively participates in constructing and manipulating the conceptual representation.

Supporting and guiding the student's own reasoning processes is the idea behind two interactive computer programs: the ANIMATE program for teaching algebra word problem solving, developed by Nathan, Kintsch, and Young (1990), and HERON, designed for tutoring story problems to younger students by Reusser, Kämpfer, and Stüssi (1990). In these tutors, which also constitute a kind of educational microworld, a graphic representation of the problem space serves as a mediator between the student's informal representation of the situation depicted by the problem text (e.g., one train overtaking another) and its formal symbolic representation as an equation. Rather than providing a ready-made graphic display, the computer uses a set of menu options to guide the student in constructing a representation of the problem space. Whether that representation accurately reflects the situation described by the text is then confirmed or disconfirmed by a computer run animation of the real-world scene.

Intelligent and unintelligent tutors. There is an important difference between this kind of computer assisted learning and the "intelligent tutors" based on expert models of successful problem solving. The geometry tutor of Anderson, Boyle, and Yost (1985), for example, provides an environment that is highly structured to keep the student on the correct solution path by providing feedback and correction during the problem solving process. Making the procedures explicit to the learner and providing multiple opportunities for error-free practice, according to Anderson (1987), should form the basis for developing automatic routines that require little conscious effort and that free up processing space for higher-level mental activities. Quite a different theoretical approach is involved here than in the less directive approach embodied in CSILE, ANIMATE, and HERON (Scardamalia *et al.*, 1989; Nathan *et al.*, 1990; and Reusser *et al.*, 1990). In the latter, it is the learners, rather than the computer, who control the learning process: the learners are in charge of setting their own goals and of planning the route to accomplish them; the learners likewise are responsible for monitoring their progress and finding and correcting errors on their own. The computer merely supports these cognitively demanding activities by making available various kinds of supports: for example, by presenting organizing structures, formats, and reminders for keeping track of information; by narrowing choices through menus; by storing and retrieving information; and by providing a means of checking the consequences of one's reasoning processes (e.g., via animations). These computerized functions serve to reduce the memory load for the user, making it possible for learners to focus their attention and efforts on difficult, but cognitively more rewarding aspects of learning.

Qualitative feedback on performance is considered important in both intelligent and nonintelligent training programs. This kind of feedback goes beyond the information that the answer was right or wrong, for example, by indicating to the learner what to change, how to proceed, how to reconceptualize the situation, and so on. Furthermore, it is important to provide feedback geared to the learner's present level of knowledge or skill. However, the cognitive scientists involved in designing intelligent and nonintelligent tutors have differing opinions concerning the role that errors should play in the learning process. To some degree, these are probably related to differences in the kind of learning that is the focus of a particular instructional theory or training program. Intelligent tutoring approaches, such as the geometry tutor of Anderson, Boyle, and Yost (1985), or Schneider (1985), emphasize extensive, error-free practice in order to develop automatization of procedural skills. In formal problem-solving domains, errors that are not immediately detected and corrected can lead to a chain of false inferences and dead ends from which it is difficult to recover and which impede learning of correct procedures. In contrast, tutors whose goal is to foster self regulation and self construction of knowledge (e.g., Scardamalia *et al.*, 1989) or to promote conceptual understanding (e.g., Nathan *et al.*, 1990) regard errors as occasions for learning. Since errors reveal discrepancies between new and existing knowledge, because they indicate shortcomings in the mental model being constructed, they provide the motivation to go after more information, to reformulate ideas, or to rethink the reasoning process.

In general, the contrast between intelligent and nonintelligent approaches to computer-assisted instruction may reflect differences in the kind of knowledge that is to be learned rather than incompatible theoretical notions. The tutors designed by Anderson and his colleagues, by Schneider (1985), and others are intended to build the kinds of proceduralized skills that form the basis for problem solving in formal and highly constrained domains, such as geometry or LISP programming. In contrast, helping learners to construct useful bodies of conceptual knowledge that can be accessed, manipulated, and applied in multiple situations constitutes the much less precisely defined goal of nonintelligent tutors.

Despite these differences, intelligent and nonintelligent tutors share the common goal of supporting the learner's own activities as a means of enhancing the learning of new skills and knowledge. That is, the notion of procedural facilitation underlies both approaches. In a sense, this theoretical construct simply expresses what most good teachers and parents do intuitively to guide a child's efforts to learn a new skill. However, the important contribution of cognitive research has been to formulate these vague notions into explicit and well specified theories of the psychological processes underlying skilled performance that can be implemented and tried out in instructional settings.

The Social Context of Learning

In addition to parents, teachers, and computer tutors, procedural facilitation can also come from the social setting in which learning takes place. The idea of cooperative learning and shared cognition, in which knowledge building is the function of group actions, rather than solely an individual effort, is being tried in a number of school classrooms. It is also a fundamental component of two of the training programs described above (Brown & Palincsar, 1989; Scardamalia *et al.*, 1989), as well as the cognitive apprenticeship approach (e.g., Collins, J. S. Brown, & Newman, 1989). In these methods learners at different levels of expertise all participate in modeling complex processes, scaffolding and guiding other learners' attempts to apply the modeled activities. In CSILE (Scardamalia *et al.*, 1989) individual learners also contribute their own ideas and the results of their independent activities to build a general pool of knowledge that can be accessed, used, and further developed by all learners.

The advantages of embedding instruction in a group setting include the following, according to Brown and Palincsar (1989): (1) Cooperative learning provides a supportive means of promoting the use of self-regulatory strategies. Anxiety is reduced and motivation increased by having the responsibility for comprehending, solving a problem, or completing a task shared by all members of the groups. (2) More complex problems can be tackled in a collaborative group than a single individual could accomplish, since the work on the subparts can be distributed across several individuals. Hence the building of knowledge is shared across a whole class. (3) The activities are modeled at differing stages of complexity in cooperative learning groups and become externalized through discussion, with members contributing according to their abilities. Thus, the collaborative group provides support for learners at different levels of expertise, enabling them to use skills that are just emerging. (4) Conflict plays an important and positive role in cooperative instructional settings as a means of building and elaborating knowledge. Unlike more directive, traditional instruction, students must assume the responsibility for explaining and justifying opposing viewpoints. In so doing they become deeply involved in the work of constructing and comparing domain models, building the inferences that deepen and extend their own knowledge. Resnick (1989) points out in addition that cooperative learning incorporates many of the advantages of traditional apprenticeship training in that it offers opportunities to experience knowledge in use, in contexts where the meaningfulness of individual elements of a task or activity to the whole is apparent to the learner. Thus it counteracts the tendency of school learning (which is also true at higher academic levels) to break down into decontextualized rituals.

Instructional Materials

Applications of cognitive research to instruction has largely focused on the development of instructional techniques (such as reciprocal teaching, cognitive apprenticeship) and the design of educational environments (such as computer microworlds, cooperative learning) to train higher-order comprehension, learning, and problem-solving strategies. These are the kinds of skills that enhance conceptual understanding, according to the constructivist model of learning. An important question that needs more attention in cognitive research concerns the role of instructional materials in educational settings. In many school classrooms textbooks seem to play a somewhat diminished role, perhaps in part because the information they contain is difficult to understand, to retain, and later make use of. Nevertheless, textbooks constitute major sources of domain knowledge and as such they become increasingly important later in the educational process. Hence, presenting information in a written form that is accessible to and usable by individual learners who represent a range of skills, prior knowledge, and cultural backgrounds is an important challenge for writers and researchers alike.

Can the insights about human information processing drawn from theoretical and empirical research also help us write more effective texts? Earlier attempts to improve the readability of instructional texts have not been a spectacular success (see, for example, a recent review of this literature by Britton, Gulgoz, & Glynn, 1991), but a more promising direction is indicated in a few very recent attempts to tackle this issue.

As discussed earlier in this chapter, lack of coherence in a text can be an important source of comprehension problems in reading. Therefore, filling in the inferential gaps for the reader by explicitly providing the knowledge that is needed to understand the text should make it easier to understand and recall the information it contains (Beck, McKeown, Sinatra, & Loxterman, 1991; Britton & Gulgoz, 1990; Kintsch, McNamara, Songer, & Kintsch, 1992). According to the van Dijk and Kintsch (1983) theory of discourse comprehension, this is because a coherent text facilitates the construction of a coherent memory representation of the content, the textbase, making it easier to retrieve textual content for tasks that assess reproductive learning.

However, the constructivist view of learning conceives a more active reader, one who builds his or her own meaning. And learning is defined as conceptual understanding, being able to construct mental models in a domain. This deeper kind of learning is fostered when readers generate their own inferences to bridge the gaps between pieces of information in the text and when they further enrich the text content with their own knowledge. Accordingly, as much as possible an instructional text should invite readers to engage in inferential processing, in order to create many links between the new knowledge and knowledge that they already possess. The problem here, of course, is to ensure that appropriate inferences and accurate domain models are formed by the reader. Recent critical evaluations of school texts (Beck & McKeown, 1991; Kintsch *et al.*, 1992) point out that a major problem with textbook writing is the tendency to overemphasize descriptions of facts, without indicating the interrelations among them or how they support a global topic, principle or concept. Hence, it is argued that instructional texts often lack global coherence. By failing to embed factual information in a broader context, they do not provide the kind of information that the reader needs to develop domain understanding.

There are conflicting demands to satisfy in order to create texts that are effective vehicles for learning for a heterogenous body of learners. On the one hand, a text must be coherent enough so that comprehension does not breakdown for low knowledge readers. At the same time, readers who have the requisite knowledge can deepen their understanding by generating gap-filling inferences on their own. Coherent for whom?—is a question with which future research will have to grapple. Yet here a solution to the problem of individualizing the presentation of knowledge is at least foreseeable within a computerized system such as hypertext. This technology can be used to free reading from the constraints of linear processing, allowing the reader to access information at more explicit or less explicit levels, as needed. Hence, content could be tailored to the individual knowledge background of different readers, as proposed by Kintsch *et al.* (in prep.).

Conclusion

In general, however, the demand to accommodate the needs of individual learners remains one of the most difficult problems we face in designing and delivering effective instruction, and cognitive research makes it clear that there are no easy solutions. It suggests that there is no single way to write an instructional text for readers with varying knowledge backgrounds; it offers no generally agreed-upon list of general learning or problem-solving strategies to instruct, indeed no unified theory of learning. Instead, our theories that describe complex human processing indicate a much more differentiated view of the learning process than that implied by traditional educational models. The success of instructional design, of instructional methods, of the educational setting, and the materials used will all depend on a detailed consideration of the multiple factors that interactively affect the learning process, including the following:

– the knowledge background, interests, goals and beliefs of individual learners;

– the goal of a particular task or learning situation defined in terms of how the knowledge is to be used;

– the specific processes and knowledge required to accomplish a particular task;

– the specification of the learning context in terms of the degree to which it involves the active participation of the learner and provides adequate outside support.

Nevertheless, detailed processing theories of learning in individual domains can guide our efforts. By helping us to discover where processing breakdowns are likely to occur in executing a particular task, and why, we will have a much better understanding of what it is we need to teach.

References

Anderson, J. R. (1987). Skill acquisition: Compilation of weak-method problem solutions. *Psychological Review, 94*(2), 192–210.

Anderson, J. R., Boyle, C. F., & Yost, G. (1985). The geometry tutor. In *Proceedings of the International Joint Conference on Artificial Intelligence-85* (pp. 1–7). Los Angeles: International Joint Conference on Artificial Intelligence.

Beck, I. L., & McKeown, M. G. (1991). Substantive and methodological considerations for productive textbook analysis. In J. P. Shaver (Ed.), *Handbook of research on social studies teaching and learning* (pp. 496–512). New York: Macmillan.

Beck, I. L., McKeown, M. G., Sinatra, G. M., & Loxterman, J. A. (1991). Revising social studies text from a text-processing perspective: Evidence of improved comprehensibility. *Reading Research Quarterly, 26*(3), 251–276.

Bereiter, C., & Bird, M. (1985). Use of thinking aloud in identifying and teaching of reading comprehension strategies. *Cognition and Instruction, 2,* 131–156.

Britton, B. K., & Gulgoz, S. (1990). Using Kintsch's computational model to improve instructional text: Effects of repairing inference calls on recall and cognitive structures. *Journal of Educational Psychology, 83,* 329–345.

Britton, B. K., Gulgoz, S., & Glynn, S. (1991). Impact of good and poor writing on learners: Research and theory. In B. K. Britton, A. Woodward, & M. Binkley (Eds.), *Learning from textbooks.* Hillsdale, NJ: Lawrence Erlbaum Associates.

Brown, A. L., & Palincsar, A. S. (1989). Guided, cooperative learning and individual knowledge acquisition. In L. B. Resnick (Ed.), *Knowing, learning, and instruction: Essays in honor of Robert Glaser* (pp. 393–451). Hillsdale, NJ: Lawrence Erlbaum Associates.

Burton, R. R., Brown, J. S., & Fischer, G. (1984). Skiing as a model of instruction. In B. Rogoff and J. Lave (Eds.), *Everyday cognition: Its development in social context* (pp. 139–150). Cambridge, MA: Harvard University Press.

Collins, A., Brown, J. S., & Newman, S. W. (1989). Cognitive apprenticeship: Teaching the crafts of reading, writing, and mathematics. In L. B. Resnick (Ed.), *Knowing, learning, and instruction: Essays in honor of Robert Glaser* (pp. 453–494). Hillsdale, NJ: Lawrence Erlbaum Associates.

van Dijk, T. A., & Kintsch, W. (1983). *Strategies of discourse comprehension.* New York: Academic Press.

Ericsson, K. A., & Kintsch, W. (1991). *Memory in comprehension and problem solving: A long-term working memory.* (Tech. Rep. No. 91-13). Institute of Cognitive Science, University of Colorado, Boulder, CO.

Glaser, R., & Bassok, M. (1989). Learning theory and the study of instruction. In M. R. Rosenzweig and L. W. Porter (Eds.), *Annual Review of Psychology* (Vol. 40, pp. 631-666). Palo Alto, CA: Annual Reviews, Inc.

Just, M. A., & Carpenter, P. A. (1987). *The psychology of reading and language comprehension.* Rockleigh, NJ: Allyn & Bacon.

Kintsch, E. (1990). Macroprocesses and microprocesses in the development of summarization skill. *Cognition and Instruction, 7*(3), 161-195.

Kintsch, W. (1988). The use of knowledge in discourse processing: A construction-integration model. *Psychological Review, 95,* 163-182.

Kintsch, W., Britton, B. K., Fletcher, R., Kintsch, E., Mannes, S., & Nathan, M. J. (in preparation). A comprehension-based approach to learning and instruction.

Kintsch, E., McNamara, D. S., Songer, N. B., & Kintsch, W. (1992). Revising the coherence of science texts to improve comprehension and learning I: Traits of mammals. (Tech. Rep. No. 92-03). Institute of Cognitive Science, University of Colorado, Boulder, CO.

Mannes, S., & Kintsch, W. (1987). Knowledge organization and text organization. *Cognition and Instruction, 4*(2), 91-115.

Nathan, M. J., Kintsch, W., & Young, E. (1990). A theory of word algebra problem comprehension and its implications for the design of learning environments. *Cognition and Instruction.*

Palincsar, A. S., & Brown, A. L. (1984). Reciprocal teaching of comprehension-fostering and monitoring activities. *Cognition and Instruction, 1*(2), 117-175.

Perfetti, C. A. (1989). There are generalized abilities and one of them is reading. In L. B. Resnick (Ed.), *Knowing, learning, and instruction: Essays in honor of Robert Glaser* (pp. 307-335). Hillsdale, NJ: Lawrence Erlbaum Associates.

Polson, P., Lewis, C., Rieman, J., & Wharton, C. (in press). A method for theory-based evaluation of user interfaces. *International Journal of Man-Machine Studies.*

Rauenbusch, F., & Bereiter, C. (1991). Making reading more difficult: A degraded text microworld for teaching reading-comprehension strategies. *Cognition and Instruction, 8*(2), 181-206.

Resnick, L. B. (1989). Introduction. In L. B. Resnick (Ed.), *Knowing, learning, and instruction: Essays in honor of Robert Glaser* (pp. 7-24). Hillsdale, NJ: Lawrence Erlbaum Associates.

Reusser, K. (1992). Tutoring systems and pedagogical theory: Representational tools for understanding, planning, and reflection in problem solving. In S. Lajoie and S. Derry (Eds.), *Computers as cognitive tools.* Hillsdale, NJ: Lawrence Erlbaum Associates.

Reusser, K., Kämpfer, A., & Stüssi, R. (1990). HERON: Ein adaptives tutorielles System zum Lsen mathematischer Textaufgaben. In A. Reuter (Ed.), *Informatik auf dem Weg zum Anwender.* Berlin: Springer.

Scardamalia, M., Bereiter, C., McLean, R. S., Swallow, J., & Woodruff, E. (1989). Computer-supported intentional learning environments. *Journal of Educational Computing Research, 5*(1), 51-68.

Scardamalia, M., Bereiter, C., & Steinbach, R. (1984). Teachability of reflective processes in written composition. *Cognitive Science, 8,* 173–190.

Schneider, W. (1985). Training high performance skills: Fallacies and guidelines. *Human Factors, 27*(3), 285–300.

Vygotsky, L. S. (1978). *Mind in society: The development of higher psychological processes* (M. Cole, V. John-Steiner, S. Scribner, & E. Souberman, Eds.). Cambridge, MA: Harvard University Press.

Chapter Three

Functions of an Automated Instructional Design System

Charles M. Reigeluth

To state the obvious, the purpose of an automated instructional design system is to automate the instructional design process. *Automating* could entail anything from providing a few tools for an instructional designer to use, to entirely replacing the instructional designer. It generally does not refer to replacing the subject-matter expert. The *instructional design process* could entail anything from the instructional strategy selection process (the design phase of the instructional systems development process) to the entire spectrum of phases, including analysis, design, development, implementation, and evaluation. Where an automated instructional design (AID) system falls on these two continua will determine how powerful a tool it is for course development.

Regardless of where an AID system falls, it must incorporate knowledge about both process and product. *Product* knowledge includes knowledge about what the instruction should be like when the design process has been completed. This knowledge is referred to as principles and theories of instruction, which prescribe different instructional strategies for different situations. *Process* knowledge includes knowledge about how to create the product. It is a set of procedures and heuristics as to how to analyze the learners' needs, how to select appropriate content for the instruction, how to use principles and theories of instruction, how to develop or produce any learning resources or instructors' guides, how to conduct a formative evaluation, and so forth. Although an AID system must incorporate knowledge about both process and product, the scope of this chapter is limited to a discussion of product knowledge: instructional theories and principles.

Instructional theories and principles are very different from learning theories and principles. They are concerned with prescribing what the instruction should be like—what instructional strategies should be used when—and therefore are prescriptive. Learning theories and principles, on the other hand, are concerned with describing what goes on in a learner's head—what learning processes a learner uses—and therefore are descriptive. John Dewey (1900) characterized instructional theory as a "linking science" between learning theory and educational practice.[1] There is a strong relationship between these two disciplines. Instructional theory provides concrete guidance for how to facilitate the occurrence of certain learning processes. And learning theory provides a rationale as to why certain instructional prescriptions are useful. Learning theory can provide a basis for the (deductive) development of instructional theory, but instructional theory can just as readily be developed (inductively) through trial and error. And instructional theory can just as readily provide the impetus for development of learning theory (for example, to explain why an instructional strategy is so effective under certain conditions).

Regardless of the scope of the AID system, its most important function is to specify what the instruction should be like for a particular situation (particular goals, content, learners, and learning environment). In other words, it must prescribe the most appropriate instructional strategies and tactics.

Organizational Strategies

In the process of designing instruction, an instructional designer or an AID system must address macro-organizational strategies first, for they include prescriptions for selecting, structuring (grouping), and sequencing the course content, which must be done before mid-level and micro-organizational strategies can be selected.

Macro-Organizational Strategies

In addition to strategies for selecting, structuring, and sequencing the course content, macro-organizational strategies include ones for synthesizing (explicitly teaching interrelationships) and summarizing (systematically reviewing) the content.

[1] Editor's note: It is just this concept of instructional theory as a linking science that inspired the choice of AIDA as an acronym—AIDA (Verdi's opera) was commissioned to celebrate the opening of the Suez Canal, which links two bodies of water.

Selecting content

The selection of content is based on needs analysis and task or content analysis. Needs analysis entails identifying the goals (the desired expertise for the learners) and identifying the learners' current knowledge (the existing expertise of the learners). The need is the gap between the two. To figure out how to fill the gap, one must perform a task analysis that identifies the specific knowledge and skills that are missing. This includes identifying procedures, causal models, and other knowledge structures that distinguish the desired expertise from the existing expertise. Selecting content is not an instructional strategy. It is concerned with deciding what to teach rather than how to teach it. However, it is included here because of its great importance in the design process.

Structuring and sequencing content

In research on structuring and sequencing a course or training program, it emerged that every pattern of sequencing is based on a single type of relationship within the content (Reigeluth, 1989). For example, the chronological sequence is based on the time relationship among events; Gagné's hierarchical sequence is based on the learning prerequisite relationship among skills; the forward-chaining procedural sequence is based on the order relationship among activities; the Reigeluth-Merrill elaboration theory's conceptual elaboration sequence is based on the parts or kinds taxonomic relationships among concepts; Scandura's shortest-path sequence (further developed and popularized by P. Merrill, 1987) is based on the simple-to-complex relationship among paths of procedures, and so forth.

In the cognitive domain, the Reigeluth-Merrill elaboration theory (Reigeluth and Stein, 1983) prescribes a holistic approach to structuring and sequencing that may enhance such goals as building stable cognitive structures, facilitating creative thought, and allowing for maximum appropriate learner control. The elaboration theory's simplifying conditions method (Reigeluth, 1987) calls for beginning the instruction with the simplest kind of typical task an expert would perform, and teaching it on the application (skill) level. The conditions which make that kind of task so simple are identified, and subsequent lessons in the course gradually relax those conditions so that ever more complex tasks are learned. These tasks can be primarily domain-dependent skills, generic skills, or understandings.

There is still relatively little known about the kinds of relationships that are most important for facilitating learning. New approaches to sequencing will probably be developed as new kinds of relationships are identified, especially for the affective domain. It seems likely that optimal sequencing strands will be developed for each of a variety of types of learning, then interwoven with each other to form a complete course or curriculum sequence.

Synthesizing and summarizing content

Synthesis is the process of explicitly teaching important relationships among ideas. Summarizing entails providing systematic review, perhaps by having the learners periodically use what they have learned. Very little attention has been paid to developing useful strategies and tactics for synthesis and summarizing (see Van Patten *et al.*, 1987). This is particularly unfortunate since they can have such a powerful impact on learners.

Mid-level Organizational Strategies

Some instructional planning is done on a level which is broader than micro-strategies (for a single idea) but considerably narrower than macrostrategies (for an entire course). Bruner's notion of a "learning episode" is a good example. A learning episode has a problem-solving character, it has a clear beginning and a clear end, it builds up to a climax of understanding, and its length should be proportional to the payoff—the magnitude of the climax of understanding (Bruner, 1960). Romiszowski's (1984) overall instruction strategies is another example, and they include such alternatives as an expositive strategy and an experiential strategy.

Merrill has also developed some mid-level organizational strategies he calls transactions (or instructional interactions), each of which is designed for a specific purpose or situation (Li & Merrill, 1990; Merrill, Li, & Jones, 1991); see especially Merrill's chapter in this volume. A transaction is a set of micro-organizational tactics and a strategy for sequencing those tactics. Transactions are configured according to several "parameters" (tactics), including:
- transaction mode (expository or inquisitory)
- instructional control (learner- or system-controlled)
- display
    - representation form
    - location of information
    - duration
- practice
    - format
    - amount
    - criteria
- feedback
    - conditions
    - types
    - durations
- guidance

> – conditions
> – types
> – amount
> – duration

Merrill has identified four major kinds of transactions: component, abstraction, association, and enterprise. A **component transaction** teaches all or part of one kind of cognitive structure, or "frame" as he calls it. An **abstraction transaction** teaches all or part of an abstraction hierarchy (ranging from instances on the lowest level of abstraction to progressively more general levels of a cognitive structure). An **association transaction** teaches two or more cognitive structures linked by an association relation. And an **enterprise transaction** teaches all cognitive structures (and their interrelations) for a given "enterprise" (task).

At present, there is very little in the way of tested prescriptions in this area. It seems likely that prescriptions will be developed for the use of such strategies as: apprenticeship, debate, field trip, game, ancient symposium, laboratory, lecture, project, simulation, role play, brainstorm, tutorial, and others (Dorsey *et al.*, 1989).

Micro-Organizational Strategies

Many instructional theorists, including Gagné, Merrill, and Gropper, have proposed that the selection of micro-organizational strategies and tactics should depend primarily on the nature of what is to be learned (see Reigeluth, 1983). Different theorists have offered different taxonomies of what is to be learned, but there is a surprising degree of similarity among those taxonomies.

Perhaps the first type of learning to be analyzed and investigated (because it is the simplest, most superficial type of learning) is what Bloom calls "knowledge" (Bloom 1956). Merrill refers to this type of learning as "remember verbatim" (Merrill *et al.*, 1979), and Ausubel calls it "rote learning" (Ausubel *et al.*, 1978). It is also one aspect of Gagné's "verbal information" (Gagné, 1985) and Anderson's "declarative knowledge" (Anderson, 1985).

A more complex type of learning is what Bloom calls "application." Merrill refers to it as "use-a-generality," Gagné calls it "intellectual skill," and Anderson uses the term "procedural knowledge." Certainly, learning to apply a rule requires very different methods of instruction from just memorizing it.

An even more complex type of learning has only recently begun to receive widespread investigation under the rubrics of thinking skills and learning strategies. It includes Bloom's higher levels ("analysis," "synthesis," and "evaluation"), Merrill's "find-a-generality," Gagné's "cognitive strategies," and Anderson's "domain-independent knowledge."

Interestingly, several of these taxonomies of learning have identified another type of learning which has been largely ignored by instructional theorists until now, and in fact was even largely ignored by learning theorists until recently. It is similar to (though somewhat more complex than) what Bloom calls "comprehension" and what Merrill refers to as "remember paraphrased," and comes closest to what Ausubel identifies as "meaningful verbal learning." It is also the other aspect of Gagné's "verbal information" and Anderson's "declarative knowledge." When students have to learn what an atom is, one hardly has concept classification (applying the concept) in mind. The learners are not expected to be in a situation where they need to say, "Oh! Look at that! That's an atom!" And their teachers certainly don't want them just to recite by rote what an atom is. There is clearly another type of learning, which is perhaps best characterized by the word "understanding." It seems to arise through the construction of meaningful (nonarbitrary) linkages or relationships between the new idea and what the learner already knows.

In sum, there are in the cognitive domain four major types of learning which require very different methods of instruction. The most intuitive labels may be: (a) memorizing information, (b) understanding relationships, (c) applying skills, and (d) applying generic skills. The various types of "domain dependent" content (content in the subject areas), such as concepts, procedures, and principles, can be acquired as any one of the first three types of learning. A concept can be memorized (either its definition or an example of it), or it can be understood (its relationships with other knowledge), or it can be applied (instances can be classified as examples or nonexamples of it). The fourth kind of learning is "domain independent" and generally requires more time to acquire. There is strong evidence that these four types of learning dictate different choices of strategies and tactics more than any other consideration or factor.

It is important to note that these types of learning are not levels of learning in the sense that one level must be acquired before another level can be acquired. People often acquire rules on an application level without being able to verbalize or state the rules. This happens to all ages, from children (e.g., linguistic rules) to experts in complex domains (e.g., problem solvers and strategists). Also, many procedures are learned on the application level without any understanding of what is happening or why it works. Math and statistics are often learned (taught) this way (unfortunately). And students clearly do not need to memorize a passage in order to be able to understand it.

Facilitating memorization
The field of instructional theory has grown out of a behavioral orientation which focused most efforts on prescriptions for memorizing informa-

tion (association tasks). Research has shown that there are three tactics which should universally be used to facilitate this type of learning (called "routine tactics"): presentation, practice, and feedback. First, present the information that is to be memorized. Second, provide the learner with opportunities to practice remembering it under conditions typical of the post-instructional requirements. Finally, provide immediate feedback on each practice, by confirming correct answers or giving the correct answer on wrong answers.

Additional tactics include: repetition, chunking, prompting, and mnemonics. Practice opportunities should be repeated until the learner has mastered the information. If more than about seven items of information are to be memorized, then the items should be chunked into groups of no more than about seven items each; and the presentation, practice, and feedback should focus exclusively on one chunk until it is mastered. Prompting is a way of helping learners when they cannot remember the information. Prompts are designed to help the learner establish retrieval cues. Mnemonics, which are based primarily on cognitive theory, can greatly decrease the amount of time and effort students need to memorize information. They include first-letter mnemonics (acronyms), phrases, visual images, rhymes,and songs.

Facilitating application of skills

The behavioral orientation of learning theory and instructional theory also yielded some valuable prescriptions for teaching skill application (especially concept classification and procedure using). For routine tactics Merrill's (1983) component display theory extends the notion of presentation-practice-feedback to generality-examples-practice-feedback. The generality is a definition of the concept or statement of the procedure or principle. The examples are instances of the concept or demonstrations of the procedure or principle. The practice is an opportunity for the learner to classify new instances of the concept; to perform the procedure in a new situation; or to use the principle to predict effects, explain causes, or implement solutions (achieve desired effects) in new situations (Merrill, 1983; Reigeluth & Schwartz, 1989). The feedback confirms a correct answer or corrects the learner's cognitive processing on wrong answers.

Additional tactics include consistency, divergence, progression of difficulty, attention focusing, and alternative representation, among others. Consistency entails making the examples, practice, and test items as similar as possible to the postinstructional requirements. Divergence entails making the examples as different as possible from each other, making the practice items as different as possible from each other, and making the test items as different as possible from each other. The examples and practice should also be arranged in an easy-to-difficult order. The learner's attention should be focused on important aspects of the generality, examples, and feedback, through use of color, comments, shading, zooming, animation, loudness, and so forth. And the generality, examples, and practice items should often be represented in a different form, such as realia, iconic, and abstract (symbolic) forms. For a review of research on each of these tactics, see Merrill *et al.* (1976).

Facilitating understanding

Behavioral theory has little to say about how to facilitate understanding. Hence, there is relatively little in the way of validated prescriptions for facilitating the acquisition of understanding (meaningful learning). What work has been done has largely been on the development of descriptive learning theory (cognitive theory), rather than prescriptive instructional theory, with the exception of Ausubel's work (see Ausubel *et al.*, 1978).

There appear to be two different kinds of understanding, which require very different instructional strategies and tactics. One is what might be called conceptual understanding, for it entails understanding an idea by relating it to other knowledge in a semantic network or schema. Crucial to this form of understanding is identifying the kinds of relationships which represent important dimensions of understanding for the new idea (Lindsay & Norman, 1977). They may include superordinate, coordinate, and subordinate relationships, as well as analogical, experiential, functional, and others. Once the important relationships have been identified, it is possible to select a tactic appropriate for teaching each. Superordinate relationships are built by relating the new knowledge to a meaningful context or advance organizer. Coordinate relationships are built through comparison and contrast, subordinate through analysis of varieties and/or components, analogical through comparison and contrast with an analogy, and experiential through description of concrete examples or case studies. It is important to select familiar "objects" for teaching these relationships. A relationship can only be taught by relating the new idea to another idea ("object") that the learner has acquired. The more familiar the learner is with the object, the easier it will be to learn the relationship.

The other kind of understanding is what might be called causal understanding, or mental model, for it entails understanding an interrelated set of causal relationships and interdependencies. Since causal models are usually quite complex, one important instructional strategy is to use an elaboration sequence based on simplifying conditions (Reigeluth, 1987; see "Micro-Organizational Strategies" above). For example, White and Frederiksen (1987) designed a progression of microworlds (computer-based simulations) for teaching the laws of motion. The first microworld was the simplest because it stipulated many simplifying conditions, such as that an object could move in one-dimensional space only and there was no friction. The conditions simplified the causal model to the point where it could be relatively easily acquired by experimenting in the microworld. Then those simplifying conditions were gradually relaxed, one or two at a time, requiring the causal model to gradually grow in complexity. Other important tactics appear to be: labeled illustrations (Mayer, 1989), demonstrations, exploration, and practice in predicting, explaining (or inferring), and solving problems (Reigeluth & Schwartz, 1989).

Facilitating application of generic skills

Behavioral theory has not contributed much to knowledge about how to teach generic skills. However, instructional theorists and cognitive scientists have recently begun to devote greater attention to generic skills: thinking skills, problem-solving skills, learning strategies, and metacognition. Of the work that has been done here, most of it has been on deciding what to teach, rather than how to teach it. It seems likely that the most important methods will be a good simple-to-complex sequencing strategy for teaching any given generic skill, and prescriptions for integrating such single-skill sequences with each other and with a range of domain-dependent content sequences (both are macro-organizational strategies). Other than this, it seems likely that a generic skill will have to be analyzed as to its skill (primarily procedure-using) components and its understanding components, and that those components will be taught using the micro-organizational strategies and tactics appropriate to each.

Affective learning

These four types of cognitive learning (memorizing, applying, understanding, and generic skills) represent important aspects of instructional theory. Martin and Briggs (1986) identify several different dimensions of affective learning, each of which seems likely to require different methods of instruction. They include: attitudes/ values, morals/ethics, self-development, emotions/feelings, and several other dimensions. Within each, they conduct a comprehensive review of literature (theory and research), and formulate some instructional strategies and tactics.

Perhaps the most commonly taught of the dimensions of affective learning is attitudes/values. The major theories that offer instructional prescriptions include:

- The Yale Program (Hovland, Janis, & Kelley, 1953), which offers prescriptions for the use of persuasive communications;
- Dissonance Theory (Festinger, 1957), which prescribes techniques for increasing or decreasing dissonance among the learner's attitude, behavior, and/or environment,
- Social Learning Theory (Bandura, 1977), which prescribes a variety of techniques for changing attitudes by influencing conse-

quences of those attitude, such as direct reinforcement, vicarious reinforcement through modeling, and verbal persuasion.

Martin and Briggs then propose three major strategies for effecting attitude change based on the review of literature: persuasion, dissonance, and modeling. And they propose specific tactics for implementing each strategy. For example, a few of the tactics proposed for persuasion include:

- Use a credible source.
- Present both sides of the attitude if the audience is hostile or when the other side will be presented also.
- Provide an opportunity for overt verbalization or action.
- Delineate the reason for accepting an attitude, as well as providing the attitude itself.
- Attempt to lower the ego-involvement of the attitude object (pp. 137-138).

Although Martin and Briggs have considerably advanced our knowledge about how to design good instruction for affective learning, much more work is needed in this area.

Other conditions for selecting tactics

However, the selection of micro-organizational strategies and tactics should not just depend on the nature of the content. The nature of the learner is important, as well as the capabilities of the media that are selected. There is growing evidence that the nature of the learner has the greatest influence on decisions about what to teach, rather than how to teach it (Jonassen, 1982). It is not desirable to teach things which the learner has already mastered, for that would be a waste of time and money, and it would demotivate the learner. On the opposite extreme, it is undesirable to teach things which are too far beyond the learner's current knowledge, for lack of important prior knowledge (including prerequisite skills— Gagné, 1985) would make learning very difficult, if not impossible.

Perhaps the second most important way that the nature of the learner influences the selection of micro-organizational strategies and tactics is in making decisions about the amount of instructional support provided to the learner, that is, how rich the the instruction should be. It is important to assess the difficulty of the content based on the learner's ability and prior familiarity with it. The more difficult it is, the richer the instruction needs to be, including the use of more examples and practice, alternative representations (especially hands-on and visuals), attention-focusing devices, hints, and shaping (or successive approximations).

A third way that the nature of the learner is important is in the selection of motivational strategies. A motivational profile of the learner is very important for selecting appropriate motivational strategies (Keller, 1983, 1987).

With respect to the nature of learning environments, significant strides in information technologies are providing educators and trainers with tools of a magnitude of power previously undreamed of. Most current micro-organizational strategies were developed with a "page" mentality for paper delivery. To take full advantage of the capabilities of new mediational systems, educational thinking must advance beyond such a static, confining level. Strategies and tactics need to be developed which take advantage of the dynamic, interactive, and artificial intelligence capabilities of computers and interactive video. When such media are available, strategies and tactics that take full advantage of them should be selected.

Computer-based simulation possesses great potential for taking advantage of advanced technologies. But most simulations fall miserably short of their potential. Prescriptions for improving their quality are under development. Alessi and Trollip (1985) and Reigeluth and Schwartz (1989) have developed some prescriptions, but much more work remains to be done to test, refine, and further develop such prescriptions.

Advances in information technologies have also made possible the design of intelligent tutorial systems which can be used alone or in combination with simulations or other instructional approaches. The major deficiency to date for such systems is an inadequate set of instructional rules for an expert tutor so it will optimally facilitate learning. There is much room for improvement in the area of operationalizing prescriptions to the level of specificity necessary for expert tutors. Merrill (1989) has made some important advances in this area, but much more work is needed.

Motivational Strategies

Another important issue that has been too little explored in research and theory is that of motivating learners. All of the above-mentioned kinds of strategies and tactics can be used to enhance motivation to learn: organizational, mediational, and management. Motivational strategies were largely ignored by instructional theorists until very recently. Keller (1983, 1987) has done much to integrate the current knowledge about motivation into a set of prescriptions for instructional designers, but more work is needed in this area, particularly regarding motivational strategies which are uniquely possible with advanced technologies.

Mediational Strategies

Given that instructional technology has strong roots in media, instructional designers have a tendency to constrain their instructional designs to certain mediational systems, particularly to such resources as print, computers, and video. However, many other types of mediational systems can be used. The source of instruction can be human or nonhuman; a human source can be a professional or an amateur; a nonhuman source can be instructionally designed or not created specifically for purposes of instruction; and the intended receiver can be an individual or a group. These characteristics yield the typology of mediational systems shown in Table 3.1. Note that the labels in the boxes are familiar concepts that do not overlap 100 percent with the concept as defined by the characteristics of the source and receiver. They are included here merely to be illustrative—the sort of approach one might think of first for each category. There is also considerable overlap between these categories and the mid-level strategies mentioned earlier. Furthermore, it is important to keep in mind that almost any medium (or combination of media) can be used within each of these categories.

Instructional designers have had a tendency to use self-instructional modules without considering that another mediational system might be better. Cost-benefit analysis is likely to be very important in making informed decisions. For practical guidelines in this area, see Romiszowski (1988). It is important to think of the instruction in terms of interactions between the mediational system and the learner, rather than to just think in terms of delivery of content by the system (Merrill, 1988).

Management Strategies

As instructional tools become more powerful and more varied, the task of managing the instruction becomes more formidable and more important. It is not just a matter of coordinating diagnosis-and-revision activities, although that is certainly very important. It is also a matter of deciding which kind of resource is important for whom and when, and which strategies and tactics are important for whom and when on each resource. A wide variety of considerations comes into play, including individual differences, mastery learning, record keeping, learner control, scheduling, incentives, and much more. With the development of expert systems, it is possible to think of designing an advisor into computer-based instruction. Such an advisor could monitor the learner's activities, intervene with advice when appropriate, answer questions about instructional management, and serve other instructional management functions. But what are the rules which should govern such an advisor? And what instructional management activities are best left to a human? Much more work is needed to develop useful prescriptions regarding such management issues.

Conclusion

To be successful, an AID system must specify what the instruction should be like for a particular situation (particular goals, content, learners, and learning environment). Instructional theory, as a ''linking science'' between learning theory and educational practice, provides the growing but

RECEIVER

		Individual	Group
Human	**Professional**	*Tutoring*	*Lecture*
	Amateur	*Peer Tutoring*	*Discussion*
Nonhuman	**Designed**	*Self-instruction Module*	*Group Activities*
	Natural	*Individual Projects*	*Group Projects*

SOURCE

Table 3.1. Typology of Mediational Systems.

still incomplete knowledge base for prescribing the most appropriate instructional strategies and tactics. An AID system can only be as good as the knowledge about instructional design that we put into it. While we already know much about how to facilitate memorization-level and skill-level learning, we know much less about how to facilitate understanding, generic skills, and affective learning of various kinds.

But advancing our knowledge about "product" (what good instruction is like for different situations) is only half of the story. We then must figure out efficient processes for applying that knowledge to particular situations, including analysis, design, development, implementation, and evaluation. The quality of these two kinds of knowledge that is built into an automated instructional design (AID) system will determine how powerful a tool it is for course development.

References

Alessi, S. M., & Trollip. S. R. (1985). *Computer-based instruction: Methods and development.* Englewood Cliffs, NJ: Prentice-Hall.

Anderson, J. R. (1985). *Cognitive psychology and its implications* (2nd ed.). New York: W. H. Freeman.

Ausubel, D. P., Novak, J.D., & Hanesian, H. (1978). *Educational psychology: A cognitive view.* New York: Holt, Rinehart, & Winston.

Bandura, A. (1977). *Social learning theory.* Englewood Cliffs, NJ: Prentice-Hall.

Bloom, B. S. (ed.). (1956). *Taxonomy of educational objectives. Handbook 1: Cognitive domain.* New York: David McKay.

Bruner, J. S. (1960). *The process of education.* New York: Vintage Books.

Dewey, J. (1900). Psychology and social practice. *The Psychological Review, 7,* 105–124.

Dorsey, L., Olson, J., & Reigeluth, C. M. (1989). Instructional theory for mid-level strategies. Paper presented at the meeting of the Association for Educational Communications and Technology, Dallas, Texas.

Festinger, L. (1957). *A theory of cognitive dissonance.* Stanford, CA: Stanford University Press.

Gagné, R. M. (1985). *The conditions of learning and theory of instruction* (4th ed.). New York: Holt, Rinehart, & Winston.

Hovland, C.I., Janis, I.J., & Kelley, H.H. (1953). *Communications and persuasion.* New Haven: Yale University Press.

Jonassen, D. (1982). Aptitude- versus content-treatment interactions: Implications for instructional design. *Journal of Instructional Development, 5*(4), 15–27.

Keller, J. M. (1983). Motivational design of instruction. In C.M. Reigeluth (Ed.), *Instructional design theories and models: An overview of their current status* (pp. 383–434). Hillsdale, NJ: Lawrence Erlbaum Associates.

Keller, J. M. (1987). Strategies for simulating the motivation to learn. *Performance Instruction, 26,* 1–7.

Li, Z., & Merrill, M.D. (1990). Transaction shells: A new approach to courseware authoring. *Journal of Research on Computing in Education, 23*(1), 72–86.

Lindsay, P. H., & Norman, D. A. (1977). *Human information processing: An introduction to psychology.* New York: Academic Press.

Mayer, R. E. (1989). Models for understanding. *Review of Educational Research, 59*(1), 43–64.

Martin, B. L., & Briggs, L. J. (1986). *The affective and cognitive domains: Integration for instruction and research.* Englewood Cliffs, NJ: Educational Technology Publications.

Merrill, M. D. (1983). Component display theory. In C.M. Reigeluth (Ed.), *Instructional design theories and models: An overview of their current status* (pp. 279–333). Hillsdale, NJ: Lawrence Erlbaum Associates.

Merrill, M. D. (1988). The role of tutorial and experiential models in intelligent tutoring systems. *Educational Technology, 28*(7), 7–13.

Merrill, M. D. (1989). Knowledge Engineering: An Instructional Design Expert System. Workshop presented at the meeting of the Association for Educational Communications and Technology, Dallas, Texas.

Merrill, M.D., Li, Z., & Jones, M.K. (June 1991). Instructional transaction theory: An introduction. *Educational Technology, 31*(6), 7–12.

Merrill, M. D., Olsen, J. B. & Coldeway, N. S. (1976). Research Support for the Instructional Strategy Diagnostic Profile (Report No. 3). San Diego, California: Courseware, Inc.

Merrill, M. D., Reigeluth, C. M., & Faust, G. W. (1979). The instructional quality profile: A curriculum evaluational and design tool. In H.F. O'Neil Jr. (Ed.), *Procedures for instructional systems development* (pp. 165–204). New York: Academic Press.

Merrill, P. F. (1987). Job and task analysis. In R.M. Gagné (Ed)., *Instructional technology: Foundations* (pp. 141–73). Hillsdale, NJ: Lawrence Erlbaum Associates.

Reigeluth, C. M. (Ed.). (1983). *Instructional design theories and models: An overview of their current status.* Hillsdale, NJ: Lawrence Erlbaum Associates.

Reigeluth, C. M. (1987). Lesson blueprints based on the elaboration theory of instruction. In C.M. Reigeluth (Ed.), *Instructional theories in action* (pp. 245–88). Hillsdale, NJ: Lawrence Erlbaum Associates.

Reigeluth, C. M. (1989). Prescriptions for designing a theoretical elaboration sequence. Paper presented at the annual convention of the Association for Educational Communications and Technology, Dallas, Texas.

Reigeluth, C. M., & Schwartz, E. (1989). A prescriptive theory for the design of computer-based educational simulations. *Journal of Computer-based Instructional Systems, 16*(1), 1–10.

Reigeluth, C. M., & Stein, F. S. (1983). The elaboration theory of instruction. In C.M. Reigeluth (Ed), *Instructional design theories and models: An overview of their current status* (pp. 335–81). Hillsdale,NJ: Lawrence Erlbaum Associates.

Romiszowski, A. (1984). *Producing instructional systems.* London: Kogan Page.

Romiszowski, A. (1988). *The selection and use of instructional media* (2nd ed.). London: Kogan Page.

Scandura, J. M. (1977). *Problem-solving: A structural/process approach with instructional applications.* New York: Academic Press.

Van Patten, J., Chao, C., & Reigeluth, C. M. (1987). A review of the strategies for sequencing and synthesizing instruction. *Review of Educational Research, 56*(4), 437–71.

White, B., & Frederiksen, J. (1987). Causal model progressions as a foundation for intelligent learning environments (Report No. 6686). Bolt, Beranek, and Newman, Cambridge, Massachusetts.

Implications for Automating Instructional Design

Martha C. Polson

As discussed in the introduction to this section, the principles and guidelines suggested by the three authors vary a good deal in what they emphasize in instructional design, and therefore the nature of the instruction produced. If one makes a list of the principles derived by Gagné, the general principles and strategies discussed by Reigeluth and Kintsch, in some cases there is fairly direct mapping from one to the other, but some of the more constructivist positions advocated by Kintsch have no equivalent in the other chapters.

The following two statements map very directly.

> And learning is defined as conceptual understanding, being able to construct mental models in a domain (Kintsch, page 38).

> The other kind of understanding is what might be called causal understanding, or mental model, for it entails understanding an interrelated set of causal relationships and interdependencies (Reigeluth, page 50).

In some cases the principles of Kintsch can be considered the rationale for the principles of Gagné and strategies of Reigeluth. The following two principles are examples.

> Learning occurs by extending existing knowledge (Kintsch, page 26).

> Stimulate recollection of previously learned relevant knowledge (Gagné, page xvi, principle 5).

In other cases, although the starting point is the same, the conclusion is quite different. In the two examples below, although Gagné and Kintsch agree on the need for feedback, they do not necessarily agree on the nature of the feedback.

> Provide varied practice with corrective feedback (Gagné, page xvii, principle 10).

> Qualitative feedback on performance is considered important in both intelligent and nonintelligent training programs. This kind of feedback goes beyond the information that the answer was right or wrong. (Kintsch, page 36).

Many of the positions put forth by Kintsch have no equivalent in the discussions by the other authors. For example:

> Contemporary discourse processing theories (e.g., van Dijk & Kintsch, 1983; Just & Carpenter, 1987; Kintsch, 1988; Perfetti, 1989) view comprehension and learning as an active process of meaning construction in which the learner creates a personal interpretation of the information in a text or discourse (Kintsch, page 25).

> Comprehension, writing, problem solving, and learning in general are strategic, rather than rule governed processes (Kintsch, page 30).

While the three authors, Kintsch, Gagné, and Reigeluth, are producing principles with some overlap, as can be seen from some of the above comparisons, they do have very different emphases with respect to the design of instructional and/or computer-aided instructional design systems. Kintsch is emphasizing principles which lead to a sophisticated learner; the others are emphasizing principles which lead to sophisticated instructional materials. While the two goals are not mutually exclusive, sophisticated instructional materials for one instructional situation may not necessarily produce a sophisticated learner—one who can learn the given material and also develop some learning strategies which will make for efficient and effective learning in other situations.

While the constructivist position might be an ideal to strive for, the research on how to implement such instruction is in its infancy and the principles espoused are very general. Therefore, implementing an AIDA which can guide an instructional designer in producing the instruction might not be within our current capabilities.

While the previous three chapters provide background information and advice on the nature of instruction that produces the most effective learners, as well as guidelines for developing effective instructional materials, there is little that can be concluded directly from these chapters about exactly how one should automate the instructional design process. However, the nature of the recommended end products of the instructional design process afforded by the automation places some lower limits on the capability of the system. For instance, it should allow for highly interactive instruction. The details of a system enabling an instructional designer to produce and implement instructional materials and methods which result in effective instruction and effective learners is the subject of the remainder of the book.

Part II

Approaches to Automating Instructional Design

Introductory Remarks

J. Michael Spector

Having laid a relatively firm foundation for instructional design in cognitive learning theory, we shall now proceed to the task of considering how instructional design might be automated. Not all possible approaches are considered. Halff's paper clearly advises against making the computer responsible for inventing new instructional designs. Rather, Halff would have the computer generate computer-based instruction (CBI) according to established instructional designs. In general, we have chosen to restrict our attention to those approaches which restrict the problem space of instructional design, applying the principle that computers should do what computers do best and people should continue to do what they do best. It will become apparent, however, that there is some disagreement about what each can do best.

A second reason for not considering other approaches is that the AIDA project was commissioned by the United States Air Force for a particular problem situation. In many cases the Air Force makes subject-matter experts responsible for the creation of computer-based instructional materials. As a consequence, the approaches considered in this part of the book all take into account that the instructional designer, although an expert in a particular technical domain to be trained, may be a novice with regard to instructional systems and technologies. This situation restricts possible approaches to automation. For example, designing a powerful set of intelligent tools for a master instructional designer (e.g., IDE, Pirolli & Russell, 1990) is not appropriate for our particular problem setting.

We acknowledge that other approaches are possible and some of those are both interesting and promising—most notably Duchastel's critic (1990), Expert CML (Jones & Wipond, 1990), and IDE (Pirolli & Russell, 1991). However, the consultants and advisors on the AIDA project agreed that AIDA should support novice instructional designers. The result of this decision to support novice instructional designers caused emphasis to be placed on the most difficult aspects of instructional design as opposed to the most tedious and repetitive aspects (see Preface). This decision to focus on novice instructional designers caused a serious reexamination of instructional design, which we hope is reflected in this volume. At the end of the conceptual phase of AIDA's development, the advisors and consultants had agreed on a general functional model, represented in the figure below. There are six functional components to AIDA: (1) student, environment, and task information, (2) content information, (3) an AIDA executive, (4) a strategies component, (5) a delivery mechanism, and (6) an evaluation component.

The papers that follow address this model directly or indirectly. Halff offers two different ways that such an AIDA could be implemented, one in a commercial instructional design environment and a second in a technical training center similar to that found in the Air Force. Halff argues that the particular environment has implications for the implementation of each of these six functional components.

Gagné conceptualizes an AIDA that gathers information from the novice instructional designer about trainees, environment, job tasks, and the types of capabilities to be trained. The system then offers guidance for implementing instructional strategies appropriate to that situation. Gagné classifies instruction into three phases: (1) setup, (2) initial presentation, and (3) practice. His assumption is that different instructional objectives require different instructional strategies. He then describes various strategies that would be appropriate for different objectives.

Merrill's version of AIDA is more complex than Gagné's. Gagné imagines guiding the user to an effective instructional design by asking about the instructional setting and offering context-specific advice and examples. Merrill believes that it is possible to automate more than just the instructional design guidance. He believes that the kind of information that Gagné collects for a specific case implies a particular kind of instructional design. Merrill argues that once the design has been selected most of the implemen-

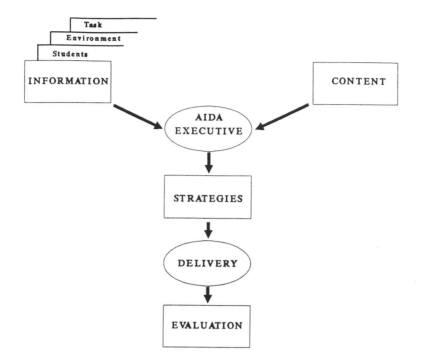

Functional Components of AIDA

tation can then be automated. His views are formulated around a second generation of instructional design that emphasizes the need to organize instruction around integrated sets of knowledge. Merrill also stresses the need to integrate the traditional five phases of instructional systems development (ISD—analysis, design, implementation, production, and evaluation).

Merrill extends Gagné's notion that different instructional strategies are appropriate for different instructional objectives by arguing that there are three kinds of things that might be the focus of instruction: entities, human activities, and processes. Each of these has a different instructional framework. If the focus is an entity, then the instruction will likely be about the names and locations of parts of the entity. If the focus is a human activity, then the instruction will most likely involve the steps in that activity. If the focus is a process, then it is likely that causal relationships will enter into consideration. Merrill proposes "transaction shells" as a means to implement these intelligent instructional frameworks, and he provides an elaboration of how they might be configured differently for a variety of instructional settings.

Tennyson offers an even more ambitious version of AIDA. He proposes the development of an intelligent tutoring system for the domain of instructional design. He does not address the six functional components directly, but it is clear from his discussion that he has accounted for all of the minimal functionality represented in the figure above and much more. Tennyson's system contains an instructional database and a content database, which roughly correspond to the strategies component and the content component. In addition, Tennyson's system would have two primary modes of operation: as a coach or as an advisor. He argues that novice instructional designers need to be coached toward effective designs, while experienced designers need only occasional advice. An intelligent automated instructional design environment would be adaptive and accommodate both kinds of users.

Tennyson also argues for the integration of the five phases of ISD. Specifically, he argues that cognitive psychology should inform the process and that evaluation should be considered a valuable aspect of each phase and subphase of ISD. In keeping with the spirit of Tennyson's remarks, we have included in Part III our own attempts to evaluate the progress of designing AIDA (see the chapter by Muraida, Spector, O'Neil, & Marlino). Tennyson also contributes a valuable list of authoring activities appropriate to a fourth generation of instructional design, which is included as an appendix to this volume.

References

Duchastel, P. C. (1990). Cognitive designs for instructional design. *Instructional Science*, 19(6), 437–444.

Jones, M., & Wipond, K. (1990). Curriculum and knowledge representation in a knowledge-based system for curriculum development. *Educational Technology*, 30(5), p. 714.

Pirolli, P., & Russell, D. M. (1991). Instructional design environment: Technology to support design problem solving. *Instructional Science*, 19(2), 121–144.

Chapter Four

Prospects for Automating Instructional Design

Henry M. Halff

Introduction

This chapter explores both the limits of and opportunities for automation in the design and development of instruction. My intention is to argue for two recommendations:

(1) Automation should assist in the generation of instruction from known designs—not the creation of designs to be implemented manually.

(2) Automation projects should support existing instructional paradigms for broad subject-matter areas (e.g., computer programming), and should not strive to implement some "universal" theory of instructional design.

First, I lay the groundwork for these arguments by reviewing the main lines of research that do or should influence the field of instructional design. I begin with an examination of theory in learning and cognition, and follow this with a discussion of some newer work on the cultural bases of instruction. Then, I examine the relationship of these theories to research and recommendations of the instructional design community.

Next, I consider two general approaches to the automation of instructional design. On the advisory approach [not the same as Tennyson's advisory approach], computers advise instructional developers, and, in particular, devise designs for instructional applications. Design knowledge is represented in a computer and implementation is primarily the responsibility of a human developer. On the generative approach instructional designers rely on computers to generate the instruction that implements an existing design. Design knowledge is primarily resident in a human designer, who uses a computer to help implement the designs. That my sympathies lie with the generative approach should be evident.

I describe two challenging but not impossible projects that illustrate this approach. I use these two cases to speculate on the conditions appropriate for automated generation of instruction and on the problem of generality in instructional design. Then I present my understanding of the proposed architecture for AIDA and elaborate the implementation of AIDA in terms of two different ways to approach automating the design of instruction.

In the final section, I recap the arguments made earlier and suggest a number of research issues. These and other issues are taken up in more detail in Part III of this volume.

Theory and the Prospect of Automation

One of the main themes of this chapter is the relationship between the automation of some instructional design function and the justification for that function. Below, I argue that both of these functions require an explicit theory of instructional design. To set the context for the argument, and for other points to be made, a brief review of approaches to instructional design is in order. For a more thorough treatment, see Part I of this volume, especially Reigeluth's chapter.

Learning Theory

From a scientific point of view, the design of systems for human learning should be founded on a knowledge of the fundamental mechanisms of learning. The study of learning mechanisms has always been a major part of psychology. Learning research has its roots in the empiricist philosophers of the eighteenth century; it dominated American psychology almost completely in the first half of this century; and it is manifest today as cognitive psychology.

Fundamental Commitments. Throughout its history, research and theory on learning have been characterized by two strong commitments:

(1) Learning should be understood in mechanistic terms. A complete theory of learning is one that describes stimuli (inputs), responses (outputs), performance mechanisms (rules for generating inputs from outputs), and the laws of learning (rules that specify how the performance mechanisms change with experience).

(2) The unit of analysis in any theory of learning is the individual organism. If one can determine the laws that govern an individual's learning, one can then (in theory) account for his or her behavior in any setting, no matter how complex.

An approach to instructional design follows quite naturally from these commitments. The general goal of instruction is to arrange for optimal behavior across a range of stimulus situations. A complete learning theory predicts the behavior that results from any particular set of learning experiences. By inverting this function, it should be possible to determine which experiences optimize behavior.

The Cognitive Revolution. Early approaches to learning theory were born of the behaviorist tradition, which proposed that learning was nothing more than the establishment, through reinforcement, of associations between observable stimuli and observable responses. Coupled with performance rules to account for generalization and motivational effects, the behaviorists met with some success both in explaining learning in the lab and in assisting with the design of instruction.

The behaviorists' success, however, was limited to simple S-R spaces and to cases where instructional objectives could be defined in a clearcut fashion. In the sixties, it became clear, on both theoretical and empirical grounds, that the behaviorist approach could not account for the learning of complex skills such as language comprehension (Gold, 1967).

What emerged from the lessons of the sixties was the realization that most behavior of interest to instructional designers is mediated by intermediate, unobservable cognitive structures, and that these structures are too complex to be induced by a simple behaviorist approach to learning. Associations form during learning not between stimuli and responses but between cognitive structures, and learning typically has as much to do with development of the structures themselves as with the formation of associations among them.

As a result, instructional objectives must, at some point in the design process, be represented as the cognitive structures that support skilled performance (see Tennyson's Fourth Generation ISD model in Part II of this volume). Simply denoting the input-output (S-R) requirements of a skill is impossible for some skills and, in the case of other skills, insufficient for instructional purposes.

Unfortunately, there is no consistent methodology for determining the cognitive structures that support skilled performance, although cognitive task analysis is aimed at just this problem. A grab-bag of methods such as thinking-aloud protocols can be used to shed light on these structures, and a number of formalisms are available for representing them. However, there is no mechanistic way of applying the methods; there are no generally applicable means of determining the uniqueness of a particular cognitive model; and, there are no general methods of determining the learning mechanisms responsible for the acquisition of cognitive structures.

Although the cognitive revolution did considerable damage to the simple behavioristic approach to learning, it did not change the learning theorist's commitment to the fundamental principles mentioned above. Like behaviorists, cognitive psychologists seek a mechanistic explanation of learning, and like behaviorists, they are committed to understanding learning as a phenomenon of the individual learner.

Instruction and Culture

In this section we view instruction, not as the manipulation of fixed learning mechanisms but as a cooperative venture, one that takes advantage of corresponding teaching and learning mechanisms. We examine three lines of research, one concerned with cooperative mechanisms for structuring student-teacher interactions, a second that provides information on the role of structure in learning, and a third that examines more global issues concerning the cultural aspects of learning.

The Structure of Classroom Interactions. We begin with Mehan's (1979) "constitutive ethnography" of lessons delivered in a first-grade classroom. His objective was to show that interactions among students and the teacher were governed by a shared "grammar" that defined the structure of a lesson. The model developed by Mehan specified:

> the grammatical rules that could be used to "parse" a lesson into its constituent parts and subparts,

> the mechanisms used by students and teachers to instantiate the grammar (i.e., to make sure that all parts were included in the right order), and

> the mechanisms used to repair the structure whenever it was compromised by external or internal interruptions.

An overview of the grammar itself may give the reader some flavor for the results. Each lesson consists of these major phases (see Gagné's model in Part II of this volume for elaboration of a similar model):

an opening that orients the students to the lesson's activities,

a body, in which the class covers the subject matter, and

a closing, that serves to inform students of the end of the lesson.

The body, as Figure 4.1 shows, can be decomposed into the treatment or coverage of any number of topically related sets of interactions. Each interaction consists of a query (usually from the teacher), a reply (usually from a student), and an evaluation by the person initiating the interaction. The grammar is flexible enough to allow for some structure in the topically related groups and, more importantly, for extended interactions in which the conversation is extended until all three components satisfy the conversants.

Mehan provided empirical support for the model as an account of all of the interactions, captured on videotape, of thirteen lessons on different subjects at different times in a single firstgrade classroom. He was able to show that the proposed structure governed the majority of interactions in the classroom and that where the interactional structure was violated, the participants invariably invoked one of the proposed repair mechanisms.

Hierarchical
Organization

EVENT	Lesson					
PHASE	Opening		Instructional		Closing	
TYPE OF SEQUENCE	Directive	Inform.	Elicit	Elicit	Informative	Directive
ORG OF SEQUENCE	I-R-E	I-R (E$_o$)	I-R-E	I-R-E	I-R (E$_o$)	I-R-E
PARTICI-PANTS	T-S-T	T-S-T	T-S-T	T-S-T	T-S-T	T-S-T

Sequential Organization

KEY: T = teacher; S = student
I-R-E = initiation -reply-evaluation
E$_o$ = evaluation optional in informative sequence

Figure 4.1. The Structure of Classroom Lessons. (Adapted from H. Mehan, *Learning Lessons: Social Organization in the Classroom.* Cambridge, MA: Harvard University Press, 1979, Figure 2.1, p. 73.)

Mehan concludes that success in the classroom depends on mutual adherence to the interactional structure. The teacher found the structuring conventions useful in instructing only because the students "bought into" them. The students found the same conventions useful in learning only because the teacher made use of them in covering the subject matter.

It is this interdependence that makes it difficult to view what goes on in a classroom from a learning-theoretic point of view. It cannot be said that the students conform to some general laws of learning, for their behavior is clearly fitted to the particular social conventions at work in the classroom. Conversely, it cannot be said that the teacher applied general design principles to the construction of her lessons. The devices that she used to cover the subject matter depended on the particular social conventions used in the classroom.

Culture and Learning. After reading Mehan's work, one cannot help but be struck by the author's complete disinterest in learning and instruction. Although he offers elaborate and convincing evidence that classroom interactions are structured by a set of cultural conventions, he makes no claim that the resulting structure has anything to do with what students learn. Mehan's analysis provides much fodder for conjecture on this point, but for a precise account of the role of culture in instruction, we turn to the work of VanLehn (1987) and the design of instruction in multi-column subtraction skills. VanLehn's early work, done in collaboration with others, is well known and can be easily summarized. The early impetus for research in the area was the observation (Burton, 1982), that children at intermediate stages of learning exhibit systematic error patterns known as mind bugs and that it is possible to give a precise procedural account of each of these bugs. One bug, for example, is manifest in a procedure that writes, in the answer row of each column, the result of subtracting the smaller digit in the column from the larger.

A second step in this research (Brown & VanLehn, 1980) accounted for bugs in terms of a general procedural representation of the multi-column subtraction procedure itself. The procedural representation was rule-based, and the account proposed that bugs arise because students who are "missing" one or more rules are brought to an impasse on certain problems. Confronted with an impasse, the students use a local problem-solving strategy to produce a "syntactically" correct response. The smaller-from-larger bug, for example, is invented by students who have no borrowing rule when they face a problem requiring borrowing.

The third step in this line of research and the one of central concern here, addressed the acquisition of subtraction skills over the four-six year span that they are taught in school. VanLehn reached three crucial conclusions. First, students acquire the skill by inducing the multi-column subtraction procedure from exercises and examples. The semantics of the procedure, its relationship to the number system, and all other teleological considerations appear to have no effect on learning. VanLehn based this conclusion largely on the fact that student's choice of bugs shows no bias towards the semantics or purpose of the procedure.

Second, VanLehn showed that it is impossible, in principle, to induce the procedure for multi-column subtraction from a random sequence of examples or, more precisely, from a sequence of examples taken by the student to be random. The induction problem in this case has two faces. First, the procedure contains disjunctions or choices needed to handle special cases such as borrowing and borrowing from zero. No finite but unstructured set of examples contains enough information to allow a student to discriminate the correct rules. Second, the procedure calls for the computation of intermediate results, the results of borrowing in particular. Examples themselves do not offer enough information to induce the intermediate calculations.

At this point we are faced with a paradox. Students appear to learn this procedure from exercises and examples, yet these exercises and examples are not, in principle, sufficient to support learning. The problem is not specific to multi-column subtraction. Many of the procedures that we acquire are learned from exercises and examples, contain disjunctions, and have intermediate computations. How, then, do we learn these procedures?

VanLehn was forced to the conclusion that the exercises and examples provided to the student are not random and were not perceived by students as random. Rather, they are structured in such a way as to permit learning, and this structure was apprehended by the student. He proposed two design principles needed to make the procedure learnable. A one-step-per-lesson rule requires that the exercises and examples in a curriculum be grouped into lessons, and that each lesson addresses a single disjunction or step in the procedure under study. Examples and exercises in a lesson require only the step addressed in the lesson and steps acquired in previous lessons. Second, a show-work principle dictates that the results of intermediate calculations be shown in all worked examples. If these two principles constrain the design of a curriculum and if they likewise constrain the learning process, then it is possible to induce the subtraction procedure from a curriculum of exercises and examples.

On the design side he showed that textbooks do indeed conform to the one-step-at-a-time and the show-work principles. On the learning side he created all possible learning trajectories admissible under these principles and showed that the bugs and bug patterns in these trajectories matched approximately, but far from perfectly, the bugs and bug patterns found in children's performance.

What is important about step theory is not so much its empirical support as the conclusion that learning mechanisms and instructional design are interdependent. The design principles (one step per lesson and show work) are needed to sufficiently constrain the learning task, but these principles are only effective if they also constrain the student's learning process. Effective instructional design and effective learning are a cooperative enterprise. The designer and the learner, although without consultation, agree to honor the conventions needed for effective learning. Conventions that thus pervade our society are, by definition, deemed to be part of our culture. In this sense, VanLehn's approach provides the vital insight that culture, at least in some cases, makes learning possible by cutting the induction problem down to size.

Situated Cognition. The implicit presumption in our consideration of both Mehan's and VanLehn's work is that certain cultural mechanisms used for instructional purposes can be abandoned once the student leaves the instructional situation. In other words, the cultural conventions that support the acquisition of a skill can be divorced from the content of the skill itself. More recently, this presumption has been called into question by those interested in the notion of situated cognition.

The roots of the situated-cognition notion can be found in Dreyfus' (1972) arguments concerning the limits of formal (computer) representations as an account for behavior in natural settings. Learning theorists (including cognitive scientists) have long been fond of pointing out that complex behavior is nothing more than the interaction of simple mechanisms with a complex environment. Dreyfus turned this very proposition on its own creators by arguing that the environment is so complex that even complete knowledge of learning mechanisms will be useless in accounting for behavior in arbitrarily-chosen natural settings. The success of any cognitive-science model, Dreyfus argued, rests on simplifying ad hoc assumptions based on the scientist's intuitions about the relevant aspects of the situation being modeled.

More recently, similar arguments have been made by cognitive scientists interested in the effect or lack of effect of instruction on cognitive functions in non-instructional settings (Greeno, 1989; Brown, Collins, & Duguid, 1989). Critical to the thinking of these scientists is the contention that non-instructional situations almost always offer contextual support for cognitive operations that completely bypass the methods taught in school to accomplish the same ends. Often cited, for example, is Lave's (1988) observation of an individual who, when faced with the task of obtaining 3/4 of 2/3 of a cup of cottage cheese, measured out 2/3 of a cup, physically divided the result into quarters, and helped himself to three of the four quarters. Because he was situated in a context that afforded him the necessary tools, he was relieved of the burden of formulating a "school" method for achieving the result.

Insights on the situated nature of cognition have two lessons. First, they lead us to the conclusion that the cultural mechanisms used to make learning possible (or easier) may also have the unintended effect of limiting its applicability. In the extreme, the argument goes, instruction is so tailored to the instructional "culture" that it is totally useless in any other culture.

The second lesson is methodological. The methods that we use to study learning and to design instruction are themselves situated. The conclusions that we reach concerning learning and the recommendations that we provide to instructional designers depend on implicit agreements on the nature of instruction. The point is important when we entertain the notion of automating the design process because a computer does not share the same understandings as a human instructional designer. Hence, the same design recommendations may be interpreted in very different manners by machines and humans.

We return to this point in the next section, but the foundation for our discussion there rests on an understanding of the research tradition concerned explicitly with instructional design.

Instructional Design

The instructional design tradition (see Gagné's remarks in the introduction) is concerned with the development of a design science for instruction. Judging from the work of this community, their goal is a set of handbooks containing step-by-step instructions for designing, developing, and maintaining instruction.

Those working in this tradition have avoided the commitments of those who proceed from learning theory and have skirted many of the problems of the learning-theoretic approach.

Instructional design researchers are not explicitly committed to mechanism. Many of the guidelines found in their work make no reference to any mechanism of learning (and sometimes have no justification whatsoever). Where learning theory applies, it can be used in design recommendations. Other bases for a recommendation must be used when learning theory is noncommittal or irrelevant to a design decision.

Instructional designers also have been more aware of the situated nature of learning and performance. The research tradition, in fact, receives much of its impetus from the fact that much of training is not oriented towards the job requirements of the students. Instructional designers examine how performance assessment is done in the job situation and orient instruction to the results of that examination.

Fundamental Commitments. This is not to say that instructional designers do not have their own commitments. Unlike learning theorists, instructional designers are concerned with the process of designing instruction. They have a fundamental commitment to the development of a uniform design process that covers the life cycle of any instructional enterprise. This commitment has profound implications for both theory and practice. In theory, when considering the balance between the power of skill-specific instructional methods and the power of general instructional principles, instructional designers weigh in on the side of general instructional principles. In practice (and to the annoyance of many consumers of instructional design), instructional designers have a tendency to begin each project anew, often putting forth a major effort only to arrive at a design only slightly different from existing instruction.

A related commitment of instructional designers is a process that separates analysis from design and development (Tennyson's model in Part II of this volume is an exception). That is, they are committed to the belief that instructional objectives can be determined without reference to instructional methods. Conversely (and related to the point made above), instructional methods are not subject-specific. How to teach can be determined by the application of general instructional principles to instructional objectives. What distinguishes the teaching of calculus from the teaching of French are the objectives to be met, and not the principles used to meet those objectives.

This analysis-design process can be found in a number of other fields that espouse a top-down, systems approach to design. The top-down approach in the ISD tradition is typically an exercise in decomposition, classification, and mapping. Primary instructional goals are decomposed into a hierarchy of primary and enabling objectives. These objectives are then classified along several dimensions, and the results of the classification are mapped onto instructional methods. Instructional design therefore seeks to advise developers as to the kind of instruction to be used. The content of the instruction is the responsibility of the instructional developer.

The Theoretical Basis of Instructional Design. A theory of instructional design (or any other theory, in fact) need not be correct in all of its details, but it must carry with it the methodology for verifying any assertion made within the theory. We need to ask then what it means to verify any or all of the numerous design recommendations proposed by researchers in instructional design. (Part III of this volume addresses this issue in more detail.)

The instructional design community has difficulty in confronting this issue, and this imposes limits on the extent to which the instructional design process, as they view it, can be automated.

The heart of the problem is that the community has been concerned with the development of good instructional design but has not been explicit about what constitutes a design to begin with. As it stands now, instructional design recommendations, when they work, rely on implicit agreements among researchers and designers on what constitutes a design. The implementation of any particular recommendation in any particular situation depends on the designer's intuitions about how the recommendation should be interpreted in the particular context. In some situations these interpretations are straightforward. However, the variety of contexts and the complex dependencies among instructional objectives make it unlikely that any theory will be able to generate the wide range of human instructional endeavors, and still preserve all important distinctions among them.

Without knowing the possibilities for any particular instructional design, it is impossible to frame a method for validating a recommendation. Even more important for our purposes, the lack of an explicit design space limits the possibilities for automating the design process. Automating the design process itself would require a method for formally representing all of the knowledge that one might want to teach and casting the principles of instructional design so that they could work with the knowledge thus represented.

Approaches to Automating Design

It is not this book's intent to explore all of the ways that automation might support instructional design. We are concerned with ways that design knowledge can be incorporated into computers and used to create instructional materials. Eliminated from consideration are the use of computers for support functions such as document processing and the use of computers simply to store and present reference materials on instructional design.

Advisory Approaches

As already mentioned, one attractive use of computers in instruction is to involve them in the process of instructional design. A design advisor seems the ideal marriage of the vast body of instructional design rules and current expert-systems technology. Such a combination might well be able to support the design process by:

eliciting, from a human developer the instructional objectives for the application,

eliciting the information needed to classify each objective, and

creating a design for the course by applying design guidelines to the information gathered by the designer.

The advantages of this approach are evident. It would relieve instructional designers of the burdensome bookkeeping associated with the conventional process. It would provide an audit trail that could be used to justify the inclusion or exclusion of material and to provide a basis for course revision. Automating the design process would help to ensure a uniform, presumably high, quality of instruction. Automation would lower the skill requirements for instructional developers. However, the viability and usefulness of advisory systems rest on certain assumptions, each of which is questionable in the light of the above discussion.

One such assumption is that instructional design principles are separable from content. At issue is the extent to which design principles must be specialized. If the same design principle is used for all objectives requiring, say, classification of individual stimuli, then an advisory system could offer a considerable advantage. If, however, the design of troubleshooting training for, say, Ford Tauruses is governed by different principles than that for Buick LeSabres, an advisory system cannot participate usefully in the design process.

The usefulness of an advisory system also rests on the assumption that such a system complements the strengths and weaknesses of human developers. Even if an advisory system could make a substantive contribution to the instructional design process, it may well be that this contribution is not the one really needed by the instructional development community. It is not difficult to envision a system that takes an hour to lead an instructional developer to a conclusion that could be reached unassisted in five minutes. Nor is it difficult to envision the same system leaving the really difficult and time consuming aspects of development to the human developer. In short, a system that provides design guidance for human developers is only useful to the extent that those developers lack design skills and possess development skills.

The advisory systems envisioned here are principled. That is, they implement certain principles of instructional design to guide the developer through a top-down design process. The relative usefulness of such an approach depends on the relative effectiveness of this philosophy in dealing with real instructional-design processes. For development *de novo*, this approach may make sense, but I suspect that little instructional development starts from scratch. New training, in one way or another, is derived from old training. In some cases, developers may draw on the culture of the training institution to create new training. For example, commercial pilots qualifying for a new type of aircraft can expect the same type of training as they received in previous, similar situations. In other cases, the subject matter itself carries its own instructional methods. A scientist faced with the responsibility of keeping her graduate students abreast of their field normally makes available to her students the same mechanisms that she used to acquire the knowledge.

Finally, the effectiveness of an advisory system rests on the availability of the information required to drive the course development along the course set by the advisor. Instructional development can and must proceed in many cases when such knowledge is incomplete. For example, a commonly agreed-upon stage in instructional design is the formulation of explicit procedures for successful performance of a task. For some instructional objectives, such as multi-column subtraction, such procedural formulations are available. For others, such as X-ray interpretation or foreign-language translation, the best that can be hoped for are rules of thumb that only roughly characterize some presumed procedure.

In summary, the usefulness of advisory systems depends on their sufficiency and on the extent to which their functions match the needs of instructional developers. One view of instruction is that of a designed object much like a computer program or spacecraft. On this view, advisory systems offer considerable promise, since it should be possible to capture effective instructional design in a set of general principles and mechanically apply those principles to create new instruction.

Another view is that instruction is a product of evolution. That is, as knowledge evolves so do the mechanisms for its transmission. Some of these mechanisms are part and parcel of the subject matter; others are cultural; still others are genetic. On this view, the power of advisory systems is definitely limited. The normal course of instructional development is that of adopting and combining existing instructional techniques, perhaps without reference to design principles.

Generative Approaches

A different approach to the role of automation rests on the observation that relatively stable instructional paradigms characterize instruction in a number of areas. Troubleshooting and foreign-language training are two examples taken up below. Data entry, geography, and computer programming are other promising examples. In each of these cases, a general paradigm is configured to fit individual instructional applications. A basic method for troubleshooting training is fitted to different classes of devices. The same can be said for language training.

These cases offer the opportunity for automation to assist in the generation of materials for broad subject areas. Generative instructional tools already exist in a number applications of computer-assisted instruction. In their simplest form, they generate exercises for drill-and-practice of skills such as typing and arithmetic. In more sophisticated form, they generate instruction from an abstract representation of the knowledge to be taught (Crawford & Holland, 1983).

Generative approaches tend to be strong where advisory approaches are weak. They can be tailored to the level of generality achieved in the design that they implement. The simple systems for generating exercises in arithmetic are clearly suitable only for arithmetic. Systems like the IMTS (Towne, Munro, Pizzini, Surmon, & Wogulis, 1988) offer instruction across a broad class of troubleshooting domains, and systems such as the CBMS (Crawford & Holland, 1983) are limited not by the domain but by the form of knowledge in that domain.

In contrast to advisory approaches, generative approaches leave conceptual aspects of instructional design to a human designer and take over the more routine chores of implementing a design. Generative systems, rather than ignoring the evolutionary nature of instruction, can be tools for accelerating that process. They provide a formal representation of an instructional design, one known to be explicit enough to support the mechanical generation of materials. These designs can be refined, combined, and adopted to different needs. Changes in the resulting instruction can be unambiguously traced back to changes in the design itself. Design principles can be induced and applied within the scope of admissible variations in the design.

Two Proposals for Automated Generation of Instruction

To illustrate the potential for generative approaches to automation, I shall describe two particular opportunities for a generative approach. The applications chosen, foreign-language training and troubleshooting, are intentionally quite different. The first is meant to illustrate what might be done with a well-developed but poorly understood instructional design. The latter is intended to illustrate how general instructional principles, combined with precise knowledge of a skill can be used for controlled, automatic generation of a curriculum.

Foreign-Language Training

A first example of the potential for generative approaches to instruction is oriented towards the achievement of literacy in a foreign language. The situation is of interest both because of what is known about the subject and what is unknown.

Current Practice in Foreign-Language Training. Much of what would be considered essential for instructional design in foreign-language training is simply unavailable. Literacy in a foreign language is necessary and sufficient for the ability to translate written material between one's native tongue and the foreign language. Unfortunately, we are far from a complete understanding of the mechanisms that might be responsible for translation skills. There is no precise standard for an acceptable translation, and, for many texts, there is genuine disagreement among experts.

Although we lack a precise model of foreign-language literacy or translation skills, we do possess a rough intuitive grasp of the major components of the process. Among these components are the following:

pattern matching to identify idioms and other common expressions,

lexical translation to determine the possible senses and roles of the individual words in the text,

syntactic analysis to determine the text's phrase structure, and

semantic and pragmatic analysis to resolve lexical and syntactic ambiguities.

Although the details of these processes and the relationships among them are unknown, they serve as the basis for the design of instruction in foreign languages. Typically languages are taught through a sequence of distinct lessons each of which addresses instructional goals relating to idioms, syntax, and vocabulary. These goals relate to the first three components listed above. Training in the fourth component is not provided on a systematic basis although students are usually required to produce translations that reflect the meaning of the original text.

Lessons roughly conform to the canons of step theory. A limited number of grammatical constructions are presented so that the grammatical knowledge is built in a stepwise fashion. In addition, texts are chosen that reflect only the vocabulary and grammar under study or that covered in previous lessons.

Opportunities for Automation. In spite of the fact that foreign-language literacy is only partly defined, there is considerable opportunity for automation to assist in the construction of curricula addressing this skill.

At the lowest level, computers could examine candidate texts for each lesson and assemble vocabulary lists. The pattern-matching capabilities of current text-analysis software is capable of identifying idiomatic expressions in text. Hence, given the target text for each lesson, a computer could take over much of the chore of constructing the vocabulary and idiom sections.

More interesting is the possibility that computers can be used to create, refine, or evaluate the syntactic content of lessons. As was mentioned above, part of a typical lesson deals directly with one or a few syntactic components of the target language. Computers are capable of mechanically generating the examples needed to exhibit both well-behaved and irregular examples of the constructions under study.

More importantly, natural-language parsers are well-enough developed that they could both generate and analyze texts to be included in each lesson. Texts used in initial lessons must be highly constrained and are usually generated by the teacher or textbook writer to conform to the limited lexical and syntactic skills of the student. These same constraints should also allow computers to undertake the task of generating sample texts. In later lessons, texts become less constrained and, at some point, are drawn from the existing literature in the target language.

In addition, the task of checking these texts for conformance to instructional objectives becomes more difficult as the students' repertoire grows. Computers could be of considerable value in analyzing candidate texts for their fit into each lesson and even suggesting modifications to eliminate vocabulary or constructions beyond the scope of the lesson. Tools such as these could ensure not only that all objectives of each lesson are covered but also that material going beyond the lesson's objectives is excluded.

Finally, at the most abstract level, computers could assist in the construction of a curriculum that systematically developed the syntax of the language. In particular, it could draw on research in computational linguistics and language learning to develop the kind of procedural representation that VanLehn developed for multi-column subtraction. Armed with such a representation, it could sequence the components of the procedure, and create exercises and examples that corresponded to the sequence.

Advantages and Disadvantages. I chose foreign-language training because it illustrates both the strengths and weaknesses of the generative approach to automation of instructional design.

The possibilities discussed above are not revolutionary. They suggest incremental improvements in both the process and product of an existing instructional design. If that design is fundamentally flawed, then the mechanisms suggested above will be of little benefit. By the same token, the approach is wed to the domain of foreign-language training. The computer programs that provide the functions suggested above would be of no use outside of this domain.

On the other hand, where large gaps exist in our knowledge of the target skills, the generative approach to automation provides some promise of improving on existing practices. The development of programs such as those suggested here would ease the development burden, provide improved instructional materials, and sharpen our conceptions of how instruction is generated within the general paradigm.

Moreover, although the approach suggested is not a "universal instruction generator," its generality is well matched to the domain. There may be some set of general instructional principles that, in addition to suggesting the current design or an improved one, will be equally specific and helpful in its suggestions for history and automobile-repair curricula.

Troubleshooting

Our interest in foreign-language training was based on the existence of an instructional design applicable to a bounded but large set of specific instructional needs. A general paradigm for troubleshooting training also exists, but the paradigm itself is far less structured than that for foreign-language training. Typically, troubleshooting training is device specific. Students are, through lectures, provided with the theory of operation of a device and perhaps some hands-on practice manipulating the device. The heart of troubleshooting training is a sequence of exercises in which students must isolate a single specific fault in the device or in a simulation. The faults are typically chosen on the basis of their importance and sequenced in order of difficulty. Importance and difficulty are typically decided on the basis of intuitions.

Our psychological knowledge of troubleshooting is far more developed than that of language learning. The performance requirements of the skill are well known, and we have a reasonably complete picture of the cognitive concomitants of the skill. It should therefore be possible to construct models of particular troubleshooting tasks and use these models to select and sequence exercises.

Troubleshooting Defined. Troubleshooting, for our purposes, is the identification of faulty components in malfunctioning equipment. Our view of equipment is deliberately simplified. We view a piece of equipment as a network of components. Each component at any time is in one or a number of possible states. Each of the components receives inputs from one or more other components and delivers outputs to other components. Each of these outputs is a function of the component's inputs and state. Troubleshooters can observe some of the outputs and the states of some components. They can manipulate the states of some components (e.g., switches). Costs can be assessed for observations, replacements, and panel manipulations.

In typical training situations, certain simplifying assumptions govern the behavior of the equipment:

> Every malfunction is the result of a single faulted component, although in real equipment multiple faults often occur.

> Faults can be characterized as a change in the state or possible states of a component, not in the topology of the equipment, although in real equipment faults can change the nature of the connections among components.

> Neither testing nor replacing a component will fault another component, although in real equipment a faulted component can protect another component from damage.

Finally, we assume that there are no faulty replacements, even though real world technicians will on occasion return a faulted component to inventory.

These restrictions are the ones traditionally used in troubleshooting training and in tests of troubleshooting competence. I suspect that they are part of the maintenance-training culture. Without them, many trouble-shooting exercises would be insoluble and many of the soluble ones would be uninstructive. In some settings, other simplifications may also apply. For example, feedback loops may be eliminated, or components may be limited to a single fault mode.

The Cognitive Psychology of Troubleshooting. Cognitively oriented studies of troubleshooting are not new. However, it is only recently that we have seen theories of skilled troubleshooting sufficiently precise to support modeling of individual performance.

One compelling account of troubleshooting skill is that of Rouse and his colleagues (Hunt & Rouse, 1984; Rouse & Hunt, 1984; Rouse, Rouse, & Pellegrino, 1980). A recent version (Hunt & Rouse, 1984) of this group's theory holds that skilled troubleshooters work with two distinct strategies. Both of these strategies are represented as sets of rules that control the focus of attention. One set of rules, called T-rules, captures device-independent troubleshooting expertise. These rules match configurations found in the device to common patterns which are, in turn, associated with trouble-shooting actions or decisions. Hunt and Rouse (1984) give the following example:

IF the output of X is bad and X depends on Y and Z and,
IF Y is known to be working, THEN check Z.

The rule potentially applies to any three components of the device that match the rule's condition.

A second strategy is embodied in rules called S-rules that capture de-vice-specific troubleshooting skills. S-rules match to specific patterns of observations in the device rather than general configurations of compo-nents. Rouse and Hunt suggest the following S-rule for troubleshooting automobiles:

IF the engine will not start and the starter motor is turning and
IF the battery is strong, THEN check the gas gauge.

Both S-rules and T-rules are local in scope. That is, their conditions contain no information on the overall impact of applying the rule. For ex-ample, the T-rule given above might match a part of the device that contains fairly little information about the fault's location and also to a pattern containing a great deal of information about the location of the fault. All other things being equal, troubleshooters should, and do, choose the latter configuration. Rouse and Hunt found it necessary to account for this effect by conditioning the rule selection process on each rule's usefulness. Towne, Johnson, and Corwin (1983) also found that observations are chosen largely on the basis of their information value.

This research indicates that skilled troubleshooters base their troubleshooting decisions on three aspects of the troubleshooting situation:

device-specific associations between symptoms and faults,

device-independent configurations of components, and

the information-theoretic value of potential decisions.

One final result worth mentioning concerns the generality of troubleshooting skills. Higher-level cognitive skills have been found to be generally resistant to transfer, but the results described in Rouse and Hunt (1984) indicate that if students are taught to troubleshoot a variety of different systems, they have an advantage in learning to troubleshoot a new system. Two factors, I believe, were critical to this finding. First, Rouse and his colleagues knew where to look for transfer in the sense that device-independent techniques (T-rules) are known to operate in the training and transfer domains. Second, the successful transfer experiments provided training in more than one domain, thus conferring an advantage on device-independent skills during training.

Computer-Aided Generation of Troubleshooting Curricula. The foregoing suggests that troubleshooting training can have either or both of two distinct objectives. Some individuals (consumer electronics technicians, for example) may need training in device-independent troubleshooting techniques. Others (advanced avionics technicians, for example) will need training in device-specific skills. The training techniques for these two objectives will be different, but computers can help in each case.

We now present principles for selecting and sequencing troubleshooting problems (as exercises and examples) and the role of computers in implementing these principles.

1. *Teaching General Troubleshooting Skills*

The results cited above indicate that general troubleshooting skills should be taught by using problems drawn from a variety of devices with a variety of structures. These problems should be selected to promote these cognitive skills:

pattern-recognition skills that enable troubleshooters to identify simple configurations of components,

skills in identifying the appropriate troubleshooting action for each of
the patterns identified, and

device-comprehension skills that allow students to choose the most
information-laden observations.

With certain extensions, current models of troubleshooting could be
used to provide specific definitions for each of these skills. The main stum-
bling block to achieving such a model at this time is the lack of a suitable
representation scheme for devices. Both intuition and evidence from studies of cognitive structures indicate that troubleshooters represent devices in
terms of a hierarchical decomposition. Such a decomposition makes device
comprehension manageable and almost automatically leads the trouble-
shooter to the most information-laden observations. Also, to the extent that
the device is designed hierarchically, a decomposition may be evident in its
documentation.

The task of creating a curriculum of problems is one of finding the
principles that apply to this situation. Note, for example, that the learning
situation envisioned here is subject to the same sources of difficulty that
VanLehn found in multi-column subtraction. Both the pattern-recognition
and device-comprehension skills involve disjunctions (choice points), and
unobservable intermediate results (the choice of a pattern) are involved in
every troubleshooting decision. This suggests that problems be grouped
into lessons that reflect the stepwise development of pattern-recognition
and device comprehension skills and that some method be used to exhibit
the intermediate results required to make each troubleshooting decision.

The availability of a psychologically valid model of device-independent
troubleshooting skills makes it possible to represent the design requirements for the curriculum in formal, computational terms. Thus, a computer could be used to generate candidate problems for each lesson that
meet the stepwise refinement requirements of the lesson. Furthermore,
given a suitable way of displaying intermediate results, computers could
generate materials that would show students otherwise unobservable steps
in the troubleshooting process.

The system sketched above could not, in itself, completely automate
the generation of instructional materials. For one thing, the system would
not generate a unique curriculum, and developers would need to choose
among those available. In addition, giving a nod to proponents of situated
cognition, some effort should be made to situate the abstract problems in

realistic scenarios. Finally, it might be wise to include a verbal description of the troubleshooting procedure and its basis.

2. Teaching Device-Specific Troubleshooting Skills

The research discussed above indicates that these recognition skills tend to develop naturally as students become familiar with the devices. Of interest here are the possibilities that training can accelerate the acquisition of device-specific strategies and, more importantly, selectively promote the acquisition of more effective strategies.

The key to realizing these training goals is to develop a specific set of device-dependent strategies; determine the troubleshooting procedure (typically a discrimination net) that best implements the strategies; and devise a curriculum targeted to that procedure. Computers can help in these ways:

by generating alternative device-specific strategies;

by evaluating the relative utility of a device-specific strategy, comparing its cost to that of its device-independent counterpart;

by evaluating an entire set of device-dependent strategies, inducing the troubleshooting procedure needed to implement the set and assessing its complexity; and

by generating the sequence of problems that will most effectively teach a device-dependent troubleshooting procedure.

3. Keys to Generative Curricula

We can summarize the suggestions made above by recapping the philosophy behind automated generation of troubleshooting curricula. Automation becomes relevant in this case because of the potential for formally representing the space of troubleshooting problems in a way that reflects the knowledge requirements of the skill. It is under these circumstances that instructional design principles, such as show-work, shed their vague character, and become tools for automatic curriculum generation. In both of the cases discussed above, we envision a system that, working from a procedural representation of the target skills, creates a sequence of troubleshooting lessons. The first lesson would start with the simplest case. Subsequent lessons would add refinements to the procedure, one step at a time, by introducing problems that exercise the use of the target refinements. In addition, for each problem generated, the computer would provide a trace of each problem's solution. These traces could form the basis for implementing the show-work principle.

The important point of this example, however, is not the extent to which instructional development is automated but the nature of the automation and its prerequisites. Required are a formal and psychologically valid model of the troubleshooting process and instructional principles that can be applied to the model. The result is a curriculum guaranteed to conform to the principles. This guarantee cannot be met if one of the three components—formality, psychological validity, or instructional principles—is missing.

Is There a Single Generative Approach? The two examples presented here are, by design, quite different. The foreign-language example shows that automation has the potential for generating and evaluating materials even when the target skill is not well specified. The opportunity for automation in this case is the existence of a well-worked out instructional design whose components can be matched with formal cognitive representations of the material needed to implement the design.

The second example, troubleshooting training, by contrast suffers from a weak instructional design and fairly complete knowledge of the skill itself. In this case instructional principles can be put in correspondence with a formal cognitive model of the target skill in order to produce a curriculum.

Thus, to the extent that we accept the promise in these approaches, it appears that there is no one set of conditions that make a generative approach attractive. The strength of the generative approach is its ability to achieve uniformity within its area of application. Its application to any one area may be almost completely *ad hoc*.

I suspect that the *ad hoc* nature of this approach has to do with the nature of instruction in general. In both of the examples above, some formal representation of cognition in the target area corresponded to some set of instructional principles or methods. Since I see no prospect for a uniform, formal interface of all instructional methods to all domains of human knowledge, opportunities for generating instruction with computers will remain a matter of judgment and intuition.

Preliminary Observations about Automating ID

Computers Should Make Things Better or Easier

The appropriate use of computers is for tasks that humans do poorly or with some difficulty. We have suggested above that one such class of tasks is the generation of large amounts of instructional materials that must, by design, conform to complex specifications. To the extent that those specifications can be formalized, a computer can be used to automate the process.

Other opportunities for automation exist in roles supportive of the instructional design process. These include document processors, authoring systems, data-analysis programs, and automated retrieval of reference materials, to name a few. One could even envision an automated procedural guide to the instructional design process that would track the design as it developed and make suggestions for completing the design.

Not useful would be any tool that pre-empted design tasks that could be done better and more easily by an unassisted human developer. A program that insisted on wending its way through a complex set of design rules and principles on the pretext of actually creating a design would be a counterproductive use of computers.

Build on Existing Instructional Knowledge

If, as I propose above, instruction develops more by evolution than by design, it would be a serious mistake to provide computer support for one design approach without examining the potential for supporting other approaches. Many courses developed today are, either explicitly or implicitly, derived from other similar courses. This imitative approach to design may be inappropriate in some instances, but in many cases it is the most effective route to a new design. More than passing attention should be given to automation efforts that support the adaptation of a design to many different applications. Not recommended would be a commitment to support with automation only those design efforts that conform to a top-down ISD process.

Generality Is a Sacred Cow

The instructional design community has made no bones about its commitment to offering guidance on the development of every sort of instruction (see Gagné & Briggs, 1979). This commitment to generality is laudable on general grounds and makes particular sense in the context of instructional design. One reason for embracing generality is that one never knows what sorts of instructional mechanisms will be needed until the design process is well underway. The general stance is also a welcome contrast to typical efforts in other research communities. More often than not educational research deals with effectiveness of a single mechanism in a single, often artificial context. Real instructional problems are only solved with a combination of instructional techniques. One of ISD's major strengths is its ability to help designers assemble and configure a variety of mechanisms to meet particular instructional needs.

However, the goal of generality in the design process itself is not necessarily a recommendation for generality in automated support for instructional design. Today's computers are simply not equipped to make many of the judgments needed to create an effective design. They can offer support for selected tasks in the design process and they can participate, in certain cases, in the generation of materials. Those interested in supporting instructional design with computers should pitch the level of generality of their efforts to those appropriate for the tool being developed, not at the level of generality of the design effort itself.

The AIDA Concept

Next, I shall examine how the AIDA concept applies in particular instructional development contexts and suggest how the concept could be most profitably automated in those contexts. I'll elaborate the AIDA concept in two specific instructional development contexts (one real, one fictional). The discussion of each context includes a thumbnail sketch of its main characteristics, a description in terms of the AIDA concept, and suggestions for appropriate automation of the Concept. As will be seen, certain important differences between the two contexts have a critical influence on the automation of instructional design within each context.

The AIDA concept (see the AIDA Concept figure in the introduction to Part II) is a description in information processing terms of instructional design, development, and delivery currently being proposed as the high level AIDA architecture. Further elaboration is required before any serious use can be made of this concept (Gagné, Merrill, and Tennyson offer alternative elaborations later in Part II of this volume).

The Content Component

In describing the Content component, we need to ask about the function of the component, about its structure, and about the practices used in particular instructional situations. All three of these issues are problematic.

A naive behavioristic view holds that content is nothing more than a description of the tasks that students should be able to perform as the result of training. Views informed by cognitive science, however, see the futility of this approach for all but the simplest of instructional situations. Most instructional developers now view course content more in terms of what students are to learn.

The switch from a behavioral to a cognitive perspective provides two advantages. First, it allows one to precisely represent complex instructional objectives, for example, that of recognizing a well-formed chemical formula. Second, it incorporates into the instructional design process, the specification of the intermediate cognitive structures that support skilled performance. For example, a behavioristic specification of the content of a troubleshooting course might be nothing more than a list of symptoms and appropriate troubleshooting actions (tests and replacements). A cognitive representation would include specifications related to interpreting block diagrams, selecting tests, and refining hypotheses lists.

Unfortunately, the more ambitious one is about the function of the Content component, the more difficult and complex are the problems of specifying its form and implementing that specification. Most instructional designers seek a language-like representation of instructional content in which structure (syntax) is clearly separated from content (semantics). This separation finds its advantage in principles of instructional design that operate on the structure or syntax of the content without having to worry about the content or semantics. In practice, the representation of content is even further constrained by instructional-design considerations. Most views of instructional design (e.g., Gagné & Briggs, 1979) require a content representation in terms of instructional objectives that can be matched to corresponding instructional methods.

Once the function and form of the Content component have been adopted, there remains the issue of actually representing a particular content area. Neither the cognitive science community nor the instructional design community has had much success in devising powerful, uniform, broadly applicable methods for inducing the cognitive structure of a skill. What we have instead is a grab-bag of empirical and formal methods with only the roughest of intuitive guidelines as to their use. A reasonably sharp cognitive or instructional scientist can usually, by dint of intensive effort, create a cognitive representation of a skill. However, another individual would probably arrive at a completely different analysis, and no one would find either of their analyses to be of much help in conducting an analysis of a different type of skill. The most hopeful statement that one can make is that skills may come in families, for example, electronic troubleshooting, foreign-language learning, and computer programming. Analysis of the family as a whole may yield significant dividends over separate analysis of individual members.

The following critical points summarize this discussion:

Content must be represented in a generative, cognitive form. It is a competence model and must, of necessity, identify the mechanisms whereby competence is to be achieved.

Instructional design methods place non-trivial constraints on the form of the Content component. They require that syntax or structure be separable from content or semantics. They also require the explicit representation of instructional objectives in the Content component.

Even within these constraints, there are no uniform methods for analyzing particular skills. Some skills may, however, fall in families that admit to a common structure.

The SET Component

The SET component represents information about **S**tudents, the learning **E**nvironment, and the target **T**asks. Different conceptions of the structure of this component lead to different approaches of the instructional design process.

The simplest conception of the SET component is that of a finite list of features that describe certain aspects of the students, instructional environment, and target tasks. The list might include level of motivation (a student feature), availability of laboratories (an environment feature), and availability of job aids (a task feature). The feature list could be quite long, but only a fraction of its members would be relevant to any particular design.

The feature-list approach to SET leaves much to be desired. In particular, it does not allow for use of content-specific aspects of students, the instructional environment, or the task. Not represented in a fixed feature list, for example, are the student's level of mastery of particular objectives, the availability of equipment for practicing particular parts of a skill, or the frequency with which particular operations are encountered on the job. Accommodating this information would, at the least require an overlay approach (Carr & Goldstein, 1977), whereby SET features are represented in a structure isomorphic to that of the Content component. Thus, if the AIDA concept is to produce instruction sensitive to particular student knowledge and compentence, particular training opportunities, and particular task characteristics, the SET component must be dependent on the Content component.

Also problematic is that aspect of the SET component that is innocuously labeled "task." As originally conceived, this aspect of the SET component specifies the goals and behavioral objectives of the skill to be learned. It therefore forms the basis for the content analysis described above. In many cases, the task has a complex structure that is imposed on the Content component.

The relationship between students, tasks, and content can be even more complex. Consider, for example the following three situations:

1. Students proficient in the maintenance of avionics systems in general are to be trained to maintain the avionics of the F-22, the Air Force's latest fighter.

2. Students not proficient in the maintenance of avionics systems in general are to be trained to maintain the avionics of the F-22.

3. Students not proficient in the maintenance of avionics system are to be trained in to maintain the avionics of the F-22 in such a way that they also acquire skills helpful in or sufficient for maintenance of other avionics systems.

These three cases, in which the primary instructional objectives are ostensibly identical, each call for vastly different representations of student knowledge, task definition, and content knowledge.

To summarize, the separation of SET from Content may be misleading. Whenever content-specific aspects of the students, environment, or task play a role in the instructional design, the SET component will acquire a structure derived from the Content component. Conversely, material in the Content component may, in part, derive from the structure and/or content of the task description. Thus, in some instructional designs, the SET and Content components will be functionally independent; in others they will be so closely related as to be inseparable; and one can envision the full range of possibilities between these two extremes.

Instructional Strategies

An instructional strategy is a procedure for teaching a single objective. It is abstract in that it is general over the class of objectives to which the strategy applies. It takes, as data, student characteristics and the material that defines the particular objective. It produces, as output, instruction to be delivered to the student.

A couple of examples may help make the concept clear. Figure 4.2 presents a strategy for teaching a serial, non-branching procedure. Note that it is applicable to any serial, non-branching procedure. Figure 4.3 illustrates a strategy for teaching computer programmers how to use a primitive of a new language when a corresponding primitive of an old language is available. Both strategies are general. However, that of Figure 4.2 is applicable to a wide range of domains; that of Figure 4.3 is applicable to one domain and only in particular circumstances. The strategies employed in most curricula are a mix of general and domain-specific strategies.

Also worth noting here is that these strategies make no commitment to media or other aspects of the training environment. Depending on the interpretation of terms such as elicit and exhibit, one could execute these procedures in a classroom, in a laboratory, or on the job.

The representation of instructional strategies is a critical issue for ISD in general and for the AIDA concept in particular. To appreciate the enormity of the problem, it is helpful to remind ourselves that a complete representational theory of instructional strategies must accommodate both the vast range of material that can be conveyed through instruction and the vast range of mechanisms available for conveying material.

OBJECTIVE

> Error-free execution of a serial, non-branching procedure.

STRATEGY

> Inform the student of the nature of the objective.
> Exhibit the entire procedure.
> For each step N,
> > Repeat until success
> > > Exhibit steps 1 to N.
> > > Have the student execute steps 1 to N.
> > Success is error-free execution.

Figure 4.2. Instructional Strategy—Non-branching Procedure.

As Merrill points out in his chapter, the instructional design research community is of two minds on the nature of strategies. The conventional approach, which he calls ID_1 is based on a set of universal instructional primitives that can be composed into strategies. One primitive, for example, might produce a verbal statement of some aspect of the material. Another might generate and exhibit an example. Others might query students in particular ways.

One might argue that the strategy illustrated in Figure 4.3 is nothing more than a specialization of some domain-independent strategy. A proponent of this argument, however, would be obligated to exhibit the operations that permit some strategies to be represented as specializations of others. She would also be obligated to show, in this case, which generalization of the strategy in Figure 4.3 is most useful in designing computer-programming instruction.

OBJECTIVE

> Use of a programming primitive, P, in a new language, L.

PREREQUISITE

> Use of the corresponding primitive, P', in an old language, L'

STRATEGY

> Exhibit the syntax and function of P.
> Exhibit the relationship of P to P'.
> Exhibit a procedure in L' using P' and the corresponding procedure in L.
> Exhibit a program in L' using P' and elicit the corresponding program in L.
> Exhibit a programming assignment in L that requires the use of P and elicit the solution.

Figure 4.3. Instructional Strategy—Language Primitive.

Merrill (1989) and I (Halff, 1989) have pointed out that an approach based on primitives leaves much to be desired. In the first place, the set of primitives is open ended; there is no principled way of generating a unique, or even a canonical set. Second, effective instruction incorporates complex constraints among instructional primitives as they are assembled into strategies. A teacher, for example, may refer to particular exercises in a textbook. Exercises and examples in most curricula are subject to sequential constraints (VanLehn, 1987). Interactive instruction also appears to be governed by complex relations among individual instructional primitives (Collins & Stevens, 1982).

Needed, therefore, to compose primitives into strategies, are not only the mechanisms for selecting the primitives but also ways of representing procedurally all pertinent constraints among them. Needed, therefore, is nothing less than a generative grammar of instruction. Although it may be possible to write such a grammar for particular objectives or fixed set of objectives, to actually write one for an interestingly large class of domains is well beyond any foreseeable advances in instructional design. This is not to say that skilled instructors do not or cannot implicitly exercise such a grammar in the course of designing instruction.

Rather than dealing with instructional primitives, it seems more promising to collect and implement instructional strategies as integral, blackbox units, which Merrill (see Merrill's chapter) calls transaction-frames. On this approach, strategies can be tailored to individual situations in specific, *ad hoc* ways, but they cannot be disassembled, transformed, and reassembled. Once configured to a particular instructional purpose, transaction frames become special-purpose procedures called simply transactions. Transaction-frames or blackbox strategies can be viewed as cultural products, subject to the methods and principles of natural science. Even if they cannot be generated, they can be collected, classified, studied, and used.

What one gains from the transaction-frame approach is feasibility. What one sacrifices is generality. By simply collecting all of the transaction-frames appropriate to an objective or domain, one can ensure effective instruction for the objective or domain. There is no principled way of applying the products of this exercise to another domain. Different objectives will almost certainly require different transaction frames, and some, all, or none of the instruction frames appropriate to one domain could be useful in another.

Neglected in the current conception of AIDA is the notion of a curriculum, the collection of strategies that generate a course of instruction. I mention it only in passing here, noting that the problems that arose at the strategy level arise also at the curriculum level. Curricula must reflect complex, often *ad hoc*, constraints among strategies. The two general approaches to representing curricula are (1) a generative grammar in which strategies are lexical items or (2) *ad hoc* existing schemata that dictate the configuration of strategies in a curriculum. See Reigeluth and Stein (1983) and Gagné and Briggs (1979) for suggestions regarding the first approach.

In summary, we have been concerned with the instructional strategies that constitute procedures for delivering objective-specific instruction in the AIDA concept. Strategies might be represented by a generative scheme based on a fixed set of instructional primitives and a grammar expressing the structure of strategies. A more feasible alternative views strategies as black boxes (transaction frames) that can be tailored on an *ad hoc* basis to meet particular instructional objectives. The generative approach has the advantage of providing a complete, principled approach to strategy representation but is infeasible for general instructional design purposes. The transaction-frame approach is potentially labor intensive and not based on explicit principles but it does offer extensibility to almost any domain.

The AIDA Executive

The task of the AIDA Executive is, in brief, to analyze any of a broad range of Content and SET and to produce a set of procedures that will effectively teach the material. The Content can be represented in any number of ways: semantic nets, production systems, uninterpreted text, and neural networks, to name a few. The procedures created by the AIDA executive must be able to transform these various representations into forms suitable for consumption by students, human instructors, and mechanical teaching devices.

The procedures must also, when run, provide effective instruction. The AIDA executive therefore has a problem somewhat more challenging than that of software design, and the central issue in the design of the Executive is how to meet this challenge.

What makes the task feasible are constraints on the representation of both the input to and output from the AIDA Executive and a judicious division of labor among the subcomponents of the Executive:

> The content is represented by a grammar that parses the subject matter into objectives.

> Instructional strategies are either generated or selected and matched to objectives.

> The strategy is configured to the content by filling slots for content-specific material.

The strategy is configured to the student(s) and the training environment by filling slots with corresponding information from the SET component.

Thus, the Executive's success lies in properly structuring the Content and SET components and providing a workable set of strategies. If strategies are generated from instructional primitives, then the Executive composes each strategy by exercising the generative grammar in the context of Content and SET specifications. If strategies are based on transaction frames, then the Executive selects the frame and configures it according to Content and SET specifications.

Instructional Delivery

The reader at this point may ask why the AIDA concept makes reference to strategies at all. Why not connect the AIDA Executive directly with the student by making it responsible for instructional delivery? The answer to this question lies in the need for interactive instruction. Because instruction is generally interactive, the product of an instructional design must have a procedural representation. That is, it must be represented as a strategy.

Current instructional design methods can be classified into one of a small number of levels of interactivity:

Some forms of instruction are non-interactive. Uninterruptable lectures, films, and other presentations are of this sort.

Most forms of instruction offer at least a moderate level of self pacing. Students can decide when to turn the pages of a text or can proceed through the steps of a laboratory exercise at their own pace.

Most forms of instruction offer some sort of local feedback. The practice of many skills (e.g., bowling) automatically provides information about performance.

Some forms of instruction offer local interactive control over the curriculum. The branching strategies used in most computer-based instruction are of this sort. I use the term local here to indicate that branching decisions in this type of instruction are context free.

Qualitative simulations such as STEAMER (Holland, Hutchins, & Weitzman, 1984) are examples of instruction that reach a context-sensitive level of interactivity. The response of such systems to student actions is a complex function of the evolving instructional context.

Some forms of instruction are conversational. They rely on strategies that query, inform, and listen to students in natural language or a medium of equivalent power and complexity. Classroom and tutorial discussions are prime examples of this level of interactivity. These forms of instruction are not only context sensitive, but also incorporate some form of planning and abstraction of the instructional context.

These levels roughly delineate the information-processing requirements of the instructional delivery mechanism(s). Self-paced instruction, for example, need only be able to determine when to undertake the next step in an instructional procedure, based on input from the student. The mechanism for delivering conversational instruction, on the other hand, must have the full power of natural language.

Also important is the interface between the instructional delivery mechanism and the curriculum. Instructional delivery systems that embody complex instructional procedures can operate with high-level representations of the curriculum. Competent human instructors, for example, can convert general written guidelines for a classroom discussion into a complex procedure for conducting the discussion. Strategies for computer delivery need to be written in machine-interpretable form. Some forms of instruction such as text and (uncoached) batting practice need no interpretation at all.

In summary, the design of an instructional delivery system must take into account two types of information-processing requirements. First, the level of interactivity with students will impose information-processing demands on the delivery system. Second, the delivery system must be able to interpret strategies in the form provided by the AIDA Executive.

Evaluation

Evaluation is commonly viewed as being either summative or formative. The distinction serves us well here even if we take some liberties with their definitions:

Summative evaluation is scientific enterprise designed to test the assumptions underlying the instructional design.

Formative evaluation is an exercise in optimization, designed to determine the best values for unknown parameters of the instructional design.

In most applications, a third aspect of evaluation, quality control, is also required:

Quality control assesses the conformance of the instructional design and delivery process to its specification.

That these three types of evaluation are interdependent is obvious but often overlooked in practice. A formative evaluation cannot be done until quality-control issues have been resolved. A summative evaluation is meaningless unless the instructional system has been optimized through a formative evaluation.

Quality control. Quality control is based on a specification of system outputs under a particular configuration, without regard to whether that configuration is the optimal or whether the underlying assumptions behind the system are valid. Quality control is achieved when the actual system outputs conform to that specification. Within the AIDA concept, quality can be assessed by determining the extent to which:

information provided for content analysis is properly converted to a content representation,

information provided about students, the training environment and the task is properly represented in the SET component,

the AIDA Executive produces specified curricula from SET and Content information, and

the instructional delivery mechanism faithfully executes the procedures produced by the AIDA Executive.

Quality can be assessed in controlled experiments or by natural observation. An appropriate experimental technique for assessing quality relies on the use of a validation suite, a set of standard inputs and outputs known to conform to the system design. Natural experiments for quality evaluation within the AIDA framework are more difficult to design since, in a natural setting, the true values of intermediate stages are unknown. Nonetheless, it may be possible in particular cases to devise indices and standards for quality that are not contaminated by uncertainty in the parameters of the system.

In evaluating quality, it is also important to keep in mind the difference between general, system-related problems, and special problems only manifest under certain circumstances. These two aspects are commonly separated by observing system performance under a variety of circumstances. Since special problems in AIDA will almost always be manifest as human error, thorough quality testing calls for observing system behavior with a number different designers, instructors, and other human elements.

Formative evaluation. Formative evaluation is a technique for optimizing system performance under conditions of uncertainty about the system's parameters. Therefore, to understand how formative evaluation might function in the AIDA concept, we need to examine sources of uncertainty in system characteristics. Among such sources of uncertainty are the following.

Indeterminacy in the derivation of content from task. Data from a content analysis will often be insufficient to uniquely determine the cognitive structures that support competent performance. At these junctures, the content analyst makes an arbitrary decision which may have downstream consequences for instruction.

Nonidentifiable parameters of students and environment. It may be theoretically impossible to determine the values of some student or environment parameters at the time of course design and development. Typically some arbitrary choice is made which may, like arbitrary content decisions, have downstream consequences for instruction.

Simplifying assumptions to remove variance. The distributions of students and training circumstances are often unknown at the time of training development. Even if they are known, it is usually infeasible to optimize a design for the entire distribution of possibilities. Typically, then, the designer simplifies the problem by designing for a typical student and typical circumstances. The performance of the system may degrade so in nontypical circumstances that this simplification is not warranted.

Arbitrary assignment of strategy to objective. The mix of strategies used to address an objective is often the result of intuition or isolated empirical results. Strategies other than the ones chosen may, in fact, provide better instruction.

Arbitrary cost-effectiveness decisions. During design, and particularly during delivery, decisions may be made to sacrifice effectiveness for costs savings (or vice versa) without complete knowledge of the trade-off function. Such practices will often lead to suboptimization of overall cost-effectiveness.

Indeterminacy is assessing student characteristics during instruction. Much interactive instruction relies on assessment-instruction feedback loops in which instruction is tailored to the results of a particular assessment. Pocedures for both testing and scoring these instruments may constitute sources of uncertainty.

Formative evaluations have three components. First, specific sources of uncertainty are identified. Second, a sensitivity analysis is conducted to determine which of the identified sources has an effect on instruction. Third, experiments are conducted to evaluate different approaches to the sources that pass a sensitivity criterion.

Formative evaluation is difficult. An inspection of the partial list above indicates the difficulty of even identifying sources of uncertainty. Typically, instructional designers encounter enough difficulty in arriving at one viable set of assumptions that consideration of alternatives is not possible within the resources allotted to the development. Nonetheless, where difficult and potentially critical decisions are made, the three-component process can help in selecting the best choice.

Summative evaluation. Summative evaluation can be used to identify where instruction or instructional designs produced under the AIDA concept meet or fail to meet expectations. A summative evaluation can be as simple as a criterion-referenced test given to students. However, one can envision more thorough summative evaluation designed to assess all stages of the AIDA concept:

Pretests of students and empirical observations of the training environment can be used to evaluate the validity of the SET component.

A number of techniques (Anderson, 1988) from cognitive psychology can be used to assess the validity of the Content component as a model of competence.

On occasion, learning models will be available to test the effectiveness of instructional strategies in particular cases, but, as I have pointed out elsewhere (Halff, 1989), opportunities for this sort of assessment are limited.

Finally, the effectiveness of instructional delivery can be evaluated by tests of student's behavior.

The evaluation model described here serves to illustrate two general points about evaluation. Performance deficiencies can result from several causes. Implementation can fail to meet design specifications. The design can be suboptimal. The assumptions underlying the design can be in error. Because different remedies apply to these different problems, an effort should be made to separately evaluate their contributions to system performance.

Performance deficiencies can arise at any stage in the development process. For this reason, evaluation efforts should provide information, not only on the nature of problems but also on their specific locus within the AIDA concept.

No matter how extensive the evaluation effort, these points cannot be ignored. The value of any evaluation instrument lies in its potential to deliver precise information on the cause and locus of deficiencies in the design and development process.

Critical Issues for AIDA

The foregoing material presents a rough description of the AIDA concept and delineates the issues critical to its implementation in any context. Before turning to context-specific considerations, a review of these issues is appropriate.

Content. The Content component is a cognitive model of what is taught. It has both structural, syntactic aspects and content, semantic aspects. Critical is the syntax governing the structure of course content and, in particular, the extent to which that structure is constrained by instructional considerations. Also critical are the methods used to determine and represent the semantic aspects of the Content component.

SET. The SET component represents information about students, the instructional environment, and the task being taught. The overriding issue in the design of this component is its relationship to the Content component. The structure of the content may or may not be reflected in information about students and the instructional environment. Conversely, the structure of the content may or may not reflect the structure of the task. Dependent on the resolution of these questions is the structural complexity of information in the SET component.

Instructional Strategies. An instructional strategy is a procedure for delivering instruction. One approach to its representation is generative in that each strategy is a sequence of instructional primitives, configured and constrained by grammatical rules. Another approach views strategies as black boxes, which we call transaction frames. Although unstructured, transaction frames are schematic and can be configured to meet any of a broad class of instructional situations. These same issues and approaches apply not only to individual strategies but also to entire curricula.

The AIDA Executive. The AIDA Executive defines the mapping from SET and Content components to instructional strategies. The Executive operates by parsing content into objectives and then matching these objectives to strategies. Identification of objectives is determined by the structure of the content. Information about objective type, students, and environment is influential in determining the strategy.

Instructional Delivery. Instruction is delivered by executing the strategies produced by the AIDA Executive. The level of interaction in these procedures is a major determinant of the information-processing requirements of the delivery system. In addition, since the Instructional Delivery component acts as an interpreter of strategy specifications, the power of the interpreter must be matched to the level of abstraction in the strategy specifications.

Evaluation. Evaluation, within the AIDA concept, is used to determine where problems exist and how to make improvements. Essential in any evaluation is to determine the cause of problems, be they in quality of implementation, optimality of the design, or validity of underlying design assumptions. Also important is the identification of the locus of any problems, that is, of the particular component of the AIDA concept that gives rise to the problem.

Resolving all of these issues in general is obviously an impossible problem. In particular contexts, however, many of the issues become irrelevant and others become tractable. To understand how these issues are manifest in particular situations, we turn now to a discussion of the context of instructional design and development. Because a systematic view of instructional development contexts is beyond me, the treatment below is limited to the analysis of two examples of particular development contexts. One of these contexts, the Technical Training Center (TTC), is real although my presentation of that context may depart from reality at several points. The second context, CAI 'R' Us, is fictional but representative of a number of instructional development organizations.

The choice of these two contexts was deliberate and intended to focus the discussion on contextual aspects of automation. The next two sections describe the contexts in terms of the AIDA concept and ask how that concept can be profitably automated.

The Technical Training Center

The Development Environment

The Technical Training Center (TTC) is responsible for the design, development and management of technical training. Training requirements are promulgated by authorities outside of the Center. When training development requests arrive at the Center, they are assigned to one of several departments known as Training Development Branches (TDB). These TDBs are organized around particular technical specialties. Some branches of the Center are involved in special projects such as exportable CAI that cut across technical specialties. Although not explicitly addressed here, these units have much in common with CAI 'R' Us, which is discussed in the next section.

When a development request arrives at a TDB, it is placed in the hands of a Training Specialist, who then assumes responsibility for developing the course. These Training Specialists are subject-matter experts in the training to be developed but have little if any expertise in training design and development.

Content. Two mechanisms define the content of courses developed at the Center. Requests for training development are accompanied by a document known as Specialty Training Standards (STS). This document, for the most part, defines the structure of the subject matter. The content (as distinct from structure) resides in the mind of the Training Specialist responsible for course development.

SET. The STS defines, in addition to course requirements, the entering capabilities of students. The Training Specialist's personal knowledge is, no doubt, used to supplement this written documentation. Constraints on the training environment (e.g., course length and method of instruction) may be provided with the training request. Otherwise, this information is developed as part of the design process. Task information resides almost completely in the Training Specialist's mind or in technical documentation available to him (Spector, 1990).

Instructional Strategies. Instructional strategies are not explicitly developed in the course of training design and development. Rather, they are implicitly embodied in lesson plans and other course materials. Other aspects of instructional strategy are represented in the instructors' minds.

The AIDA Executive. The TTC has an ISD model that is meant, among other things, to guide the selection of instructional strategies to meet particular objectives. However, this model is not appropriate to the particular needs of most Training Specialists at the Center, and their lack of training in instructional design renders them ill equipped to implement formal instructional design methods.

I suspect that tradition is the principal determinant of instructional strategies at the TTC. Since each of the TDBs develops training within a technical specialty, they accumulate schematic knowledge of instruction in the specialty. In developing training to meet a particular objective, they match the objective to one or another instructional strategy, and configure the strategy to fit the particular objective. Configuration may be largely a process of consulting old strategies that have been previously configured to similar objectives.

Instructional Delivery. Instruction is typically delivered in a conventional classroom setting to classes of about eight students. Students are provided with some written materials and instructors work from written lesson plans. Since a TDB is responsible for both development and delivery of instruction, some aspects of instructional delivery are not explicit in lesson plans or course material but rather are carried directly from development to classroom by Training Specialists. The small class size indicates that the level of interactivity in delivery is quite high.

Evaluation. The principal mechanism for quality control at the Center is documentation of the ISD process. This documentation conforms to a standard ISD model and is considered more burdensome than helpful in quality control.

Formative evaluation is difficult under most conventional ISD models since opportunities for sensitivity analyses and interim experiments are limited. Although informal evaluation of instruction may feed back into subsequent design, formative evaluation is not a large concern at the Center.

Some attention is given to summative evaluation by including measurement and standards as part of the required ISD process. Measurements are restricted to tests of student performance (usually on pencil-and-paper instruments). These tests might constitute useful summative information were it not for deficiencies in quality control and formative evaluation. There is no systematic way of tracing problems evident in these tests to their sources in the design and development process.

By way of summary, we can point to four aspects of instructional design and development at the center that have particular significance for automating these processes.

First, the division of labor for course development is of interest. The determination of objectives and their sequence is in the hands of authorities outside of the TDB. All other aspects of design, development, and delivery are the responsibility of the Training Specialist.

Second, the population of courses developed at a single TDB or by a single Training Specialist is narrowly circumscribed along technical lines. All courses written within a TDB have roughly the same objectives and address roughly the same technology. What distinguishes one development project from another are the particular technologies involved.

Third, and consistent with the second aspect, those responsible for instructional design and development are subject-matter experts and usually possess no special expertise in instructional science or practice.

Fourth, there is little in the way of automated support for either development or delivery of instruction. Tables and forms used in the ISD process offer the opportunity for some formal representation content and instructional structure. The content itself and most of the instructional procedures are not formally represented. Development and delivery procedures are implemented by the human Training Specialists.

Automated Support for the TTC

With the understanding developed above of the context governing instructional design and development at the Center, we can envision the kind of automated support appropriate for this context. The following speculations describe first how AIDA might appear to a Training Specialist at the Center and then how this vision relates to the more general AIDA concept.

Kim and the AIDA: A course development fantasy. Presented here is a brief sketch of course development using AIDA in the TDB devoted to Advanced Carbohydrate Preparation Equipment. The Training Specialist, Kim Cook, is about to prepare a new maintenance training curriculum for the latest toaster, the To-14 (including the attack model of the toaster, the To-14A).

The AIDA workstation that supports Kim's development effort has a large screen, appropriate manipulanda and output devices, access to scanners and to the toaster's technical documentation. The workstation also offers a complete complement of document preparation tools: Optical Character Reading (OCR) software, text and graphic editors, and other useful applications. AIDA itself allows Kim to operate with any of three views of the evolving course:

A Technical Description view allows her to record and edit information about the toaster itself.

A Training Requirements view allows her to record and track instructional objectives.

A Curriculum view allows her to work with the evolving curriculum.

Kim opens a window exhibiting the top level Curriculum view of the new course. At the moment, it contains nothing but the Standard Toaster Maintenance Training Curriculum Template. She also opens a window on the Training Requirements Window loaded with objectives defined in the STS. Finally, she opens a new Technical Description window for the To-14 and a window on an existing Technical Description of the To-12, the direct predecessor to the To-14.

Kim's first task is to create, in the new Technical Description window, a Dynamic Block Diagram (DBD) of the To-14. A DBD is nothing more than a qualitative simulation of the device, and it is entered using an editor similar to that described in Towne and Munro (1988).

Most of the DBD can be copied from the existing To-12 Technical Description. Kim updates the old To-12 DBD with minor technical changes. She also adds the To-14's new Digital AntiBurn Sensor (DABS) and the explosive-propelled toast-eject unit on the To-14A.

A convention adopted early on in the design of AIDA itself calls for the use of terms related to the technical domains taught at the center or to concrete instructional operations. Training Specialists confused by the term "qualitative model" instantly grasped the meaning of "Dynamic Block Diagram."

As soon as Kim completes the DBD, the Curriculum window changes in almost imperceptible ways indicating that AIDA has "roughed in" certain lessons. She ignores these changes and begins to fill in technical data on the components and connections in the DBD. Some of these data are taken from the To-14's technical documentation, others from the To-12's Technical Description. As these data are added more changes are evident in the Curriculum window.

Kim next turns to a section of the Technical Description known as Standard Maintenance Procedures. She examines a library of toaster-maintenance procedures, chooses those appropriate to the To-14 and, working from the technical documentation, configures each to fit the To-14. She also adds a procedure for testing the DABS, adapting a procedure found in a larger library of maintenance procedures. The new procedure calls for the use of special purpose DABS test equipment, which is automatically added to a list of test equipment to be covered in the course.

With the technical description essentially complete, Kim turns her attention to the curriculum. At this point, the Curriculum window contains a tentative curriculum. Some of the modules, such as the section on standard maintenance procedures are described in some detail. Others, such as troubleshooting training, are nothing more than place markers at this point.

Associated with each module in the evolving course are certain training variables, including the time allotted to the module and the media to be used. These aspects of the course were established years ago as part of the To-14 acquisition process. Kim checks these previously established values and revises one to reflect the fact that the modules on standard maintenance procedures will be provided via interactive videodisc, since production of the planned maintenance simulator has been held up pending OSHA approval.

Kim then begins a careful inspection of the material itself. A general orientation to the course is to be given in a classroom environment. Kim scrutinizes the lesson plans for that section of the course, fills in the many blanks using material from the technical documentation, and edits the material for coherence and completeness. She adds a discussion of some of the To-14's idiosyncrasies that AIDA failed to include in the course.

The second section of the course provides interactive videodisc practice in standard preventive maintenance and repair procedures. AIDA has already created the computational structure for this training and formulated a proposed videodisc design. Kim edits the material, adding warnings appropriate to some procedures. She uses electronic mail to send the videodisc design to the Center's video production unit along with a request for an initial design meeting.

The last section of the course is a computer-based troubleshooting laboratory. Kim consults the Training Requirements related to troubleshooting and selects a list of target faults for the laboratory. AIDA uses the DBD to create and sequence exercises for each of the faults. It also proposes additional exercises on faults easily confused with those in Kim's target set. She changes the instructional medium for the lab to interactive videodisc and obtains a revised disc design from AIDA. AIDA warns her that the module is too long for the scheduled time, but she ignores this warning since she knows that the students will find enough time to complete the lab.

What is important to understand about this fantasy is that AIDA is designed to talk to the Training Specialist in her terms, that is, in terms of technology and teaching, not in instructional design terms. Kim is never asked to think about facts, rules, concepts, and procedures, or about expository vs. inquisitory strategies, or about learner control. Rather, she is asked what the To-14 is like, what students must learn about it, and what the training environment is like. She is also given control over the end product and the responsibility for aspects of the course beyond the scope of automation.

We are now in a position to ask how each of the components of the AIDA concept can be designed to implement this philosophy.

Content. What makes the foregoing description a feasible picture of automated instructional development at the TTC, is the organization of the Center's activities around technical specialties and subject-matter expertise. A typical TDB may, for example, be responsible for the development of maintenance training for each of a class of electronic devices (e.g., radar, avionics). Because maintenance skills are the targets of instruction in each case and because the devices being maintained are all of a kind, the cognitive structures that support skilled performance can be represented in the same fashion in all courses. The initial development of a representational system may be difficult, but the uniformity of maintenance skills across courses offers the promise that a few common representational systems can serve to represent the content of training in a large number of courses. The content of a typical maintenance course, for example, might employ the following devices:

qualitative models of the type devised by Forbus (1984) to represent equipment functionality;

procedural representations of the type described by Kieras (1987) to represent preventive maintenance and repair troubleshooting procedures of the type discussed by Hunt and Rouse (1984);

text models of the type discussed by van Dijk (1980) for the representation of technical documentation; and

materials relating procedural and conceptual representation to the equipment itself, test equipment, and ancillary materials (simulators, photographs, etc.), perhaps based on some of Baggett and Ehrenfeucht's (1985) suggestions.

Some of these representational devices apply to contexts other than equipment maintenance. However, the key to successful representation here is the development of structures that are specialized to maintenance as taught for a particular organization. A system for automating the representation of technical documentation should be based not on a general van Dijk (1980) model but rather on a van Dijk-like model specialized to represent the appropriate technical documentation. A calibration procedure should not be represented within a framework that covers all goal oriented procedures but rather with a schema specific to calibration.

SET. Individuals being trained in similar technological skills are normally drawn from populations with similar backgrounds. Thus, to the extent that courses under the purview of a single TDB address similar technological skills, student and environment variables in one course will usually be the ones that are important in others developed in the same TDB. Furthermore, the treatment of these variables in designing instruction will also be the same across courses.

This is not to say that there is no variation from student to student or training environment to training environment, but simply that the important sources of variation will remain the same from course to course and can be dealt with in the same fashion in different courses. Students deficient in digital logic will be given the same sort of remediation in a course devoted to one sort of radar system as they will in a course on a different sort of radar system. Likewise, the availability of a maintenance simulator for one type of equipment will have the same impact on instruction as the availability of a simulator in a course addressing a different piece of equipment of the same class.

As the consequence, the opportunity exists for determining how to treat SET considerations in, say, a maintenance-training context and automating that treatment implicitly in the AIDA Executive. The general problem of remediating deficiencies or assigning media to instructional objectives is difficult and probably beyond effective automation. Fortunately, these general problems are not of concern to the Training Specialist at the TTC. Of interest to him are particular students deficient in digital logic and availability of particular maintenance simulators. These specific issues, because they are constrained to the context of maintenance training, can be handled automatically and may even benefit from automation.

Instructional Strategies. Earlier I suggested that the fundamental issue in the development of curricula and instructional strategies was that of generation vs. schema selection. When the space of instructional objectives is highly circumscribed (as it is at the TTC) and when computers are used to develop curricula, then the latter approach is the one to be favored.

A schema for a maintenance-training curriculum, such as the one described above for the To-14, might have the following main components:

an orientation to equipment structure, function, and documentation;

hands-on training in preventive maintenance and repair procedures; and

a troubleshooting laboratory.

Each of these components will have a structure of its own and will, at the lowest level, consist of particular transaction frames. The orientation component, for example, might have a structure dictated by elaboration theory (Reigeluth and Stein, 1983). The procedure-training component might be organized around the occasions for invoking each procedure, but would have an otherwise flat structure. The troubleshooting laboratory could consist of problems that are organized and sequenced in such a way as to promote the development of an effective troubleshooting strategy. The further development of this curriculum for a particular maintenance course could be automated by a mechanism that would sequence and configure transaction frames from a computer model of the equipment in the Content component, material in the equipment's technical documentation, and some material supplied by a Training Specialist.

It is easy to underestimate the importance of restricting the scope of automated curriculum development to a particular domain, in this case, maintenance. To appreciate the importance of this restriction, consider the following:

The top level structure of the curriculum is, itself, specific to maintenance.

Assume one chose to use elaboration theory to structure the orientation component. Automating elaboration theory in general is a major undertaking. Much more feasible is the development of an automated procedure, conforming to elaboration theory, for generating an orientation to the structure, function, and documentation of a piece of equipment.

Many, although not all, of the transaction frames, particularly those for troubleshooting practice, can only be profitably automated as maintenance-specific procedures.

An additional benefit of domain-specific curricula and transaction frames is the possibility of automatically configuring the same instructional strategy to different media. Within a domain, each transaction frame can be assigned a set of alternative media and can be automatically configured to any member of that set. A troubleshooting transaction frame, for example, could be configured to run a qualitative simulator like STEAMER (Holland, Hutchins, and Weitzman, 1984) or a videodisc-based simulator like GMTS (Towne, 1987). It could also be configured to generate lesson plans for a classroom implementation of a troubleshooting exercise. The possibility of these alternate configurations, however, depends on knowing enough about what is being taught to be able to specify the set of applicable media and the configuration procedure.

To summarize, instructional strategies in technical training can be given a formal representation and, moreover, a representational scheme can be devised to adequately cover the instructional strategies used within a particular technical domain. Strategies represented in such a scheme will need further specialization to particular material, and some may, themselves, be specializations of more general strategies.

However, in practice, AIDA will achieve maximum advantage by representing instructional strategies at the most specialized level that covers the population of courses developed by the Training Specialist.

The AIDA Executive. In the previous section I noted that the task of the AIDA executive is to produce a curriculum of strategies from Content and SET specifications. It also describes a general technique for this task based on decomposition of the content into distinct objectives, assignment of strategies to objectives, and configuration of those strategies to fit the content.

This top-down approach can be feasibly implemented by humans, but presents significant and perhaps insurmountable problems to machines. The source of difficulties in automated top-down planning is that of ensuring conformance of the plan to constraints that cross the boundaries of plan components. In instruction, for example, the inclusion of say an illustration in one part of the course may be critical in selecting and configuring a transaction frame in another part of the course.

The simplest solution to the machine planning problem is to avoid it by providing ready-made plans, and that is the solution suggested for AIDA as described here. The templates and procedures that represent curricula and instructional strategies are nothing more than plans for instruction in particular domains. The AIDA executive, instead of having to reason from abstract instructional principles need only invoke a suite of slot-filling procedures to configure the curriculum and its transaction frames. These procedures, like the curriculum templates and content descriptions would be *ad hoc* and specific to a domain. For example, a slot-filling procedure for a troubleshooting exercise would first select and sequence faults using a procedure to maintain coherence and then, for each fault chosen, run an optimal troubleshooting model to generate the correct sequence of troubleshooting actions to isolate the fault.

Instructional Delivery. I see two opportunities for AIDA to advance instructional delivery in settings like the TTC.

First, AIDA can provide direct support of advanced, computer-based instructional techniques. The information-processing requirements of computer-based simulators, intelligent tutoring systems, adaptive testing, and other techniques are such that their implementation requires computer support. A training device such as the IMTS (Towne and Munro, 1988) cannot be feasibly configured for any application without the support of its computer-based authoring facilities.

This is not to say that AIDA in this context should restrict itself to computer-based delivery. One of AIDA's strong points here is that of providing a complete solution to technical training problems. Restricting the media that it addresses to computers would make it inapplicable to any situation requiring the higher levels of interactivity that only "live" systems and human instructors can provide in some circumstances.

A second opportunity for AIDA to advance the delivery of instruction is by helping instructional developers deal with turbulence in training environments and student characteristics. For example, it is seldom the case that all training devices for a piece of equipment are available when the first students need to be trained in the operation and maintenance of that equipment.

A single transaction frame, appropriately configured, should be able to generate equivalent instructional procedures for alternative media. This capability, to reconfigure transaction frames for different circumstances, would greatly ease the burden of producing revised materials as new media become available.

Evaluation. The previous section describes three aspects of evaluation: quality control, formative evaluation, and summative evaluation. The quality-control issues discussed there arise more in connection with the design of AIDA as conceived of here than with its use. Validation of the sort discussed in that section should be carried out on the initial implementation of AIDA and on each extension to a new technical area. It should also be possible to check the conformance of courses to quality standards such as those found in the IQI (Montague, 1983). Partial support for this validation can be provided by AIDA itself.

AIDA, as sketched in the fantasy above, offers numerous opportunities for formative evaluation. Training Specialists can create different qualitative models of the same device and compare the curricula created by the two models. They can play the same what-if games with other aspects of the design such as media assignment and problem selection. Automated generation of curricula provides a far greater measure of control in empirical comparisons of different design approaches.

Summative evaluation is not particularly relevant to the concept of AIDA as presented here. In the TTC, AIDA should be viewed as a development tool whose validity should be established prior to implementation. Although AIDA can support the continuous evaluation of students both before and after training, it offers no special advantage in some of the more precise summative evaluation techniques suggested above.

In summary, training development contexts like the TTC, where training requirements, content structure, and curriculum structure vary little from course to course, are prime candidates for effective automation of instructional design. AIDA, in these contexts, should support instructional design and development through conversations with the developer that address the particulars of the subject matter, the training requirements, and instructional materials. The implementation of this philosophy calls for the representation of both content and instruction at the most specialized level that covers the population of courses under development. Instructional design theory may play a key role in the development of these specialized representations, but it should not play an explicit role in their implementation.

The viability of this conception depends on some nontrivial assumptions of how instruction changes across technical domains and specialties. One way of expressing these assumptions is shown in Figure 4.4. Technical domains and specialties fall in a hierarchy and close relatives in the instructional hierarchy share more in the way of instruction than do distant cousins.

Thus, for example, the changes needed to adapt To-12 maintenance training to To-14 maintenance training are trivial compared to the changes needed to adopt To-12 maintenance training to a course in Ada programming. This assumption is violated to the extent that small changes in content or training requirements lead to large changes in instructional design. One can expect some such violations but I doubt that they are numerous enough to threaten the viability of AIDA as described here.

The level of generality of AIDA within the hierarchy of Figure 4.4 is an open question. An AIDA that addresses, for example, only the maintenance training for one particular device is too specialized. An AIDA that addresses all of technical training is too general. I suggest above that AIDA be specialized at the branch level, thus making the question something of an organizational issue. One could envision more general versions of AIDA, for example, one capable of designing maintenance training for any electronic device or maintenance training for all devices. AIDA ceases to become useful, however, when its level of generality exceeds that of the technical knowledge of the subject-matter expert designing the course. A way of having one's cake and eating it too is to rely on a configurable AIDA that could be specialized for development of training in particular specialties. (The computer program responsible for creating specialized AIDAs would be known as the Automated AIDA Design Assistant, or AAIDADA).

CAI 'R' Us

The Development Environment

CAI 'R' Us is a fictional firm engaged in the development of Computer-Assisted Instruction (CAI). It was founded in 1975 by a group of computer programmers and educators who had formerly worked in a university-based CAI lab. The lab was dissolved due to lack of funding, and CAI 'R' Us bought the lab's computer along with rights to the TeachWrite authoring language. TeachWrite, now updated to run on microcomputers, is considered the cornerstone of CAI 'R' Us' success. The language's many design flaws—among them, lack of recursion, block structure, scoping, and structured variables—are masked by the availability to the author of 2,436 powerful TeachWrite commands.

CAI 'R' Us writes courseware mainly for the government or for its contractors. Jobs vary in content but are constrained by suitability of the media. Most of their contracts are awarded through competitive procurement.

Content. CAI 'R' Us obtains most of its work through competitive procurement. They concentrate more on development than front-end anal-

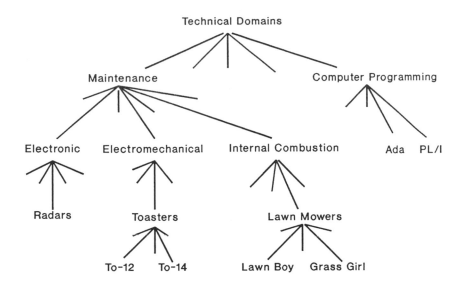

Figure 4.4. Technical Domains Hierarchy Fragment.

ysis and usually start work with a preliminary needs analysis in hand. This analysis, in addition to identifying and structuring instructional objectives, tailors the scope of the project to the media available to CAI 'R' Us.

In spite of the computer-based nature of CAI 'R' Us' work, formal representations of the instructional objectives are usually not provided with the front-end analysis. Cursory verbal descriptions of each objective (in behavioral terms) are provided via the RFP, and additional definition is obtained in consultation with subject-matter experts during the course of design and development.

Instructional strategies. In spite of TeachWrite's 2,436 powerful commands, the strategies used in any particular job are small in number. Some of these strategies are common to all of CAI 'R' Us' jobs and, indeed, to most conventional CAI. Sequential displays of graphic or text, multiple-choice queries, and so-called interactive, branching simulations are among these common devices. In addition, most jobs require the development of specialized, job specific instructional strategies, usually based on simulation.

The AIDA Executive. The design and development of courseware at CAI 'R' Us follows an engineering model. A conceptual design document is developed that describes the curriculum and specifies the strategies to be used for each lesson or unit. A brief description of the content of each unit is also provided with this document. Curriculum design is informal but tied to the instructional objectives provided by the client. A quality control check associates each unit in the design with its associated objective(s) and vice versa. The selection of strategies is guided implicitly by a few simple rules of thumb, such as those found in Merrill (1989). Neither CAI 'R' Us nor its clients have ever felt the need to make these rules explicit.

A detail design document is produced after client approval of the conceptual design. This detail design is typically a storyboard description of those parts of the course administered via conventional CAI and a detailed description of any special simulations or strategies. The detail design document then, represents the configuration of strategies selected in the conceptual design phase. This configuration process is, like the conceptual design, informal. Material is written or selected in consultation with subject-matter experts engaged by the client or by CAI 'R' Us.

Instructional delivery. CAI 'R' Us makes available to its clients the full range of automated instructional delivery devices including interactive videodisc, computer-generated graphics, and a variety of manipulanda (mice, touchscreen, etc.). The level of interactivity is local interactive, to use the terms introduced earlier. Since TeachWrite itself is a general-purpose language with no explicit means of representing instructional content, the translation from detailed design specification to code is done by a humans.

Instruction by humans is not a central part of CAI 'R' Us' offerings. The firm does, however, provide some support and training for instructors in automated classrooms.

Evaluation. The typical CAI 'R' Us project contains procedures for quality control, for formative evaluation, and for summative evaluation. Clients and CAI 'R' Us review both the conceptual and detailed design of the project. Pilot experiments of some or all units allow for formative evaluation. Incorporated into each course are both formal and informal evaluation instruments. Clients are provided with summary statistics of student performance and students' subjective ratings of the course. Although the development context at CAI 'R' Us shares some important features with that at the TTC, they are different in many ways critical to the issue of automated instructional development and design.

Like the TTC, CAI 'R' Us usually receives something in the way of a front-end analysis from its clients. This analysis provides the firm with instructional objectives that presumably can be met using the media available to CAI 'R' Us.

Unlike the TTC, however, there are no domain restrictions on the projects undertaken at CAI 'R' Us. The company may, on one occasion, take a job addressing the training of Social Workers in dealing with drug addicts and, on another occasion, undertake to provide training of budget analysts on electronic spreadsheets.

Also in contrast to the TTC, subject-matter expertise then is not what CAI 'R' Us brings to their work. Rather, they provide expertise in instructional design and development and the development of computer-assisted instruction in particular.

Automation plays a much more critical role at CAI 'R' Us than at the TTC. Since all instruction is delivered by computer, the instructional strategies involved are only those that can be automated. Although these strategies do not themselves have formal representations, they could be formalized and automated with appropriate software.

Automated Instructional Design at CAI 'R' Us

We can now try to envision, as we did in the previous section for the TTC, what AIDA might be like if it were designed for use at CAI 'R' Us. As the reader might suspect, the aspects of the CAI 'R' Us context just reviewed imply quite a different model of AIDA.

Harry, Mud, and the AIDA: Another course development fantasy. Harry Hylton-Ashcroft, a Senior Design Consultant at CAI 'R' Us is working with an RFP from the Department of Energy requesting a self-contained CAI package to train geologists and petroleum engineers in methods for reservoir analysis for use with new secondary-recovery methods. Reservoir analysis is the process of estimating how much oil or gas can be recovered from a prospective or existing oil field. Secondary recovery techniques are those used to recover minerals once the primary flow has been exhausted. Among the most important are water or gas injection and horizontal drilling.

According to the RFP, students need to be able to:

collect data needed for reservoir analysis,

select an analysis method based on data available and recovery method,

make use of a DoE-furnished computer program, RESEVAL2, for reservoir analysis, and

interpret the output of the program.

Harry, recognizing that his meagre knowledge of the oil industry extends only to his local gas station, brings in an expert reservoir engineer, Mud Doogan, as a consultant. Harry, Mud, and AIDA work together under a tight deadline to provide a conceptual design for RFP.

Harry's AIDA workstation presents three views of a project:

A SET view permits entry and editing of information about students.

A Content view permits entry and editing of course content.

An Instructional Strategies view permits inspection and editing of the evolving course design.

Harry and Mud begin with the SET view. Harry opens an Enterprise frame and asks Mud, "What, basically, are we trying to teach people to do?"

Mud replies, "Estimate petroleum reserves recoverable using various secondary-recovery methods."

Harry enters Mud's words into the Enterprise frame of the SET view. Harry does not understand what Mud is saying; Mud does not understand what Harry is doing. However, both feel that they have made substantial progress.

Harry then turns to the Content view and begins to elaborate the knowledge needed to succeed in the enterprise. They inform AIDA of a top-level description of the estimation procedure, the result is depicted in Figure 4.5. Harry then defines the output of the first step depicted in Figure 4.5, "Gather Data." These data are different sorts (seismic, logs, scouting reports, etc.). AIDA has the capability to represent the structure of each in considerable detail.

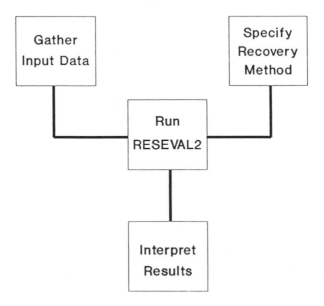

Figure 4.5. Top-Level Instructional Objectives.

Harry is beginning to feel that the job will be a piece of cake, when Mud remarks, "Of course, most of the time, you don't have all that stuff [the data to be gathered]." In the conversation that ensues, Harry learns of some of the complexities in this first step. Some data are always available; some are available at a cost; and some are unavailable at any cost. Depending on the situation, some data are less useful than others. Some data, taken under less than ideal conditions, must be adjusted based on the engineer's professional judgment. Sometimes a first analysis indicates that more data and subsequent analyses are needed. The basis of many of these judgments and decisions is a complex geological model of "what's down there." Harry decides that he cannot respond to the RFP with a complete course on reservoir engineering. He turns his back on AIDA and, in consultation with Mud, formulates a simplified model of the job. Students will be taught how to run the DoE programs and interpret their output under a restricted range of standard conditions and existing data.

Harry and Mud return to AIDA and the elaboration of the first step. They use AIDA's standard forms for describing the data to be gathered in the first step. Mud allows that since gathering the data itself is outside the scope of the course, its preparation for input into the DoE programs is the only aspect of the step that needs to be taught. Harry can use AIDA to represent the data-preparation procedure for some types of data. Others require perceptual skills or complex procedures outside the scope of AIDA's procedure-representation facilities. Harry indicates to AIDA that sample materials can be made available for training and testing.

Moving on to the second step of the process illustrated in Figure 4.5, Harry learns that the heart of the process is that of specifying the parameters of each secondary-recovery method under consideration. Harry has no trouble in informing AIDA of the structure of the parameters of each possible method and of rules for providing their values. He also finds it easy to specify how the results of this specification should be prepared for input to the DoE programs.

Harry is unable to complete the "Run DoE Program" step in Figure 4.5, because the DoE programs have not been released yet. However, consultation with DoE reveals that the programs are menu-driven, run on personal computers, and have all of the characteristics of programs for which CAI 'R' Us has developed training in the past. He makes a note to include references to earlier work in his proposal.

Moving on to the "Interpret Output" step in Figure 4.5, Harry learns from Mud that students will need to learn the output format, the assumptions of the analysis method, and how to assess the accuracy of the analysis. Harry chooses to represent DoE program output as a part-whole structure in AIDA so that students will be taught the components of the output and their location in the output report. AIDA assists Harry in elaborating the analysis methods used in terms of a causal model describing data flow among the program's modules. Finally, Harry uses AIDA's rule-based representational system to construct a procedure for assessing the accuracy of RESEVAL2's estimates. Mud, by this time, is totally overawed and completely confused.

The content analysis is complete enough to warrant some curricular recommendations. AIDA first makes some general curriculum recommendations. In particular, it recommends the five module course depicted in Figure 4.6.

Both Mud and Harry accept AIDA's top level recommendation. Harry, noting that considerable text and graphic material will be needed to complete the Introduction module, delays further development until after contract award. He asks AIDA to open the second module for further development. AIDA suggests two techniques for teaching students how to format input data. The first is exploratory in that students provide their own data, the second is generative in that sample data are provided to the student. The decision, according to AIDA, should be made on the basis of motivation. It engages Mud and Harry in a series of simple questions about students' jobs and the potential impact of instruction, finally concluding that

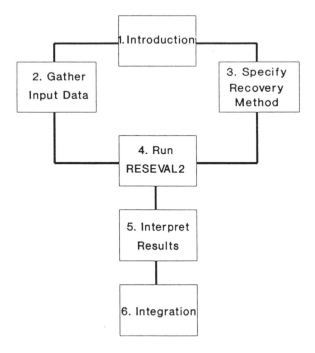

Figure 4.6. Course Map for DoE Project.

student motivation is "high." Mud remarks that AIDA apparently doesn't know how petroleum engineers feel about DoE software, so Harry resets student motivation to "low."

AIDA accepts Harry's revised evaluation and his request to generate a sample of the problems that students would be given to practice preparing data for input to RESEVAL2. AIDA reminds Harry that some graphic data (sample electronic log records) have not yet been provided. It then presents a few sample exercises from the module just as they would appear to students. Mud is impressed; he is particularly impressed by one problem in which students are given data from a Sprayberry well that yielded half a million barrels of oil. (The term "Sprayberry" refers to a formation found at about 7,000 feet. Wells drilled in this formation normally produce about 70,000 barrels during their lifetime.)

Harry, realizing that not all combinations of inputs are realistic, assesses his options for obtaining reasonable problems: develop off-line, realistic data sets, construct or purchase a geological model that will generate plausible values, or construct an approximate rule-based generator within AIDA that will generate realistic data for perhaps 95% of the problems. He decides that the last choice is the least costly and makes a note to cost out the development of the rules.

Harry and Mud continue their work with AIDA and, within a short time, are able to generate a conceptual design for the project and enough sample materials to support a response to the RFP. Although Module 3 is not in the design (because RESEVAL2 is not complete), the design for Module 4 is quite impressive. AIDA generates an entire interactive lesson on different parts of RESEVAL2's reports. Also part of the design is a hypertext facility that students can use to inspect the methods used by RESEVAL2 to generate each result. Finally, AIDA automatically designs a lesson with integrated practice that teaches students how to assess the accuracy of the figures produced by RESEVAL2. Since CAI 'R' Us won the contract and were, with Mud and AIDA's help, able to finish the work on time and under budget, a summary of AIDA's contribution to the project is worth mentioning.

AIDA took CAI 'R' Us from an enterprise that depended primarily on hand-crafted instructional strategies to one in which machines are responsible for a large part of curriculum design and development. This transformation was accomplished by explicitly automating all of the strategies previously used only implicitly at CAI 'R' Us (plus a few more) and interfacing the strategies thus automated to a collection of knowledge representation mechanisms that cover most of the content of interest to CAI 'R' Us' clients. Representation of some material is awkward at best, and not all content can be represented in the system, but enough content goes directly from AIDA into courseware to have a major impact on the design and de-velopment process at CAI 'R' Us.

How AIDA might be designed for effectiveness in the CAI 'R' Us de-velopment context is taken up in the rest of this section.

Content. The nature of CAI 'R' Us' business dictates the criteria that apply to representation of its content. AIDA must provide generality in the sense of being able to represent content from a number of different subject domains. It must provide parsimony in using as few knowledge-representa-tion devices as possible. It must provide knowledge structures that are use-ful in instructional design. These three constraints cannot all be met by the same system.

As a compromise, AIDA offers one knowledge-representation mecha-nism for each of three major classes of knowledge:

Production systems are used to represent procedural knowledge.

Schema are used to represent declarative knowledge.

Qualitative-process theory (Forbus, 1984) is used to represent causal knowledge.

AIDA also provides, at the most concrete level, for the inclusion of uninterpreted text, graphics, and computer programs.

Because these mechanisms are general, they are useful in the represen-tation of much of the knowledge in each of CAI 'R' Us' projects. They fail when specialized knowledge, such as geology, is too complex to be feasibly analyzed within the scope of the project. The three mechanisms are obvi-ously parsimonious since they are almost completely unencumbered with *ad hoc* mechanisms.

In the initial version of AIDA, knowledge representation was com-pletely unencumbered with special-purpose mechanisms. Later versions have incorporated certain mechanisms, such as iteration, that are found in almost every application.

Perhaps most important are the availability of instructional strategies that can be directly linked to the knowledge structures so that they are useful in designing instruction.

Content representation in AIDA are further constrained by a decom-posability requirement. The content of a project must have a hierarchical representation since the AIDA executive (described below) decomposes the content along hierarchical lines.

SET. Recall that earlier we discussed two approaches to representing information about students, environment, and task. One approach is to use a fixed vector of features, such as motivation, to represent these aspects of the instructional situation. A second approach provides more precise information by using structures in the SET component that reflect the structure of the content. This latter approach would, for example, support an intelligent tutoring system that concentrates instruction on a student's individual weaknesses.

AIDA at CAI 'R' Us uses the former, simpler model. Data on student features are gathered as needed to select instructional strategies, as we saw above when AIDA's recommendation of a generative strategy depended on student motivation. Information about the instructional environment is handled in the same way. For example, certain strategies are not recommended if an instructor is not available for consultation. AIDA's representation of the task is even more simplistic, consisting of nothing more than an uninterpreted statement of the overall goal of training. AIDA relies on this statement to orient students to the training situation.

Instructional Strategies. AIDA's instructional strategies at CAI 'R' Us are similar to those described in connection with the TTC. A collection of instructional schemata are available within AIDA. Each of these schemata, once configured, becomes a procedure that implements a particular instructional strategy. The schemata are specialized to different levels of abstraction. That is, some schemata are transaction frames that embody particular interactions with students. Others handle lessons or collections of transaction frames. Still others handle entire curricula. Configuring a schema is a matter of drawing on appropriate subject matter from the Content module, selecting subschemata, and selecting media.

The AIDA Executive. In contrast to the TTC, AIDA at CAI 'R' Us is a top-down course designer. AIDA's knowledge of how to teach is embedded in a system for matching schemata to elements of the content hierarchy. The main criterion for matching is the correspondence between the knowledge structure to be taught and the candidate strategy. That is, each strategy knows the kind of knowledge that it can teach. More general strategies match objectives at higher levels of the content hierarchy, and more specific strategies match low-level elements of the hierarchy. For example, a general curriculum strategy, shown in Figure 4.5, matched the first-level content decomposition shown in Figure 4.6. a specific hypertext transaction frame matched the specific content element representing RESEVAL2's models and assumptions.

In most cases, conflicts will arise when several strategies match a content element. The converse situation, an impasse where no strategy matches a particular element, is one about which we do not like to think.

AIDA uses three mechanisms to resolve these conflicts. If the element being matched has descendants, AIDA can often eliminate strategies that cannot be matched at lower levels. Decisions among those remaining can often be made using rules of thumb that reference student and environment features. As a last resort, the human developer can be asked to resolve the conflict.

Instructional Delivery. One of the key's to AIDA's success at CAI 'R' Us is the restriction of instructional delivery mechanisms and the consequent restriction of instructional strategies. CAI 'R' Us does not deal with instructor-delivered instruction or it's computer-based equivalent. Hence, it has no need to consider or represent the dialogue structures required to implement this sort of instruction. Nor does CAI 'R' Us deal, in any serious way with noninteractive media such as text and videotape. These media are used in CAI 'R' Us' instructional system, but their structure is never a design problem for AIDA; AIDA never generates text or a shooting script for a videotape. Rather, the delivery mechanisms available for use at CAI 'R' Us are those that achieve the middle levels of interactivity described in an earlier section.

Of interest is the fact that these middle levels of interactivity are fairly new to the instructional enterprise. Conversation and discourse have been with the human race for tens or hundreds of thousands of years. As the consequence they may have a complexity that has heretofore defied all attempts at automation. Human-computer interaction is newer to the human scene and is governed by simpler and less elaborate structures. It is this simplicity that renders feasible the automated design of computer-based instruction.

Evaluation. AIDA at CAI 'R' Us offers considerable opportunity for evaluation. Because AIDA itself undertakes much of the design, quality control issues arise mainly in connection with the assistance provided by human instructional developers. Quality can be assessed in experiments using standard course materials, and defects can be traced to specific points in the design and development process. Naturalistic assessments are also possible by sampling materials or decisions provided by instructional designers and assessing the quality of the sample. For purposes of formative evaluation, most "degrees of freedom" in a project occur in the design of the Content component and the choice of instructional strategies. AIDA can support the evaluation of various options in each cases by producing designs that implement each option. The resulting designs can be submitted to a sensitivity analysis, and the ones that differ in significant ways can be implemented and tested empirically.

Three aspects of summative evaluation are pertinent to AIDA as it functions at CAI 'R' Us. Of primary interest is the scope of AIDA's capabilities. Some courses can be designed and developed using AIDA's standard capabilities. For others AIDA serves as little more than a shell for *ad hoc* instructional methods implemented outside of its normal mechanisms. In some cases these failures will be those of the Content module to represent the subject matter. In others failure can be traced to lack of a suitable strategy. In all cases it is important to examine where, in each course or project, AIDA fails to provide an appropriate representational or instructional method.

Second, there will be cases in which AIDA has the potential for designing adequate instruction but in which design proves impossible because the system is simply unusable. Failures of this sort can be traced to low-level developer-AIDA interface problems, to the lack of suitably strong mechanisms for developer-AIDA interaction, to lack of training, or to a host of other issues.

Finally, there will be cases in which design tasks are well within AIDA's capabilities, and no problems arise in implementing the design, but the instruction produced is simply not effective. These problems will be manifest in performance measures taken from students after all other sources of deficiencies have been eliminated.

In summary, the AIDA found at CAI 'R' Us is quite a different beast than that found at the TTC. CAI 'R' Us brings a relatively restricted set of instructional mechanisms (those available through CAI) to bear on an almost unrestricted content population. AIDA therefore offers general mechanisms for representing subject matter that can accommodate a large portion of the subject matter presented to the firm in a way that offers considerable leverage on the design of instruction. Instructional strategy selection within CAI 'R' Us' AIDA relies on explicit selection rules and top-down approach to instructional design. These commitments are required to handle the range of subject matters of interest to CAI 'R' Us and are feasibly implemented because of the restricted range of instructional mechanisms available to the firm. Because design principles are explicit in CAI 'R' Us' AIDA, evaluation can be quite precise.

Also worth noting is the nature of the interaction between developer and AIDA. In contrast to AIDA at the TTC, AIDA at CAI 'R' Us organizes the design process around an explicit model of instructional development. Developers delineate instructional objectives and have direct control over the entire design process.

Automating the AIDA Concept

As I hope the reader has noticed, however, the design goals of AIDA, the means of reaching those goals, and the issues associated with the design, depend critically on the implementation context.

AIDA at the TTC

In both this section and the next, we will address four questions. What characteristics of the development context are critical to AIDA's design goals? What should AIDA be like in the context? What kind of design will satisfy the design goals? What research is needed to arrive at a design?

Characteristics of the context. Recall that the TTC is organized along technical lines. Each TDB is responsible for training in a narrowly defined technical area. Courses are designated by outside authority to meet specified primary objectives. Subject-matter experts, unskilled in instructional systems design, are responsible for course design and development. Courses are delivered in lecture-discussions to small classes, but other media can be and are employed.

Design goals. AIDA will function best in this context if it is aligned to the mission and experience of its users. It should be conversant in the technology being taught and be prepared to create instruction from technical descriptions of the subject matter. AIDA's recommendations should conform to the principles of effective instructional design but its users should not be required to be conversant in those principles. Rather, AIDA should provide, to its users, the specialized representations of content and instruction that promote efficient automatic generation of instruction and control over the final instructional product.

Design. These design goals can be met by developing, for each subject-matter domain:

> specialized curriculum templates appropriate to the domain or specialty,

> both specialized and general instructional strategies addressing particular skills known to be critical to course objectives (but which can be configured for different media), and

> content representations designed to provide material needed to implement the curricula and instructional strategies.

The AIDA Executive should operate in a bottom-up fashion. That is, it should start with a curriculum template for the course, select instructional strategies and then configure those strategies from the Content component.

Research issues. The most critical research issue for AIDA, as conceived of here, is the nature of the hierarchy illustrated in Figure 4.4. Needed is an understanding of how instruction becomes progressively constrained as content becomes progressively more specialized. Although this issue can be partially illuminated by analytical means, instructional analyses of actual or proposed courses will be needed for a complete resolution.

Once Figure 4.4 has been mapped out for a course population of interest, and once it is known how instruction is successively constrained as one moves down the hierarchy, one can resolve certain critical design issues for AIDA:

> circumscribing the subject-matter domain(s) to which particular versions of AIDA apply,

> determining the instructional strategies and media needed for effective instruction in these domain(s),

> formulating the knowledge structures that support the configuration of instructional strategies, and

> developing the conceptual and computational mechanism for the generation of multiple specialized versions of AIDA.

AIDA at CAI 'R' Us

Characteristics of the context. Unlike the TTC, CAI 'R' Us must develop courseware for a wide range of subject matters. However, the media and instructional methods available to them are limited to those that can be implemented with conventional computer-based media. Development personnel are available that have considerable skill in all aspects of instructional design, but subject matter experts are supplied by clients or engaged as consultants.

Design goals. AIDA at CAI 'R' Us must meet two main objectives. First, it must provide a means of constructing curricula for a wide range of subject matters. Second, it must implement these curricula using the mechanisms available through computer-based instruction. Because of its general scope and because CAI 'R' Us relies on experienced developers, AIDA should speak the language of instructional design, make explicit its design decisions and their basis, and give developers control over the design process.

Design. To accommodate these design goals, AIDA should be based on:

> a set of instructional strategies that define the course at various levels ranging from a top-level decomposition of the curriculum down to individual transaction frames,

> transaction frames that are tailored to the methods and media available with conventional computer-assisted instruction, and

general knowledge-representation mechanisms for representing content.

The AIDA Executive should function in a top-down manner. It should use a production system or a similar type of pattern-matching mechanism to select and assemble instructional strategies, starting with a general plan for the curriculum and proceeding to successively lower levels of detail.

Research issues. Three major issues must be at least partially resolved for AIDA, as conceived of at CAI 'R' Us, can be developed in a systematic fashion.

The first of these issues is the domain of application of AIDA. Defining this domain as whatever might come to CAI 'R' Us for development or even whatever is amenable to instruction via conventional CAI may be sufficient for the purposes of this exposition, but it is not sufficient to support the actual design of AIDA. If the boundaries and structure of AIDA's domain are not defined, then design decisions will be made arbitrarily to support whatever applications are used for development and validation. Specialization, of the type made explicit in the TTC's AIDA, will occur implicitly in the development of CAI 'R' Us' AIDA. Design decisions made prematurely on the basis of a limited sample of applications will face reconsideration or hacking under stress from other applications.

The second issue is that of knowledge representation. For purposes of exposition, we proposed a small number of general knowledge-representation mechanisms. Although such mechanisms might, in principle, be adequate for a broad range of applications, in practice, the complexity of many domains will render them infeasible for representation with a few general mechanisms. However, specialization of knowledge-representation mechanisms entails specialization also of instructional strategies. Carried too far, one might find oneself with all of the disadvantages of a specialized AIDA and none of the advantages.

The third issue is that of the instructional design process itself. Top-down planners face the problem of incorporating constraints across widely separated elements of the plan. The solution to this problem that we suggested above is by no means new and involves the hierarchical refinement of the instructional plan using strategies pitched at various levels of the hierarchy. Needed to implement this approach is a collection of strategies that is broad enough to cover all applications without reaching impasses in the design process and yet specific enough to usefully constrain the course design.

To call these issues "research issues" is something of a misnomer, for I see no way of resolving them through a systematic research program. Rather, their resolution will lie in a combination of arbitrary decisions and cut-and-try R&D.

Conclusion

The discussion above has pointed out some of the opportunities for and limitations on automation in instructional design. In our discussion of theory, we saw that conceptions of instruction have developed from a mechanistic learner-centered approach to one that recognizes the importance of cultural mechanisms in both the acquisition and exercise of skill. The picture that emerges of the instructional enterprise is one more of evolution than design. The methods for transmitting knowledge are part and parcel of the knowledge itself. As a bit of knowledge changes, interacts with other bits, and assumes different forms in different contexts, the instructional methods that keep the idea alive will change in corresponding ways.

The implications of this view for the instructional design community are relevant to the question of automation. The effectiveness of top-down instructional design methods is not at issue; they clearly work when applied appropriately in the appropriate situations. What is of interest is the reason for their effectiveness. I contend that the key to their success is the human designer, who can interpret general recommendations in specific contexts. Because humans can appreciate the dependencies among different aspects of a domain of instruction, and because they can work out the implications of these dependencies for an instructional design, the presence of people in the loop guarantees that the complexity and variety of instructional designs will be sufficient to meet the complexity and variety of domains to be taught.

Computers, however, have none of the context needed for effective design of instruction. The uniform, general implementation of a body of instructional design principles in a computer would require a uniform, general method of representing all that might ever need to be taught. Also needed would be an interface between this representation and the body of instructional design principles. Neither of these components is within the grasp of current approaches to knowledge representation.

Offered here were two very distinct approaches to the functions and design of AIDA. Both approaches conform to my bias that AIDA should be more of a tool in the hands of a course developer than a development engine. Because of this bias, I recommend that developers with different backgrounds working in different contexts be given different types of tools, even if they have similar short-term goals. A subject-matter expert developing instruction in a context defined by his technical specialty needs a tool that talks to him in technical terms and isolates him from unnecessary instructional considerations. An instructional designer working in a context defined more by instructional technology needs precise and explicit control over most instructional-design decisions and a system that does not restrict him to particular content domains.

Those pursuing the development of AIDA must be aware that it will have different functional specifications in different contexts. This awareness may permit the judicious choice of one or more contexts for further research and development, or, at the least avoid the disaster of developing AIDA for one context and evaluating it in another.

It is my hope to have introduced some moderation and humility into efforts at automating instructional design. It may help to recall that we, almost without knowing it, are the consummate teachers and students of the animal kingdom. We have, depending on how you count, several million years of collective experience in teaching and learning from each other. Nearly every communicative act among us has some instructional aspect. Hence, it should come as no surprise that we face some difficulty in expressing our knowledge of instruction in the precise, formal terms needed for computer implementation.

References

Anderson, J. R. (1988). The expert module. In M. C. Polson & J. J. Richardson (Eds.), *Foundations of intelligent tutoring systems* (pp. 21–53). Hillsdale, NJ: Lawrence Erlbaum Associates.

Baggett, P., & Ehrenfeucht, A. (1985). *A multimedia knowledge representation for an "intelligent" computerized tutor* (Tech. Rept. No. 142). Boulder, CO: University of Colorado, Institute of Cognitive Science.

Brown, J. S., Collins, A., & Duguid, P. (1989). Situated cognition and the culture of learning. *Educational Researcher, 18*(1), 32–42.

Brown, J. S., & VanLehn, K. (1980). Repair theory: A generative theory of bugs in procedural skills. *Cognitive Science, 4,* 379–426.

Burton, R. R. (1982). Diagnosing bugs in a simple procedural skill. In D. Sleeman & J. S. Brown (Eds.), *Intelligent tutoring systems* (pp. 157–183). New York: Academic Press.

Carr, B., & Goldstein, I. P. (1977). *Overlays: A theory of modeling for computer-assisted instruction* (AI Memo No. 406). Cambridge: Massachusetts Institute of Technology.

Collins, A., & Stevens, A. L. (1982). Goals and strategies of inquiry teachers. In R. Glaser (Ed.), *Advances in instructional psychology* (Vol. 2, pp. 65–119). Hillsdale NJ: Lawrence Erlbaum Associates.

Crawford, A. M., & Holland, J. D. (1983). *Development of a computerbased tactical training system* (Spec. Rep. NPRDCSR-83-13). San Diego, CA: Navy Personnel Research and Development Center.

Dawkins, R. (1976). *The selfish gene.* Oxford: Oxford University Press.

van Dijk, T. A. (1980). *Macrostructures.* Hillsdale, NJ: Lawrence Erlbaum Associates.

Dreyfus, H. L. (1972). *What computers can't do.* New York: Harper & Row.

Forbus, K. (1984). Qualitative Process Theory. *Artificial Intelligence, 24,* 85–168.

Gagné, R. M., & Briggs, L. J. (1979). *Principles of instructional design.* New York: Holt, Rinehart, & Winston.

Gold, E. M. (1967). Language identification in the limit. *Information and Control, 10*, 447–474.

Greeno, J. G. (1989). A perspective on thinking. *American Psychologist, 44*, 134–141.

Halff, H. M. (1989). Prospects for automating instructional design. Arlington, VA: Halff Resources, Inc.

Holland, J. D., Hutchins, E. L., & Weitzman, L. (1984). Steamer: An interactive inspectable simulation-based training system. *AI Magazine, 5*, 15–27.

Hunt, R. M., & Rouse, W. B. (1984). A fuzzy rule-based model of human problem solving. *IEEE Transactions on Systems, Man, and Cybernetics*, SMC-14, 112–120.

Kieras, D. E. (1987). *The role of cognitive simulation models in the development of advanced training and testing systems* (Tech. Rept. TR-87/ONR-23). Ann Arbor, MI: University of Michigan, Technical Communication Program.

Lave, J. (1988). *Cognition in practice.* New York: Cambridge University Press.

Mehan, H. (1979). *Learning lessons: Social organization in the classroom.* Cambridge, MA: Harvard University Press.

Merrill, M. D. (1989). *Project AIDA: A concept paper.* Logan UT: Utah State University.

Montague, W. E. (1983). Instructional Quality Inventory. *Performance and Instruction, 22*(5), 11–14.

Reigeluth, C. M., & Stein, F. S. (1983). The elaboration theory of instruction. In C. M. Reigeluth (Ed.), *Instructional design theories and models: An overview of their current status* (pp. 335–381). Hillsdale, NJ: Lawrence Erlbaum Associates.

Rouse, W. B., & Hunt, R. M. (1984). Human problem solving in fault diagnosis tasks. In W. B. Rouse (Ed.), *Advances in man-machine systems research* (Vol. 1) (pp. 195–222). Greenwich CT: JAI Press.

Rouse, W. B., Rouse, S. H., & Pellegrino, S. J. (1980). *IEEE Transactions on Systems, Man, and Cybernetics*, SMC-10, 366–376.

Spector, J. M. (1990). *Designing and Developing an Advanced Instructional Design Advisor* (AFHRL-TP-90-52). Brooks AFB, TX: Training Systems Division, Air Force Human Resources Laboratory.

Towne, D. M. (1987). The generalized maintenance trainer: Evolution and revolution. In W. B. Rouse (Ed.), *Advances in man-machine systems research* (Vol. 3, pp. 1–63). Greenwich CT: JAI Press.

Towne, D. M., Johnson, M. C., & Corwin, W. H. (1983). *A performance-based technique for assessing equipment maintainability* (Tech. Rep. 102). Los Angeles, CA: Behavioral Technology Laboratories, University of Southern California.

Towne, D. M., & Munro, A. (1988). The intelligent maintenance training system. In Psotka, J., Massey, D. L., & Mutter, S. A. (Eds.), *Intelligent tutoring systems: Lessons learned.* Hillsdale, NJ: Lawrence Erlbaum Associates.

Towne, D. M., Munro, A., Pizzini, Q. A., Surmon, D. S., & Wogulis, J. (1988). ONR final report: *Intelligent maintenance training technology* (Tech. Rep. 110). Los Angeles, CA: Behavioral Technology Laboratories, University of Southern California.

VanLehn, K. (1987). Learning one subprocedure per lesson. *AI Journal, 32*, 140.

Chapter Five

Computer-Based Instructional Guidance

Robert M. Gagné

General Assumptions

What is desired as an ultimate goal of AIDA is a computer-based system that advises inexperienced personnel who are engaged in designing technical training in the application of methods and procedures of instructional design. The AIDA system aims to make use of any and all available technological developments in computer and media delivery subsystems.

The operations to be described make two basic assumptions: (1) that the six-block AIDA architecture presented in Spector's introduction to Part II is adopted for AIDA, and (2) that the instructional designers score at or above the 75th percentile on the Academic scale of ASVAB (Armed Services Vocational Aptitude Battery). In addition, designers should also be experienced in categorizing job-tasks into learnable capabilities. My remarks concerning a computer-based instructional guidance system are organized according to the first five blocks of the six block architecture. I do not address the evaluation component here, but it is addressed in Part III of this volume.

Information

The design of instruction for technical training requires information about (a) characteristics of the *trainees* who are to receive the training; (b) the setting or *environment* for the training to be designed; and (c) the nature of the *task* or job for which training is being given. These different kinds of information will influence the choice of instructional strategies (to be described later).

Trainees. A great variety of trainee characteristics can be assessed. Among others that may occur to the instructional designer are such personality characteristics as achievement motivation, locus of control, anxiety tolerance, and others of this general variety; current motivation to learn; spatial orientation ability; perseverance. In line with the work of Snow (Corno & Snow, 1986; Snow & Lohman, 1984), I assume that, except in cases of particular and unusual tasks, these personal characteristics of trainees need not be taken into account. The amount of difference any of them would make in the choice of instructional strategy is very small.

In contrast, some characteristics of trainees as learners are likely to make considerable difference in the choice of instructional strategies. Two of these are (1) Reading Ability, that is, ability to comprehend prose like that of the *Reader's Digest*; and (2) Reading Comprehension Test score, as measured by well-known standardized tests. Fortunately, these two abilities are captured by a single test score, such as the Word Knowledge subtest of ASVAB. Reading Ability in its first meaning is critical because the instruction being designed is going to be delivered largely by prose statements. The second meaning, Reading Comprehension Test score, is a measure that correlates highly with what may be called ''learning aptitude.'' It therefore carries implications about the relative ease with which new ideas can be learned by the trainee, when they are presented in connected discourse form. While a continuous range of Word Knowledge scores is available, the important distinction is assumed to be the dichotomy between good readers and poor readers, which I call Reader–Non-Reader. On this basis, reasonable choices of instructional strategy can be made.

Environment. The assumption is made that most instruction will be delivered to the individual trainee via a station containing a monitor, a sound delivery system, and a console of keys (or an alternate mechanism). It is assumed that provision will be made for trainees to interact with these components not only individually, but also in learning pairs, or perhaps by interconnected small groups. However, the delivery of some parts of instruction in an instructor-led class is not ruled out. The introductory portions of courses, and instruction designed to establish attitudes, are examples of instructional types for which instructor presentations may be most effective.

With respect to micro-instruction having specific and singular objectives, three parts of the learning environment need to be distinguished, because they require different sets of instructional strategies. The first is *setup*, the second is *initial presentation* of the material to be learned, while the third is the *practice* period. The setup period is to assure learner readiness. Initial presentation includes the display of the stimuli to be responded to by the trainee (such as an instrument panel, a technical order) and a set of directions that tell the learner what he is expected to do. This period of initial presentation ends at the point when the learner actually executes the targeted performance, initially.

The practice period provides a number of additional occasions in which the trainee carries out varied instances of the activities he has learned to do. This period is one which strengthens the learned capability, refines it, and endows it with elaborations. Provision is made in this period for the feedback which gives reinforcement to the learned capability. This may be done in an automatic fashion, or it may require the judgment of a teacher, or it may be provided by other trainees, when practice is done in pairs or teams.

In summary, the critical values for the learning environment, assuming that most learning takes place at an individual station, are: (1) a setup period which sets the stage for learning, (2) initial presentation period, and (3) practice period. The first two of these can be accomplished by almost any medium of delivery, while the third requires a situation which can provide interactive feedback.

Task. In considering the range of activities involved in technical training, it is necessary to recognize as an initial caution, that some training is being given for tasks in which there are *serious consequences for error* (for example, piloting an aircraft, disarming an explosive device, fire fighting). When such tasks occur, transfer of training to the job situation must be 100%. Such tasks require, during the practice period, practice on the actual equipment or on a simulator (Reiser & Gagné, 1983). Otherwise, task characteristics that have implications for instructional design pertain to the *stimulus* mode inherent to the task. Is the trainee learning to respond to: (1) shapes, (2) spatial configurations, (3) objects or pictures of objects, (4) people, (5) information presented aurally, (6) information in printed form, or to some combination of these? These task characteristics will determine the stimulus mode in which major portions of instruction are presented, particularly during the period devoted to practice. For example, if the task is one which includes replacing a transformer in a larger assembly, the assembly and the transformer, or a suitable picture of them, will be required as displays during the period of practice.

Summary—Information. Table 5.1 presents a summary of the forms of information required in the planning of instruction for technical training. The first column lists the kinds of information needed, while the second indicates the characteristics to be considered, and variations of them.

Content

What information is needed by AIDA to describe the "content" to be acquired by trainees in the technical training area? The entities that are

Class	Characteristics
Trainees	Reader Non-Reader
Environment	Individual Station Instructor Led Setup Period Initial Presentation Practice Period
Task	Serious Error Consequences Stimulus Mode Shapes Spatial configuration Objects, Pictures of objects People Aural presentation Print presentation

Table 5.1. Classes of Information for AIDA.

learned are stored states called *capabilities* (sometimes, dispositions). Capabilities make possible different sorts of performances, as may be required by the task or job. For a number of reasons, both theoretical and practical, it is convenient to distinguish several types of capabilities, corresponding to different types of performance or learning outcomes (Gagné, 1985, p. 67). The major distinctive types of capabilities are listed in Table 5.2, along with examples. Some alternate designations for these five types of capabilities are shown in parentheses.

The nature of content. If the five kinds of capabilities of Table 5.2 represent what is learned, what has become of "content?" The answer is,

Type of Capability	Example of Performance
Intellectual Skill (Procedural Knowledge)	Identifying a transformer: Demonstrating a procedure for testing a transformer.
Verbal Information (Declarative Knowledge)	Matching a capacitor with its name: Stating the transformer's function.
Cognitive Strategy (Control Process)	Using split-half to check for a malfunction in an electric circuit.
Motor Skill	Making a fine adjustment of a volume knob.
Attitude	Choosing to wear gloves when pouring a caustic liquid.

Table 5.2. Types of Learned Capabilities with Examples.

the conception of "content" is not useful. If what is referred to is the presentation made to the learner, it is evident that this is not the same as content to be learned. Communications to the learner such as "notice the resistor in the top part of the diagram" are guidance for the learner, but they are not what is learned. Likewise, a verbal definition such as "the locus of points equidistant from a given point" is not desired as a statement to be learned; instead, the hoped-for learning is the *capability* of demonstrating the meaning of the concept "circle." It happens that there are a few instances of correspondence between "what is said to the learner" and "what is learned" such as the names of days of the week, or months of the year. But in general, the "content" of communications to the learner do not become "content" that is learned. What is learned are capabilities for performance.

The Integrative Control Capability

Besides the single capabilities listed in Table 5.2, another important capability is one that *integrates* them and controls their application to some unitary activity. This may be called an *integrative control* capability. For example, an airman who has responsibility for maintenance of a particular airborne radio set must have learned capabilities like the following: (1) verbal information, the names of the radio set and its components; (2) intellectual skills such as the measurement of resistance, the procedure for adjusting RF gain; (3) cognitive strategies for finding malfunctions; (4) an attitude of using safety precautions with high voltage circuits. Assuming all of these single capabilities have been well learned, they must still be integrated into a total purposive activity. *Integrative control* is provided by a "radio-functioning schema." This schema continues to remind the mechanic that maintaining the radio in working order requires using all of these capabilities in such a manner as to meet the goal. The schema that performs the function of integrative control consists of more than a single capability; it is an integrated complex of capabilities, organized around the central concept of the goal. In view of the purposive nature of activities to be engaged in by graduates of technical training courses, the schema that must be acquired may be categorized as an *enterprise schema* (Gagné & Merrill, 1990). Summarizing, what needs to be learned by trainees in technical training are five kinds of capabilities (Table 5.2), and the capability of integrative control representing a productive goal, called an enterprise schema.

The AIDA Executive

The function of the executive is to identify instructional strategies and to categorize them so that they can be selected to achieve the most effective learning. Selection will be determined by the requirements generated by variations in the characteristics of (a) trainees, (b) environment, (c) task, and (d) content (capabilities to be learned).

This becomes a multi-dimensional operation, however. Strategies for optimal learning differ with the stage of instruction being designed (see Table 5.1). What is presented to the learner, and how it is presented, obviously depends on whether the designer is making preparations for learning (setup), introducing the item to be learned and getting the learner to show what he has learned (initial presentation), or providing for feedback that will reinforce a performance (practice). Whatever is to be learned, the communications made to the learner go through a number of stages. These stages have been described as the nine events of instruction (Gagné, 1985, pp. 246–256; Gagné, Briggs, & Wager, 1988, pp. 194–198). For present purposes, I will deal with the somewhat abbreviated set of stages already mentioned, and listed as factors of Environment in Table 5.1.

Stages of Instructional Communication

The following paragraphs describe stages of instruction that require different instructional strategies:

Stage A: Setup. The instructional events of this period include gaining learner attention, informing learners of the learning objectives, and stimulating recall of prior learning. The latter two purposes may in most cases be combined in the establishment of an enterprise schema that integrates previously learned knowledges and skills and communicates a scenario delineating the goal of the learning.

Stage B: Initial Presentation. This stage includes the instructional events of presenting the stimulus situation, providing guidance to learning, and eliciting an initial performance. Some of the most critical instructional strategies are brought to bear in this stage. Also, the differences in instructional strategies appropriate for different learned capabilities (Table 5.2) take on particular significance during this stage (Gagné, 1985, pp. 246–256).

Stage C: Practice. During this stage, practice provides additional occasions for performance by the learner, in each case followed by informative feedback. Number of performances involved in practice may be few or many, depending on the capability. Performances may also be elicited after some designated time period (retention) and in some novel contexts (transfer). Also, some of the performances will provide the basis for evaluation.

Instructional Strategies

The factor that determines differences among selected instructional strategies is, above all, the type of capability being acquired (in the AIDA guidance material, called "content-characteristics"). Strategies have to be identified for each kind of capability (Table 5.2, and also for an enterprise schema); strategies must also be selected for each of the stages A, B, and C of the instruction. The need for a matrix is seen, but it is a very complex one, requiring a large spatial array. The tactic adopted here is the following: Potential strategies will be listed and described for each of the stages of instruction, intended to cover any and all capabilities (Table 5.2 and enterprise schema). Then, in a following section, the *selection of strategies* will be described, for each kind of capability objective.

Possible Strategies for Stage A

The setting-up stage, Stage A, has the following strategy possibilities:

A1: Grabber. An event (statement, picture, demonstration) that commands attention by capturing the trainee's interest.

A2: Scenario. A verbal description, and demonstration, of what the learner will be able to do when learning is complete, and how that performance relates to the system or organizational goal. Importance of accomplishment of the goal is emphasized.

A3: Reminder. A verbal statement beginning "You remember that . . . ," reminding the learner of previously acquired knowledge that is in the general area of the job (for example, measuring voltage is in the general area of "circuit testing"). The knowledge should be chosen to be as familiar as possible to the learner.

A4: Recall. Present examples of the concepts or procedures that are prerequisite (components) of the skill to be learned, each requiring the trainee to make a response.

Possible Strategies for Stage B

The presentation stage, Stage B, has the following strategy possibilities:

B1: Statement. A verbal statement of a rule, procedure, principle, or definition (Merrill calls this a generality). "A triangle is a closed figure with three sides" is an example. "To increase resistance, decrease the diameter of the conducting wire" is another. Verbal statement may be accompanied by a picture or diagram, when clarity of comprehension is judged to be aided thereby.

B2: Example. A particular instance of a concept or principle is described verbally, pictured, or both. "Figure XYZ (diagram) is not a triangle, because it is not a closed figure." The statement can be made so as to require a learner response.

B3: Label. Actual objects, pictures, or diagrams, are associated with labels that name them. The parts of a piece of equipment may each have a label; different knobs may be associated with such names as "volume," "frequency," "power," etc.

B4: Mnemonic. A sentence, meaningful phrase, or picture, to assist the verbatim memorization of a set of labels, or labels in a series. GSC45V can be remembered using the mnemonic "General service cart, Victory in '45."

B5: Discourse. A series of sentences that are logically and meaningfully connected. The discourse may be relatively short, as in "Small resistors have three colored bands", to quite long, as in a description of the connectedness of the parts in a complex electric circuit.

B6: Analogy. A verbal statement such as "_____ is like _____" presents the analogy. An example is "Constricting the flow of water in a pipe is like inserting a resistor in the conductor of electric current."

B7: Elaboration. Verbal discourse which relates a concept, rule, or set of ideas in a discourse to other things or events that are likely to be highly familiar and easily remembered. "Magnesium oxide is formed rapidly in a bright flash, whereas iron oxide (rust) forms slowly." A picture may be employed.

B8: Model's Choice. Presentation or description of a respected human model. After being identified, the model states and/or demonstrates a choice of personal action that reflects a targeted attitude. For example, an attractive male model chooses to be a "designated driver," refusing alcoholic drinks. An aircraft mechanic (model) refuses to "give up" until he is convinced that a replaced component works well.

B9: Question. A statement is presented that requires the trainee to respond by making a choice, completing a statement, or otherwise showing that something has been learned.

Possible Strategies for Stage C

The practice stage, Stage C, has the following strategy possibilities:

C1: Practice. Presentation of examples (of a concept or rule), few or many, each one different in its characteristics, and each a previously unencountered instance requiring a learner response. Each learner response is given feedback with correction. Number of examples required depends on the complexity of the learning task, and is arrived at by judgment based on experience with similar tasks. Also, increased precision in motor skills is attained by increased practice.

C2: Assessment. Additional trials of practice, without accompanying feedback, are given to permit assessment of performance.

C3: Telling. The learner is asked to tell the gist, or main points, of a discourse that has been presented. This may be done by presenting partial cues, as in a test requiring the trainee to fill in the blanks.

C4: Transfer. The trainee is required to apply learned concepts or procedures to a novel problem, or in a novel situation. Example: applying the rules of trigonometry to the task of sailboat tacking. Evaluation may also be carried out with transfer trials.

Selecting Instructional Strategies

The selection of strategies for particular learning objectives (capabilities) requires consideration of characteristics of the trainees, the environment for training, and the nature of the task. Since these determinations are complex, I propose that they be done in sequence. The proposed sequence is described here in terms of steps to be taken by the instructional designer. Presumably, each step will be aided by an advisory communication from the AIDA advisor.

In the following, Step 3 asks the instructional designer to classify each capability listed in the job-task analysis which is to be included in the training. Two assumptions are made here, and I know of no simple way of avoiding them:

Assumption 1: A job-task description has been done, and is available to the instructional designer.

Assumption 2: The designer has had sufficient training and experience to be able to classify specific job-tasks in the categories of Table 5.2.

Step 4 indicates the instructional strategies applicable to each category of capability being learned, in the order for their employment. For example, when instruction is being designed to teach a Concept, the designer begins with A1 (Grabber), then proceeds to A2 (Scenario), then to A3 (Reminder), and so on, taking note in each case of the advisory information that is displayed.

Step 1. Choose Media

Readers: Provide pictures when judged to aid comprehension and recall.

Non-readers: Use pictures and diagrams whenever possible. Use audio communications when possible.

Consequences of Error Serious: Use real equipment or simulator.

Step 2. Establish Integrative Control

Present the enterprise schema.

Describe, demonstrate, the purposive activity aimed for as a result of
training.

Reminders of relevant concepts, previously learned. Reminders of relevant rules and procedures, previously learned.

Reminders of relevant cognitive strategies, previously learned. Reminders of suitable attitudes, previously acquired.

Note: If the relevant concepts, procedures, and attitudes have not
been previously learned, design remedial training for them, as outlined in the following steps.

Step 3. For Each Enterprise, Classify the Single Capabilities to Be Learned

See job-task descriptions. See Table 5.2. Reflecting the enterprise scenario, place the capabilities to be learned in a suitable order for learning.

Step 4. Select and Order Appropriate Instructional Strategies for Each Capability

In following the sequence of strategies for each capability, use an informal conversational style. Strive for a coherent, interactive set of
communications with the trainee, helping to carry him from the setup
stage (A) on to presentation (B) and into practice with feedback (C).

Concept (Identify)

A1	Grabber.	Omit if considered unnecessary.
A2	Scenario.	Include, unless enterprise schema is well recalled.
A3	Reminder.	Include, unless Recall (A4) is necessary.
A4	Recall.	Include to strengthen prerequisite learning.
B1	Statement.	State, or demonstrate. Order can be B2, B1.
B2	Example.	
B3	Label.	Include if not already known.

B4	Mnemonic.	Include for a set of concept labels, or a series.
C1	Practice.	Use variety in examples and non-examples. Use novel examples, not previously employed.
C2	Assessment.	

Procedure

A1	Grabber.	Omit if considered unnecessary.
A2	Scenario.	Include, unless enterprise schema is well recalled.
A3	Reminder.	(Or A4).
A4	Recall.	Include unless A3 is sufficient.
B1	Statement.	Describe or demonstrate.
B2	Example.	Order can be B2,B1.
B4	Mnemonic.	Include if necessary for recall of sequence.
B6	Analogy.	Include if helpful for recall.
B7	Elaboration.	Include if helpful for recall; consider picture, diagram.
B9	Question.	
C1	Practice.	
C2	Assessment.	
C4	Transfer.	Use a novel problem, novel situation.

Verbal Information (Label)

A4	Recall.	Distinguish some other labels, previously learned.
B2	Example.	
B4	Mnemonic.	Include if helpful for recall.
B7	Elaboration.	Include if helpful for recall. Consider picture, diagram.
B9	Question.	
C1	Practice.	
C2	Assessment.	
C4	Transfer.	Ask question in a novel setting.

Verbal Information (Discourse)

A1	Grabber.	Include if necessary to arouse interest.
A2	Scenario.	Describe, demonstrate relationship of discourse to enterprise.
A3	Reminder.	Remind learner of larger meaningful context into which discourse fits.
B5	Discourse.	Use pictures for clarity, to aid recall.
B6	Analogy.	Include if helpful for recall.
B7	Elaboration.	Include if helpful for recall.

B9	Question.	Ask for recall of main idea.
C3	Telling.	Ask for another recall of the gist.
C4	Transfer.	Application of discourse in a novel situation.

Cognitive Strategy (Control Process)

A1	Grabber.	Include if necessary to arouse interest.
A2	Scenario.	Describe, demonstrate how cognitive strategy relates to job-task.
A3	Reminder.	Remind about concepts and procedures involved in the activity to which the cognitive strategy obtains.
A4	Recall.	Include unless A3 is sufficient.
B1	Statement.	Describe or demonstrate.
B2	Example.	Order can be B2,B1.
B6	Analogy.	Use if appropriate.
B9	Question.	
C1	Practice.	
C2	Assessment.	
C4	Transfer.	Use a new problem, new situation.

Motor Skill

A1	Grabber.	Omit if considered unnecessary.
A2	Scenario.	Include unless enterprise schema is well recalled.
A4.	Recall.	Ask for recall of prerequisite part-skills.
B1	Statement.	Demonstrate the procedure involved in the motor skill.
B9	Question.	Ask trainee to execute the procedure involved in the motor skill.
C1	Practice.	Continue repeated trials until adequate precision is attained.
C2	Assessment.	
C4	Transfer.	Ask for execution of skill in new setting.

Attitude

A1	Grabber.	Emphasize attitudinal aspects of the enterprise.
A2	Scenario.	Relate attitude to the enterprise.
A3	Reminder.	Remind trainee of human model who is attractive, credible, powerful. Remind about concepts or procedures involved in the action to be chosen.
B7	Elaboration.	Describe, demonstrate the situations in which the targeted choice behavior is usually made.

B8	Model's Choice.	Model describes, demonstrates the targeted choice of personal action. Display or describe the achievement and satisfaction of the model.
B9	Question.	In a described situation, ask trainee to make the appropriate choice of personal action.
C1	Practice.	Present additional situations for choice of personal action.
C2	Assessment.	
C4	Transfer.	Present an unfamiliar situation calling for targeted choice of action.

Conclusion

Constructing an AIDA to implement the scheme sketched in the preceding sections is both possible and affordable. The primary advantage of building such a system is that doing so would provide a relatively inexpensive research platform to use in elaborating and testing specific instructional guidance. In addition, such a system would provide the means to begin exploring exactly where practitioners actually need guidance and what kind of guidance is needed. Both areas of research are mentioned in Muraida's concluding section in Part III as worthy of research.

I have proposed a relatively simple AIDA. It contains no elements of artificial intelligence. It does not employ an expert system. It does not use case-based reasoning. It does not perform dynamic user modeling. What this system does is to engage the user in a dialogue which is intended to coax him or her into designing and developing effective instructional materials. Robust examples illustrating each step can be provided to users in a hypermedia environment. Since this system is based on offering on guidance, it shall be called GAIDA, for Guided Approach for an Instructional Design Advisor.

[Editor's Note: Professor Gagné has been named a National Research Council Senior Research Fellow at the Armstrong Laboratory to carry out the design and development of GAIDA.]

References

Corno, L., & Snow, R. E. (1986). Adapting teaching to individual differences among students. In M. Wittrock (Ed.), *Third handbook of research on teaching.* New York: Macmillan.

Gagné, R. M. (1985). *The conditions of learning* (4th ed.). New York: Holt, Rinehart, & Winston.

Gagné, R. M., & Merrill, M. D. (1990). Integrative goals for instructional design. *ETR&D, 38*(1), 23–30.

Gagné, R. M., Briggs, L. J., & Wager, W. (1988). *Principles of instructional design* (3rd ed.). New York: Holt, Rinehart, & Winston.

Reiser, R. A., & Gagné, R. M. (1983). *Selecting media for instruction.* Englewood Cliffs, NJ: Educational Technology Publications.

Snow, R. E., & Lohman, D. F. (1984). Toward a theory of cognitive aptitude for learning from instruction. *Journal of Educational Psychology, 76,* 347–376.

Chapter Six

An Integrated Model for Automating Instructional Design and Delivery

M. David Merrill

Background

The purpose of this chapter is to provide an initial concept for an automated instructional design advisor and to indicate the functions it should perform, including knowledge acquisition and strategy analysis. An attempt is also made to identify the principles of knowledge theory, learning theory, and instructional theory that underlie these functions. The model that will be elaborated is an outgrowth of our work on ID EXPERT and second generation instructional design. This model represents a much more integrated and holistic vision of instructional design. The ideas presented here are primarily those of the Utah State University Instructional Technology Development Team and includes M. David Merrill, Mark K. Jones, Zhongmin Li, and their associates.

This chapter is condensed from several working papers, some of which have been reworked individually and published separately. This material, however, represents the history, evolution, and current status of our instructional development theory. A shorter treatment without such a complete background can be found in the February 1992 issue of *Educational Technology* (Merrill, Li, & Jones, 1992b). The new vocabulary introduced for ID_2 is still evolving. The reader's indulgence is requested for those terms which are not consistent with other publications.

Theoretical Foundations for an AIDA

First Generation Instructional Design (ID_1)

The use of contemporary instructional design methodologies results in instruction that is more effective than that based only on folklore and trial-and-error. However, these methods have not provided the hoped for increase in instructional effectiveness that would enable learners to more adequately and efficiently grasp, and to apply, the content presented. Most are based on the psychology of the 50s and 60s; they are analytical, not synthetic; they are components rather than model or schema oriented; and their application requires considerable effort. Because the theories upon which these methods are based predates the development of highly interactive, technology-based delivery systems, little guidance is provided for developing instruction for these systems.

The most widely applied instructional design theory is based largely on the work of Robert M. Gagné and his associates at Florida State University (see the previous chapter in this volume). This work is often equated with the term Instructional Systems Development (ISD). It assumes a cumulative organization of learning events based on prerequisite relationships among learned behaviors. Gagné's principal assumption is that there are different kinds of learned outcomes, and that different internal and external conditions are necessary to promote each type. Gagné's original work (Gagné, 1965) was based on the experimental learning psychology of the time, including concepts of paired associate learning, serial learning, operant conditioning, concept learning, and gestalt problem solving. Recent versions (Gagné, 1985) have incorporated some ideas from cognitive psychology, but the essential characteristics of the original work have remained. The best example of Gagné's current thinking is probably the previous chapter in this volume.

Our own work, Component Display Theory (see Merrill 1983, 1987a, 1988), built directly upon Gagné's principal assumption. We extended the outcome classification system by separating content type from performance level. We also added a more detailed taxonomy of presentation types and clarified the prescriptions of the Gagné position. Nevertheless, Component Display Theory has the same roots as the Gagné position.

Other contemporary instructional design theories (see Reigeluth, 1983, 1987) are consistent with the Conditions of Learning and Component Display Theory. Gagné extends cumulative prerequisite analysis by including

Information Processing Analysis as suggested by Paul Merrill (Gagné, 1985). The recommendations for Structural Analysis by Scandura (Scandura, 1983; Stevens and Scandura, 1987) and Algorithm/Heuristic Analysis by Landa (1983, 1987) are similar to Information Processing Analysis. Markle (1983), Gropper (1983, 1987), Engelmann & Carnine (1982) and Collins (Collins & Stevens, 1983; Collins, 1987) provide a set of recommendations for teaching concepts and rules that are similar to the recommendations of The Conditions of Learning and Component Display Theory. Most of these theories were developed relatively independently of one another, yet produce similar recommendations, thus providing some rough confirmation of the validity of the recommendations.

In this chapter we refer to this body of theory and methodology as First Generation Instructional Design (ID₁). These First Generation ID Theories were preceded by a series of transitional theories including "Operant Conditioning" and "Programmed Instruction" based on Skinner (1953, 1957), the "Meaningful Verbal Learning Theory" of Ausubel (1963), and the instructional theories of Bruner (1966). While there is a remarkable similarity in their prescriptions, they share a number of limitations:

content analysis focuses on components, not integrated wholes;

limited prescriptions are set forth for knowledge acquisition;

there are superficial prescriptions for course organization strategies;

the theories are closed systems, asserting principles based on a subset of available knowledge, and are unable to accommodate new knowledge as it becomes available;

each phase of instructional development is performed essentially independently of other phases, as the theories provide no means for integration or for sharing data;

the resulting instruction teaches components but not integrated knowledge and skills;

the resulting instruction is often passive rather than interactive;

and all of these theories are very inefficient to use because an instructional designer must build every presentation from fundamental components.

Limitations of ID₁

Limitation 1. Content analysis does not use integrated wholes which are essential for understanding complex and dynamic phenomena. First generation instructional design methods attempt to identify the components of subject matter. These constituent components are then used to prescribe course organization and sequence. The elements of this analysis are individual content components such as facts, concepts, principles (rules), or procedures. The resulting instruction may be effective in teaching these pieces of the content, but is often not effective in helping students to integrate these components into meaningful wholes. New scientific knowledge is often complex and dynamic. As a result, it is difficult to understand such knowledge with only isolated concepts and principles. An integrated understanding is essential. As elaborated in Part I of this volume, cognitive psychology, in postulating the notion of schema or frame, suggests that cognitive structure consists of mental models. Learning results in the construction and elaboration of these models which serve to organize the knowledge, and to facilitate recall and further learning. No ID₁ content analysis procedure takes this notion of mental models into account.

Limitation 2. Limited prescriptions for knowledge acquisition. While ID₁ methods prescribe content structure as a result of the content analysis, none prescribe the subject matter components necessary to build a complete knowledge base for this structure. Hence the resulting structures are little more than content outlines for which the designer must still gather considerable additional material in order to build the course.

The content structure resulting from content analysis is rarely used directly in the course materials. The form of representation, usually some diagram, is not in a form that can be used by the presentation. In fact, current design methodology often requires three different and separate specifications of the content: first, as a set of task descriptions or objectives; second, as a story board or script; and third, a program written in some computer or authoring language. In addition to being time-consuming, this separation of content analysis from course development decreases the correspondence between these two activities, resulting in course content that is not represented in the content structure, or content structure elements that are not contained in the course materials.

Limitation 3. Limited prescriptions for course organization. For most ID₁ methods there is a gap between content analysis and course organization strategies. The prescription for course organization strategies is either not present or superficial. Prescriptions range from a one-to-one correspondence between content structure elements and instructional modules, to the bottom-up sequences suggested by hierarchies of enabling objectives. None of these ID₁ methods adequately accounts for different levels of instructional outcomes, such as familiarity versus basic instruction versus remediation. None of the ID_1 methods considers the highly interactive nature of the new technologies and how to prescribe highly interactive sequences.

Limitation 4. Existing theories are essentially closed systems. There is no means of incorporating fine-grained expertise about teaching and learning, gained from research, and applying this in the design process. While there remains much to understand about how people learn, we in fact know a great deal already. The designer of instruction must, however, apply this knowledge separately from the application of ID_1 theory, as no hooks are built into the theory to incorporate and apply new and better knowledge as it is discovered.

Limitation 5. ID_1 fails to integrate the phases of instructional development. Methodology based on ID_1 defines five phases of instructional development: analysis, design, development, implementation, and evaluation. While the outcomes of each phase are inputs to the next, and the development cycle is iterative, that is the extent of the integration of the phases (Tennyson's fourth generation ISD in the following chapter is an exception). Separate tools are used, and separate knowledge representations are maintained in each phase. Theory provides no prescriptions for how changes made in one phase should lead directly to changes in another. For example, in the analysis phase, information about the content to be taught is gathered, and represented in terms of the tasks that are performed by someone skilled in the subject matter to be taught. In the design phase, learning objectives are developed for each task. While the task analysis is preliminary to the objectives development, theory does not prescribe how the task analysis should be used. Guidance is available to the designer on the form to write an objective, but its actual selection and content is a matter of judgment and experience. At the next phase, development, learning activities are designed for each objective. Again, guidance is limited to what should go into an activity; there is no prescription for selecting activities. Moreover, at this point there is no direct connection whatsoever between the task analysis and the learning activities, and no possibility that information could flow directly from the one to the other.

Limitation 6. ID_1 teaches pieces but not integrated wholes. Each of these ID_1 methods attempts to prescribe the characteristics of the stimulus presentation to the student. These presentation components consist of elements such as definitions, examples, non-examples, practice problems, attention-focusing help, and prerequisite information. In every case the instructional designer must compose an instructional strategy from such elements to make a complete whole. Often these strategies take on a disjointed character in which one content element is taught after another, but little is done to integrate a series of elements into a whole. Elaboration theory (Reigeluth, 1983, 1987) is an exception to other first generation theories in that it does attempt to provide some integration.

Limitation 7. Instruction is often passive rather than interactive. Most of the ID_1 theories were formulated before interactive media (computer-based instruction, interactive video, intelligent tutoring systems) were readily available. As a consequence most of these models concentrate on the stimulus elements of the presentation rather than on input elements. Instruction based on ID_1 is frequently passive rather than interactive, requiring little mental effort on the part of the student. ID_1 theories are display orientated (our own work is called Component Display Theory) rather than transaction or interaction oriented. Collins' (1983, 1987) inquiry-based prescriptions is the only theory in the Reigeluth collection that is concerned with dynamic on-line adaptation of the instruction based on student interaction with the materials. They prescribe examples and non-examples but have little to say about the use of experiential interactions, simulated environments, or controllable worlds (see Merrill, 1988).

There is evidence that learning is directly related to the level of mental effort put forth by the student. This mental effort must bear a direct relationship to the concepts and principles being taught. When the instruction is passive, learners are not forced to examine their cognitive structure, and the resulting learning is poorly retained, does not relate well to previously learned materials, and is not easily transferred to new situations. Furthermore, much new scientific knowledge is dynamic in character and cannot be understood without a more active representation and student involvement.

Limitation 8. Every presentation must be constructed from small components. With ID_1 methods the designer must always compose every instructional strategy from basic display elements, e.g., definitions, rules, examples, and helps. This means that for each lesson the designer must analyze and select every display element for presentation to the student. If one were to consider a larger content element, a mental model, then it is conceivable that there is a corresponding instructional transaction for promoting the acquisition of this mental model. Composing instruction from larger transaction units would mean considerable savings in development time and resources. By analogy first generation instructional design is a little like limiting a chemist to the basic elements. The chemist can make anything but to get water you must start with hydrogen and oxygen and make the compound first. We need some instructional compounds that can be used as wholes. However, none of the ID_1 methods identify such transaction wholes.

Limitation 9. Current ID is labor intensive. Current instructional design and development practices are extremely labor intensive. Even though the hardware is affordable, the courseware frequently is not. A development/delivery ratio of more than 200:1 is too high. The current ratio for designing and developing instruction for the new interactive technologies exceeds 200 hours of design/development for each 1 hour of delivered instruction (Lippert, 1989). Some estimates suggest ratios exceeding 500:1 just for programming.

The impact of computerization on other fields has been to increase productivity by reducing labor costs, or allowing greater production from the same labor. Personal computers probably owe their success to the electronic spreadsheet. Every financial planner could immediately see the efficiency of using an electronic spreadsheet. Tasks that at one time might require days or weeks could now be accomplished in minutes or hours.

In education and training the ratio is just the opposite. Educational experiences which can be planned and delivered in a few hours using conventional methods and technologies require days or weeks with the computer. It is often argued that the quality of the instruction justifies the increased effort. However, when data is gathered it often shows only a marginal advantage for the computer. This data rarely justifies the enormous increase in effort. Until now, computer-based instruction has only been cost effective when large numbers of students are taught by the same program over a considerable period of time and the cost is justified by reducing personnel costs.

Second Generation Instructional Design (ID₂)

If interactive instructional technologies are to provide a significant part of the increasing amount of education and training demanded by society, then there is a critical need for significantly improved methodology and tools to guide the design and development of high quality interactive technology-based instructional materials. There is a need for second generation instructional design (ID₂).

ID₂ would build on the foundation of ID₁, but would address the shortcomings noted above. Specifically, ID₂ will:

> be capable of analyzing, representing, and guiding instruction to teach integrated sets of knowledge and skills;

> be capable of producing pedagogic prescriptions for the selection of instructional strategies and the selection and sequencing of instructional transactions;

> be an open system, able to incorporate new knowledge about teaching and learning, and to apply these in the design process; and

> integrate the phases of instructional development.

ID₂ will comprise the following components:

a theoretical base that organizes knowledge about instructional design and defines a methodology for performing instructional design;

a means of representing domain knowledge for the purposes of making instructional decisions;

a collection of mini-experts, each contributing a small knowledge base relevant to a particular instructional design decision or a set of such decisions;

a library of instructional transactions for the delivery of instruction, and the capacity to add new or existing transactions to the library; and

an on-line intelligent advisor program that dynamically customizes the instruction during delivery, based on a mixed-initiative dialogue with the student.

Analyzing and Representing Instruction for Integrated Goals

Our orientation is cognitive rather than behavioral. We start from the basic assumption that learning results in the organizing of memory into structures, which we may term mental models. To this we adopt two propositions about the learning process (see Kintsch, Part I, this volume):

organization during learning aids in later retrieval of information, and

elaborations generated at the time of learning new information can facilitate retrieval.

Organization refers to the structuring of knowledge, while elaboration refers to the explicit specification of relations among knowledge units.

From ID_1 we retain Gagné's fundamental assumption:

There are different learning outcomes and different conditions are required to promote each of these different outcomes (Gagné 1965, 1985).

We propose to extend these fundamental ideas as follows:

a given learned performance results from a given organized and elaborated cognitive structure, which we will call a mental model;

different learning outcomes require different types of mental models;

the construction of a mental model by a learner is facilitated by instruction that explicitly organizes and elaborates the knowledge being taught during the instruction; and

there are different organizations and elaborations of knowledge required to promote different learning outcomes.

However, we make no claims about how cognitive structure is organized and elaborated, as this is not well understood. We stand on the weaker, and more defensible, assumption that we can analyze the organization and elaborations of knowledge outside the mind, and presume that there is some correspondence between these and the representations in the mind.

Addressing the limitations of ID_1 in regards to the teaching of integrated wholes, we propose that ID_2 should be capable of teaching the organized and elaborated knowledge needed to facilitate the development of mental models. A necessary precondition to the design of such instruction is the development of detailed prescriptions for a knowledge acquisition process to identify all of the information necessary for a student to build a mental model. The outcome of this process would be a representation of the knowledge to be taught in terms of its structure and its elaborations.

Classes of Knowledge Representations

The means chosen to represent knowledge about a domain depend upon the use to which that knowledge will be put. We distinguish for the purposes of this analysis three classes of knowledge representation (KR).

KRr is a class of representation for the purpose of retrieving the knowledge in various formats. A representation of this class would be most appropriate for database applications, and would emphasize descriptors, keys, and relations.

KRe is the class most often used in artificial intelligence, where it is desired that the representation be executable. The emphasis here is on modeling the domain in terms of propositions, scripts, etc., which can be executed under the constraints of several variables in order to simulate a natural or hypothetical system. (See Brachman & Levesque, 1985, for a review of this area.)

KRi is the class of interest here, in which key information about the domain is represented in a way so that instructional decisions may be made. Here the emphasis is on categorizing the elements of the domain for the purposes of selecting instructional strategies, and identifying the semantics of links among domain elements in order to prescribe instructional sequences. ID_1 approaches to knowledge representation (referred to as content, or job/task analysis, see Bloom *et al.*, 1956; Gagné, 1985; P. F. Merrill, 1987) are insufficiently precise and comprehensive, and are particularly lacking in describing linkages among domain elements.

Knowledge Representation for ID_2

The key to ID_2 is the acquisition and representation of course content. We propose to represent knowledge in terms of objects which we call frames; each frame has an internal structure (slots, which contain values for the structure), and links to other frames. These (both internal and external) are termed elaborations of the frame. The set of all elaborated frames together, which contains all the knowledge to be instructed by a course, is called an elaborated frame network.

We hypothesize that there are three fundamental frame types:

entities, which correspond to some thing, for example a device, object, person, creature, place, or symbol;

activities, sets of related actions to be performed by the learner; and

processes, sets of related actions which are entirely external to the learner.

There are also three types of elaborations. These are:

components, which correspond to the internal structure of a frame; for an entity, the components would be parts of the entity; for an activity, steps; and for a process, events and causes;

abstractions, which correspond to a "kinds-of" class/subclass hierarchy into which the frame may be classified; and

associations, which are meaningful links to other frames in the network.

The network structure of the knowledge representation allows information to move through the structure, so that data contained in one part of the net affects the data stored elsewhere. Two principal means by which this occurs are:

inheritance, in which attributes of a class or superclass in an abstraction hierarchy are passed to a subclass or instance, and

propagation, in which the contents of a frame influence the contents of another frame connected to it via an association link.

Knowledge analysis and acquisition is the process of gathering and organizing all of the information required for the student to acquire a given mental model or set of mental models. The product resulting from the knowledge analysis and acquisition process is an elaborated frame network. Each elaborated frame in this network corresponds to the knowledge required to facilitate the development of a mental model in the cognitive structure of the student.

By representing the organization and elaborations of knowledge structures, it will be possible to select and sequence instructional units which make the structure of the knowledge explicit to the student. However, in order to do so effectively, we need more than just a description of the knowledge structures. We need instructional strategies for teaching integrated wholes, and rules, or prescriptions, for selecting these strategies. In addition, we need larger instructional units, or transactions, designed to teach an entire knowledge structure, rather than a single knowledge component.

Transactions

A transaction is defined as a mutual, dynamic, real-time give-and-take between the instructional system and the student in which there is an exchange of information. The purpose of a transaction is to promote the acquisition of one or more mental models. Instruction designed using ID_2 is in terms of a sequence of these transactions.

The adequacy of a transaction is determined by a number of factors including the degree of active mental processing involved, the completeness with which the transaction promotes acquisition of the target mental model, the degree to which the transaction elaborates a prerequisite mental model, and the degree to which the transaction can be customized to the special needs of individual students or groups of students. Transactions are categorized by the content elements instructed (for example, the component—parts—elaboration of an entity frame); and by the instructional strategy implemented for that content.

Frequently the effective implementation of a particular instructional strategy will require more than a single transaction. The set of transactions that implements a given instructional strategy to teach a particular elaborated frame in a particular domain, in order to promote the acquisition of a given mental model by a given student, is referred to as a transaction frame set. Similarly, the set of transactions necessary to achieve a given instructional goal is referred to as a transaction goal set.

Note that these terms refer to the effects of the transactions, not to collections of code segments. A transaction is not a piece of code or an instructional artifact but the effect of executing a piece of code or an instructional artifact. It is a logical construction, not a physical one.

The code segment which when executed causes a transaction to take place is called a transaction instance. This is created by the transaction generation system (TGS) as a result of an object-oriented design process. A class "transaction" is defined, with a subclass structure beneath it corresponding to the different types of possible transactions that can be generated by the system. A given transaction is instantiated by the TGS from this class hierarchy, and the capabilities of the transaction instance are inherited through the class structure. The instructional artifact thus created may be stored in a library of such artifacts for reuse. For efficiency, the TGS may access the library and recommend instantiated transactions in place of generating new transactions. The ability to assemble courses from such previously prepared standard components will be a major source of economy in the instructional design process using ID_2.

It is important to recognize that the delivery method for a transaction is not constrained by ID_2. In addition, existing instruction, not created with ID_2, may be categorized, placed in the library, and recommended by the system. In order to be included in the library, it is only necessary that a transaction be describable in terms of its intended instructional outcomes and the type of domain knowledge instructed.

Pedagogic Prescriptions

Instructional strategy specifies a pedagogy for selecting, sequencing, customizing, and integrating instructional units. Strategy exists at several levels. There is strategy embedded into a transaction that controls the presentation of the transaction. This may be termed micro-strategy. Above this level, there is the strategy which directs the assembling of a set of transactions into a transaction frame set, to instruct a particular elaborated frame. There is the higher-level strategy which integrates the instruction for a set of elaborated frames, each with its own transaction frame set, into a larger instructional unit which corresponds to an instructional goal. At the highest level there is strategy to integrate all goals into a course. These levels may be termed macro-strategies. In this section we are concerned only with macro-strategies.

The identification of instructional goals is critical to the design of instruction for ID_2. A goal corresponds to some learned capability or performance which the student will attain as a result of the instruction. The achieving of a goal may require the acquisition of one, or a set, of mental models by the learner.

An instructional (macro-) strategy is implemented with one or more transaction frame sets. A transaction frame set, as discussed above, is constructed to include all the transactions necessary to promote the acquisition of a given mental model. The pedagogic strategy determines which of the possible transaction instances should be generated to achieve the instructional goal. Any given frame set will include only a few of the transaction instances which could be generated for that type of knowledge structure. Hence the pedagogic strategy serves to direct and constrain the application of the transactions. In addition, because each transaction requires only certain elements of the knowledge structure, the strategy also directs and constrains the knowledge acquisition to just the portions of the knowledge structure required for the goal. Without such constraint, the knowledge acquisition process would be completely open-ended.

A limitation of ID_1 is the lack of pedagogic prescriptions. ID_2 will contain rules for prescribing instructional strategies, which in turn will prescribe transactions. The prescription of instructional strategies will result from an analysis of the requirements and constraints of a particular instructional situation, and will lead to the identification of instructional goals.

Information gathering is the first requirement of strategy analysis. Relevant information includes an analysis of the application to which the learning will be put, the characteristics of the learner population, and the environmental conditions under which the instruction will be administered.

Using this information about a particular instructional situation, strategy analysis provides both prescriptions and filters for the knowledge acquisition process. The knowledge acquisition process is general, that is, a Knowledge Acquisition System knows about frame components, organization and elaboration but not which of these elements may be appropriate for a given situation. A prescription indicates that a particular goal requires a given level of abstraction (organization) and certain links between frames (elaboration). A filter indicates that a particular goal does not require certain frame components, certain organizational structures and certain elaborative links. ID_2 would provide rules for selecting prescriptions and filters that correspond to particular kinds of goals. A Strategy Analysis System would guide the user to select a goal type consistent with the course to be developed and would then provide prescriptions and filters which would direct the knowledge acquisition process.

Based on the constrained knowledge structure and information about the students and environment, ID_2 would prescribe sequence rules for ordering the resulting elaborated frames which comprise the knowledge structure (elaborated frame network). A Strategy Analysis System would recommend a course organization consistent with the eventual role of the learners and the particular knowledge to be taught. These rules would take into account the interrelationships between frames in the knowledge structure and the propagation among these frames. Propagation means that information contained in one frame, for a certain goal, must also be included as part of another frame for that goal. For example, if a certain course included an activity frame for "creating a budget," this frame may be linked to an activity frame for "using a spreadsheet." If a step in building a budget is to "identify personnel" then "entering the names of the personnel in the spreadsheet" would be an associated activity. In other words, steps for "using a spreadsheet" frame would propagate to the "building a budget" frame. A Strategy Analysis System would know such propagation rules and use them in building a course sequence.

Finally, the particular transactions and their sequencing necessary to acquire a particular mental model for one student with one set of expectations, abilities, previous preparation and attitudes, may be considerably different from the sequence of interactions needed by a student with a different set of these attributes. ID_2 should include rules relating student attributes with available interactions and their sequence. A Strategy Analysis System would construct appropriate transaction frame sets and configure these for students with different values on these relevant characteristics.

An Open System

A limitation of ID_1 is that there is no means of incorporating fine-grained expertise about teaching and learning, gained from research, and applying this in the design process. An example of this type of expertise would be a set of rules for determining the level of motivation of a student, and prescriptions for adjusting the instruction based on that level. Most knowledge in ID_1 systems is not of this type. To the extent that such knowledge is incorporated, it is "hard-wired" into the system. There is no means to easily upgrade such knowledge as new findings appear in the literature.

Integration of the Phases of Instructional Design

A critical limitation in the systematic application of ID_1 theories has been the lack of integration of the phases of instructional design. The work in each phase is relatively independent of the work in other phases. When similar data is used across phases, it typically must be translated into another form. This translation process is manual, hence no direct linkage exists among these different representations. Thus changes made in one phase cannot automatically cause corresponding changes in another. The practicing designer, working to a schedule, will usually maintain up to date only the data for the phase currently worked on, and is reluctant to revisit decisions made at earlier phases. These earlier phases, over time, become outdated and not representative of the actual instruction as developed. Because each phase of design results in a sharpening of focus to smaller and smaller units of instruction, important contextual information is lost when data from earlier phases cannot be manipulated concurrently. This is in no small measure responsible for the shortcomings in developing instruction that teaches integrated goals.

A Single Knowledge Representation

ID$_2$ resolves this limitation by maintaining a single representation of the data throughout the development process. Changes made in one area automatically flow through to other areas and create corresponding changes. Consistency and completeness checks are facilitated. And the designer may more easily return to earlier decisions and observe the effects of changing these without having to redo large portions of the design manually.

In addition, there are close interconnections among the phases. As discussed earlier, the strategy analysis phase directs and constrains both the knowledge acquisition and the authoring of transactions.

An Intelligent Advisor

This integration continues through to the delivery of instruction by means of an on-line advisor program.

The prescriptions made at design time are based on the designer's best estimate of the learner population. During the delivery of instruction, information about the learner, his or her aptitude, specific goals, motivation, familiarity, and other factors, as well as the learner's expressed preferences, may be taken into account to modify those prescriptions.

The advisor would have access to the knowledge base, both for the domain and the pedagogic prescriptions. In addition, it would maintain a student model that contained information about the learner. Using the information gathered about the student, the advisor would adjust design decisions to customize the instruction to more adequately meet the characteristics of the student. The advisor could also engage in a mixed-initiative dialogue with the student which would allow the student to participate in this decision-making.

Similarly to the approach to the domain knowledge representation, we propose to implement in the advisor what would be characterized as a "weak" student model: one that is not capable of simulating the actual state of the student's knowledge, or identifying as a result of such simulation the faulty conceptions, or bugs, in that knowledge. Rather, information about the student would be gathered, categorized, and entered as data for the mini-experts responsible for pedagogic strategy decisions, in particular selection and sequencing of transactions.

Comparison with Other Approaches

We have characterized the solution of ID_2 to the problems previously stated as the development of a theory capable of producing pedagogic prescriptions for integrated learning goals, and being an open system so that research results may be incorporated into the design process in the form of rule-based mini-experts.

The problem of effective instructional development for interactive technologies could be and is approached in other ways. We will examine two classes of alternative approaches.

One major approach is to improve the efficiency by which current instructional design theory and methods are applied, by developing expert systems for advice and guidance of designers (for example, Gustafson & Reeves, 1990; Jones & Massey-Hicks, 1987; Ranker, 1990). This is a conservative, knowledge engineering approach which focuses on representing existing expertise about instructional design in an expert system. The drawback of this approach is the state of knowledge about instructional design, which we believe is inadequate for the task to which it is put.

Other approaches which have received considerable attention are the development of micro-worlds to simulate a domain, and intelligent tutoring systems (Polson & Richardson, 1988; Sleeman & Brown, 1982; Wenger, 1987). These approaches attack the far more difficult problem of creating strong domain and student models capable of executing the knowledge of the domain (KRe). There are a number of difficulties with these approaches. First is the inherent difficulty of the problem, and the expense of creating these systems. Second is an overreliance on discovery learning as a means of teaching. Discovery learning (Bruner, Goodnow, & Austin, 1967; Dewey, 1937; Papert, 1980) is without question useful, but is not equally desirable in all situations. Important limitations of discovery learning are the additional time that is usually required, the fidelity of the simulation that is required, and the inability to easily overcome large gaps in prerequisite knowledge or skills. It is not difficult to imagine situations in which discovery is inappropriate and inefficient: for example, a learner experienced in a related domain may be best served by a simple presentation of the similarities and differences on critical aspects; while a learner with no knowledge of a subject may benefit from an organization of the knowledge to be learned so that a mental model into which further knowledge can be related can begin to be built.

We would contend that the most appropriate instructional strategy is a function of the domain to be instructed, a given learner's knowledge of that domain, and the instructional setting. Discovery learning is one strategy among many; the key from an instructional design point of view is having a basis for knowing when to prescribe discovery, and when to prescribe another method.

Note, however, that an ITS or a microworld simulation, or another means of discovery learning, can be used as a transaction in ID_2. It would be necessary to describe the ITS or microworld in terms of the types of domain knowledge instructed, the strategy implemented, and the specific elaborated frames instructed (as these simulations are typically not domain-independent).

Metatheoretical Elaboration of ID_2

Theory consists of two primary components: objects (entities) and relationships between these objects. The identification and description of the objects involved might be called descriptive theory. The identification of the relationships between these objects might be called prescriptive theory. When the objects involved in a theory are clearly understood (meaning that the reader can easily identify instances of a particular class of objects) then only prescriptive theory (principles or propositions) is required. However, when a theory attempts to explain the world in a new way then the definition of the objects involved is critical and the theory is meaningless without a careful definition of the entities about which the theory is involved.

In our graduate schools we emphasis methodology aimed at testing propositions (hypotheses) but we almost never teach students how to invent new concepts (that is, identify and describe the objects that the theory will be about). Yet, the identification of the right objects is critical if the theory is to have any validity. When physical science was concerned with fire, water, earth, and air little progress was made. When someone postulated atoms and molecules as the components of matter considerable progress was made. The identification of appropriate objects is at least as important as the identification and testing of relations between these objects.

In instructional theory one of our problems may be that we are dealing with the wrong objects, objects that will not enable us to make the kind of progress that we would like. The first step in theory building is to identify those objects which enable more powerful propositions. Instructional theory is weak precisely because the objects we have identified are either ambiguous or inappropriate. To progress this theory needs more appropriate instructional objects about which to build our theory.

Theoretical Interpretation

Instructional Objects

In the previous section we listed several limitations of first generation ID theory (ID_1). Many of these limitations address the objects of which instructional design theory is constructed. This set of limitations identifies instructional objects which we feel are inadequate concepts on which to build instructional theory. In the following table (Table 6.1) I will list the instructional objects which we think are inadequate and the instructional objects which we feel will enable more powerful second generation theory (ID_2):

INSTRUCTIONAL OBJECTS

ID_1	ID_2
(Inadequate concepts)	(More adequate concepts)
Individual content components: facts, concepts, principles, procedures	Integrated knowledge/skills: frames, schemata, mental models
Content outlines: hierarchy diagrams	Knowledge structures: knowledge base
Course organization: loosely defined	Course organization: based on content structure
Small presentation components: definitions, examples, practice	Integrated interactions: transactions, and transaction sets
Passive presentations	Interactive transactions
Basic display elements: rules, examples, etc.	Integrated interactions: transaction sets

Table 6.1. Comparison of Instructional Objects.

An essential step in an adequate second generation instructional design theory is to describe these new instructional objects including their attributes and relationship to other objects in the system. These descriptions constitute instructional design theory.

Instructional design theory must confront two major decisions: what to teach (content), and how to teach (pedagogy). We suggested that ID_2 will have the following capabilities:

(1) Be capable of analyzing, representing, and guiding instruction to teach integrated sets of knowledge and skills.

(2) Be capable of producing pedagogic prescriptions for the selection of instructional strategies and the selection and sequencing of instructional transactions.

The first relates to content decisions, the second to pedagogy decisions. These two capabilities incorporate the new instructional objects identified in the limitations. The first includes integrated knowledge/skill sets and knowledge structures represented in a knowledge base. The second includes course organization based on transactions and transaction sets.

Content—Analyzing and Representing Integrated Goals

Theories start with assumptions, untested axioms, on which the rest of the logical structure will be based (Merrill, 1991). What are our assumptions about the new entities we have identified? What are the propositions that follow from these assumptions?

Assumptions Adopted from Cognitive Science:

* Memory consists of both declarative and procedural knowledge. "Declarative knowledge is knowledge that something is the case, whereas procedural knowledge is knowledge of how to do something." (E. D. Gagné, 1985)

* Memory is organized into integrated sets of declarative and procedural knowledge called mental models.

Principles (Propositions) Adopted from Cognitive Science:

* Organization during learning aids in later retrieval of information.

* Elaborations generated at the time of learning new information can facilitate retrieval.

See E. D. Gagné's Cognitive Psychology of School Learning (1985) for an elaboration of these two principles and the research support for these principles.

ID₂ Content Assumptions:

Assumptions and propositions followed by a double asterisk (★★) are significant modifications of existing ideas or are original contributions from our own research efforts.

* There are different learning outcomes and different conditions are required to promote each of these different outcomes (Gagné, 1965, 1985).

* Significant learning outcomes consist of complex human activities which require integrated sets of knowledge and skill. We call such a complex human activity an enterprise. The term *enterprise* was not used in the previous section. We feel that this instructional object is less ambiguous than the term *goal* or *integrated goal*. The cognitive representation of all the knowledge and skill required for engaging in this enterprise is called a mental model.★★

Enterprises are characterized by the human activity involved. Different enterprises require different kinds and combinations of knowledge and skill. Hence, different learning activities are required to promote the acquisition of mental models required for different kinds of enterprises.★★

ID₂ Content Propositions:

Instruction should focus on helping the learner acquire mental models that enable them to engage in complex human enterprises.★★

The acquisition of a mental model by a learner is facilitated by instruction that explicitly organizes and elaborates the knowledge being taught during the instruction.★★

The above assumptions and propositions represent our fundamental theory of cognitive organization and knowledge structure. These are fundamental propositions on which ID₂ is built.

ID₂ Content Objects:

In the previous section we tried to begin identifying the objects involved in a theory of knowledge structure. Following are more careful definitions of these objects. This section is primarily a glossary identifying the key theoretical entities for ID₂. A more complete exposition of each of these entities is required. In most cases they are complex objects with several attributes and methods attached. The purpose of this section is merely to identify these entities and to provide a very brief definition of each. A more complete presentation of the theory is required to completely present each of these instructional objects but such a presentation is beyond the scope of this section.

Enterprise. An enterprise is some complex human activity. Webster defines enterprise as ''. . . an undertaking that is difficult or complicated . . .'' or ''. . . any systematic or purposeful activity.'' An enterprise is sometimes described by an integrated goal. An enterprise involves a set of related instructional objectives. An enterprise has a sense of belonging and can be bounded in some way that defines those activities that are part of a particular enterprise and those activities which are not. The terms goal and objective are not technical terms in ID₂ but are used for purposes of clarification.

Enterprise class. A set of enterprises that are characterized by the nature of the human activity involved. Five learned enterprise classes have been identified: denote, manifest, execute, discover, or design. When the term class is used we imply a class hierarchy which may be comprised of several levels of classes and subclasses. For purposes of this section we have identified only the top level of this class hierarchy. For example, the class entity enterprise has as subclasses persons or creatures, places, events, symbols, objects, or devices. Similarly, activities and processes have subclasses and these subclasses have further subclasses. A more complete presentation of ID₂ will involve careful definition of these enterprise classes together with all of their attributes. Such a complete presentation is beyond the scope of the current task (see Gagné & Merrill, 1990).

Mental model. The cognitive representation of all the knowledge and skill necessary to carry out an enterprise. A mental model is composed of a set of individual cognitive schema.

Elaborated Frame Network (EFN). A knowledge base (knowledge structure) containing representations of all the knowledge and skill necessary to carry out an enterprise. An EFN is an external representation of the same knowledge and skill which comprise a mental model. We make no claims about how cognitive structure is organized and elaborated, as this is not well understood. We stand on the weaker, and more defensible assumption, that we can analyze the organization and elaborations of knowledge outside the mind, and presume that there is some correspondence between these and the representations in the mind. An EFN is comprised of knowledge frames including their internal structures and the connections (organization and elaboration) among these frames. Abstraction is the class/subclass hierarchy into which the frame may be classified. Association is the linking of frames to other frames in the network.

Frame. Fundamental object for representing knowledge in an instructional knowledge base (knowledge structure). Each frame has an internal structure (slots which contain values for the structure) which contains the content (knowledge) components represented by the frame. Frames also contain methods which prescribe inheritance and propagation. Inheritance is the method by which attributes of a class or superclass in an abstraction hierarchy are passed to a subclass or instance. Propagation is the method by which the content of one frame influence the content of another frame connected to it via an association link. A frame is the external representation of the knowledge and skill of a single schema in a mental model.

Frame class. A set of frames that are characterized by the nature of the subject matter content involved. Three knowledge structure frame classes have been identified: entity, activity and process.

Content Rules (Principles):

ID_2 consists of two major sets of propositions or rules. Since ID_2 presupposes intelligent tools then the propositions underlying ID_2 are in the form of expert system rules. The rules identified here represent the rules that would comprise a strategy knowledge base for ID_2. When specified these rules comprise two strategy knowledge bases for an intelligent ID Expert system. The first set of rules governs the selection of subject matter content (What to teach?). This first set of rules provides filters and prescriptions for the knowledge acquisition process. The general form of the proposition is as follows:

$$EFN = F \text{ (Enterprise Class and Attributes)}$$

The frames included, the level of abstraction and the elaboration links of an elaborated frame network (EFN) are a function of the class of enterprise involved and the value of the attributes associated with this enterprise class. These rules include those governing inheritance and propagation among frames in the elaborated frame network. These rules together with the slots in the frames themselves identify all of the knowledge and skill which must be represented in the EFN if it is to be able to promote the mental model associated with the enterprise.

A detailed list of these knowledge structure principles will consist of hundreds of individual rules. It is this level of detailed learning and/or instructional principles that will be necessary to build an AIDA-like system. Broad principles will have value only when they are translated into these detailed rules in a strategy knowledge base. Nevertheless, some of the broad-based learning principles which will be considered in building these more detailed rule-based principles follow. This list is representative rather than exhaustive. Furthermore, a detailed explanation of how these very general learning principles relate to the specific entities identified for ID_2 is beyond the scope of the current task.

*The short-term memory principle: The magic number seven plus or minus two represents short-term memory limits. The number of subclasses at any level should be limited to approximately seven or less. The number of steps in an activity at any level, the number of parts associated with an object at any level, etc., should be limited to approximately seven or less. A knowledge acquisition system must know about and promote this "chunking."

*Inheritance principle: All instances within a class inherit (share) all attributes of the class. Instances may have their own unique attributes in addition. Learning the attributes of the class facilitates generalization to instances of the class. It is not necessary for the learner to learn each instance as unique. It is this property of classes that makes abstraction possible and promotes transfer. Transfer occurs when the learner learns the "abstraction model" represented by a class or superclass and then via the inheritance principle makes application to previously unencountered instances of the class. Generalization is the inverse of inheritance. It occurs when a set of individual instances which all share one or more attributes have been learned and the learner then is able to form a class for these individual cases.

*The entity principle: Entities are required for any enterprise. There cannot exist a human enterprise without at least one entity. Therefore, "identifying" an entity is the fundamental enterprise, required as a prerequisite of all other enterprises. Activity and process frames must always have at least one associated entity frame.

★The tool principle: You cannot teach a tool without an application and you cannot execute an application without a tool. Activity frames can be either "application" or "tool" activities. Every application requires at least one tool (thereby prescribing a link between frames) and every tool must be associated with two or more applications.

★The prerequisite principle: New mental models must be built from previously acquired mental models and the schemata which comprise these. New enterprises are constructed from more fundamental previously acquired enterprises.

★The process principle: Underlying any human activity is a process (sometimes not yet known) which provides an "understanding" of the activity. However, knowing the process is not prerequisite to executing the activity.

Pedagogy Transactions

ID_2 *Pedagogy Assumption:*
* Instructional interactions should be organized around all those activities necessary to promote the acquisition of a particular mental model.**

ID_2 *Pedagogy Propositions:*
* Integrated interactions which focus on all of the knowledge and skill which comprise a particular elaborated frame network (EFN or knowledge structure) aid the formation of a corresponding mental model and hence enable the learner to acquire the ability to engage in enterprises requiring this mental model.

* There are different classes of transactions required for efficient and effective acquisition of different types of knowledge frames.

The above assumption and propositions represent our fundamental theory of pedagogy. These are fundamental propositions on which ID_2 is built.

ID_2 *Pedagogy Objects:*
In the previous section we tried to begin the process of identifying the objects involved in a theory of pedagogy. Following are more careful definitions of these objects. (A more complete presentation of the theory is required to more completely present each of these instructional objects but such a presentation is beyond the scope of this report.)

Transaction. A transaction is characterized as a mutual, dynamic, real-time give and take between the instructional system and the student in which there is an exchange of information (Li & Merrill, 1990). A transaction instance is a piece of computer code which, when executed, causes a given transaction to take place. In ID_2 the word transaction is often used to mean transaction instance.

Transaction class. Different transactions involve different kinds of interactions with students. All transactions which require a particular type of interaction are grouped into a transaction class. The specific implementation of this interaction may differ widely depending on the nature of the specific entities, activities or processes involved; depending on the delivery system involved; and depending on the characteristics of the learners. Several transaction classes have been identified including: naming, classifying, predicting, executing, judging, designing, and discovering.

Transaction Frame Set (TFS). A transaction frame set is the specific individual transactions selected from one or more transaction classes which are required to promote the acquisition of a particular instantiated elaborated frame from the knowledge structure. A transaction frame set implements those interactions necessary to promote the acquisition of a particular schema in a particular domain. A transaction frame set corresponds roughly to a lesson in ID_1, however the term lesson is not part of the technical vocabulary of ID_2.

Interaction strategy. A given interaction can be controlled by a student or by a system. The individual content segments can be selected for the student (tutorial) or the student can interact with the content directly (experiential). The interaction can be for the purpose of presenting the information to the student (expository) or for the purpose of allowing student practice or testing the student (inquisitory). The amount and kind of guidance provided to the student can vary.

Pedagogy rules (principles):

Pedagogy (How to teach?) is the second set of rules which guides the selection and configuration of transactions. The general form of the proposition is as follows:

$$TFS = F \text{ (EF, EA, SA, and GA)}$$

The frames included in a transaction frame set (TFS) and the strategy involved for managing traversals through these transactions are a function of the attributes and content included for the elaborated frame involved (EF). TFS is also a function of environmental attribute values (EA), student attribute values (SA), and enterprise (goal) attribute values (GA).

$$\text{Goal Strategy} = F \text{ (EFN, SA, and EA)}$$

The strategy involved for sequencing the transaction frame sets included in the goal frame set and for managing traverse through these TFSs is a function of elaborated frame network attribute values (EFN) as well as student attribute values (SA) and environmental attribute values (EA).

A detailed list of these pedagogy principles will consist of hundreds of individual rules. It is this level of detailed learning and/or instructional principles that will be necessary to build an AIDA like system. Broad principles will have value only when they are translated into these detailed rules in a strategy knowledge base. Nevertheless, some of the broad-based learning principles which will be considered in building these more detailed rule-based pedagogy principles are as follows:

* **Role/function principle.** Learners enter instruction with different expectations about how they will use the knowledge and skills learned following instruction. These different roles require that the instruction serve different functions. The transactions used must be consistent with these role/function types.

* **Principle of least effort.** All else being equal, learners follow the path of least effort. Hence, learners with low motivation, aptitude, previous experience require more structured transactions; learners with high motivation, aptitude, previous experience prefer less structured transactions.

* **Learner control principle.** Students do better if they control their own learning; hence, maximizing learner control should be a meta-objective of instruction. However, students should only be given as much learner control as they can use to their advantage. Poor instructional decisions should lead to less control; good instructional decisions should lead to more control.

* **Active learning principle.** Amount of learning is a function of amount of relevant mental effort. Transactions should promote "active" rather than "passive" interactions.

* **Practice principle.** Learners learn what they do. A primary purpose of learning is to provide guided practice in activities as close as possible to the final integrated skilled performance. Transactions must provide opportunities for gradually increasing levels of guided experiential practice.

* **Feedback principle.** Practice without performance feedback is not practice and promotes very little learning. Learners should have access to performance feedback. However, transactions should guide learners in obtaining intrinsic feedback and gradually eliminate extrinsic feedback.

* **Primary presentation principle.** Learners learn best when information is represented in all three primary presentation forms: generality, instance, and practice. Transactions should include all three primary presentations.

* **Guidance principle.** In early stages learners benefit from extensive attention focusing information. However, such guidance can be detrimental in later stages of learning. Transactions should provide for the gradual

transfer of guidance from the instructional system to self guidance provided by the learner.

* **Representation principle.** Learning is improved when information is represented in more than one way. Transactions should provide for multiple representation of ideas. Learning is suppressed when representation is incomplete, i.e., when critical attributes are not adequately represented.

* **Matching principle.** Learning is improved when instances are carefully matched with non-instances; or when correct execution of activities is carefully matched with incorrect execution or activities; or when correct interpretation of processes is carefully matched with common misinterpretations.

* **Divergence principle.** Learning is improved when a divergent set of instances is presented.

* **Elaboration principle.** Learning is improved when simple knowledge and skills are elaborated to form complex knowledge and skills; when specific knowledge and skills are elaborated to form abstract knowledge and skills; when static knowledge and skills are elaborated to form dynamic knowledge and skills.

In this section we have attempted to outline the primary assumptions, objects, and principles which we feel underlie the design of an AIDA type system. To our very brief list could be added hundreds or even thousands of specific principles. We believe that an adequate instructional design theory must, in fact, be built on such detailed principles. A list of very general learning principles will do little to facilitate building an instructional design expert system. Hence, we chose to provide the architecture of a second generation instructional design theory and to identify the principal instructional entities involved and briefly define those entities which we felt were necessary to construct AIDA.

Elaboration of an AIDA

Approach

This section provides an index of variables, parameters, and values (values for a given attribute are set off by square brackets [ ]) which may comprise an "AIDA" like system. The organization of this section is keyed to the six block modular representation of the AIDA functional architecture represented in the six block figure in Spector's introduction to Part II.

This list of variables and parameters is neither exhaustive nor fixed. In our own work this list is continually evolving. As the rules of the system become more specific, we find it necessary to revisit these attributes and the legal values for these attributes. The list included here should be considered representative of the type of attributes appropriate for a given part of the system rather than an exhaustive list.

The legal values specified should also be considered a first cut. For example, for motivation, familiarity, etc., we have indicated high, moderate and low as values. As the rules become more sophisticated these values will probably be configured on a continuous scale from 1 to 10. Scaling these values becomes more important when the sophistication of the rules moves from IF-THEN rules to rules which cumulate evidence based on certainty factors. We have explored both types of reasoning in earlier prototypes. We find that we start with simple rules and then evolve to more complex rule structures as our experience with a given decision matures.

We have not provided complete definitions for all of the attributes listed. Where we have introduced attributes which are unique to our own work we have tried to provide some minimum level of definition or to include a paper which describes the attributes involved in more detail.

The content representation for the proposed knowledge acquisition system and the transactions which will be selected and configured by the executive system represent frames. A detailed description of these frames is beyond the scope of this chapter. We have tried to provide at least an index of the key technical terms that we use to describe these frames and some of the attributes (slots and values) that comprise these frames. This information is woefully inadequate for adequate communication, but perhaps this outline can provide a guide for further development as the AIDA concept evolves.

Interpretation Notes

In the following six subsections, square brackets ([ ]) indicate legal values for an attribute. Curly brackets ({ }) indicate slots in a frame which can assume some value.

In several of our other publications we have suggested the idea of using mini-experts. For every decision or piece of information requested by the system the system should provide assistance for the user to make this decision. This assistance is in the form of a mini-expert related to this decision. Each mini-expert would gather additional relevant information and then recommend a value for a given attribute. We have not completed very many mini-experts for our prototype systems. These attributes related to motivation illustrate the type of information that may be requested by such a mini-expert.

Information Component

As shown in the figure in the Introduction to Part II (page 65), the information component consists of three components: Audience (students), Environment (instructional setting), and Task (enterprise to be trained). The attributes, parameters, and values associated with this component are represented below.

Audience (students)

Role [consumer, supervisor, technician, problem-solver]
Motivation [high, unconcerned, unmotivated]

Some attributes contributing to motivation:

Why instruction [volunteer, required]
Job promotion [yes, unrelated]
Pay increase [yes, unrelated]
Job change [yes, unrelated]
Request job change [yes, no, no job change]
Familiarity [high, moderate, low]
Mastery Level [high, moderate, low]
Ability [high, moderate, low]

Environment (settings)

While recognizing their importance we have not implemented environment attributes in our previous prototype systems. The following list has not been carefully considered and should be considered as merely a suggestion of the type of items which should be considered.

Location [school, on-the-job, remote]
Group size [individual, teams, small group, large group]
Delivery system [individual study, platform, computer, video, interactive video, etc.]
Budget [   ]
Schedule [   ]
Resources [   ]

Task (enterprise, job)

We do not believe that behavioral objectives or goal lists are the place to start for instructional design. Rather we feel that it is important to identify some bounded, complex, integrated human activity as the target of the instruction. If this complex human activity is adequately described and classified, then the goals and objectives for this enterprise can be derived from the description of the enterprise rather than the other way around. Furthermore, we feel that it is more natural for a subject-matter expert to describe the activities that are to be trained rather than trying to list goals or objectives.

Enterprise class [denote, manifest, interpret, discover, execute, evaluate, design]

The term enterprise (Gagné & Merrill, 1990) has been extended to include the following seven enterprise classes:

For entities:
Denoting—communicating the identity, describing the form and structure of some entity, activity or process, or some class of entities, activities, or processes.

For activities:
Executing—performing some activity.
Evaluating—judging the performance of an activity.
Designing—devising a novel activity.

For processes:
Manifesting—making a process evident by showing its phases and sequence.
Interpreting—analyzing the cause and effect relationships of a process (thus enabling predictions).
Discovering—bringing to light a new process.

An adequate description of an enterprise will include the identification of other attributes that are necessary in using this information to provide prescriptions and filters for knowledge acquisition and analysis or for selecting and configuring transactions. The generality attribute [specific case or general case] is one such attribute.

Content Component

We are currently working on a Knowledge Acquisition and Analysis System as a component of an IBM Course Development System. We have taken a somewhat different approach to the representation of knowledge in an instructional knowledge base. Our approach (Jones, Li, & Merrill, 1990) is admittedly incomplete and leaves the following questions to be explored:

Association rules: What are the rules governing necessary and sufficient associations with other frames.

Propagation rules: What are the rules governing the propagation of information from one frame to an associated frame.

Consistency rules: What are the rules for cross-checking information to assure that information supplied at one point in the EFN is consistent with information supplied at some other point.

Elaborated Frame Network (EFN)

An elaborated frame network contains all of the content information necessary to teach some human enterprise. The advantage of an elaborated frame network over other forms of representation is that is contains all of the interrelationships necessary to characterize the integrated knowledge (knowledge and skills) necessary for the enterprise.

An elaborated frame network is comprised of a network of associated frames. A frame with its links to other frames identified is called an "elaborated frame." Each frame has three types of elaboration: associations with other frames, membership in an abstraction hierarchy, and components consisting of all the knowledge and skill associated with the frame.

Frame class [entity, activity, process]

Entity class [symbol, object, creature, place]
Activity class [execute, judge, design, advocate]
Process class [discrete, chained, cyclical, recursive]

Frame Association

Required associations. Certain associations are required by certain enterprise classes. Each enterprise class is characterized by a "minimum frame set," the types of frames minimally necessary to represent the enterprise. An adequate knowledge acquisition system would include the rules for required associations and use these rules to guide the knowledge acquisition process.

Propagation. The process of propagation operates within the elaborated frame network. Propagation means that information in one knowledge structure (frame) is transferred or affects the knowledge in an associated knowledge structure (frame). For example, an application activity is almost always linked to a tool activity. Each step of the application activity is executed via steps of the tool activity. Propagation would identify those tool steps required to execute each application step. An intelligent knowledge acquisition system would identify the rules of propagation and use them to guide the knowledge acquisition process.

Types of association. Types of association include the following:

[uses/used by,
 involves/involved in,
 applies/applied by,
 analogy for/analogy of,
 alternative to/alternative for,
 proximal to/proximal to,
 interacts with/interacted with,
 associates with/associated with]

Frame Abstraction

Abstraction attributes. In addition to the frame components, frames in an abstraction hierarchy require attributes for determining class membership and relationships. Instances can be ordered along one or more dimensions associated with the class to which the instance belong. Members of one class are discriminated from members of a coordinate class on the basis of one or more attributes that are associated with the superclass. A class can also be treated as an instance of a superclass and hence ordered along one or more dimensions associated with the superclass. Superclasses can be classes or instances of a higher superclass for as many levels as necessary.

Inheritance. An important characteristic of an abstraction hierarchy is that instances inherit components from classes, and classes inherit components from superclasses. That is, each instance in a class will have all of the components (parts, paths, episodes) associated with the class. There can be exceptions to inheritance for a given instance or a given class.

instance
        {dimensions, relative position of each instance on each dimension}
    class
            {attributes, value on each attribute which determines class membership}
            {dimensions, boundaries for each superclass}
            {attributes, legal values for each attribute}

Frame Components

A knowledge acquisition system, unlike first generation instructional design analysis procedures, attempts to acquire all of the content required for the instruction to occur. Frame components represent all of the detailed information related to each frame.

for entity frame
    {part {name, location, function}}
    {properties {name, description, set of legal values}}

for activity frame
    {path {steps decision, decision, loop}}
    {action, object, tool, consequence, object}

for process frame
    {episode {event [action, condition, loop]}}
        {actor, action, object, consequence, object}
        {causal net}}

AIDA Executive

The executive is the expert system which takes the information and content and prescribes strategies (transactions) for the student. Two functions are important for an executive function: (1) prescriptions and filters for knowledge acquisition, and (2) selection and configuration of transactions.

Prescriptions and Filters

The knowledge acquisition system, as we conceive of it, knows how to acquire knowledge but does not know where to stop. That is, each piece of information indicates to the system how this piece of information could be associated with other pieces of information. A given enterprise, for a given student population, for a given situation, will require only a subset of the possible information which could be acquired. The first role of the executive is to use its knowledge about enterprises, students, and situations to send to the knowledge acquisition system filters which indicate that a given frame, frame association, abstraction, or component is not required for a particular instructional implementation. In addition a given enterprise, student population and/or environment may require some additional frame, frame association, abstraction, or component. The executive must be capable of reminding the user during the knowledge acquisition that a new piece of information is required and to request the necessary content knowledge.

Transaction Selection and Configuration

The second function of the executive is to use its knowledge about the relationship between student characteristics, environmental characteristics, enterprise characteristics, and the nature of the content to select appropriate transactions and configure them for the student. This transaction configuration is what comprises a course with the enterprise transactions determining course organization, providing synthesis and summary functions, providing integrative assessment, etc., and primary transactions providing detailed interactions with the detailed content material.

Strategies Component

Strategies for us consist of transactions with a student.

Definition

A transaction is the mutual, dynamic, real-time give-and-take between an instructional system and the student in which there is an exchange of information. We distinguish several other terms as well:

A *transaction shell* is the structure of a transaction identifying the parameters, interactions, content needed, etc. for a given class of transaction. When a transaction shell is instantiated with a particular subject matter for a particular instance. Both a transaction shell and a *transaction instance* are pieces of computer code that, when delivered to a student via an appropriate delivery system, cause a transaction to occur. We are not always careful to distinguish the computer objects which cause a transaction to occur from the transaction, which is the actual interaction with the student.

Our definition of transactions is still very much in progress (Li & Merrill, 1990). However, we provide an initial elaboration in the next section.

Parameters for All Transactions

All transactions share certain parameters which enable the transaction to be configured in a number of ways. Some of these parameters are unique to a particular transaction class but others are shared by all transactions.

mode [expository, inquisitory]

Expository (presentation) is the ability to present the content information to the student. This does not mean there is no interaction but rather that the primary focus of the interaction is for the student to acquire some new information.

Inquisitory means to require the student to demonstrate that they have acquired the desired capability (knowledge or skill).

A given transaction may have several different expository or inquisitory modes. Which of these modes is provided to a given student for a given frame depends on the executive rules for configuring a transaction. The system may determine which mode of the transaction is appropriate at a given point in the instruction or the student can be given control over transaction mode selection. Again the degree of control allowed is determined by the rules governing transaction configuration.

control [learner . . . system]

System control means that the mode, sequence of interactions within a mode, type and amount of guidance is determined for the student.

Learner control means that the mode, sequence of interactions within a mode, type and amount of guidance is determined by the student with or without performance information provided by the system.

method [tutorial . . . experiential]

Tutorial method means that the system selects and portions the content to be presented to the student. Using a tutorial method the system would lead the student carefully through the content. The tutorial method does not imply that the sequence is fixed or rigid. An intelligent tutorial may respond to the student's performance in selecting the next item for presentation or practice. The key characteristic of tutorial method is that the system makes the selection of the next content to be presented.

Experiential method involves putting the student into a simulation or microworld where the student can interact with the content in a more natural way. The student can explore the domain in a variety of ways and usually has access to a much wider range of content. The experiential environment can be intelligent enabling the student to see what happens if or can be merely a controllable visualization.

display [location, source, timing]

All transactions must be able to accommodate a wide variety of message design parameters. While a given transaction may have a default display configuration, this configuration must be able to be modified to accommodate a variety of subject matter representations.

All transactions should be multimedia (this does not imply a delivery system) in the sense that a transaction should be able to accommodate a wide range of display and response characteristics. That is, the display should accommodate text, graphics, audio, and video in any combination. The transaction should also accommodate a wide variety of student response methodologies including constructed responses, pointing, graphing, device simulations, etc.

Enterprise Transactions

An enterprise transaction comprises all of the interactions necessary for a student to acquire the mental model necessary for a given enterprise. An enterprise transaction performs the following functions:

1. Knows all of the frames required for a minimum and optimal EFN for the enterprise.

2. Knows which frame should be the next area of study for a given student or group of students and when a given student should switch to this frame. This sequence function is controlled via primary and secondary sequence rules.

3. Knows how to synthesize the entire EFN for the student to enable the student to acquire the "big picture" of the enterprise to be learned.

4. Sends messages to appropriate primary transactions to execute all or part of their methods at appropriate times.

An enterprise transaction is the control structure for the course or unit level instruction.

minimum and optimal EFN

A minimum EFN is the type and association of frames required by a given enterprise. An optimal EFN is the type and association of all of the frames that may be associated with a given enterprise. A given instructional situation or student population often requires less than the optimal EFN.

primary sequence [encyclopedic, case study, naturalistic]

In our opinion there are three primary sequencing techniques: encyclopedic, case study, and situational.

Encyclopedic sequences involve the presentation of organized, cataloged knowledge. Encyclopedic sequences systematically present each tool, each concept, each activity, each process in a logical manner. This is typically the reference manual or text book sequence. Encyclopedic sequence is the sequence most frequently used in formal schooling.

Case Study sequences involve the presentation of a series of carefully selected examples, scenarios, cases which serve to introduce successively elaborate paths or episodes. Case studies are usually accompanied by a graded secondary sequence. Case studies may be a series of exercises, demonstrations, etc. Case study sequences frequently require propagation transactions.

Situational sequences are characterized as on-the-job. New information is introduced as it is encountered in a "real world" setting. Instruction is often introduced on an "as-needed" basis. There is no gradation of sequence (requires a chronological secondary sequence). Instruction can be solicited by the learner or the learner can be monitored and instruction provided when inadequacies are observed.

secondary sequences [vertical, temporal, abstraction]

Secondary sequences are nested within the primary sequences.

vertical sequence [elaboration (top down), prerequisite (bottom up), flat]

Vertical sequence refers to the introduction of prerequisite information. An elaboration sequence starts with the simplest complete representation of the activity or process and adds layers of complexity as the instruction progresses. Prerequisite information is introduced an as-needed basis. A prerequisite sequence presents prerequisite skills first then combines them together into more complex activities.

temporal sequence [chronological, graded]

A chronological sequence is in the order of occurrence or according to order of execution. A graded sequence means that the sequence has been contrived on one or more dimensions.

Dimensions of graded sequence:

familiarity [known . . .unknown]
frequency [most frequent . . . least frequent]
criticality [most critical . . . least critical]

abstraction sequence [concrete to abstract, abstract to concrete, flat]

Abstraction sequence refers to whether the specific or general case is taught first. This determines the direction of traverse in an abstraction hierarchy.

synthesis interaction {learner control, epitome variation}

Two variations of a synthesis interaction exist at an enterprise transaction level. A learner control transaction would give the student access to the EFN and allow the student to explore the network at will in order to get a picture of the domain.

An epitome variation (based on Reigeluth's Elaboration Theory) would provide a systematic view of the network stressing the elaboration of the subject matter in a systematic way rather than merely letting the learner wander.

primary transactions [component, abstraction, association]

A primary transaction comprises all of the interactions necessary for a student to acquire the content represented by a frame or a set of related frames. A primary transaction performs the following functions:

1. Knows all of the frames required for accomplishing its particular mission (the transaction frame set).

2. Knows which frame or frame component should be the next area of study for a given student or group of students and when a given student should switch to this frame. This sequence function is controlled via primary and secondary sequence rules.

3. Knows how to synthesize the entire transaction frame set for the student.

4. Sends messages to other primary transactions to execute all or part of their methods at appropriate times.

Parameters for All Primary Transactions

The level of performance required by a transaction depends on the level of instruction. Too often we assume basic instruction for naive learners when in the real world much of our learning requires a much less intense learning activity. Instructional level is a parameter which determines the intensity with which the student must interact with the material and the consequent level of performance acquired.

Because a transaction can be either expository or inquisitory the same transaction can serve one or more instructional functions. The mode, level of learner control, and other parameters are determined in part by the function. The same transaction may be activated at different points in the instructional process and serve a different function each time it is activated.

instructional level

[overview,
 remediation,
 familiarity,
 assessment,
 basic instruction [LC, SC]]

instructional function (interaction mode)

[presentation [LC,SC],
 practice,
 Ieg assessment,
 IG assessment,
 remediation]

component transactions [identification, execution, interpretation]

Component transactions enable the learner to acquire all of the components which comprise a given frame. There are three classes of component transactions corresponding to the three types of frames: identification for entity frames, execution for activity frames, and interpretation for process frames.

Identification transactions enable the student to acquire the names, functions, properties, relative location of all the parts which comprise an entity.

Execution transactions enable the student to acquire all of the paths in an activity.

Interpretation transactions enable the student to acquire all of the episodes in a process.

The term *acquire* in this context has a range of meanings all the way from a verbal information (Gagné's term), that is, for example, remembering or recognizing the paths in an activity, or episodes in a process to being able to actually perform the activity; or being able to interpret a process by predicting what will happen in a given situation; or being able to explain what is happening in a given situation. The level of performance required of the student is determined by the executive in configuring the transactions. A component transaction can also apply to a frame at the instance level (the specific case) or at a higher level in an abstraction hierarchy such as a class or super class. In the later case the components being acquired are generalized components which apply in a variety of specific cases.

abstraction transactions [judging, classification/decision, generalization, transfer]

Abstraction transactions enable the learner to acquire skills that require the content from several frames in an abstraction hierarchy.

Judging transactions require a class frame with two or more subordinate instance frames. These frames can be entity, activity, or process frames. Judging transactions enable the student to acquire the ability to order the instances of a given class on the basis of some dimension (criterion). The dimensions can be any attribute or combination of attributes. Judging the performance of others as they perform an activity is an example. Ordering a set of entity instances is an example.

Classification/decision transactions require a superclass frame with two or more subordinate class frames each of which have two or more instance frames. These frames can be entity, activity or process frames. Classification transactions enable the student to acquire the ability to sort or identify instances as to class membership. Concept identification is an example. Selecting among alternative activities to accomplish some goal is an example. Editing (selecting the appropriate usage) is an example.

Generalization transactions require a superclass frame with two or more subordinate class frames each of which have two or more instance frames. These frames can be entity, activity, or process frames. Generalization transactions enable the student to acquire the ability to combine instances of two or more classes into a more general class. Generalization is the inverse of classification.

Transfer transactions require a superclass frame and one or more class frames. These frames can be entity, activity, or process frames. Transaction transactions enable the student to acquire an abstraction model, that is, a generalized path or generalized episode and apply this to a previously encountered class or instance.

association transactions [propagation, analogy, substitution, design, discovery]

Association transactions enable the learner to acquire skills that require several different associated frames.

Propagation transactions enable the student to acquire one set of skills in the context of another set of skills. While learning an application activity the student can simultaneously learn a tool activity for doing the application. Or while learning a tool the student can simultaneously learn application activities for the tool. Or while learning a process the student can simultaneously learn a method activity for studying or observing the process. Or while learning a method activity the student can simultaneously learn the process for which the method was devised.

Analogy transactions enable the student to acquire the paths from one activity by likening it to an analogous activity; or to acquire the episodes in one process by likening it to an analogous process or activity.

Substitution transactions enable the student to learn an alternative activity or process by comparison, elaboration, extension of a previously learned activity or process.

Design transactions enable the student to use given frames in the EFN to invent new activity frames not previously included.

Discovery transactions enable the student to use given frames in the EFN to find new process frames not previously included. Given a method activity the student creates new instances of the application of this method and for each instance identifies a causal network eventually identifying an abstraction model or class process frame for the instances. Discovery transactions enable the student to expand the EFN by adding new frames as the result of creative activity.

Delivery Component

Two characteristics should characterize instruction which is delivered as a result of an AIDA like system. First, the transactions should be independent of any specific delivery system. Second, the instruction should be capable of being adapted to an individual student on-the-fly via an intelligent advisor system.

System Independent Delivery

Transactions which are prescribed by an "AIDA" like system should be device independent. This means that all of the interactions are captured by a computer program which is capable of expressing the nature of these interactions via a set of generic commands. Each delivery device with which the system interacts would have its unique output driver which is capable of understanding the generic commands from the transaction and interpreting them in terms of the specific characteristics of delivery device. A separate driver would be necessary for each specific delivery device but a single output driver would be able to interpret any of the possible transactions prescribed by the automated design system. We are all familiar with this concept in that we often must configure our computer systems with a driver for a particular printer. Each type of printer must have its own driver capable of interpreting the output from our word processor, spreadsheet, etc.

An Intelligent Advisor

An intelligent advisor is like an "AIDA Executive" that operates on-the-fly while a student is engaged in the actual instruction. An intelligent advisor is not the same as an intelligent tutoring system. An intelligent advisor contains pedagogy rules but not specific information about a particular subject matter. An intelligent advisor monitors a student's performance and on the basis of data gathered concerning the student's performance and interaction with the instruction can provide guidance to the student about what frame should be next and when the student should shift to this frame; or what type of transaction should be next and when the student should shift to this transaction. In addition the advisor has the capability of selecting, instantiating, and configuring a new transaction for the student as may be required by the student's performance.

Evaluation Component

Evaluation is of two types: evaluation of student performance and evaluation of system effectiveness.

Student Performance

In our concept of instruction we do not separate student evaluation from instruction. Each of the transactions described for the system should have the capability of both expository and inquisitory modes. An inquisitory mode can be used both for practice or for assessment. Since all of the transactions we envision for such a system are interactive, they must be capable of determining the nature of the student's capability or performance at a given moment in time.

That is, the student must either be provided information about the nature of his/her performance in order to make judgements about the adequacy of their own capability state or performance level, or the system must assess the adequacy of the performance or capability state in order to continue or adjust the interaction until a satisfactory level of learning has been achieved. In other words, assessment of student capability and performance is an integral part of the transaction and advisor system. We do not see the need for a separate student assessment system apart from the components already described.

System Evaluation

An adequate delivery system must have the capability of gathering and interpreting performance data on students as they interact with the system. This data can then be used to evaluate the adequacy of the system itself. We have entertained the idea of a system that is capable of interpreting this data via its own expert evaluation system and updating itself. Such a self-correcting system is difficult to conceive or build. A more feasible approach, at least in the short run, is a system that gathers and interprets information and then in cooperation with an instructional designer provides information which will enable the designer to modify a given rule set or to add or modify a transaction.

An adequate system must allow the rules that comprise its expertise to be easily modified and updated as evaluation data becomes available as to the adequacy of the decisions made by the system.

We have suggested that such a system should consist of a set of mini-experts, each of which have knowledge about a particular instructional decision. Further, that these mini-experts should use expert system type representations that easily allow the addition or deletion of rules. In this way the maintenance and continual improvement of such a system should be facilitated.

References

Ausubel, D. P. (1963). *The psychology of meaningful verbal learning*. New York: Grune & Stratton.

Bloom, B. S. *et al.* (1956). *Taxonomy of educational objectives*. New York: David McKay.

Brachman, R. J., & Levesque, H. J. (1985). *Readings in knowledge representation*. San Mateo, CA: Morgan Kaufman.

Bruner, J. S. (1966). *Toward a theory of instruction*. New York: W. W. Norton.

Bruner, J. S., Goodnow, J. J., & Austin, G. A. (1967). *A study of thinking*. New York: Science Editions.

Collins, A. (1987). A sample dialogue based on a theory of inquiry teaching. In C. M. Reigeluth (Ed.), *Instructional theories in action: Lessons illustrating selected theories and models*. Hillsdale, NJ: Lawrence Erlbaum Associates.

Collins, A., & Stevens, A. L. (1983). A cognitive theory of inquiry teaching. In C. M. Reigeluth (Ed.), *Instructional design theories and models: An overview of their current status*. Hillsdale, NJ: Lawrence Erlbaum Associates.

Dewey, J. (1937). *Experience and education*. New York: Macmillan.

Engelmann, S., & Carnine, D. (1982). *Theory of instruction: Principles and applications*. New York: Irvington.

Gagné, E. D. (1985). *The cognitive psychology of school learning*. Boston: Little, Brown, & Co.

Gagné, R. M. (1965). *The conditions of learning* (1st edition). New York: Holt, Rinehart, & Winston.

Gagné, R. M. (1985). *The conditions of learning* (4th edition). New York: Holt, Rinehart, & Winston.

Gagné, R. M., & Merrill, M. D. (1990). Integrative goals for instructional design. *ETR&D, 38*(1), 23–30.

Gropper, G.L. (1983). A behavioral approach to instructional prescription. In C. M. Reigeluth (Ed.), *Instructional design theories and models: An overview of their current status*. Hillsdale, NJ: Lawrence Erlbaum Associates.

Gropper, G.L. (1987). A lesson based on a behavioral approach to instructional design. In C. M. Reigeluth (Ed.), *Instructional theories in action: Lessons illustrating selected theories and models*. Hillsdale, NJ: Lawrence Erlbaum Associates.

Gustafson, K. L., & Reeves, T. C. (1990). IDiOM: A platform for a course development expert system. *Educational Technology, 30*(3), 19–25.

Jones, M., & Massey-Hicks, M. (1987). Expert CML: the next generation. Paper presented at the Computer-assisted Learning in Tertiary Education Conference, Sydney Australia, Nov 30–Dec 2.

Jones, M. K., Li, Z., & Merrill, M. D. (1990). Domain knowledge representation for instructional analysis. *Educational Technology, 30*(10), 7–32.

Landa, L. N. (1983). The algoheuristic theory of instruction. In C. M. Reigeluth (Ed.), *Instructional design theories and models: An overview of their current status.* Hillsdale, NJ: Lawrence Erlbaum Associates.

Landa, L. N. (1987). A fragment of a lesson based on the algoheuristic theory of instruction. In C. M. Reigeluth (Ed.), *Instructional theories in action: Lessons illustrating selected theories and models.* Hillsdale, NJ: Lawrence Erlbaum Associates.

Li, Z., & Merrill, M. D. (1990). Transaction shells: A new approach to courseware authoring. *Journal of Research on Computing in Education, 23*(1), 72–86.

Lippert, R. C. (1989). Expert systems: tutors, tools, and tutees. *Journal of Computer Based Instruction, 16*(1), 11–19.

Markle, S. M. (1983). *Designs for instructional designers.* Champaign, IL: Stipes.

Merrill, M. D. (1983). Component display theory. In C. M. Reigeluth (Ed.), *Instructional design theories and models: An overview of their current status.* Hillsdale, NJ: Lawrence Erlbaum Associates.

Merrill, M. D. (1987a). A lesson based on the component display theory. In C. M. Reigeluth (Ed.), *Instructional theories in action: Lessons illustrating selected theories and models.* Hillsdale, NJ: Lawrence Erlbaum Associates.

Merrill, M. D. (1987b). The new component design theory: Instructional design for courseware authoring. *Instructional Science, 16,* 19–34.

Merrill, M. D. (1987c). An expert system for instructional design. *IEEE Expert,* Summer, 25–37.

Merrill, M. D. (1988). Applying component display theory to the design of courseware. In D. H. Jonassen (Ed.), *Instructional designs for microcomputer courseware.* Hillsdale, NJ: Lawrence Erlbaum Associates.

Merrill, M. D. (1991). Constructivism and instructional design. *Educational Technology, 31*(5), 45–53.

Merrill, M. D., & Li, Z. (1988). Implementation of an expert system for instructional design (phase 2). Army Research Institute technical report.

Merrill, M. D., & Li, Z. (1989a). Implementation of an expert system for instructional design (phase 3). Army Research Institute technical report.

Merrill, M. D., & Li, Z. (1989b). An instructional design expert system. *Journal of Computer-Based Instruction, 16*(3), 95–101.

Merrill, M. D., Li. Z., & Jones, M. K. (1990a). Limitations of first generation instructional design. *Educational Technology, 30*(1), 7–11.

Merrill, M. D., Li, Z., & Jones, M. K. (1990b). Second generation instructional design (ID$_2$). *Educational Technology, 30*(2), 7–14.

Merrill, M. D., Li, Z., & Jones, M. K. (1992). Instructional transaction shells: Responsibilities, methods, and parameters. *Educational Technology, 32*(2), 5–26.

Merrill, P. F. (1987). Job and task analysis. In R. M. Gagné (Ed.), *Instructional technology: Foundations.* Hillsdale, NJ: Lawrence Erlbaum Associates.

Papert, S. (1980). *Mindstorms: Children, computers, and powerful ideas.* New York: Basic Books.

Polson, M. C., & Richardson, J. J. (1988). *Foundations of intelligent tutoring systems.* Hillsdale, NJ: Lawrence Erlbaum Associates.

Ranker, R. A. (1990). A computer based lesson development advisor. *Educational Technology, 30*(30), 46–49.

Reigeluth, C. M. (1983). The elaboration theory of instruction. In C.M. Reigeluth (Ed.), *Instructional design theories and models: An overview of their current status.* Hillsdale, NJ: Lawrence Erlbaum Associates.

Reigeluth, C.M. (1987). Lesson blueprints based on the elaboration theory of instruction. In C.M. Reigeluth (Ed.), *Instructional theories in action: Lessons illustrating selected theories and models.* Hillsdale, NJ: Lawrence Erlbaum Associates.

Scandura, J. M. (1983). Instructional strategies based on the structural learning theory. In C.M. Reigeluth (Ed.), *Instructional design theories and models: An overview of their current status.* Hillsdale, NJ: Lawrence Erlbaum Associates.

Skinner, B. F. (1953). *Science and human behavior.* New York: Macmillan.

Skinner, B. F. (1957). *Verbal behavior.* New York: Appleton-Century-Crofts.

Sleeman, D., & Brown, J. S. (1982). *Intelligent tutoring systems.* New York: Academic Press.

Stevens, G. H., & Scandura, J. M. (1987). A lesson design based on instructional prescriptions from the structural learning theory. In C.M. Reigeluth (Ed.), *Instructional theories in action: Lessons illustrating selected theories and models.* Hillsdale, NJ: Lawrence Erlbaum Associates.

Wenger, E. (1987). *Artificial intelligence and tutoring systems.* Los Altos, CA: Morgan Kaufman.

Chapter Seven

A Framework for Automating Instructional Design

Robert D. Tennyson

Introduction

This chapter presents framework specifications for an instructional systems development (ISD) expert system and tutor. The design proposed here is not restricted to the provisional architecture for AIDA outlined in Spector's introduction to Part II of this volume. While the influences of that architecture will be obvious, I felt that it was important to offer a more ambitious undertaking that incorporated elements of artificial intelligence (AI). The goal of this ISD expert system is to improve the means by which educators design, produce, and evaluate the instructional development process.

In the past several decades, research and theory development in the fields of instructional technology and cognitive science have advanced the knowledge base for instructional design theory such that we now believe that learning and thinking can be significantly improved by direct instructional intervention (see Polson and Kintsch in Part I, for example). Unfortunately, these advancements have increased the complexity of employing instructional design theory, making instructional development both costly and time consuming. Through the application of expert system and intelligent tutoring methods, it is now possible to develop an intelligent computer-based ISD expert system that will enable educators to employ instructional design theory for curricular and instructional development. I propose a framework for the development of an ISD expert system that will assist both experienced and inexperienced instructional developers in applying advanced instructional design theory.

Advancements in cognitive psychology and instructional technology in the past three decades have aided in the building of a literature of instructional design theory that can provide educators with sophisticated means to improve learning in all levels and conditions of education and training (Tennyson, 1990d). However, along with this theoretical growth in instructional design has come the problem of instructional developers (i.e., educators producing instruction) learning how to apply the new knowledge.

In response to this growth in the field of instructional design theory and practice, universities have developed graduate programs to produce instructional design (ID) experts. Even at the master's degree level, these graduate programs require at least two years of full-time study. Therefore, if an organization is to employ this body of knowledge to improve learning, it must either: (a) develop in-service training programs to teach instructional design theory and practice; or (b) develop a means by which educators can employ the knowledge without necessarily having to become ID experts.

This rapid growth in the instructional design field has also occurred in hundreds of other technical fields. To help maintain high levels of sophistication and to bring into application the most advanced knowledge from their respective fields, many of these other fields have employed expert system methods. An expert system is a computer-based representation of the domain-specific knowledge of an expert in a form that can be accessed by others for assistance in problem solving and decision making. An implication of this definition is that an inexperienced person can, with the aid of an expert system, perform tasks that would normally require the direct involvement of a domain-expert. Proposed in this chapter is a framework for the development of an expert system to help instructional developers (i.e., authors) use the most advanced knowledge in the field of instructional design theory when designing and producing computer-based curriculum and instruction.

Instructional Systems Development

The process of designing, producing, and evaluating instruction is referred to in the literature as instructional systems development (ISD). The main components of ISD include the following: (a) analysis of the instructional (and/or curricular) problem/need; (b) design of specifications to solve the problem; (c) production of the instruction; (d) implementation of the instruction; and (e) maintenance of the instruction. Embedded in each component of ISD are specific types of evaluation to insure quality control (Tennyson, 1978).

There are in the current literature several examples of computer-based tools intended to improve the productivity of the ISD process. Hermanns (1990) describes Computer-Aided Analysis (CAA), a computer program which aids in job task analysis. Based on a hierarchically-organized list of job tasks entered by the instructional designer, CAA produces as output a set of preliminary terminal learning objectives that can be further reviewed and edited by the developer. Ranker and Doucet (1990) describe SOCRA-TES, which allows the user to fill in information that is used by SOCRA-TES to create an instructor's lesson outline including objectives, events of instruction, samples of student behavior and test questions. Perez and Seidel (1990) present an overview of their specifications for an automated training development environment that will be based on the Army Systems Approach to Training (SAT) model of instructional design. The main features of the environment are a set of tools for developing the components of instruction and an expert design guide for assisting the designer in using the tools. Merrill and Li (1990; see also the previous chapter in this volume) propose ID Expert, a prototype rule-based expert system for instructional development that makes recommendations about content structure, course organization, and instructional transactions (tutor/student interactions) based on information supplied by the designer.

The systems just referred to differ greatly in function and scope and in the degrees to which each makes use of expert system methods to reduce the level of knowledge required of instructional designers. In contrast, my ISD expert system will employ adaptive interface and intelligent tutoring techniques to allow even the most inexperienced author to immediately begin to develop quality instruction. Labeled ISD Expert, the proposed system will make expert knowledge about the most sophisticated ISD methods readily available to potential authors, thus minimizing or eliminating the need for formal instructional systems development training.

The ISD model proposed for ISD Expert (see Figure 7.1) was developed to reflect an application (functional) model rather than a teaching model. That is, most ISD models are based on the assumption that developers will learn ISD. Thus, they resemble a linear process that attempts to include all possible variables and conditions of ISD. The result is that they do not take into account any other ISD situations other than complete start to finish instructional development. The assumption is that in all ISD situations, ISD starts at the analysis phase and proceeds step-by-step to the final completion of the implementation phase. The proposed ISD model, in contrast, views the author's actual situation as the beginning point of any possible ISD activities. For ISD Expert, the proposed ISD model is an associative network of variables and conditions, which can be addressed at any point in instructional development depending on the given situation.

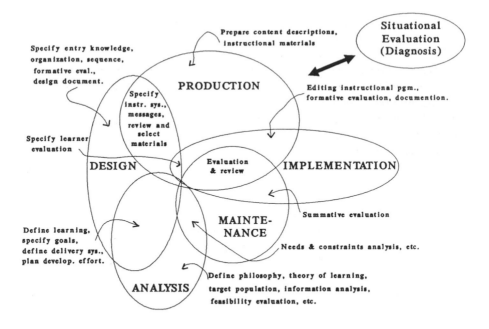

Figure 7.1. ISD-4th Generation.

This chapter does not provide complete specifications for ISD Expert. Instead, it provides a framework from which specifications can be designed and developed. The content of this chapter includes both the philosophy of the proposed ISD Expert and the framework specifications. Given the complexity of ISD and the effort necessary to develop an expert tutoring system, this chapter will also serve as a means for extending the dialogue on the concept of automated ISD systems and tools that forms the general subject of this volume.

Philosophy of ISD Expert

Expert systems are designed for domain experts to aid them in dealing with complex processes that are either time consuming or which require specific experience and expertise (e.g., in a subdomain). In practice, expert systems have been successful when the content is narrowly focused and when the situations have clear rules for decision making (Smith, 1984). Because of the range of experience and training in ISD among instructional developers, I am proposing an expert system that will be designed for authors who are content domain experts but not necessarily ISD domain experts. This is not a contradiction of previous expert system efforts, but a reflection of the fact that the user of ISD Expert will not be an ISD expert initially. Rather, the proposed ISD Expert would take into account a range of expertise and experience in instructional design theory and practice.

To accomplish this goal, I propose an expert system that will employ intelligent (adaptive) human-computer interface techniques. The intelligent ISD Expert will operate at two basic levels: (a) first, a coaching expert will direct inexperienced authors through the acquisition of ISD skills while helping them deal with their specific situation; and, (b) second, an advising expert will assist experienced authors by making recommendations for their specific situation. For example, for an inexperienced author, the coaching function will deal with basic ISD skills and direct the development effort. In contrast, ISD Expert will function as an advisor for an experienced author, making recommendations while the author controls the actual ISD decision making. In this environment, both inexperienced and experienced authors will be exposed to opportunities to increase their individual expertise through a process of learning ISD while using the system (Schiele & Green, 1990).

The importance of the distinction between the coaching and advisement functions is based on a review of research findings in expert systems. An example from this body of research is Clancey's (1979, 1983) work with MYCIN, a medical diagnosis consultant program, and GUIDON, a tutorial program designed to make use of MYCIN's rule base for teaching purposes. Clancey found that the rules encoded in MYCIN were inadequate for teaching because the knowledge required for justifying a rule and explaining an approach was lacking. He found it necessary to add additional components to GUIDON to help organize and explain the rules (Clancey, 1989).

In a similar fashion, ISD Expert will have the ability to support and explain its recommendations and prescriptions in the language of ISD, not merely by enumerating the rules applied to make a recommendation. An example of one approach to providing this ability can be found in Swartout (1983). Swartout combined declarative and procedural knowledge, in the form of domain principles, to create the knowledge base for XPLAIN, a drug prescription consultant which provides detailed justification of its prescriptions.

Although ISD Expert cannot be considered a means for teaching ISD, the very nature of the system's philosophy, which assumes that authors will gain knowledge with experience, will result in continuing improvements in ISD applications. That is, as authors gain experience in ISD, the system would exhibit the characteristics of a conventional expert system. Therefore, it should increase the efficiency of instructional development and help in those areas where even experienced ISD authors initially lack specific expertise.

ISD Expert Intelligent Author-Computer Interface

ISD Expert, as proposed, will operate as an expert system employing intelligent author-computer interface (ACI) methods between the author and the system (Anderson, 1988). The ISD Expert intelligent ACI model (see Figure 7.2) consists of four modules: the author's model of instruction, an ISD tutor (with both coach and advisor capabilities), an ISD knowledge base, and an instructional content knowledge base. Both knowledge bases have knowledge acquisition capabilities. The ISD Expert tutor is responsible for the interface between the individual authors and specific activities associated with developing their respective instructional needs.

ISD Expert System

In addition to the intelligent ACI component, the ISD Expert system has three functions (see Figure 7.3). The first function is to aid in the diagnosis of a given author's situation. This diagnostic function evaluates the current situational conditions of the author (e.g., does the author want to prepare a computer-based graphic program for use in a lecture; does the author want to design a new course?). Following the situational evaluation, the second function recommends prescriptions along the lines associated with the level of author experience. That is, instead of trying to force all situations into a single solution, the prescriptions are individualized, based on situational differences and ISD experiences of the author. The third function, ISD Expert, through the system's tutor, helps the authors in accomplishing the prescriptions. As authors become increasingly more sophisticated in using ISD Expert, they will be ready to accept increasingly

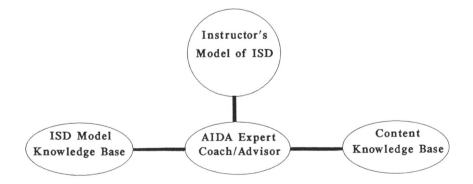

Figure 7.2. ISD Expert Components.

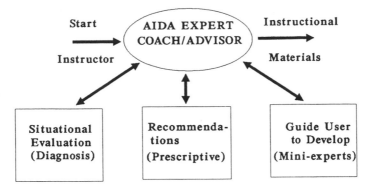

Figure 7.3. Intelligent Interface Model.

more advanced variables and conditions of instructional design theory and practice.

ISD Model

The proposed content for ISD Expert is the fourth generation ISD model (Tennyson & Christensen, in press). This ISD model is designed to adjust to future growth in instructional design theory and therefore does not become obsolete as new advancements are made, unlike earlier models. Figure 7.1 presents an illustration of the fourth generation ISD model. Briefly, the four generations of ISD models can be described as follows:

–First generation (ISD_1, Figure A.1, Appendix). The main focus of the first generation model was the implementation of the behavioral paradigm of learning (Glaser, 1966). The system consisted of four components: objectives, pretest, instruction, and posttest. The system was completed with an evaluation loop for purposes of revision.

–Second generation (ISD_2, Figure A.2, Appendix). Advancements in instructional technology led to the need to increase the variables and conditions of the ISD model. The second generation adopted systems theory to control and manage the increasingly complex ISD process (Branson *et al.*, 1976). The behavioral learning paradigm remained, but was of secondary importance to the focus of the system: developing instruction.

–Third generation (ISD_3, Figure A.3, Appendix). In practice, the ISD process was too linear and did not account for situational differences among applications (Tennyson, 1977). To account for situational differences, the external control of the system gave way to phases of

ISD, that could be manipulated in any order by the instructional designer. This model assumed that ISD was an iterative process that could be entered at any point depending on the current state of the author's situation (Allen, 1986). Learning theory was still considered behavioral but cognitive theory was making some appearances (e.g., use of simulations for acquisition of cognitive skills in decision making).

–Fourth generation (ISD_4, Figure 7.1). Advancements in cognitive psychology have made major changes in many of the ISD variables (e.g., content analysis, objectives, measurement, instructional strategies), making the ISD model yet more complex (see Tennyson, 1990a,b; Tennyson & Rasch, 1990). Using AI technology, the fourth generation model handles the complexity of ISD with a diagnostic/prescriptive system. Extending from the second and third generations, the ISD_4 model provides the knowledge base for the proposed ISD Expert system.

Cognitive Theory

With growth of research and theory in cognitive psychology (Bonner, 1988), ISD Expert will exhibit a strong cognitive learning theory basis in both its ISD content and its approach to author-computer interaction. Early ISD models had a strong behavioral paradigm as their learning theory foundation (e.g., the first generation ISD model). The instructional strategies embedded in the first generation ISD models followed closely the behavioral paradigm of small incremental steps with emphasis on reinforcement of correct responses. For example, a task analysis in the ISD_1 paradigm favored a sequential approach that included student exposure to all possible attributes in a domain of information. For the most part, situational context and higher order cognitive knowledge and strategies were not considered because they did not fit the behavioral paradigm that dealt only with temporal content and observable performances (Brown, Collins, & Duguid, 1989).

In many other aspects of instructional development, ISD_1 models also incorporated the behavioral paradigm, especially in the evaluation of learners. The focus of learner evaluation was on attainment of performance objectives that were isolated from meaningful applications or situations. By the 1970s, however, the ISD models exhibited more characteristics of systems models, the result being a separation of ISD procedures from a given learning theory paradigm. This growth in the "systems" of ISD characterized the second generation ISD model.

Although the learning theory foundation of the ISD_2 models remained basically behavioral, the inflexibility of the flowchart nature of the models limited their utility. In response to this inflexibility, the ISD_3 models actually proposed the elimination of the linearity of ISD by including phases of development that could be manipulated according to the unique conditions of given situations. The third generation ISD model identified phases of ISD that included direct links to specific forms of evaluation (see Figure A.3, Appendix), and therefore allowed user control of the procedures based on situational need. The third generation focused on an increased emphasis on evaluation without basic changes in the learning theory foundation, although the flexibility of the model made it possible to include the growing literature in cognitive psychology.

By the end of the 1980s, there had been sufficient empirical and theoretical work in cognitive psychology and instructional technology to once again see the possible effects of learning theory on ISD (Glaser & Bassok, 1989). The effects can be seen in such things as the importance of macro (i.e., curricular) level activities in ISD, contextual analysis of the information to be learned, evaluation of the learners, employment of interactive media, instructional strategies for higher order thinking, employment of structured and discovery instructional methods, effect of the affective domain on the cognitive, influences of group interactions on learning, and context and situational variables on knowledge acquisition (Tennyson, 1990b). The result has been the development of fourth generation ISD models that resemble a schematic structure (see Figure 7.1) and have a cognitive learning paradigm foundation for the various procedures of instructional development.

Along with a cognitive learning foundation for the ISD content, the human-computer interface of ISD Expert should exhibit a cognitive approach as opposed to a behavioral one. The contrast between the two approaches is the assumption made in regard to the interaction between the author and ISD Expert. In a behavioral approach the interaction between the author and the ISD expert system would be made at a reductionist level, that is, small incremental steps in linear sequence of instructional development in which the author is simply, and constantly, filling in requests for information without understanding the individual ISD tasks in relationship to the given situation. This is a common approach employed in expert systems for novices where the task is relatively concrete and the user is simply filling in information. However, it must be assumed that the ISD task is complex and requires an author who can intelligently use the system more productively as he/she gains experience. Therefore, a cognitive approach assumes, even initially, that the author can connect the individual ISD tasks with his/her given situation.

To summarize, a cognitive psychology implication for ISD Expert is an expert system that assumes that the author can initially function in the role as an instructional designer. This implies that even at an initial level of ISD, the author will have a real instructional problem/need and that he/she will be able to solve the situation with the prescription(s) offered by the ISD Expert system. As the author becomes more experienced with ISD Expert, he/she will be able to make increasingly sophisticated use of the system. ISD is a complex process, but the complexity is in part due to the given situation. Thus, for the initial, inexperienced author, the potential employment of ISD Expert will focus on noncomplex situations, but with the author feeling that he/she is participating in real ISD decision making.

This approach to the author should limit training for ISD Expert to a set of basic software functions and activities. Instead of viewing training on ISD Expert in the conventional linear fashion where the author works through a set of meaningless practice situations, the training will be embedded in the initial individualized ISD situation. For example, if the author wants to develop a test, his/her initial entry into ISD Expert will deal with test construction. In other words, training and gaining experience will be driven by the individual author's situation. Rather than a two-year graduate program as prerequisite to being an instructional designer, the ISD Expert author will function as an instructional designer beginning with his/her first use. Because ISD is a complex environment and the needs of individual authors will vary at any given time, over an extended period of time, the individual authors will acquire more ISD knowledge as situational needs occur.

Computer Technology

Because ISD Expert is intended to improve the performance of instructional designers, rather than to advance the state of the art in expert systems techniques and methods, it is most productive to make use of existing, standard computer hardware and software architecture whenever possible in the development of ISD Expert.

Certain restraints are imposed on the hardware and software choices by the requirements of the environment in which ISD Expert will most often be applied. These requirements are summarized as follows:

–Support for several simultaneous authors at both local and remote sites;

–Large data storage capacity for knowledge bases and programs;

–Sophisticated graphics capability;

–Provision for incorporating special-purpose programs (for example, to support research projects) into ISD Expert on an ad hoc basis; and

–Employment of interactive media.

Where hardware is concerned, a basic decision is whether to implement ISD Expert on a central mainframe or minicomputer, or on microcomputers. Simons (1985) and Harmon, Maus, and Morrissey (1988) address the expanding role of the microcomputer in AI development, citing growing hardware capacity, wider availability of sophisticated software tools and increasing user familiarity with microcomputers as the forces contributing to the growth in expert system development for microcomputers.

I am proposing that ISD Expert be implemented in a network of PC's (e.g., Intel 80386-based microcomputers) connected to a central network and file server with one or more large-capacity hard disk drives for program and knowledge base storage. This configuration is generally compatible with the Air Force's Base Level Computing facilities and with many common university arrangements.

There are a number of physical network topologies that could be used to implement ISD Expert with networked PCs. There are some trade-offs involved in using this configuration as contrasted with a network of "dumb" terminals connected to a central mainframe and data storage. For example, transmitting large quantities of data to/from the central file server to the PC's does require system overhead. However, the advantages outweigh the drawbacks. The intelligence of the system will be distributed throughout the system, minimizing the demands on the central unit. In addition, AI software for PCs is affordable and PC graphics are generally superior and affordable.

The software used to create ISD Expert must provide an open architecture. That is, it must be practical to write local programs for special purpose functions (e.g., as research projects) and link them into the standard software with a minimum of effort. Also, the knowledge bases must be accessible to local programs as well as to the standard software. Expert system development is done either by using expert systems shells, which are commercially-available skeleton systems that can be instantiated with the specific domain knowledge required for an application, or by writing the expert system from scratch in a general or special purpose programming language. Harmon *et al.* (1988) report that of 115 expert systems surveyed in actual use in the United States in 1986, 92 were produced using shells while 23 were written using programming languages (chiefly LISP).

ISD Expert will be implemented using commercially-available expert system shells. However, in view of the fact that ISD Expert must also support customization, the shells that are chosen must support local exits to facilitate the linking in of custom programs. These custom programs will be written in a high-level computer language, preferably one with extensive AI features (e.g., LISP; PROLOG).

Summary

To establish a framework for ISD Expert, it is important to clearly specify the philosophy of the system (Morgan, 1989). A well specified philosophy will help keep the system under control during development and later when doing revisions. Proposed in this section is that ISD Expert have a foundation in cognitive psychology (Newell & Card, 1985). And, that this foundation specifies for the system both the content and the author-computer interface (Norman, 1986). Specific areas of the proposed philosophy are as follows:

–An expert system that has both diagnostic and prescriptive functions

–An expert system that will serve experienced and inexperienced authors

–An intelligent ACI system with both advising and coaching capabilities

–Knowledge base content will employ the fourth generation ISD model

–Employment of interactive media

–Cognitive learning theory as the foundation of the ISD procedures

–Cognitive paradigm approach to ACI Entry to system based on individual author situation

–Training as a concurrent activity with ISD activities

–A computer-based network system with remote capabilities

–Software tools that provide an open architecture

–Employment of a high-level language (e.g., an AI language)

–Commercial shells that include access to own-code programs

–Data dictionaries for knowledge acquisition components

The above discussion on a proposed philosophy for ISD Expert provides the foundation for the following section describing the system framework.

ISD Expert: System Framework

Because of the range in authors knowledge of ISD, ISD Expert will be designed using the methodology of intelligent human-computer interface systems. That is, rather than either attempting to teach ISD to the author or to develop a system around one linear approach that restricts and narrows the richness of ISD, I argue for a system that begins with the individual author's given situation. An adaptive computer-human interface will be concerned with improving authors' applications of ISD and their own models of instruction.

Furthermore, the proposed system will encourage the growth of the author's knowledge of ISD, but with the complexity of ISD being transparent. The purpose of ISD Expert will be to diagnose the given situation of the author and then prescribe recommendations for dealing with his/her individual situation. It is assumed that each author will present a different situation and, therefore, will require a unique prescription.

Heuristics will be used to accomplish this goal (see Bonnet, Haton, & Truong-Ngoc, 1988; Waterman, 1986). Two important features of the heuristic method, as contrasted with production rules, are: (a) the flexibility needed to implement prescriptions in conditions of uncertainty or novelty (i.e., prescriptions are established in real time by integrating best available information from the system's knowledge base); and (b) the elimination of the need for an exhaustive reduction of ISD content knowledge to production rules.

One of the serious problems in expert systems design for nonmathematical areas has been the attempt to reduce complex and abstract concepts to production rules (e.g., Merrill's ID Expert, 1986). Even though I am proposing the use of a network and file server system for the operation of ISD Expert, it is the programming time involved in trying to apply the reductionist approach to an environment as complex as ISD that rules out the exclusive use of the production rules programming methodology. The software architecture of ISD Expert must be open to allow for future extensions. For example, it may be deemed necessary to append a case-based module to advise authors in the area of curriculum decomposition. The production rule method may not be suitable for this type of complex situation (Clancey, 1983). Much of the ISD process is context bound; therefore, the system must be adaptable, allowing for prescriptions to be finalized by the author.

ISD Expert is an expert system with four main components: an intelligent author-computer interface component, a diagnosis function component, a prescriptive function component, and an instructional production guide component (Figure 7.2). The intelligent ACI component will be the means by which authors will interact with ISD Expert. Rather than use a menu driven system, I propose a tutorial interaction between the author and ISD Expert. The diagnostic component will function as the evaluator of each author's situation and provide an evaluation report (Guba & Lincoln, 1986). This report will serve as the guidelines in preparing the prescription. Additionally, the prescription will be based on the author's ISD model as well as the diagnostic report. The fourth component will provide the author with assistance in the production of materials from the prescription(s). The level of assistance will again be influenced by the author's ISD model.

Intelligent Author-Computer Interface Component

The intelligent ACI component for the ISD Expert is illustrated in Figure 7.2. The main modules are as follows: (a) an author's model of ISD; (b) the ISD tutor; (c) the ISD knowledge base model; and (d) the content knowledge base. I will now discuss the role of each component of the ISD Expert tutor.

Author's Model of ISD

The purpose of this module is twofold: (a) to establish the level of ISD expertise of the author, and (b) to help the author improve his/her own model of instruction. This is necessary because no formal attempt is to be made to directly train the authors in ISD. The individual author's model will be updated with each use of the system. This profile of the author will help the system in its prescriptive recommendations. For example, experienced authors will have a narrow and limited knowledge of ISD and, also, of the ways in which their instruction could be improved. Prescriptions should be at their level of understanding. On the other hand, more experienced authors would be able to use more advanced prescriptions. It is important to keep the ISD prescriptions at the level of the author's experience and also to provide an opportunity for creativity and the possible use of different ideas generating from the author (Russell, Moran, & Jordan, 1988). A key feature of the proposed ISD Expert is the power of the author to disagree with a given prescription and still to be able to continue with the ISD process.

ISD Tutor

Intelligent interface systems work on the premise that a meaningful dialogue must be established between the user and the system. An important feature of this dialogue is that it is mixed initiative, where the user has an opportunity to query the system as well as being controlled by the system. The ISD Expert tutor will approach the diagnostic function from the context (situation) of the author. Personalizing the diagnostic activity will provide the opportunity for the tutor to search the content knowledge base to include specific references in the prescription to available existing materials and resources.

Because of the range of knowledge and experience in ISD of potential authors, two basic modes of interface are proposed. At one extreme will be authors who are completely inexperienced in ISD. For these individuals, a coaching mode is proposed. The coaching mode is a well established method of instruction used in intelligent computer-assisted instruction (ICAI). This mode assumes that the author will need direct and controlled assistance in dealing with his/her given situation. The function of the tutor as coach is to approach the ISD activity in a disciplined way while helping the author develop ISD skills. Prescriptions for the situation are specific and the coach is responsible for the decision making.

In contrast is the advising interface. For the experienced author, the tutor as advisor would offer alternative prescriptions, with the final decision(s) in the hands of the author.

The tutor, as part of the intelligent ACI component, is the point of contact between the author and the other ISD Expert components (see Figure 7.2). In the proposed design, the tutor gathers information about the author's specific situation and, by interaction with the Situational Evaluation component, prepares a report of the given problem/need. This evaluation report is sent to the Recommendations component where a prescription(s) is prepared. When the prescription(s) is prepared, the tutor presents it to the author; at that point, depending on the mode of the tutorial interaction (i.e., coaching or advising), there may occur a dialogue between the author and the tutor to finalize the prescription. Once a final prescription is prepared, the tutor interacts with the ISD model knowledge base to set up the authoring activities. The tutor also assists the author in certain aspects of materials production through the fourth component of the ISD Expert system. Updating of the author's model will be the continuing role of the tutor in ISD Expert.

ISD Model Knowledge Base

The content knowledge of ISD Expert will reside in the ISD model knowledge base (KB) (Figure 7.3). Once the prescription(s) is decided upon, the necessary authoring activities are compiled by the tutor from the ISD model knowledge base and presented to the author. (Authoring activities of the knowledge base are presented in the Appendix.) Information within this KB will be stored as structured data files, organized as an associative network. The purpose here is to efficiently locate information without the restrictions of rigid production rules. That is, the ISD model knowledge base should exhibit the heuristic search characteristics of an information retrieval system.

Content Knowlege Base

The fourth module of the proposed intelligent ACI system for ISD Expert, the content knowledge base, is a source from which curricular and instructional materials resources may be obtained. These materials may be included in the implementation of prescriptions developed by ISD Expert or they may stand alone. For example, if an author wants a simulation for a given lecture, he/she could query the content knowledge base to see what might be available. In another situation, ISD Expert may develop a prescription and obtain the necessary materials from the content knowledge base without the author explicitly requesting the action. Access to the content knowledge base may be either by direct author query via the tutor or indirectly as a result of the implementation of prescriptions.

The content knowledge base will help eliminate duplication of effort in instructional development by providing a catalog of available materials. Information in the content knowledge base would come from two sources. Material that is developed with ISD Expert is automatically added to the content knowledge base. Material may also be input from sources external to ISD Expert. For example, many materials and resources that are developed in R & D efforts independently of ISD would be useful in course applications if authors had access to them. General information manuals and other media-based resources (e.g., video disc materials) are another example of materials from external.

Situational Evaluation Component

The first activity in the proposed ISD Expert system is the evaluation of the given author's situation. The assumption is that each author will have a different need or problem, depending on his/her given situation. As the ISD Expert tutor establishes the author's model of instruction, the Situational Evaluation Component will diagnose the situation employing AI techniques. Again, it is assumed that the tutor will determine the experience level of the author and in turn adjust the report of the evaluation. For example, if the tutor determines that the author is experienced in ISD, and the situation is to develop a lesson on troubleshooting, the report would indicate those two conditions, which would influence the type of prescription(s) recommended. By focusing on the given situation, ISD Expert can employ the complexity and richness of the fourth generation ISD model without directly training the author about the entire model.

Recommendations Component

The purpose of ISD Expert is to help authors improve their instructional product development by applying the most advanced variables and conditions of instructional design theory. This is made possible by the recommendations component, which interacts with the ISD knowledge base to interpret the situational evaluation diagnosis and recommend a prescription to deal with the given instructional situation. Also, the prescription is adjusted to the author's level of experience. This is an important feature of the proposed ISD Expert because it prescribes an effort of development that can be efficiently accomplished by the author. For example, if an inexperienced author is presented with a prescription that would fit an experienced author's profile, the novice author would not be able to adequately follow the production activities. The result would be that the prescription is implemented inefficiently or not at all. Presentation of the prescription will likewise be based on the experience of the author. The experience level of the author will determine the program control (i.e., coaching or advisement) employed in the production component.

Production Component

The term production is used here to reflect a variety of different types of instructional situations that might occur. ISD includes, in addition to instructional development, test development, computer-based management development, print materials development, instructional aids, visual aids, etc. The function of this component is to guide the author in the production process. As such, this part of the expert system directly interacts with the tutor. Because of the range of ISD activities, this component will be composed of mini-experts, each reflecting a different authoring activity (see Appendix). That is, the mini-experts will be the various activities within the ISD model. For example, if the situation is to develop a test for troubleshooting, the author's model indicates an experienced author, and the prescription recommends a simulation, then a mini-expert on design of simulations would guide the author in the production of an appropriate simulation. An important feature of ISD Expert will be to facilitate the employment of knowledge-based technologies for instructional delivery. For example, for computer-based instruction, this component would directly produce the courseware (Tennyson, 1990c).

Once the production effort is completed, a report is sent to the tutor to update the author's model and to reference the effort in the content knowledge base. To further improve the efficiency of ISD Expert, instructional strategy (IS) shells will be accessible by the mini-experts to do the actual product development: IS shells will only require that the author enter into the system content information and the system would develop the product (much like Merrill's transaction shells discussed in the previous chapter).

The above four components of the proposed ISD Expert system will be designed and programmed as independent expert systems so as to allow for future additions and elaborations. This is necessary because of the continuing growth in the instructional design theory field.

Central Network System

The computer environment includes a centrally-based network and file server for both local and remote PC workstations. Because of the proposal for a content knowledge base (see Figure 7.3) with acquisition capabilities and an author's instructional model within ISD Expert, a large capacity disk storage should be an integral part of the system. Also, given the computing power of PCs, much of the intelligent interfacing would take place at the workstation.

Although there are a large number of commercially-available shells for program development, many do not allow for local exits and returns. With such software, the development effort becomes constrained by the closed architecture of the given shell; the shell becomes a methodology in itself rather than a tool to be used in implementing multiple methodologies. ISD Expert should be programmed in a high-level language with artificial intelligence features; commercially-available shells should be used when feasible to augment the system features.

Development Plan

The framework presented here offers a complete expert system for automating instructional development. To produce such a system, there are two possible approaches. The first would be to develop the ISD Expert system as presented. The second would be to follow an incremental approach in which an initial prototype is developed that only has a minimal set of features and is aimed at an experienced author. That is, an ISD Expert that would only have an advisor level tutor and the situational evaluation and recommendations components. The content knowledge base and acquisition features of the intelligent interface tutor and the production component would be added in subsequent elaborations.

Although the first approach seems possible, there are a number of problems that need to be considered that might favor the second approach. An initial problem is the cost factor. As stated earlier the majority of expert systems are developed using commercial shells. Cost in terms of software is the time required to produce a product that will be timely and profitable. That is, the proposed ISD Expert would most likely be a software product that would need to generate income within a reasonable time frame. Rapid prototyping is a procedure to develop software employing shells that are linked by some general language (Hewett, 1989). Thus, instead of five years to produce a complete version of ISD Expert, an initial prototype could be developed in much less time.

A second major problem in producing a complete ISD Expert in the first approach is the necessary research needed for the new system. There has been minimal empirical research to date on instructional variables and conditions associated with the extension of cognitive learning theory to instructional design theory (see Muraida's concluding section in Part III). Even though it is possible to develop an initial prototype, research in cognitive instructional design theory needs to be done as well as the interaction of media within this theoretical framework. A third problem area relates to the specification of the human-computer interaction variables and conditions necessary to run and manage the complex environment of ISD Expert.

Cycling through an incremental approach to development of ISD Expert will produce an initial product for employment and research within the constraints of costs and system knowledge. The initial prototype (or ISD Expert1) would exhibit many standard characteristics of the third generation ISD model (see Figure A.3, Appendix) with successive versions taking on more of the ideas associated with the fourth generation ISD model.

Summary

The purpose of ISD Expert is to improve learning by aiding authors in the employment of contemporary instructional design theory. This chapter presented a framework for an expert system to implement the concept of ISD Expert. This system will interact with authors on an individual basis according to their respective experience with principles and variables of instructional design theory. Inexperienced authors will be coached to develop basic ISD skills while the more experienced authors will be advised on the employment of advanced instructional design variables and conditions.

An author's instructional design model is a necessary module for an intelligent human-computer interface component because it replaces the need for a separate training program for authors. The sophistication of ISD Expert's prescriptions will be directly influenced by the author's instructional design model. Therefore, both ISD novices and experts will be able immediately to use ISD Expert. That is, the proposed system would take into account experience in instructional design theory and practice.

The fourth generation ISD model (see Figure 7.1) provides the instructional knowledge base for ISD Expert. The content knowledge base is proposed as a database for instructional materials within subject matter areas. Both knowledge bases will have acquisition capabilities.

The basic proposed ISD Expert system will have four interactive components: (a) an intelligent author-computer interface component; (b) a situational evaluation component (diagnosis), (c) a recommendations component (prescriptions), and (d) a production component. ISD Expert will be designed for a computer-based network system using a high level, AI language and expert system shells.

To implement the concept of the fourth generation ISD model, the situational evaluation component of ISD Expert will diagnose each author's given problem and/or need. This will make the system application-orientated rather than the conventional lock-step system that is most suited for the teaching of ISD. From the diagnosis perspective, ISD Expert will generate a prescription. For those authors who seek assistance in implementing the prescription, especially those requiring the development of instructional materials, the fourth component will guide the production effort. This production component will be composed of mini-expert systems that have specific functions (e.g., instructional strategy shells).

Conclusion

In conclusion, I am proposing an expert system that will bring the power of instructional design theory and practice to educators who would not normally have the opportunity to employ such knowledge in their instructional efforts. The proposed ISD Expert will improve learning by making instructional development both effective (i.e., by employing the most advanced principles and variables of learning and instructional theories) and efficient (i.e., by reducing the time and cost of conventional methods of instructional development).

References

Allen, M. W. (1986). Authoring aids: The means to improved authoring procedures. *Proceedings of the SALT Conference*. Orlando, FL: Society for Applied Learning Technology.

Anderson, J. R. (1988). The expert module. In M. C. Polson & J. J. Richardson (Eds.), *Intelligent tutoring systems* (pp. 21–53). Hillsdale, NJ: Lawrence Erlbaum Associates.

Bonner, J. (1988). Implications of cognitive theory for instructional design: Revisited. *Educational Communications and Technology Journal, 36*, 3–14.

Bonnet, A., Haton, J. P., & Truong-Ngoc, J. M. (1988). *Expert systems: Principles and practice*. Englewood Cliffs, NJ: Prentice-Hall.

Branson, R., Rayner, G. T., Cox, J. L., Furman, J. P., King, F. J., & Hannum, W. H. (1976). *Interservice procedures for instructional systems development* (5 Vols.) (TRADOC Pam 350-30 and NAVEDTRA 106A). Fort Monroe, VA: U. S. Army Traning and Doctrine Command. (NTIS No. ADA-019 486 ADA-019 490).

Brown, J. S., Collins, A., & Duguid, P. (1989). Situated cognition and the culture of learning. *Educational Researcher, 18*(10), 32–42.

Clancey, W. J. (1979). Tutoring rules for guiding a case method dialogue. *International Journal of Man-Machine Studies, 11*, 25–49.

Clancey, W. J. (1983). The epistemology of a rule-based expert system framework for explanation. *Artificial Intelligence, 20*, 215–251.

Clancey, W. J. (1989). The knowledge level reinterpreted: Modeling how systems interact. *Machine Learning, 4*, 287–293.

Corno, L., & Snow, R. E. (1986). Adapting teaching to individual differences among students. In M. Wittrock (Ed.), *Third handbook of research on teaching*. New York: Macmillan

Gagné, R. M., & Merrill, M. D. (1990). Integrative goals for instructional design. *Educational Technology Research and Development, 38*(1), 23–30

Gagné, R. M., Briggs, L. J., & Wager, W. (1988). *Principles of instructional design* (3rd ed.). New York: Holt, Rinehart, & Winston.

Gagné, R. M. (1985). *The conditions of learning* (4th ed.) New York: Holt, Rinehart, & Winston.

Glaser, R., & Bassok, M. (1989). Learning theory and study of instruction. *Annual Review of Psychology, 40*, 631–666.

Glaser, R. (1966). The design of instruction. In J. I. Goodlad (Ed.), *The changing American school: NSSE 65th Yearbook* (pp. 215–242).

Guba, E. G., & Lincoln, Y. S. (1986). The countenances of fourth-generation evaluation: Description, judgment, and negotiation. *Evaluation studies review annual, 11*, 70–88.

Harmon, P., Maus, R., & Morrissey, W. (1988). *Expert system tools and applications*. New York: Wiley.

Hewett, T. T. (1989). Towards a rapid prototyping environment for interface design: Desirable features suggested by the electronic spreadsheet. In A. Sutcliffe & L. Macaulay (Eds.), *People and computers* V (pp. 305–314). Cambridge, UK: Cambridge University Press.

Hermanns, J. (1990). Computer-aided instructional system development. *Educational Technology, 30*(3), 42–45.

Merrill, M. D. (1986). Prescriptions for an authoring system. *Journal of Computer-based Instruction, 12*, 90–96.

Merrill, M. D. (1990). Introduction to special issue: Computer-based tools for instruction design. *Educational Technology, 30*(3), 5–7.

Merrill, M. D., & Li, Z. (1990). An instructional design expert system. In S. Dijkstra, B. van Hout Wolters, & P. C. van der Sijde (Eds.), *Research on instruction: Design and effects* (pp. 21–44). Englewood Cliffs, NJ: Educational Technology Publications.

Morgan, C. C. (1989). *Programming from specifications*. Englewood Cliffs, NJ: Prentice-Hall.

Newell, A., & Card, S. (1985). Prospects for psychological science in human computer interaction. *Human Computer Interaction, 1*, 209–242.

Norman, D.A. (1986). *Cognitive engineering. In User-centered system design* (pp.31–62). Hillsdale, NJ: Lawrence Erlbaum Associates.

Perez, R. S., & Seidel, R. J. (1990). Using artificial intelligence in education: Computer-based tools for instructional development. *Educational Technology, 30*(3), 51–58.

Ranker, R. A., & Doucet, R. M. (1990). SOCRATES: A computer-based lesson development advisor. *Computers in Human Behavior, 6*, 162–171.

Reiser, R. A., & Gagné, R. M.(1983). *Selecting media for instruction*. Englewood Cliffs, NJ: Educational Technology Publications.

Russell, D., Moran, T., & Jordan, D. (1988). The instructional design environment. In J. Psotka, L. Massey, & S. Mutter (Eds.), *Intelligent tutoring systems: Lessons learned* (pp. 96–137). Hillsdale, NJ: Lawrence Erlbaum Associates.

Schiele, F., & Green, T. (1990). HCI formalisms and cognitive psychology: the case of Task-Action Grammar. In M. Harrison & H. Thimbleby (Eds.), *Formal methods in human-computer interaction.* Cambridge, UK: Cambridge University Press.

Simons, G. L. (1985). *Expert systems and micros.* Manchester, UK: NCC Publications.

Smith, S. F. (1984). Adaptive learning systems. In R. Forsyth (Ed.), *Expert systems: Principles and case studies.* New York: Chapman & Hall.

Snow, R. E., & Lohman, D. F. (1984). Toward a theory of cognitive aptitude for learning from instruction. *Journal of Educational Psychology, 76,* 347–376.

Swartout, W. R. (1983). XPLAIN: A system for creating and explaining expert consulting programs. *Artificial Intelligence, 21,* 285–325.

Tennyson, R. D. (1977). Instructional systems: Development, evaluation, and management of learning environments. In D. J. Treffinger, J. K. Davis, & R. E. Ripple (Eds.), *Handbook on teaching educational psychology* (pp. 215–242). New York: Academic Press.

Tennyson, R. D. (1978). Evaluation technology instructional development. *Journal of Instructional Development, 2*(1), 19–26.

Tennyson, R. D. (1990a). A proposed cognitive paradigm of learning for educational technology. *Educational Technology, 26*(6), 12–17.

Tennyson, R. D. (1990b). Cognitive learning theory linked to instructional theory. *Journal of Structural Learning, 13,* 362–371.

Tennyson, R. D. (1990c). Computer-based enhancements for the improvement of learning. In S. Dijkstra, B. H. A. M. van Hout Wolters, & P. C. van der Sijde (Eds.), *Research on instruction: Design and effects.* Englewood Cliffs, NJ: Educational Technology Publications.

Tennyson, R. D. (1990d). Integrated instructional design theory: Advancements from cognitive science and instructional technology. *Educational Technology, 26*(6), 18–28.

Tennyson, R.D., & Christensen, D.L.(in press). Four generations of instructional systems development. *Educational Technology Research and Development.*

Tennyson, R. D., & Rasch, M. (1988). Linking cognitive learning theory to instructional prescriptions. *Instructional Science, 17,* 369–385.

Tennyson, R. D., & Rasch, M. (1990). Instructional design for the improvement of learning and cognition. In H. Feger (Ed.), *Wissenschaft und Verantwortung* (pp. 71–90). Goettingen, Fed. Rep. of Germany: Hogrefe-Verlag.

Waterman, D. A. (1986). *A guide to expert systems.* Reading, MA: Addison-Wesley.

Implications for Intelligent Instructional Assistance

J. Michael Spector

As indicated in the introduction to this section, we have restricted our treatment of approaches to automating instructional design to those which implement existing established instructional designs (Halff's generative systems). Our reason for this restriction is that we do not believe that machines are capable of truly the creative, adaptive, and innovative activities required in devising effective instructional designs. However, we do see ways for using intelligent machine techniques to assist in the process of designing and developing instructional materials.

We further restricted our focus to a target population which consisted primarily of subject-matter experts with limited expertise in the areas of instructional technology and educational psychology. The advantage of this restriction is twofold: (1) it coincides with an actual and significant instructional design population, both in the military and the academic sectors; and (2) it cause the important concerns in automating instructional design to be raised explicitly, rather than relying on a human expert to make up for system deficiencies.

Within these restrictions we have treated in detail a variety of possibilities. Gagné argues for automating only the guidance framework. This kind of automation consists primarily of two kinds of assistance: (1) specific instructions pertaining to programming meaningful events of instructions; and (2) elaborate examples of how those instructional events can be automated. The advantage of this sort of automation is that it is relatively inexpensive. Indeed, the Armstrong Laboratory already has several prototypes of GAIDA (Guided Approach: Instructional Design Advising) which required less than six person-months to create in Tool-Book.™

Merrill argued for a more extensive kind of intelligent framework for instructional design. His proposal incorporates instructional transactions, which are intelligent object-oriented frameworks for creating specific kinds of instructional interactions in a computer-based environment. The notion of a transaction shell, together with that of a rule-based advisor to interact with a subject-matter expert/courseware author and configure appropriate transactions, forms the basis of the AIDA (Advanced Instructional Design Advisor) project. AIDA is now in the prototyping and evaluating phase (1992–1993), and it is expected to be fully operational and in use in the Air Force in 1997. While AIDA costs more than GAIDA, it will place fewer demands on courseware authors to be experts in the areas of instructional technology or educational psychology.

Tennyson's approach was clearly the most ambitious: an intelligent tutoring system (ITS) for the domain of instructional design. Such a system would adapt to the user, distinguishing novice designers from expert users. In addition, it would provide a variety of context-specific and domain-pertinent instructional design aids. The construction of Tennyson's intelligent tutor for instructional design is a desirable goal, but it is most probably out of reach in the near term. Along the way to Tennyson's system, the issues raised in the implementation of Gagné's and Merrill's systems will have to be resolved.

In order to resolve these issues, prototypes must be implemented, problematic areas identified, and then rigorous evaluation methodologies must be put into motion. It is no secret that the evaluation of new instructional technologies often gets slighted, partly because those accountable for the funds do not want to appear frivolous and partly because those accountable for the products do not want to appear foolish. We remain convinced, however, that the key to genuine progress in the automation of instructional design is the disciplined evaluation of the effectiveness of the various attempts at automation. As a consequence, that topic is the focus of the concluding part of this volume.

Part III

R & D Issues in Automating Instructional Design

Introductory Remarks

Daniel J. Muraida

From the broadest perspective the research issues that must be addressed in the automation of instructional design involve the knowledge base content and structure, and user interfaces. The former category encompasses questions of what can legitimately and usefully be included in a corpus of instructional design guidance. Recent efforts have focused on optimal methods for adapting computerized instruction to learner characteristics (Ross & Morrison, 1988; Steinberg, 1989) and producing transfer effects (Phye, 1989; Jelsma, van Merriënboer, & Bijlstra, 1990). The latter category concerns the problems surrounding the most accurate, facile, and effective means of conveying instructional design guidance to the nonexpert designer. The research in this area has generally proceeded more slowly with fewer available empirical studies (Bovair, Kieras, & Polson, 1990). Obviously a section of this length cannot provide an exhaustive treatment of the research issues which surround the development of instructional design resources. In this section, however, the authors provide a sampling of the more critical problems confronting researchers in automated instructional design. Each chapter is briefly sketched below.

In her chapter entitled "Task Analysis for an Automated Design Advisor," Martha Polson attacks the problem of determining the optimal approach to assessing the cognitive demands of a task in the domain of equipment maintenance training. Polson subsequently addresses the significant concomitant problem of representing the task analysis in a form congruent with a representation or simulation of a piece of equipment. The utility of cognitive task analysis lies in the its ability to zero in on the critical components of complex procedural tasks, and its ease of application for technically naive users. Polson presents suggestions for determining what the appropriate granularity for a task analysis should be, and for determining how to make the analysis manageable for the user.

Halff addresses the appropriate use of scenarios in instructional design for maintenance training. He identifies the requirements for scenario-based instruction that provide the cognitive underpinnings for their effectiveness quite apart from contextual realism. He then delineates a sequence of instructional activities which he asserts would optimize the student's benefit from the scenario.

Friedman's chapter examines what is known about the utility of graphics for presenting and teaching factual knowledge and procedural skills. Friedman points out that much of the effectiveness attributed to graphics is based on anecdotal or over-generalized evidence. She goes on to explain the complex interplay of content structure, human information processing characteristics, and instructional goals that moderate the instructional effectiveness of graphics materials.

The chapter by Muraida *et al.* explores an evolving role for evaluation in automated instructional design and development. Taking a cue from Tennyson's work (Part II) evaluation is viewed as a constant function throughout the development process. It is proposed that evaluation should begin with the development of the functional specifications for an instructional design (system). The authors describe how the evaluation of functional specifications was addressed in an actual R&D project, resulting in an explicit analysis of tradeoffs. Secondly, the authors discuss how one of the higher priorities of the tradeoff analysis (transaction shells) was submitted to preliminary evaluation for proof of concept.

The final section provides a discussion of the development of a preliminary version of a cognitive model of the automated instructional design process. The development of this model was occasioned by the results of the preliminary evaluation. The purpose of the model is to develop a reliable tool which will enable evaluators to match users, design environments, and interfaces for optimal efficiency and productivity.

References

Bovair, S., Kieras, D. E., & Polson, P. G. (1990). The acquisition and performance of text-editing skill: A cognitive complexity analysis. *Human-Computer Interaction, 5,* 148

Jelsma, O., van Merriënboer, J. J. G., & Bijlstra, J. P. (1990). The ADAPT design model: Towards instructional control of transfer. *Instructional Science, 19*(2) 89–120

Phye, G. B. (1989). Schemata training and transfer of an intellectual skill. *Journal of Educational Psychology, 81*(3) 347–352

Ross, S. M., & Morrison, G. R. (1988). Adapting instruction to learner performance and background variables. In D. H. Jonassen (Ed.), *Instructional designs for microcomputer courseware.* Hillsdale, NJ: Lawrence Erlbaum Associates.

Steinberg, E. R. (1989) Cognition and learner control: A literature review. *Journal of Computer-Based Instruction, 16*(40) 117–121

Chapter Eight

Task Analysis for an Automated Instructional Design Advisor

Martha C. Polson

The first step in the design of any instruction is a task analysis to determine what should be taught. From the cognitive science information processing approach, it is argued that a behavioral analysis is not sufficient. A cognitive analysis needs to be performed because education and training should take into account the cognitive processes involved in learning and performance, not just the objective behaviors required (see Glaser & Bassok, 1989, as well as several chapters in Psotka, Massey, & Mutter, 1988 for recent discussions of this issue).

Halff (1990) identified three types of cognitive structures important to the maintenance enterprise: the execution of procedures, a mental model of the equipment, and fault isolation skills. Thus an adequate cognitive task analysis should identify the information and skills that must be imparted to the student to support the acquisition of these cognitive structures. This paper will address only the areas of procedures and mental models (see Halff, Part III, for an extended discussion of fault isolation skills).

While the current walk-through is based in part on Kieras's cognitive task analysis, little attention has been paid to date to specifying the nature of the task analysis in the AIDA system. The primary focus of this paper is to explore the task analysis conducted by Kieras as a basis for specifying the task analysis requirements in an AIDA designed for maintenance training. The questions to be considered include:

–What is the nature of the cognitive task analysis?

–How detailed does the analysis need to be?

–How should that task analysis be represented in AIDA?

–How do you map the representation onto the instructional materials?

–What kinds of aids and/or guidance could be provided to a novice instructional designer, who might also a subject-matter expert (SME), to perform the task analysis?

This paper does not attempt to provide complete or final answers to the above questions, but primarily strives to spell out the issues that need to be addressed and some of the relevant literature.

Cognitive Analysis of Procedures

The analysis of the troubleshooting procedures done by Kieras is a particular type of analysis known as a GOMS (Goals, Operators, Methods, and Selection Rules) analysis, which derives from the Cognitive Complexity Theory (CCT) of Kieras and Polson (Bovair, Kieras, & Polson, 1990) and has as its intellectual predecessor the work of Card, Moran, and Newell (Card *et al.*, 1983). This approach entails analyzing the tasks to be accomplished into a meaningful series of goals and subgoals. Each goal to be accomplished is recursively broken into a series of subgoals until a level is reached in which accomplishing the subgoal can be achieved by either a primitive level motor or mental act.

Goals represent a person's intention to perform a task, subtask, or single cognitive or physical operation. Goals are organized into structures of interrelated goals that sequence methods and operations. An example goal from troubleshooting the engine would be to determine if the ignition system is functioning correctly.

Operations characterize elementary physical actions (e.g., pressing a button, setting a switch, or attaching a probe) and cognitive or mental operations (e.g., perceptual operations, retrieving an item from memory, or reading a voltage and storing it in working memory). The most primitive mental operations are actions such as receiving perceptual information, making a basic decision, depositing facts from working memory into long term memory, retrieving facts from long term memory and activating them in working memory, forming a goal, etc.

Methods generate sequences of operations that accomplish specific goals or subgoals. The goal structure of a method characterizes its internal organization and control structure. The GOMS model assumes that execution of a task or procedure involves decomposition of the task into a series of subtasks. A skilled person executing a procedure has effective methods for each subtask. A novice may have less efficient methods. Accomplishing a task involves executing the series of specialized methods that perform each subtask. There are several kinds of methods. High-level methods decompose the initial task into a sequence of subtasks. Intermediate-level methods describe the sequence of functions necessary to complete a subtask. Low-level methods generate the actual user actions necessary to perform a function.

A person's knowledge of how to do a complex task is a mixture of task-specific information—the high-level methods—and system-specific knowledge, the low-level methods.

Then, a high-level method for troubleshooting a jet engine would be:

–check out the starting operations of the engine

Intermediate-level methods which are part of the high-level method for checking out the symptom of no start would include

–check for bad ignition
–check for fuel flow problem
–check for defective starting system
–check for altitude limitation problem

Low level methods for the intermediate methods include

For checking for bad ignition
–apply shorting stick to AB plug
–check the ENGINE IGNITION, AUTOSYN INST & IGNITION
INVERTER circuit breakers for proper engagement
For fuel flow problem
–check fuel system circuit breakers for proper engagement

Selection rules determine which method to select. In an expert, selection rules are compiled pieces of problem-solving knowledge. The selection rule must state the appropriate context for using any given method. If there is more than one method, the rule must state when each method is appropriate.

In summary, the GOMS model characterizes the user's knowledge as a collection of hierarchically organized methods and associated goal structures that sequence methods and operations. The knowledge captured in the GOMS representation describes both general knowledge of how the task is to be decomposed and specific information on how to execute the methods required to complete the task.

One of the greatest advantages of this approach for our purposes is that Kieras has prepared a detailed guide for doing task analysis of procedures using the GOMS methodology (Kieras, an unpublished 1990 edition of this document can be obtained from David Kieras, Technical Communications Program, TIDAL Bldg. 2360 Bonisteel Blvd, University of Michigan, Ann Arbor, MI 48109-2108). He has also defined a language (NGOMSL) or "Natural" GOMS Language which is relatively easy to read and write. Kieras's guide also includes procedures for doing a GOMS analysis by using a breadth-first expansion of methods rather than trying to describe goal structures directly.

Mental Models Analysis

Halff (1990) summarized the importance for maintenance training of imparting correct and adequate mental models of the equipment. Kieras (1988b, 1990) pointed out that the most accurate way of determining the mental model to be taught would be to do a complete cognitive simulation. However, realizing that this is not always a feasible approach, Kieras (1988b) spelled out some heuristics that could be used to determine the mental model that should be taught in lieu of a complete simulation. The heuristics are:

   −relevance to task goals
   −accessibility to use
   −critical procedures and inference strategies

All of these heuristics involve doing an analysis equivalent to a GOMS analysis of the task at hand. In addition, two other hierarchical cognitive analyses are required: an explanation hierarchy and a hierarchical decomposition of the device structure and mechanisms. The *relevance to task goals* heuristic states that explanations should only be given if they are relevant to a task goal. To carry out this heuristic an explanation hierarchy is constructed. The first pass at what goes into this hierarchy can be what is in the existing documentation. The goals of the GOMS analysis are then mapped to the explanation hierarchy, which will reveal any missing explanatory information as well as any extraneous material which need not be taught. Constructing the explanation hierarchy is not really extraneous work since this material is needed for the instructional material.

The second heuristic, *accessibility to use*, implies that the device, illustration, or simulation which is presented to the technician should not contain parts which he cannot access. Again, this involves mapping the GOMS analysis, but onto the device description, rather than the explanation hierarchy.

The third heuristic says that the GOMS analysis should be examined for procedures that will be difficult to learn due to what appears to be arbitrary content. These procedures should then be analyzed to determine what inferences would need to be made in order for the content to appear logical rather than arbitrary. The information necessary to make those inferences should then be made explicit in the training materials. This information will need to be included either in the explanation hierarchy or the device description.

Level of Detail of the Task Analysis

Kieras (1990) as well as Anderson (Anderson, Boyle, Corbett, & Lewis, 1990) have advocated doing a complete cognitive simulation of a given task which is based on a cognitive analysis of the task in order to determine the content of instructional materials and training procedures. The advantage of a simulation is that it insures that the analysis is complete. Also, as Kieras and Polson (Bovair, Kieras, & Polson, 1990) have shown, a tremendous amount of information about the task at hand can be gained if the analysis is completed down to the level of simple operations or operators for most aspects of the task. The information that can be derived from the simulation includes the time to learn the task, the amount of transfer of training from one procedure to another, and the execution time for various procedures or methods. The disadvantage is that a complete cognitive simulation requires a tremendous amount of effort to implement, even after the cognitive analysis of the content of the instruction is complete. However, as can be seen from the GOMS analysis of Kieras (1988a), the use of the GOMS method for cognitive analysis of procedures does not require that it be followed through by a complete simulation or that all tasks be analyzed to the level of simple operators.

How low level the analysis needs to be for the procedures for any given instructional package will be determined in large part by the level of expertise of the trainees. For instance, for the problem of No Start with the Probable Cause of no ignition or poor ignition (page 6-7 of Technical Manual for Engine Conditioning of the T38) the first step is to check ignitor plugs for firing and proper spark rate. This is followed by a note that the proper spark rate is three sparks in two seconds. Presumably this is as low as the analysis needs to go. In terms of a computer-based instructional system, this detail could be represented by clicking on a designated ignitor plug icon handle (handles are mouse sensitive areas) which will give its status. If the status had been set to bad then the simulation would continue with the procedure (the next step if the ignitor plugs do not fire is to check the static inverter). The actual motor and perceptual operations necessary in checking the spark rates would not have to be explicitly laid out. However, for a novice technician some of the steps in the T38 troubleshooting manual, such as *remove the engine,* do seem rather high level and may need to be broken down into subtasks. Anderson (Anderson, Boyle, Farrell, & Reiser, 1984) refers to this as adjusting the grain level of the instruction.

As a way of decreasing the workload of authoring the simulation and/or doing the GOMS analysis for a given domain, a library of generic low-level procedures such as testing ignitor plugs (as well as their corresponding simulations) could be provided in an AIDA configured for that domain. In fact these could be a set of separate modules that are given as screening tests to insure that these low-level methods or methods which occur in many different troubleshooting situations such as *remove the engine* are learned before entering simulations which are higher level or aimed at specific problems. A problem for a generic system, as opposed to a system written explicitly for a domain such as electronic maintenance or airplane maintenance, is knowing what skills and knowledge can be assumed. If the domain is known, there is probably a reasonably finite set of testing skills, mechanical procedures, etc., that are known to be required to perform the task. For instance, if the student is said to be at such and such a skill level in a particular field, is there a list of basic procedures that the student can be expected to know and which would not have to be represented in detail in a particular domain?

Representing the Task Analysis

In the CCT approach of Kieras and Polson, a simple production system is used to implement the results of a NGOMSL analysis into a working simulation. The device knowledge necessary to carry out the simulation is represented in a Generalized Transition Network (GTN). An example of the representation of a device in the GTN formalism is given by Kieras (1990) and Kieras & Polson (1985). However, a number of representation schemes are possible. A scheme used by Anderson in his PUPS system is a candidate representation that is probably compatible with the Transaction Shell representation discussed by Merrill (Jones, Li, & Merrill, 1990; see also Merrill's chapter in Part II). Anderson's PUPS (Penultimate Production Systems) theory holds that procedures are acquired by compiling declarative knowledge (Anderson *et al.,* 1990). The declarative knowledge necessary for compiling the procedures which model task performance is represented in schema-based structures called PUPS structures. These schema include slots for the function of the entity being represented by the schema, a form slot for the physical appearance of the entity, and a precondition slot which states the preconditions necessary for the function to be achieved. In compiling the productions which are the basis of procedural knowledge, the function slot maps to the goal to be achieved, which will require knowledge of the entity represented; the precondition slot maps onto the condition of the condition-action pair in a production; the form slot in the PUPS tutors holds the form of the current action to be carried out such as a particular Lisp function. A similar scheme could be used for representing the GOMS analysis. Merrill has proposed an activity frame that has paths or sequences of actions. This frame could also have slots for the function, the operators, and the outcome. The values for these slots could probably be automatically generated from a NGOMSL analysis just as it is technically feasible to generate a running production rule based simulation from a NGOMSL analysis.

The explanation hierarchy can be represented in numerous different ways. From my limited understanding it appears that the representation scheme already proposed by Merrill for AIDA (see Part II, this volume) would be adequate to represent the explanation hierarchy. The device knowledge will ultimately be represented in the graphical simulation. The initial representation may be a hierarchical listing of the names of the device components or perhaps a block diagram, which can serve as a guide for constructing the sketch which will guide the construction of the graphical simulation.

Mapping the Content of GOMS
and Mental Model Analysis
to the Device Simulation

Following Kieras's approach will yield three hierarchically arranged representations. The GOMS analysis will spell out the steps to be followed in carrying out procedures for operating, calibrating, troubleshooting, or repairing the equipment, starting with the highest level goals and methods. These are succesively decomposed to lower level subgoals and methods. The GOMS analysis will also identify any device components that need to be included in the representation of the device structure as well as the declarative knowledge that needs to be conveyed about them: function, location, name, etc. The explanation hierarchy will contain the causal and declarative knowledge necessary to execute the procedures, support inferences necessary for constructing a mental model of the equipment, and definitions of the attributes and rules of objects, etc.

The device simulation contains a graphic representation of the device structure and qualitative simulations of its functioning. Authoring in the simulation starts with a temporary sketch which is derived from the prior cognitive analysis, particularly the mental model analysis, which entails interrelating the GOMS analysis, the explanation hierarchy, and the hierarchical device structure decomposition. However, the construction of the simulation is done in bottom-up fashion starting with the lowest level of the device hierarchy. The lowest level objects are the bottom items in the device structure analysis. These correspond to the objects manipulated by the lowest level operators in the GOMS model. For this reason, it is not feasible to develop the simulation and do the GOMS analysis and explanation hierarchy in parallel, which might be tempting to the novice instructional designer, who wants to get on with "real" work. The analyses have to be complete before the construction of the simulation can begin.

The behavior of the objects are defined by attribute handles and rules. These aspects of the simulation are drawn from the explanation hierarchy. Once the basic simulation is complete, procedures which are carried out on the device are authored by carrying out a sequence of actions which correspond to actions spelled out to accomplish the goals in the GOMS analysis. The individual actions correspond to the operators. What is missing from the simulation representation is any indication of the function or purpose, i.e., goals, of the procedure. These have to be represented in the dialogue windows.

Implications for a Task Analysis Capability

The major difficulty that will be faced in developing a successful transactional shell for developing courseware for procedural learning skills will be performing a successful task analysis. It has been widely recognized in the educational literature since Gagné (1968) that successful instruction in a complex task involves decomposing the task into a collection of *meaningful subtasks*. Modern cognitive theories (Bovair *et al.*, 1990; Card *et al.*, 1983) require that a theorist provide a *correct* goal structure for a complex task in order to be able to successfully model the acquisition and performance of that task.

The terms *meaningful* and *correct* are what make things difficult. A complex task can obviously be divided up into an arbitrary collection of hierarchically arranged components. A meaningful and correct decomposition reflects the actual underlying structure of the task in a comprehensible manner that can be learned by a student. For example, a given subtask cannot be arbitrarily complex. If it contains more than four or five major components the subtask in turn must be decomposed into a collection of sub-subtasks (Kieras, 1988a).

Experts have a large amount of knowledge about relevant task decompositions in the domain of their expertise. However, much of this knowledge is implicit, i.e., highly compiled, which presents a problem for instruction. The task of decomposing the knowledge and making it explicit so it could be incorporated successfully in instructional manipulations is a very different skill from the skill of successfully performing the task.

The problem of doing a successful task analysis in collaboration with the subject matter expert who is not a trained educator or cognitive scientist is equivalent to the problem of developing an expert system where the domain expert is not a knowledge engineer, but must communicate his/her knowledge to the knowledge engineer in order for it to be incorporated into the expert system. This process is long and tedious and is often a severe test of even successful collaborations. During an initial phase the domain expert describes to the knowledge engineer his/her understanding of the knowledge underlying his/her performance. The knowledge engineer then attempts to incorporate this description into an expert system. The initial version of this system is incomplete; it contains errors because the domain expert may not have explicit understanding of the expertise, or because of miscommunications between the domain expert and the knowledge engineer. Successive iterations of the developing expert system require that the domain expert gain a more explicit understanding of his expertise and that the knowledge engineer require extensive knowledge of the application domain. It should be clear why this is a long and painful process.

We have the identical problem in performing the critical useful task analysis that is necessary to develop successful instructions in the procedural skills necessary to carry complex maintenance tasks and other skills of interest to the Air Force, with the added difficulty that we want a machine to be able to extract the domain knowledge. As demonstrated above, modern cognitive theory provides us with a partial solution to this very difficult problem and suggests the design of knowledge acquisition tools that can be incorporated into the transactional shell.

The goal structure of the GOMS model is the modern representation of such a successful task analysis. Since the GOMS model has been rigorously formalized as a production (Bovair *et al.*, 1990) and Kieras (1988a) has developed a set of explicit heuristics for doing a GOMS analysis, we are in a position to incorporate these results into a transactional shell that would support doing task analysis by deriving an appropriate goal structure for the skill being tutored. Kieras's (1988) heuristics could be incorporated into the shell and coach a domain expert during the process of deriving the goal structure from a task analysis. Thus, if the domain expert defined a single subtask that violated the complexity criteria for a subtask, i.e., more than five steps, the shell could prompt the instructional designer with a suggestion, 'consider decomposing the current subtask into a collection of less complex sub-subtasks.' Furthermore, the tool could also check that the developing task decomposition was syntactically correct.

Kieras has invested a large amount of time in writing a manual on how to do GOMS analysis and in developing an English-like language for representing the analysis. Included in the guide are many rules of thumb which could be implemented in a knowledge-based shell to give guidance to the SME or instructional designer. For instance, Kieras recommends that a given method contain no more than five steps. If there is more than that some may need to be grouped into a higher level method. There is also guidance on creating generic methods to represent methods which occur often in slightly different context. For instance, rather than a method for checking each specific circuit breaker, there would be a check circuit breaker method, which has as a variable which circuit breaker to check. This variable information is held in working memory.

This shell could do much of the bookkeeping necessary for a GOMS analysis such as creating a list of methods and information identified by the methods that need either already to be known or taught, such as their location, etc. A more sophisticated shell could automatically map the results of the analysis into the knowledge representation system. A less sophisticated system would create a paper guide for what should be hand entered into the representation system. Similar shells could also be created for the explanation hierarchy and the device structure and function knowledge. However, no explicit guidelines for doing such analyses have been developed to date.

Conclusion

The task analysis approach developed by Kieras and his colleagues appears to have much to recommend it as the basis for a task analysis module of an automated instructional design advisor. This includes a GOMS analysis for the procedural aspects of the task, and a mental model analysis. The mental model analysis consists of the development of an explanation hierarchy and a decomposition of the device structure and function. The hierarchy and the decompositions are then related to the GOMS analysis. Developing shells to aid in the cognitive task analysis is technically feasible. However, a great deal of care will need to be taken to be sure that the shells are implemented in such a way that the instructional designer perceives them as an aid, not a hindrance or an extraneous useless requirement.

References

Anderson, J. R., Boyle, C. F., Corbett, A. T., & Lewis, M. W. (1990). Cognitive modeling and intelligent tutoring. *Artificial intelligence*, *42*, 7–49.

Anderson, J. R., Boyle, C. F., Farrell, R., & Reiser, B. J. (1984). Cognitive principles in the design of computer tutors. In *Sixth Annual Conference of the Cognitive Science Society Program* (pp. 2–16).

Bovair, S., Kieras, D. E., & Polson, P. G. (1990). The acquisition and performance of text-editing skill: A cognitive complexity analysis. *Human Computer Interaction, 5,* 1–48.

Card, S. K., Moran, T., & Newell, A. (1983). *The psychology of human computer interaction.* Hillsdale, NJ: Lawrence Erlbaum Associates.

Gagné, R. M. (1968). Learning Hierarchies. *Educational Psychologist, 6,* 1–9.

Glaser, R., & Bassok, M. (1989). Learning theory and the study of instruction. In M. R. Rosenzweig & L. W. Porter (Eds.), *Annual Review of Psychology* (Vol. 40 pp. 631–666). Palo Alto, CA: Annual Reviews, Inc.

Halff, H. M. (1990). *Automating maintenance training.* Arlington, VA: Halff Associates.

Jones, M. K., Li, Z., & Merrill, M. D. (1990). *Knowledge representation for ID₂: Part 2.* Logan, UT: Department of Instructional Technology, Utah State University.

Kieras, D. E. (1988a). Towards a practical GOMS model methodology for user interface design. In M. Helander (Ed.), *Handbook of human-computer interaction* (pp. 135–157). North Holland: Elsevier.

Kieras, D. E. (1988b) What mental model should be taught? Choosing instructional content for complex engineered systems. In J. Psotka, L. D. Massey, & S. A. Mutter (Eds.), *Intelligent tutoring systems: Lessons learned* (pp. 85–111). Hillsdale, NJ: Lawrence Erlbaum Associates.

Kieras, D. E. (1990). The role of cognitive simulation models in the development of advanced training and testing systems. In N. Frederiksen, R. Glaser, A. Lesgold, & M. Shafto (Eds.), *Diagnostic monitoring of skill knowledge acquisition* (pp. 51–74). Hillsdale, NJ: Lawrence Erlbaum Associates.

Kieras, D. E., & Polson, P. G. (1985). An approach to the formal analysis of user complexity. *International Journal of Man-Machine Studies, 22,* 365–394.

Psotka, J., Massey, L. D., & Mutter, S. A. (Eds.) (1988). *Intelligent tutoring systems: Lessons learned.* Hillsdale, NJ: Lawrence Erlbaum Associates, 5–41.

Chapter Nine

Supporting Scenario- and Simulation-Based Instruction: Issues from the Maintenance Domain

Henry M. Halff

In another paper focusing on the problems associated with automating instructional design (this volume, Part II, "Prospects for Automating Instructional Design") a case was made for defining instructional objectives for maintenance training in cognitive terms. In particular, a three-part model of maintenance competence was proposed for use in an initial effort to represent the required characteristics of an automated instructional design system in this domain.

Qualitative Model

The device itself should be represented by a formal, qualitative model. A qualitative model describes the behavior of individual components, that is, how they change in response to changes in input and how their outputs vary according to state. It also describes the behavior of the device as a whole, that is, how the outputs of one device are connected to the inputs of another. These models consist of:

- a collection of components, each with its own device model, and
- the input-output relations among the components.

Inference in these models is accomplished with a qualitative reasoning scheme that infers the effects of changes in some components on the behavior of others. These inferences are derived by propagating changes in outputs of components to the inputs of components connected to those outputs. This scheme, although not providing a general approach to equipment modeling, can deal with a large class of interesting equipments. In essence this model depicts the *device structure.*

Coupled with the device structure is the device function or functional hierarchy which focuses on the various purposes of a device. This hierarchy may span several structural systems for a given function.

Yet another component of a qualitative model is the *imagery,* which includes the appearance (in sight, sound, and other senses) of the equipment, the physical actions that implement observations and repairs, and knowledge of the physical location of systems and subsystems. Direct formal representation of the imaginal aspects of a mental model are well beyond current methods of knowledge representation (see the next chapter, by Friedman). What can be constructed, however, is a systems of tokens that stand for different perceptual chunks (e.g., animated flame representing the ignition of a furnace pilot light).

Of particular importance to maintenance training is the capability to model malfunctioning equipment. Such models are constructed by allowing for fault modes as possible component states.

Fault Trees

The use of fault trees permits one to further bound the problem of creating a first approximation to an on-line instructional design capability for maintenance. Fault-tree based troubleshooting, as the name implies, is based on a hierarchical decomposition of the malfunctioning device. For each node in the tree there is a particular test for the functioning of the corresponding component or module of the equipment. The troubleshooting procedure calls for a depth-first traversal of the fault tree. If a module tests faulty, the submodules of that module are tested. Otherwise the procedure moves to the next module. Once a fault has been isolated to a terminal in the tree (corresponding to a replaceable component), the equipment is repaired by replacing or repairing the component.

Because fault trees do not, in general, cover all possible faults, the procedure can reach an impasse. In particular a module can test faulty and yet all of its submodules can test OK. When this occurs, context-free troubleshooting methods must be used to isolate the fault. It remains an open question as to whether it is possible to develop context-free models for troubleshooting. How robust should one expect a context-free method to be? If automated instructional design is to make inroads in the area of scenarios for troubleshooting, it will be necessary to find a flexible solution to the problem of impasses.

Procedures

Needed to implement fault-tree based troubleshooting are particular procedures for test and for repair. Generally, these procedures will be complex and will invoke subsidiary procedures for operation, disassembly, and other manipulations of the equipment.

These procedures need to represented in a formal scheme, such as GOMS, that can be implemented in the context of the qualitative model. That is, the elementary observations and actions of the procedures must correspond directly to observations and manipulations of the qualitative model. A possible relaxation of this requirement might allow procedures to call for attention-switching actions that would permit the maintainer to take different viewpoints not formally represented in the qualitative reasoning scheme.

In summary, a scenario, for maintenance training as constrained above consists of:

- a qualitative model of some particular equipment,

- a fault tree for that equipment, and

- the test, repair, and subsidiary procedures that support troubleshooting.

Criteria for Scenarios

With the above brief definition in mind, it can now be asked what sorts of scenarios are appropriate at the proof-of-concept stage. Three criteria are suggested as a point of departure.

Representability

As trivial as it may seem, a prime criterion is that a scenario conform to the above definition. In particular such conformity requires a formal representation of all three components of a scenario.

For the fault tree itself, this criterion is not difficult to meet since the tree is noting more than, well, a tree structure. There has to be, however, a commitment to a particular representation scheme for qualitative simulations and for procedures before settling on a specific scenario.

It is critical that the representation schemes adopted at the proof-of-concept stage not be implementation specific. That is, the specification documents need to specify a language for representing qualitative simulations and one for representing procedures. It is vital to make sure that the prototype works by interpreting at least a subset of the scenarios expressible in that language. It would not, therefore, be acceptable to deliver simply an authoring system for qualitative simulations.

This is not to say that implementation considerations should not play a role in the design of representation schemes. Obviously, it will be necessary to develop computer programs that can interpret the representations of equipment and procedures. Specifically, these programs must be able to carry out qualitative reasoning and execute the maintenance procedures in the scenario. The choice of representation schemes will obviously be constrained by how close the programs can come to implementing them.

Also worth mentioning in this regard is the fact that large classes of equipment cannot in principle be represented using qualitative simulation. Feedback, for example, is particularly difficult to simulate since it is, in principle, impossible for a qualitative reasoning scheme to determine the terminal behavior of feedback loops. Thus, many devices with feedback and similar features cannot be considered if the development of an initial prototype is to proceed under simplified conditions.

Feasibility

Even if it is theoretically possible to represent a piece of equipment and its associated maintenance procedures, it may not be feasible to do so for the purposes of a given development project. The representation chosen must be simple enough to make the project manageable for researchers, developers, and students. At the same time, the scenario must be complex enough to exercise all of the instructional functions that will be included in the prototype.

Based on personal experience, the author estimates that the goal of simplicity can be met by limiting the equipment chosen to 100 components and limiting the branching factor to 10; that is, no component would have more that 10 outputs. Fault trees should be limited to at most four levels with at most 10 tests at each level. Naturally, these guidelines are general and preliminary. Finding the right level of instructional complexity would seem to be mainly a matter of ensuring the appropriate variety of procedures. As long as particular candidates for devices are checked for these opportunities, ensuring an appropriate variety of instructional methods would not appear to present a major problem.

Interest

In addition to being feasible, it is important that the equipment chosen for the scenario be of some interest to an actual user community. The prime considerations in this respect are for equipment whose importance is clear to decision makers in the user community and for a training program with sufficient volume to provide a potential field-test site.

Instructional Material and Methods

Halff (see Part II, this volume) proposes certain methods for using computers in maintenance training. The discussion there and here is organized around three aspects of a computer-based instructional system.

Infrastructure

An instructional infrastructure for computer-based maintenance training consists of computational representations of the instructional objectives. In particular, it contains mechanisms that can simulate and describe the equipment under maintenance in both qualitative and physical terms. It also contains mechanisms that can interpret and describe procedures to be learned. In addition, an expert troubleshooting system should be available for teaching troubleshooting as problem solving.

Qualitative and Physical Simulation

Recall that the mental model consists of a qualitative model of device behavior, a description of device function, and a collection of tokens that stand for imaginal (perceptual) aspects of the device. The qualitative model can be implemented in a computer using available qualitative simulation systems such as that described in Towne, Munro, Pizzini, Surmon, Coller, and Wogulis (1990). These systems have the following basic capabilities.

- They can instantiate any qualitative model of the sort described in Halff (Part II).

- They can carry out qualitative reasoning on the model and thereby determine the states and outputs of specified components based on information regarding states and state-changes in the rest of the device.

- They present to the student a graphical depiction of the system being simulated. This depiction does not generally resemble the physical appearance of the system. Rather, it represents components as icons that can be manipulated by the student and whose appearance reflects the states of the corresponding components.

- They provide different views of the system. Presented to the student not just as one view of all components, but rather a collection of views, each showing only the components selected for that view. Some of these views might show the behavior of major subsystems, and thus conform to a structural breakdown. Others, might conform to a functional breakdown in that they show all of the components involved in a particular function.

Constructing a qualitative model of a piece of equipment, then, is a matter of entering the qualitative model of the equipment into a qualitative simulation system, designing the graphical representation of the model, and constructing the views needed for instruction. For troubleshooting training, three types of views are needed.

1. Global subsystem views are needed that present each major subsystem as an independent unit.

2. Schematic views should be constructed to show all of the components involved in the functions and malfunctions selected for troubleshooting.

3. A third type of view conjoins the first two and thereby depicts only the components involved in particular lower level nodes of the fault tree.

Needed to support the imaginal aspects of the model is a physical (as opposed to qualitative) simulation of the equipment. This physical simulation presents to the student, through appropriate media, the sights, sounds, and manipulanda associated with each of the tokens in the imaginal model. These requirements include:

- a simulation of all observations that might be made in the course of troubleshooting;

- a simulation of all actions that might be undertaken in the course of troubleshooting; and

- a simulation of transitions that refocus attention from one component of the equipment to another, including views of major panels and gross changes of view such as descending from the top and moving to the rear of the equipment.

As a development strategy, the team developing instruction should walk through every branch of every troubleshooting procedure, noting the views and manipulations needed to support the procedure. These notes can then form the basis for production of the physical simulation in appropriate media. Naturally, the physical and qualitative simulations should be linked in their implementation so that manipulations of the physical simulation are manifest as state changes in the qualitative simulation, and manipulations in the qualitative simulation are manifest in displays of the physical simulation.

Procedure Interpretation

A second component of the instructional infrastructure is a computational implementation of the procedures needed for, in this case, troubleshooting. Recall that the formalism used for representing these procedures is the fault tree described above. The components of this formalism are:

- a fault tree interpretation schema, represented in GOMS or some similar formalism;

- the fault-tree itself, represented in both procedural and declarative forms; and

- the observation and repair procedures attached to nodes in the fault tree, also represented in GOMS or some other appropriate formalism.

Needed to computerize these formal models are an interpreter that can execute the troubleshooting procedure, appropriate links to the simulation models discussed above, and a means of presenting the structure of the procedures themselves to the student. The first two items pose no particular challenges since interpreters are available for this purpose and since the simulations themselves possess the mechanisms needed to link them to a procedure interpreter.

The third item, the means of presenting the procedure itself to the student, is a critical aspect of the instructional design proposed here. Mechanisms are needed for explicit presentation of each of the three parts of the fault-tree approach. Research on the instructional impact of varied presentation modalities is only beginning to determine the degree to which they moderate the effectiveness of instructional strategies (see Friedman, Part III, this volume). Specifically needed are studies which map particular presentation methods with particular classes of procedures.

Presenting the Fault-Tree Interpretation Schema

Support for navigating the fault-tree interpretation schema should be provided by a display that either indicates the major milestones in the schema or allows the student to indicate these milestones. These milestones include:

- checking the functionality of the component under consideration;

- isolation and repair of a component;

- troubleshooting the subcomponents of a component line; and

- dealing with unsolved cases.

We can distinguish several ways of presenting milestone transitions to students, depending on the level of guidance required.

- In heavily guided practice, the computer should be capable of dictating the next milestone to be reached in the procedure. For example, in the simulation of a fuel pump it has been determined that no fuel is flowing. Each of the potential causes of this problem would be examined in turn.

- In more relaxed guidance, the student should be required to indicate the next milestone. For example, it has just been determined that no fuel is flowing. What should be done next in the fault tree?

- Under even more relaxed guidance, the computer might simply note milestones as they occur and check to ensure that the students' actions are consistent with the schema. For example, it has been determined that no fuel is flowing. You are checking the Starter Air Inlet Duct. Re-examine the fault tree to make sure that this is the next step.

Presenting the Structure of the Fault Tree

As with the interpretation schema, both a declarative and procedural interpretation of the tree itself is needed. The declarative presentation is perhaps best done graphically. As the procedure traverses the tree, the active elements can be highlighted in some way and/or subtrees can be displayed as a means of focusing attention. An example for an aircraft ignition system appears in Figure 9.1.

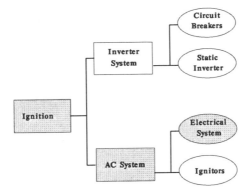

Figure 9.1. Use of Subtree and Highlighting to Focus Attention.

At minimum the procedural aspects of fault tree structure should implement the following functions.

1. Retrieve the procedure for checking the functionality of a component.

2. Retrieve the procedure for repairing a terminal component.

3. Decide whether or not a component is terminal.

4. Retrieve successive subcomponents of a nonterminal component.

A computer implementation of these functions should make their results available to students and should be able to query students about the structure of the tree. In particular, the computer should have the means to

- Inform the student of the procedure needed to check the functionality of any component—for example, "To check for low fuel flow, use the procedure that checks fuel mist in the exhaust."

- Ask the student to designate or execute the procedure needed to check the functionality of a component—for example "Select the procedure for checking the overspeed generator."

- Inform the student of the procedure for repairing any faulted component—for example, "To repair the static inverter, use the procedure for replacing the static inverter."

- Ask the student to designate the procedure for repairing a faulted component—for example, "Select the procedure used to repair the disengaged IGNITION INVERTER circuit breaker."

- Etc.

These functions can, like those listed in the previous section, be used in guided practice to ensure that the student learns how to properly manipulate the fault tree.

Presenting Procedures for Observation and Repair

As instructional objectives, procedures for repair of faulted system components, and procedures for checking the functionality of components should be represented in some formalism such as GOMS. In a computer-based instructional system, these procedures need to be given a declarative, verbal description, such a plain-English paraphrase of the GOMS representation, and a procedural implementation in the qualitative and physical simulations. In this way students can be shown or asked how the procedure unfolds through interactions conducted in verbal terms, in terms of physical actions and observations, or in qualitative, conceptual terms.

The power of these separate presentation schemes is multiplied by joining them together in complete or partial presentations of the entire troubleshooting procedure. As the procedure is presented and practiced, the system or the student can focus on any of five critical aspects of the procedure:

- strategy—the status of the procedure with respect to the fault-tree interpretation schema;

- tactics—the status of the procedure with respect to the fault tree itself;

- stepwise descriptions—the elementary observation and repair procedures;

- conceptual aspects—the theoretical description (in the qualitative model) of the procedure; and

- implementation—the physical actions and observations (in the physical simulation) that implement the procedure.

With the computer implementation suggested above, each of these aspects is viewed as being potentially available for presentation or practice at any point in the procedure.

Problem Solving and Troubleshooting

The concern of this section is for troubleshooting as a problem-solving activity in which the technicians need to discover the appropriate fault isolation strategy. In particular, the literature in this area suggests a problem-solving procedure with three main components:

- context free rules for isolating faults based on topological patterns;

- device-specific rules for troubleshooting based on known symptom-fault associations; and

- procedures for choosing the most information-laden actions at particular choice points.

This problem-solving approach to troubleshooting relies only on connectivity information in the mental model and a set of device-specific observation-action associations. By contrast, the focus of this paper is on troubleshooting *procedures*, in which the isolation strategy is provided through documentation and instruction and need only be implemented by the technician.

Troubleshooting as problem solving is an important aspect of skilled troubleshooting and therefore of maintenance training, even when a large body of troubleshooting procedures is available. In a system of any complexity, no troubleshooting guide offers complete coverage of the possible faults, and seldom will a guide offer procedures for dealing with complex situations such as test-equipment unreliability, multiple interdependent faults, and intermittent faults.

Schemes are available for representing troubleshooting as problem solving (Hunt & Rouse, 1984; Towne, Johnson, & Corwin, 1983), and instructional systems are available for implementing these schemes. Of central concern, however, is the relationship between the fault-tree approach to troubleshooting and problem-solving approaches such as those of Hunt and Rouse (1984) and Towne, Johnson, and Corwin (1983). The fault-tree approach, by sacrificing generality, provides the structure needed to render the troubleshooting process manageable with limited time and cognitive resources. Methods for troubleshooting as problem-solving have greater generality but are expensive in terms of both time and resources. A combination could use the fault-tree procedure in the initial stages and invoke a problem-solving process to deal with cases not covered in the fault tree.

Last-resort faults have been employed as guards against the impasse that might occur if a component malfunctions but each of the tested sub-components functions properly. In addition to guarding the procedure against impasses, these last-resort faults may also play the role of place holders that mark occasions for troubleshooting as problem solving. If so, then the fault tree could be redesigned to eliminate the last-resort faults, and an impasse itself could signal the occasion for invoking a problem-solving process.

The implications of this suggestion for curriculum design are clear. That is, troubleshooting as problem solving should be taught after, and in conjunction with, procedures based on fault trees, and students should be explicitly taught when to enter a problem-solving mode of troubleshooting.

Based on the points made above it appears that troubleshooting as problem solving requires a troubleshooting expert based on the problem-solving methods that students should master to solve particular problems. Two examples of such experts are available, namely, PROFILE (Towne, Johnson, & Corwin, 1983) and the Fuzzy Rule-Based Model of Hunt and Rouse (1984). The former is an almost pure information-theoretic approach that achieves not only efficient troubleshooting but also an impressive match to human troubleshooters. The latter, however, offers more face validity in that it incorporates some of the heuristics known to be used by human troubleshooters.

At present determining the more appropriate model for maintenance training would be an empirical question. Whatever model is used, however, that model should operate within the context of the qualitative simulation described above. It should also be able to start in mid-problem, and in particular, when the fault-tree procedure reaches an impasse. It should also be able to present or explain its choice of each troubleshooting action as problem-solving proceeds.

Instructional Methods

Instructional methods constitute the procedures for engaging the student in instructional interactions. The view of instructional objectives described in Halff (Part II, this volume) proposes that some of these procedures address the acquisition of a mental model of the equipment. Some should address acquisition of procedures. Some should address the problem-solving skills needed for effective troubleshooting.

The foregoing section has provided a powerful set of tools for addressing these goals. To specify the instructional methods completely, these tools need to be configured and assembled into a curriculum. The discussion above suggests that the curriculum for troubleshooting training should be organized around a few major types of activities that reflect advancing levels of knowledge and skill.

System Behavior and Structure

The first level of understanding to be attained by students is that of a mental model of the device. Activities promoting such attainment include exercises with both the qualitative and physical simulations within a framework of the structural breakdown of the device (e.g., an aircraft). Students at this stage will master fundamental qualitative reasoning tasks such as predicting the behavior of individual components and determining the implications certain states of the equipment. Exercises to be used in this phase of the curriculum include the following:

1. **Physical and Conceptual Structure.** Students are shown images of the physical equipment and asked to identify individual components, their function, and their immediate connections.

2. **Causal Reasoning.** Students are given information about all inputs to a component or subsystem and required to predict the state of the component or subsystem, its outputs under normal operating conditions, and its outputs in each possible fault mode.

3. **Functional Reasoning (a).** Students are shown some of the inputs to an element of the device and asked how its other inputs must be set in order to achieve a desired function or state.

4. **Functional Reasoning (b).** Students are shown the actual outputs and inputs to an element and asked to determine whether or not the element is faulted.

5. **Physical and Conceptual Appearance.** Students are asked to discriminate among component states on the basis of some physical depiction of those states.

The exact sequence of these exercises should be designed to reflect and convey the overall structure of the equipment. In the typical case, where the equipment can be hierarchically decomposed, the exercises can traverse this decomposition in a depth-first fashion so that students learn to reason about a subsystem immediately after learning to reason about each of its components.

These exercises should also be implemented with a view to whole-task training. Many if not all of them could be embedded in mini-troubleshooting problems in order to illustrate the application of qualitative reasoning to troubleshooting.

System Function

A second phase of the curriculum should give students an understanding of how components function, or fail to function, together to meet the operational purposes of a device. Put differently, students in this phase should learn:

- what the system and its components are supposed to do;

- how to make the system fulfill those functions; and

- how to determine when the system is not meeting its functions.

Activities at this level are organized around the functional breakdown of a device, illustrated schematically in Figure 9.1. By making this structure evident in instruction, students should be able to induce the basic operations of the system and how its components are involved in those operations.

Activities addressing system function are operational in nature. Some exercises provide guided practice in procedures such as starting the engines in an aircraft. Practice should begin with the qualitative simulation alone, pass to a stage with joint qualitative and physical simulations, and end with the physical simulation alone. Each subphase should begin with demonstration of the procedure followed by practice.

The order of presentation of different procedures in this phase should conform to a depth-first traversal of the functional breakdown, and more importantly to the subgoal structure of the procedures themselves. Specifically, the GOMS representation of each procedure breaks the procedure into small manageable subgoals that can be mastered individually. The curriculum should obviously take advantage of this feature of the representation. A second type of activity in this phase should teach the students the tests or observations needed to check the functionality of each component of the device. Several types of exercises can be used to effect such teaching.

- Students can participate in qualitative reasoning exercises that address the test procedures. Using the domain of jet engine maintenance again, they might be asked to predict the behavior of the Right Fuel/Oxygen Indicator in aircraft that have normal or faulted static inverters.

- Students can practice observational procedures, such as checking fuel flow in the overspeed governor, in the context of testing the system's functionality. Exercises that place the student in an apprenticeship role can be used to implement this strategy.

- Students can be asked to both select and execute test or observational procedures. For example, where a beginning student would practice testing the AC bus by being informed that the test involved checking Pin N in the engine ignition and accessories disconnect plug, more advanced students would practice the same operation by simply being instructed to test the AC bus.

By the end of the second phase of training, students should have many of the component skills of fault-tree based troubleshooting procedures. In particular, they should know how to test any of the device's components and subsystems for normal functioning, and they should have a good idea, based on exposure to functional breakdowns of the device, of the structure of the fault trees to be used in troubleshooting.

Troubleshooting Procedures

In the third phase, students should be introduced to fault-tree interpretation and to the fault trees that define the set of troubleshooting procedures to be learned. The activities that address these topics are described in some detail above in the section titled "Problem-Solving and Troubleshooting."

Arranging these exercises into a curriculum is not a difficult task. The following guidelines seem reasonable in this respect.

- Every malfunction in a fault tree should be covered first in a depth-first traversal of the tree and then in a random order.

- Initial exercises should provide explicit support for use of the fault-tree interpretation schema. This support can be withdrawn after practice with a few malfunctions.

- The first exercises with each malfunction should rely heavily on an explicit representation of the fault tree for the malfunction. This support should be faded with advanced practice.

- Exercises should begin first in the qualitative simulation. As students master the structure of the fault tree, use of the physical simulation can be phased in and support from the qualitative simulation can be faded.

- Documentation that is normally available in the field should be available on-line.

Problem Solving

We have noted above the importance of teaching troubleshooting as a problem-solving activity. It was suggested above that problem-solving activities have a particular place whenever fault-tree methods arrive at an impasse. Although students in the trouble-shooting procedure phase of the curriculum should be protected from such impasses, students ready for this, problem-solving level should be presented with impasses as opportunities to practice problem solving. Halff (Part II) contains proposals for instruction in troubleshooting as problem solving. The following is a list of suggested exercises consistent with that chapter.

1. Troubleshooting. Students are provided with a conceptual simulation containing a single faulted component. At each point in the trouble-shooting exercise, students would choose an action and exhibit the consequences of the action. The exercise could take many forms. For example, students might be prompted to select actions diagnostic of a particular faults or sets of faults. Other forms of troubleshooting practice can be found in Brown, Burton, & de Kleer (1982).

2. Reverse Troubleshooting. Students are told that a particular component is faulted. They are required to predict the results of certain observations based on this information. Causal reasoning patterns can be elicited or exhibited during the course of these exercises.

3. Case Studies. Students could be given real case studies of intractable troubleshooting problems. Computer support could be provided for collaborative problem solving and for peer and expert critiques of proposed solutions.

A typical troubleshooting curriculum might have the following lessons:

1. A set of reverse troubleshooting and troubleshooting problems that cover the major topological patterns found in the device. Each pattern would be addressed first by reverse troubleshooting exercises and then by troubleshooting exercises.

2. A set of reverse troubleshooting and troubleshooting problems that cover the equipment's mission-critical faults and their nearest neighbor. Students would first reverse troubleshoot each major fault and its neighbor and then troubleshoot the pair.

3. A repetition of Lesson 1 without reverse troubleshooting.

4. A repetition of Lesson 2 without reverse troubleshooting.

5. A mixture of Lessons 3 and 4.

Reverse troubleshooting in this curriculum plays the role of a cognitive support which is gradually faded from the curriculum. Other cognitive supports (e.g., external hypothesis lists) should also be withdrawn in the last lesson.

What needs to be added to this description is:

- that these exercises should only be introduced in the context of an impasse in the fault-tree procedure;
- that the exercises should only be introduced when the student has mastered the fault tree for the malfunction; and
- that the exercises should be conducted in the presence of a tutor working the problem under the same set of initial conditions as is the student.

Conclusion

This chapter has posited that training should begin, not with the procedure itself, but rather with instruction oriented to the structure and behavior of the equipment and its components. This initial instruction establishes the students' mental model and can be implemented using qualitative and physical simulations of the equipment.

Training on elementary observation and repair procedures should be introduced in conjunction with instruction on device functionality. This instruction should teach students how the equipment is used, how components operate together to achieve the functions of the equipment, and how to determine when the device or any of its components is not functioning properly.

Training in the use of fault trees should be based on guided practice. Initially the interpretation schema and the trees should be made explicit in the instruction. As students advance this explicit support can be withdrawn.

When students are ready to master troubleshooting as problem solving, practice opportunities should be provided in the context of fault-tree procedures. In particular each problem-solving exercise should begin by driving the fault-tree procedure to an impasse in which a component malfunction cannot be traced to a malfunction in any of its components.

References

Brown, J. S., Burton, R. R., & de Kleer, J. (1982). Pedagogical, natural language and knowledge engineering techniques in SOPHIE I, II, and III. In D. Sleeman & J. S. Brown (Eds.), *Intelligent tutoring systems* (pp. 227-282). London: Academic Press.

Hunt, R. M., & Rouse, W. B. (1984). A fuzzy rule-based model of human problem solving. *IEEE Transactions on Systems, Man, and Cybernetics, SMC-14,* 112–120.

Towne, D. M., Johnson, M. C., & Corwin, W. H. (1983). *A performance-based technique for assessing equipment maintainability* (Tech. Rep. 102). Los Angeles, CA: Behavioral Technology Laboratories, University of Southern California.

Towne, D. M., Munro, A., Pizzini, Q. A., Surmon, D. S., Coller, L. D., & Wogulis, J. L. (1990). Model-building tools for simulation-based training. *Interactive Learning Environments, 1,* 33–50.

Chapter Ten

Designing Graphics to Support Mental Models

Alinda Friedman

Background

Designers of instructional systems (automated or otherwise), as well as designers of courseware, often assume that graphic materials and media almost always play a useful and even necessary role in the development of educational materials, and, by inference, in the acquisition of knowledge and skills. However, in reviewing the educational, psychological, and human factors literatures, there is scant evidence to support this view. This chapter surveys these three literatures, and focuses on data relevant to understanding how and when graphic and other non-text representations can support the acquisition of factual knowledge and procedural skills. It then goes on to describe aspects of the human information processing architecture that need to be taken into account in the selection of any media of instruction; this part of the chapter is based upon principles of cognitive science. Third, a framework for the use of graphics in the development of courseware is presented, using data surveyed as well as the architectural considerations. Several of the modules within this framework could be implemented in an automated instructional design system as "mini-experts." Suggestions for research that would provide the necessary information to implement these experts are proposed throughout this chapter.

Introduction

Graphics and other forms of non-text representations undoubtedly play an important role in the acquisition of factual knowledge and procedural skills. It goes without saying, then, that guidelines for the design of courseware, technical manuals, and other instructional materials should include prescriptions for the use of graphics that maximize the efficiency with which individuals learn the material at hand. These guidelines should prescribe, among other things, (a) when using a graphic is preferable to using text, (b) what sort of graphic representation (realistic, schematic, etc.) is best suited to the particular educational applications and goals, (c) what sort of graphical conventions (e.g., that we read figures from left to right) may be assumed to be known by the targeted student population, and (d) when it is desirable for a graphic to be redundant with text information and when it is desirable for the graphic to supplement the text. Some of these prescriptions will be specific to a particular content area (e.g., in teaching chemistry, some notational schemes are more useful than others), whereas others will generalize across content areas.

In developing an automated instructional design system, such as AIDA, the principles underlying the role of graphics in knowledge and skill acquisition must be incorporated into the system. The system should allow subject-matter experts, who may not necessarily be aware of the educational and psychological issues underlying the role of graphics in learning, to make the most efficacious use of graphics in the courseware they develop. In addition, a system for automating the selection of graphics for courseware must be designed to be able to dovetail with those parts of the system in which the course modules themselves are developed. In the theoretical framework outlined in the second section of this chapter, several of the components (e.g., the information parser, the representation analyzer) could be developed as ''mini-experts'' and incorporated into a larger system. These ''mini-experts'' can be construed as ''graphics technologists'' for the system as a whole. However, as will be seen, there exist sufficient gaps in our knowledge about the role of graphics in the learning process that much research is required before such ''mini-experts'' will be able to inform the courseware development process. Some suggestions for the areas in which research is required are given throughout the discussion.

That educators believe graphics are important for learning is evident from the fact that pictures, graphs, diagrams, symbols, and other non-text information is found in all levels of instructional materials, from first-grade readers to senior- and graduate-level university course materials; the inclusion of graphics in these materials is obviously intended to facilitate learning. Pictorial representations are also ubiquitous in training manuals, consumer products, assembly instructions, and the like; businesses that devise or use such materials operate under the implicit or explicit assumption that it is easier to understand, follow, or remember information that is presented this way. In addition, more and more information in the media available to the lay public is being presented in graphic form, and is meant to be combined with nonredundant information from text, the assumption being that the intended information and the appropriate inferences are acquired as a matter of course.

Despite the widespread use of non-text representations, however, the psychological literature about how adults acquire knowledge and make inferences from graphics is sparse, as are data about how people integrate nonredundant text and non-text information and whether their ability to do so interacts with their level of literacy or their expertise within a specialized domain. For example, comparisons of novice and expert physics problem-solvers indicate that the use of graphics to present problem information to novices might be contraindicated because the graphics draw attention to superficial problem features (Larkin, McDermott, Simon, & Simon, 1980). Yet, most guidelines for constructing non-text learning materials are based on the largely intuitive (and uncritical) assumptions that (a) pictures are good, (b) more pictures are better, and (c) realistic pictures are best of all (e.g., Dwyer, 1972; see Friedman, 1979; Holliday, 1973; and Moore & Nawrocki, 1978, for review).

There is also a lack of research about which aspects of non-text representations best convey different types of information; little is known about the kinds of graphical conventions implicit in many representations (e.g., that we read diagrams from top to bottom and left to right; that size can convey relative quantity; that physical contiguity often implies temporal contiguity); nor is there much information about how these conventions are acquired or best employed in the construction of learning materials. Related to this issue is the fact that there are few empirically-based guidelines about how best to convey different substantive categories of information using graphics. For example, to convey that DNA is structured like a double helix, with two sets of complementary base pairs that separate to form templates for daughter strands, one must convey information about appearances, states and state changes, structures, functions, processes, etc. To do this successfully requires a principled means of choosing one or another portrayal method as being better suited to a particular application. This, in turn, will likely require shifting the research emphasis from concerns about the specific physical characteristics of a particular graphic media (e.g., color or monochrome; drawings vs. slides; large vs. small format) to the type of information that needs to be conveyed and the known (or to be learned) conventions available to portray that type of information.

In the first section of this chapter, I survey the psychological, educational, and human factors literatures relevant to understanding how non-text representations can support the acquisition of factual knowledge and procedural skills. In surveying these literatures, several things became dismayingly apparent. First, for the most part, these are three distinct literatures with different (though occasionally overlapping) sets of emphases, methods, empirical constraints, applied concerns, subject populations, theoretical objectives, and so on. These and other differences render cross-literature comparisons difficult. Second, common to all three literatures is an adherence to the almost uncritical assumption that graphics are better, whether for memory and learning (psychology), conceptual understanding and motivation (education), or ergonomic considerations (human factors). Moore and Nawrocki (1978) discuss several reasons often cited for an adherence to this assumption, including the beliefs that pictures are effective because (a) they are easier to perceive than verbal stimuli, (b) they can be realistic (the assumption here being that learning should be somehow proportional to degree of "pictorial fidelity"), (c) pictures can decrease memory load (or increase "channel capacity") by providing redundant codes, (d) individual differences in spatial ability are important, so some students will profit from pictorial materials and others will not, and (e) students are more motivated to learn from pictorial materials.

In the present review, it will become apparent that almost all of these reasons are too broadly stated and all can be questioned on empirical grounds. For example, although iconic or pictorial materials might produce better speed and accuracy than verbal materials for some tasks (e.g., perceptual vs. memorial comparisons, Moyer & Bayer, 1976; speeded inferences, Friedman & Bourne, 1976), there are clearly other tasks (e.g., naming words vs. objects, Potter & Falconer, 1975 [see Snodgrass, 1980]) for which verbal stimuli produce superior performance. Indeed, in picture naming tasks, variables such as the frequency in print of the pictures' names have been shown to influence performance (Oldfield & Wingfield, 1965). Similarly, although individual differences in spatial ability should be important *a priori* in some educational contexts (e.g., solid geometry), they certainly might not be in others, including contexts in which pictures have been shown to facilitate performance (e.g., learning how to identify and classify dinosaurs, Winn, 1982). The main objectives of this chapter are as follows:

(a) to determine the general conditions under which graphics are an effective educational tool;

(b) to specify which types of graphics (e.g., line drawings, grey-scale images, photographs, etc.) facilitate learning in particular knowledge and skill domains; and

(c) to develop a theoretical framework that provides guidelines for the use of graphics in the development of courseware that incorporates the information from the first two objectives.

Limitations of Current Research

All three of the literatures reviewed have limitations. In the psychological literature, the main emphasis has been on how graphical information is perceived and remembered, rather than on how different types of graphics convey different types of information more or less efficiently, or how graphics can be used to best represent information about a particular subject domain, or indeed, what information should be represented to achieve certain educational goals. Thus, the main limitation on the usefulness of this literature can be characterized by the fact that people investigate, for example, how, whether, or why picture memory is better than verbal memory, but not how, whether, or why pictures should be used in the service of learning a particular topic or type of information.

A second limitation in the psychological literature is that the current emphasis is on trying to characterize knowledge and process differences between novices and experts in a variety of domains, and not necessarily on how expertise is best acquired. Thus, the direct educational implications of such work are often missing. Finally, the research emphasis has been almost entirely placed on the psychological differences that may exist between pictorial representations and other representations, such as text. Comparisons among different types of graphic representations (e.g., photos vs. line drawings) are relatively rare.

Research in education has also focused rather heavily on picture-text differences and physical variables (e.g., large vs. small displays), to the virtual exclusion of such psychologically relevant factors as differences in the type of information to be learned, the interaction between acquisition and testing media, how to determine equivalencies in information content across media, etc. In addition, variations in the subject matter tested, the learners' characteristics, the stimulus variables manipulated, the type of test given, the educational objectives of the research, and many other factors make it exceptionally difficult to make comparisons across studies in this literature, or, indeed, to generalize at all.

As might be anticipated, in the human factors literature the emphasis has been on the principally ergonomic implications of using different display media. In addition, much of the literature is focused on extremely specific applications. Perhaps most dismaying is the tendency to make recommendations in the absence of empirical evidence. Again, this reflects an inherent assumption that the more graphics there are, the more ergonomically sound will be the application. There are a few enlightening exceptions here, though, which will be taken up in turn.

Despite these caveats, each of these literatures has contributed to understanding the role that graphical information plays in acquiring new knowledge and skills. Each has also contributed to the development of the theoretical framework to be presented. In the section that follows, I discuss constraints imposed by the human information processing system architecture and the implications these have for acquiring information from graphic and other media. In particular, I discuss the implications of (a) working memory (WM) capacity limits, (b) the manner in which information is organized and represented in long-term memory (LTM), and (c) the potential existence of qualitatively different types of processing resources. Within each section, a few selected studies in which learning from different types of graphic media was specifically investigated will be discussed, where possible. The section will close with a section on theoretical and methodological issues that preclude making strong generalizations at this point, as well as with recommendations for future research.

System Architecture

Views regarding the architecture of the human information processing system have changed considerably over the last two decades. Nevertheless, there are three enduring aspects of the system that are relevant to the role of graphics in education:

Limits on WM capacity have implications for the use of graphics as organizational aids for memory and problem solving, and also bears on issues of stimulus complexity and the highlighting of information through the use of color or other means. The hierarchical organization of LTM has implications for the perception and comprehension of graphic displays, and LTM representational differences between text and graphics have implications for the attainment of expertise through the use of analogy and metaphor. Finally, the existence of different types of processing resources has implications for the relative efficacy of providing information presented in different media, or to different modalities.

Working memory. Chase and Simon (1973) showed that chess experts can remember about the same number of randomly placed chess pieces as can novices, illustrating that the source of expertise does not rest with differences between novices and experts in some innate or acquired WM capacity. Rather, at least one source of expertise lies in the fact that experts have a vast amount of information stored in LTM about legal configurations of chess pieces; when they view a board that is structured legally with respect to the rules of chess, they can "parse" it into chunks based on these configurations. They then merely need to retrieve the configurations, and generate the pieces that comprise them, at recall. The novice, or course, has no recourse to this strategy. These findings have now been replicated in many domains of expertise, ranging from other types of games (e.g., GO;

Reitman, 1976) to more "real-world" situations, such as recall of maps depicting tactical battlefield situations represented by graphical symbols (e.g., Badre, 1982).

There are several implications that the relationship between WM capacity and expertise has for the effectiveness of graphics in problem-solving and learning. To the extent that a graphic representation of a problem facilitates chunking, it should lessen the burden on WM and facilitate problem-solving in domains for which WM limitations directly constrain solution speed or accuracy (i.e., most real-world situations). For example, Schwartz and Fattaleh (1972) found that when subjects were given deductive reasoning problems in two-dimensional arrays, they solved the problems faster than when the problems were presented in prose form.

A second implication of the relationship between WM capacity and expertise has to do with information acquisition and decision-making. It is not sufficient merely to present to-be-learned information in arbitrary chunks; it is necessary that the chunks be meaningful. For example, Bower and Springston (1970) gave subjects auditory lists of letters to repeat back; identical sequences of letters were chunked into either arbitrary (e.g., IB MPH DFB IX) or meaningful (e.g., IBM PHD FBI X) groupings. Although there were the same sequence and number of letters and the same number of chunks in each case, the meaningful groupings produced much better performance.

Moreover, there is evidence that units of information are best presented in a familiar sequence. For example, Badre (1982) tested the recall of subjects who were experts in tactical decision-making by presenting either meaningfully chunked information in a meaningful sequence, or in the reverse of the meaningful sequence, or nonmeaningful chunks presented in an arbitrary sequence, or all of the information at once. He found that the correct sequence was recalled better than the same sequence in reverse order, which was no different than recall of nonmeaningful chunks. Importantly, recall in the group who received the correct sequence did not differ from that of the group who received all the information on the same screen. Thus, if graphics can be used as aids to chunking information, then they may prove additionally useful if the chunked information can be presented in meaningful, familiar sequences.

These examples illustrate the importance of taking the level of expertise of the subjects as well as the semantics of the stimulus displays into account when investigating manipulations that allegedly make a display more comprehensible. Many investigations of physical variables, such as color coding and stimulus complexity, fail to do this. For example, Knapp, Moses, and Gellman (1982) investigated the effect of display complexity on comprehension. They recognized that complex displays might prove burdensome because of WM limitations, among other things, and recommended several guidelines for highlighting information to make displays easier to comprehend. One such suggestion was that a complex display should be segmented to show one segment at a time. However, Knapp *et al.* (1982) suggested segmenting the displays using a grid; it is likely that a grid might cross an expert's chunk boundary and actually interfere with comprehension. A better approach would be to segment the display into chunks that were based upon units of information that were meaningful according to some criteria of expertise.

All three literatures under review suggest that under many circumstances, "less is better," which has implications for the role of complexity in graphical and mixed-mode media presentations. For example, Borg and Schuller (1979) showed that subjects who were learning the names and locations of parts of a relatively complex object did better when the inner details of those parts were omitted from the stimulus than they did with a photograph of the actual object. Similarly, Dwyer (1972) found that either simple line drawings or oral instructions alone were more effective than realistic graphics (e.g., shaded drawings and photographs) on tests of drawing, identification, terminology, and comprehension in the domain of heart physiology (his results are quite a bit more complex than this and should be examined in detail). Other investigators have found that less complex stimulus materials lead to equal or better learning than more complex versions of the "same" subject matter (e.g., Moore, Nawrocki, & Simutis, 1979), and at least some of these findings are likely to be reflecting WM capacity limitations. There are also studies showing that less complex stimuli are easier to identify from brief presentations than are more complex stimuli (e.g., Ryan & Schwartz, 1956). Thus, it may be that for many applications in which designers have striven for increased veracity of detail in their graphics, exactly the opposite approach is warranted.

On the other hand, there certainly may be some circumstances (e.g., learning a difficult discrimination) in which a complex display is not only warranted, but is necessary. An example of such a circumstance may be found in the work of Marcel and Barnard (1979). They showed subjects pictographic sequences of various actions and the states that would result from those actions, using an experimental apparatus that actually paralleled the actions and states of a pay telephone. The pictured instructions could show either the part of the apparatus that was relevant to each particular step in the sequence, or else it could show the entire (more complex) apparatus at each step. Subjects who received only relevant part information produced poorer verbal descriptions of what the instructions meant and also performed the task more poorly than subjects who received pictures of the entire apparatus. One possible explanation for this finding is that Marcel and Barnard (1979) did not parse their graphics properly, so that their "part" information did not include information necessary to place the parts in context. A more interesting possibility is that Marcel and Barnard's subjects were novices trying to learn a procedural sequence, whereas, for example, Badre's (1982) tacticians, whose performance did not suffer from their having received partial information sequentially, were experts trying to integrate declarative information over time.

Related to the issue of stimulus complexity is the issue of whether using color in displays can contribute to their perceptibility or comprehensibility (Dwyer, 1975; El-Gazzar, 1984; Lamberski & Dwyer, 1983; Luder & Barber, 1984; Reid & Miller, 1980; Stone, 1983). For example, Reid and Miller (1980) had children write descriptions of the subject matter of either monochrome or colored photographs of biological subjects. They found both positive and negative effects of color, and both were due to what they believe is the ability of color to act as a distractor. The positive effects were that color displays yielded less of a tendency to merely name (identify) objects or their parts, which has been interpreted as a less optimal outcome than an actual description. The main disadvantage of the addition of color to the stimuli was that it tended to distract subjects towards describing features that were less biologically significant. It should be noted, however, that the photographs used by Reid and Miller (1980) were of the objects in their "natural" state; that is, they represented appearance information rather than assisting chunking. In principle, color coding might be used to highlight parts of displays that are significant, thus possibly reducing the amount of attention or capacity that might be required to extract this information from a display.

An example of this principle can be found in the results of Luder and Barber (1984), who investigated the effectiveness of redundant color coding in search vs. identification tasks. Redundant color coding refers to the situation in which color is perfectly correlated with some other physical cue (e.g., shape). Luder and Barber (1984) had subjects perform a continuous compensatory tracking task while periodically making judgments about the state of valves in a fuel system. Identification judgments involved questions like "valves 2 and 6 are closed," whereas search judgments involved questions like "there are three valves open." The valves could be in three states (open = green, closed = blue, emergency = red). It should be noted that these color choices are nonarbitrary. It should also be noted that identification of state information (e.g., open) is a subset of the search task.

Luder and Barber (1984) found that identification was faster than search in the monochrome conditions, whereas the reverse was true in the color conditions. Essentially, since the locations of the valves were fixed, redundant color coding offered no advantage over either shape or location for purposes of identifying the valves or their states; however, color did provide substantial gains when subjects had to search for information across the entire display. This is an illustration of the principle that the effectiveness of a particular type of graphic variable will be highly sensitive to the task demands. In addition, the color group performed the tracking task more accurately than the monochrome group in both search and identification conditions. This could be interpreted as meaning that redundant color coding enabled some capacity (or resources) to be freed for use on the tracking task.

In the framework developed below, general questions such as "when is it better (for learning or comprehension) to use color graphics as opposed to black and white graphics?" are seen as typically inappropriate. Instead, it will be necessary to determine, for example, what the WM requirements of a given task environment are, whether the information to be learned lends itself to chunking, and if so, what are the appropriate chunks to use for the targeted student population. It is only at this juncture that it makes sense to develop instructional materials, via color coding or other means (e.g., highlighting), to try to determine which of several methods facilitates chunking of displays in learners at various levels of expertise. The knowledge gained by this sort of research could be incorporated into a "mini-expert" that would enable courseware developers to use graphics appropriate to how the material to be learned was to be chunked.

To summarize, WM capacity limitations imply that the efficiency of any media for both learning and problem solving will vary as a function of how well-suited or sensitive that media is for transmitting information in chunks or configurations. For instance, unretouched photographs require the viewer to perform all of the chunking operations, whereas photos with irrelevant areas masked out, or with lines drawn around what is to be considered a chunk alleviate this operation. Conversely, any media representation that obscures or otherwise precludes such chunking should interfere with efficient learning and problem solving. It should be noted, however, that in this approach, to test relative efficiency for performance across or within media requires knowing how the information to be transmitted should be parsed into chunks for any given domain and achieved or desired level of expertise. There is a notable absence of research on this issue, although the methodology for determining how an individual has chunked a particular display is reasonably well-established (see Badre, 1982; and Chase & Simon, 1973 for examples).

Long-term memory. Research on the perception, comprehension, and memory of pictorial material has been intimately related to issues concerning the representation of knowledge. Although no single theory of LTM representation has been accepted as clearly preferable to its competitors, some general principles have emerged. Those relevant to the role of graphics in education include the fact that knowledge in LTM is organized, that the organization is hierarchical, and that there are different types of knowledge represented in LTM.

At least three types of LTM knowledge are potentially relevant to studying the role of graphic and pictorial information in acquiring new factual knowledge and procedural skills: General world knowledge (e.g., Friedman, 1979), domain-specific knowledge (e.g., Hegarty, Just, & Morrison, 1988), and knowledge about graphic conventions that are either domain-specific or not (e.g., Winn, 1982). I will discuss each of these in turn.

Most memory theorists have agreed that there are abstract structures within LTM that represent everyday knowledge about the real world. The term "schema" is often used to refer to these knowledge structures (see Polson, Part I). A schema is a data structure that represents those properties, objects, actions, events, roles, and so on, that are most commonly encountered in a particular instantiation of the schema. The schema for an object, for example, might represent typically encountered visual properties and relations among parts, or it might "point to" procedures that can be used to detect such properties and relations. An object schema might also represent what the object does, where we are likely to find it, and how we can interact with it.

Thus, there are constraints on schema variables that define the range of values it is most likely to have. We know about likelihoods, ranges, and distributions of properties, objects, and events; indeed, this is typically what is referred to as world knowledge. This knowledge is structured hierarchically, and plays an important role in perception, comprehension, and memory of both linguistic and pictorial information.

Both the organizational properties of LTM and the default knowledge represented therein will influence the acquisition of new material. It has been known for a long time that comprehension and memory are both facilitated when new information can be readily organized and assimilated into extant knowledge structures, but the primary evidence for this has come from studies in which information is to be acquired from text (e.g., Haviland & Clark, 1974). That this assertion is true about information presented graphically can be illustrated in several ways. At the perceptual level, Biederman, Glass, and Stacy (1973) had subjects identify target objects in briefly presented scenes that were either coherent or jumbled . This manipulation preserved the amount of "physical" information in the pictures (e.g., contours, brightness changes, etc.) while destroying the semantic relationships among the objects. This means that a high-level schema could not be used to aid identification of the objects. In one study, Biederman *et al.* (1973) found that even when subjects knew what to look for (i.e., they had been shown the piece with the target object in advance of the slide) as well as where to look, they were still more accurate with the coherent displays than with the jumbled displays.

In a similar vein, Mandler and Johnson (1976) have shown that subjects remember more about black and white line drawings that are coherently arranged (according to some schema) than they do when given drawings of the identical objects arranged haphazardly. Their results are especially noteworthy because their drawings contained relatively few objects (e.g., 6-8) that were not too detailed, and according to some accounts of visual LTM (e.g., Shepard, 1967) subjects might have been expected to remember them rather well, regardless of how they were arranged.

A final example of how organizing new information makes it more comprehensible and memorable comes from the work of Bransford and Johnson (1973). They showed that prose passages that were virtually impossible to comprehend, let alone remember, could be rendered easy and memorable through the addition of advance information that supplied some necessary contextual and organizational support (see Mayer, 1979, for a review of the role of advance organizers in learning). They were able to demonstrate these effects by providing a title for some of the passages, and for others, by providing a picture that "set the scene" for the actions that were described in the passage (unfortunately, they never compared the two methods directly). In summary, the more that a graphical display can be made to correspond to or take advantage of the way in which information is organized in LTM, the better will the information in that display be apprehended and remembered.

In addition to the role played by the organization of LTM, there are three broad classes of LTM expectations, or world knowledge, that are relevant to the role of graphics in education. The first, of course, is the "everyday" type of knowledge just discussed. Expectations about the world govern what people look at in a picture (Loftus, 1972), how long it takes them to recognize what they see (Friedman, 1979), and the duration of subsequent fixations to the same objects (Friedman & Liebelt, 1981). More generally, when schemas guide perception (as they do in most real world situations), then objects in the environment that correspond to "slots" in an activated schema could be perceived and comprehended relatively automatically. In contrast, without context, or in an unusual context, object identification usually requires more visual details (Friedman, 1979; Palmer, 1975).

One implication of this approach is that people should take less time to identify expected objects than unexpected objects. This should hold for objects in the environment as well as objects depicted graphically. This conjecture has been supported by eye fixation data recorded from subjects who viewed shaded line drawings depicting common scenes and places. First fixations to expected objects were half as long as first fixations to unexpected objects (Friedman, 1979). Since all objects had roughly equivalent amounts of detail, subjects either processed such details more quickly when identifying expected objects, or, more likely, such details were unnecessary for identifying expected objects in context. The latter interpretation was supported by recognition memory data. Subjects virtually never noticed changes made to the details of expected objects whereas they often noticed changes of details to the unexpected objects. Indeed, changes of details to unexpected objects were noticed more often than when expected objects were deleted altogether.

These findings indicate that the expected portion of a stimulus might be stored as an instance of the particular global schema it instantiates, without regard to specific episodic (occurrence) or descriptive details, since it is not normally useful to take note of such already expected information. Thus, in an educational context, it may be unnecessary, or even detrimental in certain circumstances, to present graphical stimuli that are rich in detail, especially when that detail is only for the purpose of embellishment.

A case in point can be found in the education literature about what is learned from a text that either is or is not accompanied by illustrations. Some authors find that graphics facilitate written or oral text comprehension and memory (e.g., Holliday, 1975; Lesgold, Levin, Shimron, & Guttman, 1975; Pressley, Levin, Pigotte, LeCompte, & Hope, 1983; Rigney & Lutz, 1976; Royer & Cable, 1976; Ruch & Levin, 1977) and others find that they do not (Alesandrini & Rigney, 1981; Edyburn, 1982; King, 1975; Lang & Soloman, 1979; Rohwer & Harris, 1975). Haring and Fry (1979) claimed that previous studies were in disagreement because the subjects were different ages, the picture manipulations ranged from one relevant picture per passage that either was specific or general to 37 pictures per passage, the texts varied in difficulty and type (e.g., whether they were narrative or expository), and the measures of comprehension varied from multiple choice to free recall. Using fourth- and sixth-grade subjects, they demonstrated that additional details in a picture do not facilitate text comprehension if those details are at a "low level." In the present context, the details they refer to are those that embellish expected items.

The second class of expectations that are relevant to the role of graphics in education is knowledge about the substantive domain to be learned or about domains that are analogous to it. We have already seen, for example, how the amount of information that is acquired from a display is related to the amount of information that can be chunked and held in WM. This in turn, is a positive function of the amount of prior knowledge that the observer has about the domain being displayed and how that information is organized.

Educators take advantage of this principle by exploiting analogies between an already known domain and a to-be-learned domain. Of interest for the role of graphics in these efforts is a study by Royer and Cable (1976). They were investigating the role of transfer in learning from prose passages and were trying to establish whether illustrations and physical analogies could facilitate transfer. They conjectured that transfer between two passages would require that the first passage somehow be able to establish a "knowledge bridge" to the second. They had college-age subjects read an abstract passage about the internal structure of metals and electroconductivity after reading either an irrelevant (control) passage, another abstract passage about electroconductivity, a passage about the topic that used concrete physical referents, a passage that was abstract but that used analogies to known concepts, or the same abstract passage accompanied by line drawings showing the structural relationships being referred to. The latter three manipulations all improved performance relative to the control group and to the abstract passage, and they did not differ from each other. Thus, it was the concreteness per se that facilitated transfer—whether by physical referent, by analogy, or by illustration. This study is important because it illustrates that it is sometimes not the use of graphics per se, but rather, a property of graphics (such as concreteness) shared by other media that has benefitted performance. The exact componential aspect of a graphic manipulation that has helped (or hindered) performance has been rarely researched or discussed.

The third class of LTM knowledge that is relevant to the communicative effectiveness of graphics in education is knowledge about graphical conventions (e.g., the use of lines streaming away from a figure to indicate motion; the assumption that we will read a table from left to right, top to bottom; the assumption that occlusion will be interpreted as a depth cue in a line drawing, etc.). That is, in the text comprehension literature a distinction has been made between the knowledge needed to comprehend the events that occur in a story and the knowledge we have about how stories are typically structured (e.g., that a story consists of a setting and episodes; that episodes consist of conflicts and resolutions, etc.; Mandler & Johnson, 1977). A similar distinction can be made for graphical stimuli: a graphic will normally attempt to convey some substantive information, and it will do so using a "grammar" and "syntax" which are assumed to be shared between the designer of the graphic and the targeted observer. This is clearly an area that lends itself to automatization in the development of courseware; in the theoretical framework proposed below, for example, it is the task of the information parser to determine, for a given course module, which graphical conventions can be assumed to be known, and which are novel. When novel conventions are required, the system might suggest to the courseware developer that a submodule be created.

Although there are certainly substantive domains in which information is principally graphic and in which it is obvious that there are conventions that need to be learned before comprehension is easy or even possible (e.g., map reading, Potash, 1977; radiography, Carmody, 1985; aerial photography, Way, 1973, cited in Perkins, 1980), for most of the domains we are concerned with here, it is not even clear whether graphics are an appropriate means to convey information, let alone which graphical conventions might or might not be appropriate for doing so.

There has not been much systematic research conducted on the relative comprehensibility of various graphical conventions for conveying different kinds of information. Evidence that there are such conventions, and that certain experiences (or training) might be necessary to perceive accurately things that are normally encountered in three dimensions when they are pictured in two dimensions comes from the cross-cultural literature on picture perception (see Pick & Pick, 1978, for a review). Although interpreting cultural differences in picture perception is difficult, in the present context, the etiology of such differences is far less important than the fact that they exist at all. Their existence underscores the importance of not presuming that the conventions implicit in a particular method of depicting information will be known to the audience for which that graphic is intended.

An almost poignant, though revealing, example of the importance of this principle comes from a study by Lang and Soloman (1979), who investigated whether pictures would facilitate the process of learning to read common nouns. In one study, only children who had been told that the pictures were representations of the objects named by the words showed improved performance. Thus, at least for young children, it cannot even be assumed that they understand the conventional use of proximity (and simultaneity in time) to indicate that two things should be taken as having the same referent.

In another example of the role that learned graphic conventions play in acquiring new knowledge, Winn (1982) investigated several means by which diagrams could be structured to convey different types of information. His grade nine subjects were to learn to identify dinosaurs as well as to learn their correct sequence of evolution. All subjects received flow diagrams with dinosaur names; half the subjects saw pictures of the dinosaurs above their names. In addition, for half of each of these groups, the flow diagram presented the dinosaurs in the "canonical" (conventional) left-to-right, top-to-bottom order, whereas the other half received the flow diagrams in the reverse of this "expected" sequence. Winn (1982) found that the conventional order produced better performance on the test of evolutionary sequence than the reverse order, but only for subjects who had received pictures in addition to names. This result is reminiscent of the Badre (1982) findings described earlier. Both findings are especially interesting because they illustrate how entrenched a convention can become; in principle, a reverse order has identical sequence information as a non-reversed order, yet they are clearly psychologically different.

That graphic conventions are not automatically comprehended, and that such comprehension is necessary for certain types of learning is nicely demonstrated in an experiment by Brooks (1977). She showed second, sixth, and ninth graders 18 black and white line drawings that each contained two normally inanimate objects, one of which was drawn with arms and legs. The objects were shown engaged in interactive relationships, and half the subjects saw the pictures with "action lines," such as vertical lines drawn above an object to indicate that it is falling. It should be noted that, though action lines are not entirely arbitrary (for example, vertical lines are not used to indicate horizontal or diagonal motion), they are nevertheless relatively arbitrary conventions used to depict the direction and amplitude of motion. Brooks' (1977) rationale for the manipulation was that action lines could be used as clues to the interactions between objects if, and only if, subjects understand this particular convention. Thus, older children, who presumably had more experience with comics and cartoons, would benefit from the action lines more than younger children. She found that action lines only facilitated recall for the ninth grade subjects.

Action lines represent an example of a pictorial convention that is acquired relatively late, so that their use as a mechanism to improve the "readability" of a graphic needs to be constrained by this fact. Indeed, several conclusions that may be reached from this literature are that (a) different pictorial devices or conventions need to be explicitly identified, (b) different pictorial conventions need to be scaled along a dimension of "readability," (c) this scale may differ according to the skills and experience of the observers (Perkins, 1980), and (d) the conventions that might be particular to a given subject matter domain might need to be explicitly taught, much as a mathematical notation is taught prior to (or at least simultaneously with) its use in a proof. Each of these conclusions could easily serve as a focus of future research.

To summarize, the organization of LTM and its representation of world knowledge, special domain knowledge, and knowledge of graphic conventions will clearly have a profound influence on perceptibility, comprehensibility and memorability, both inside and outside of a formal educational context. Thus, media representations that exploit this organization, that take advantage of conventions and default knowledge to make analogies between what is known and what is to become known should facilitate learning.

Processing resources. Until 1979, most accounts of the architecture of the human information processing system assumed that the processes that took place within the system all drew on the same general pool of processing resources (e.g., Kahneman, 1973; Norman & Bobrow, 1975). Then, Navon and Gopher (1979) wrote a seminal article in which they proposed that the human information processing system probably has access to several qualitatively different types of resources, each of which was limited in amount. Processes that required the same type of resource to execute, when performed together, would have to compete for that particular resource, with the possibility that there would not be enough for all competitors and hence there might be a decline in performance relative to a noncompetitive situation. In contrast, processes that required qualitatively different resources might be able to be executed concurrently with no loss of either efficiency or accuracy.

Navon and Gopher (1979) did not specify what the qualitative properties of different resource pools might be, and indeed, their model is somewhat intractable because it has no mechanism for the *a priori* specification of which types of resources will be required to perform a particular task. In part as an effort to address this problem, both Friedman and Polson (1981) and Wickens (1984) have proposed multiple resource models in which the nature and number of resource pools have been specified. In Friedman and Polson's (1981) model, two independent resource pools are assumed to exist that are each associated with a particular cerebral hemisphere. In Wickens' (1984) model, separate resource pools are hypothesized to exist for information input to different modalities (e.g., auditory vs. visual), for different types of stimulus codes (e.g., verbal vs. visuospatial), and for different stages of processing (e.g., early vs. late).

These approaches are relevant to the role of graphics in education because two longstanding hypotheses in the education literature regarding why the addition of graphics to a text or aural presentation should facilitate information acquisition are that (a) learning is facilitated when stimuli are input to different "channels," which usually is interpreted to mean different modalities, and (b) learning is facilitated when, either because of input to different modalities or because stimuli are of qualitatively different types (e.g., pictures and text), their processing results in more than one code. Both hypotheses are typically tested by augmenting a verbal passage (presented either aurally or visually) with some sort of graphic stimuli (e.g., Nugent, 1982; Pressley, Levin, Pigott, LeCompte, & Hope, 1983; Rohwer & Harris, 1975). From a multiple-resources view, processing stimuli in different modalities or of different types might indeed imply that different types of resources are necessary. The question is whether this is beneficial or not.

Just as the issue of redundancy of codes has been relevant to the literature concerned with the relative merits of color vs. monochrome displays, the costs and benefits of redundancy is an issue in the "multimedia" literature. It should be noted that there can be several types of redundancy, which are often confused. In the "pure" cases, there can be redundancy of input channel, as when pictures and text are presented visually, or redundancy of code, as when the same text is presented aurally and visually.

There can also be hybrids, as when aurally presented verbal material is supplemented by pictures. An example of the latter is a study by Pressley *et al.* (1983). They read aloud lists of concrete sentences to second and third graders. The sentences were either presented by themselves, or with pictures that matched their content. They found that the matching condition produced better recall than either of the other conditions, which did not differ from each other. Thus, Pressley *et al.* (1983) confirmed that pictures that are redundant with the semantic content of a sentence facilitate memory for that content. However, they had no real control over the degree of mismatch; indeed, some of the mismatched pictures directly contradicted the sentences they were shown with. This illustrates an important issue in this literature: How is one to know, either across or even within-media, what meaning is afforded by each instance of a given concept?

Rohwer and Harris (1975) also investigated the effects of presenting information in different modalities and media, and their study is notable because they used single-media control groups. They presented high and low socioeconomic status (SES) fourth-graders with three expository prose passages. In the single-medium versions, the passages were either presented with a tape recorder, or printed versions were presented via slides of the text of the passage, or picture versions were presented that consisted of 10 pictures per passage. In multimedia presentations, all possible combinations of media pairs were presented, as well as a condition in which the information was presented in all three media simultaneously. It should be noted that each passage contrasted two related concepts (e.g., two types of monkeys) on each of five attributes (e.g., type of tail), so that the correspondence between the semantic content of the passage and its pictures was made more feasible.

Although the results of their study were complex, the main findings were that, for single-media, either oral or printed presentations produced better performance that the picture presentation. For combined media, although the outcome depended a bit on the SES of the subjects, both the oral plus picture and the print plus picture presentations produced better performance than the oral plus print conditions. Rohwer and Harris (1975) concluded that presenting the same semantic content in two different codes (or what we have been referring to as "code redundancy") is generally better than presenting the identical (verbal) information to two different modalities.

Nugent (1982) came to a similar conclusion, although from slightly different findings. She pointed out that a medium is seldom associated with only one symbol system. For example, a visual medium, such as film, can be used to display still or animated graphics in addition to text. She conjectured that when semantic information is redundant, then presenting it to different modalities via different symbol systems (i.e., presenting prose to the auditory system and pictures visually) should maximize learning. Using a design similar to that of Rohwer and Harris (1975), she found positive evidence for this conjecture. In a second study, Nugent (1982) found that when semantic information was nonredundant, then presenting it to different modalities did not augment learning, relative to a single-media control, but neither did it interfere with learning. That is, subjects who received different information orally and visually performed as well as subjects who received only the oral or only the visual information.

There has not been enough research in this area to come to any firm conclusions regarding the role of either redundancy of modality or code in efficient learning. A major problem may be that it is difficult to specify exactly what information is being conveyed by a particular media. This problem will be taken up below.

Theoretical and Methodological Issues

There are several methodological problems that plague the literature as a whole and that require resolution before questions regarding the role of graphics in education can be answered. Indeed, some of these problems preclude making almost any generalizations at all from extant data.

One particularly vexing problem, mentioned above, is that of *stimulus equivalence*: it is difficult to determine exactly what information is being conveyed by different stimulus materials. This is particularly so when comparisons are made between different classes of representations (e.g., comparisons of text with flowcharts or movies or a series of pictures), but it is also difficult when comparisons are made between two different types of graphic stimuli that are alleged to portray identical substantive information in merely different formats. What is more, very few investigators make an effort to substantiate claims of equivalence by subjecting their materials to norming studies, for example.

The problem of stimulus equivalence between media has been studied in its own right (Baggett, 1979, 1986; Baggett & Ehrenfeucht, 1982). Baggett and Ehrenfeucht (1982) point out that there has basically been no method of preparing information for experimentation which is the same in content but which can be presented in two media (e.g., either pictorially or verbally). Thus, similarities and differences in performance as a function of media of presentation may be due to differences in content, and/or differences in the way the two media convey messages; they certainly may not be unequivocally assigned to media differences.

Baggett (1979) devised a method for constructing a text that was structurally equivalent to a wordless movie (The Red Balloon), insofar as subjects could agree that both the movie and the constructed text contained the same 14 episodes, each with an exposition, complication, and resolution, and that episodic boundaries in one medium had exactly specified locations in the other. New subjects then either watched the movie or heard the text, and then recalled as much as they could. Recall of structural statements was similar in both media, but there were differences in content recall, which were attributed to different degrees to which different world knowledge was activated in the two groups.

In a second series of studies, Baggett and Ehrenfeucht (1982) specifically tried to equate content as well as structure between a narrative movie (*The Unicorn in the Garden*) and a text. They developed four measures of empirically-determined content equivalence: (a) ratings of how well-represented each of 350 sentence fragments was in the movie (or vice versa), (b) for each fragment, which photo (taken from the movie) best corresponded to it or vice versa; (termed "bi-directional touchpoints),'' (c) which of the 350 sentence fragments or photos were in the top 20% in terms of importance to the story, and (d) the similarity of importance ratings of the characters in the two medias. It should be noted that these methods allow assessment of degree of equivalence, and are not limited to comparisons between movie and text media (e.g., two texts or two films could be compared). New subjects recalled the stories, and the summaries based on different media were indistinguishable.

Baggett's work is notable because the development of materials was not based on intuition (as it usually is in this literature) but rather, it was based on several empirical measures. Although it is not clear whether her conclusions will hold in a context in which non-narrative information is to be learned, nor is it clear whether her methods could be adapted to other graphic media, it would be a great help in interpreting research if other investigators would take as much care to determine in what ways their materials were or were not equivalent. Otherwise, any between- or within-media differences obtained are at best ambiguous. Thus, one possibility for future research is the development of methods and measures for assessing stimulus equivalence.

The second methodological issue shall be referred to as *domain specificity*, and concerns the choice of subject matter to be learned. It is almost overwhelmingly true that either between- or within-media comparisons are made in one and only one subject-matter domain, and often on only one particular topic or lesson within that domain. So, for example, Lamberski and Dwyer (1983) contrasted color vs. monochrome presentations of the physiology of the heart; Holliday, Brunner, and Donais (1973) compared picture-word vs. block-word diagrams of the oxygen, carbon, nitrogen, and water cycles; Nugent (1982) compared the efficacy of print, audio, and movie media (and their combinations) on the topic of cheetahs; Rohwer and Harris (1975) compared text alone with text plus analogies or pictures for learning about electroconductivity, and so on. The point is that there needs to be much more attention paid to content domains in comparing different media presentations. It would also be useful to compare more than one topic or lesson within the same domain, so that proper item analyses could be conducted. The ability to generalize findings either within or across substantive domains will be severely constrained unless specific empirical work is conducted to compare these domains. Thus, here is another area that is ripe for future research.

Third, there is a notable lack of research on the issues of (a) what *graphical conventions* exist or are assumed to exist in the presentation of information from any particular substantive domain, (b) whether these conventions can be taught and if it is helpful to do so, (c) what conventions are being implicitly compared with each other in any given study, and (d) how graphic conventions can themselves be exploited to facilitate information acquisition. These issues have already been discussed (e.g., see Winn, 1981, for an explicit comparison); they become methodological issues for reasons similar to those for issues of stimulus equivalence. That is, if two types of graphics are being compared and some sort of behavioral difference is observed, one needs to determine whether at least one of the reasons is that one type of graphic exploits or enlists a particular convention (known or unknown to the subjects) whereas the other does not. Once again, unless this is known and/or controlled, interpretations of differences between conditions cannot be made unambiguously.

A fourth area of concern has to do with the *encoding-test relationship*; i.e., the relationship between how information is presented and what sort of knowledge is being tested. There are several psychological principles (e.g., encoding specificity) as well as several studies (e.g., McDaniel, Friedman, & Bourne, 1978; Stein, Morris, & Bransford, 1978) indicating that unless there is compatibility between the way materials are encoded and how they are tested, degree of learning (indeed, even what is learned) may be incorrectly estimated. For example, Lamberski and Dwyer (1983) gave subjects color or monochrome pictures of the human heart, and tested them on terminology, comprehension of heart function, identification of structures, and their ability to draw the heart. They found more of a difference between presentation conditions on tests requiring greater visualization (e.g., identification of structures and drawing). Similarly, Jeon and Branson (1981), who investigated whether movies, slides, or text would be better for acquisition of a motor skill, criticized previous between-media studies on the grounds that many written behavioral measures do not match the instructional objectives (i.e., actual motor performance). They cite Allen and Weintraub (1968) as suggesting that the "use of motion in a display is definitely indicated when the particular content to be learned consists of the movement itself or its characteristics, or where the content is enhanced or differentiated by the cues provided in the action of the movement." Jeon and Branson (1981) found that no differences between acquisition conditions were obtained when subjects were asked to write down the procedure they just learned. On the other hand, the film produced much better performance of the actual task than did either the slides or the text, and with 37% savings in time to learn. Thus, in addition to the media of presentation, it might be profitable to have routinely several types of knowledge tests.

Fifth, even if investigators attend to the four problem areas just discussed, there is no guarantee that a conclusion regarding the relative merits of a certain type of graphic can be reached unless it is clear that the information being presented has been "packaged" suitably with respect to the particular domain of expertise to be learned and the level of knowledge of the learner. This is the problem of *domain parsing*. Thus, research on the role of graphics in education cannot really take place outside the context of curriculum research in general.

Conclusions

Each of the issues raised above converges on a principal conclusion: Given the current state-of-the-art, it is probably premature for educators to contrast different media and look for student aptitude by media of presentation interactions. Similarly, it may be insufficient for psychologists to theorize about differences between pictorial and verbal memory as if such differences were generalizable across substantive domains, or for human factors engineers to assert that particular types of media or display technologies will, under all circumstances, be better than others. This conclusion is, by no means, unique to the present article. For example, in a 1973 review of the education literature on pictorial research, Holliday stated that "It is probable that certain kinds of pictures facilitate the learning of certain types of objectives for certain students with certain characteristics. However, the precise relationships have not been established." Unfortunately, the substance of this statement is still principally true.

As stated earlier, most studies investigating the role of graphics in learning and education have tested the effects of supplementing verbal material (usually written text) with representational (i.e., realistic) pictures. The goal has usually been to verify the assumption that graphics increase instructional effectiveness. What seems to be absent from the literature in general is a systematic analysis of what types of information graphical, as contrasted to some other representations, can convey, and under what circumstances or task domains or sets of educational goals it is necessary or desirable to convey this information. Thus, the issue should probably not be stated as: Under what circumstances and with what sorts of learners are graphical media an effective educational tool? Rather, there needs to be more emphasis placed on analyzing the types of concepts to be conveyed within a given subject matter domain, and then to investigate the circumstances in which graphical media can be used to convey these concepts.

It should be clear that, when considered in terms of the architectural hardware of the human information processing system, the role played by graphics in learning is really no different, in principle, than the role played by text or any other media. Thus, for example, we know that chunking new information, organizing it, giving it contextual support, relating it to prior knowledge, and so on, are all useful devices for facilitating knowledge acquisition. It should come as no surprise that these principles are true across media. What is notably absent from the literature is a sense of the circumstances under which a particular type of media presentation is better than some other type for chunking or organizing or activating prior knowledge. There are no empirical or theoretical guidelines for determining what sorts of information are uniquely afforded by graphics and when it is important to present such information. That is, despite hundreds of studies, the question still remains as to exactly what, if anything, is special about graphics qua graphics.

Theoretical Framework

There is a growing consensus among cognitive scientists that to perform successfully in a particular task domain, a person must have an accurate mental model of that domain. Domains that have been investigated in this context include solving arithmetic or physics problems (Greeno, 1983; Larkin, McDermott, Simon, & Simon, 1980), learning to use a hand-held calculator (Mayer & Bayman, 1981; Young, 1983) or a computer's text editor (Egan & Schwartz, 1979; Gentner & Gentner, 1983), and navigating around large-scale environments (Chase & Chi, 1981). If accurate mental models underlie successful performance, then understanding the role of graphics in education requires determining what the relevant mental models are within particular knowledge and skill domains and which type of representations best convey them. Thus, to the extent that mental models can be conveyed with pictures, graphics, diagrams, and the like, then optimizing the use of graphics in education requires a framework that describes the relationship between different types of graphics and different educational goals. This will require a careful analysis of each knowledge domain and a more sophisticated view than has been adopted in the past toward the potential utility of graphic representations. That is, there will likely be some domains for which graphics are the method of choice for presenting information and others in which their use is even contraindicated.

Teaching physics is a good case in point. Physics problems are often conveyed to students with pictorial diagrams of objects like springs, pulleys, inclined planes, etc. Yet this type of presentation may not be optimal because it focuses the student on superficial features (e.g., "This is an inclined plane problem") rather than the physical laws that are relevant to the problem's solution (Larkin, McDermott, Simon, & Simon, 1980). Similarly, as discussed in the previous section, there may be certain educational goals (or conveyance needs) for which it is better to use simple rather than complex graphics, or in which the use of "enhancements" such as color are actually harmful.

In the previous section, I concluded that many issues need to be resolved before the role that graphic representations play in the educational process can be fully understood. The five particular issues raised were: (a) stimulus equivalence: the necessity of ensuring that two or more media being compared portray the same information, or else, of knowing which information is unique to each; (b) graphical conventions: the need to identify and make explicit the graphical conventions that are employed either within a particular experimental manipulation or as part of the domain knowledge to be learned; (c) encoding specificity: the need to be aware of the relationship between how information is presented and how it is tested; that is, the need to acknowledge the likelihood that there will exist interactions between acquisition media and test media; (d) domain specificity: the necessity of comparing particular methods of portrayal (e.g., photographs vs. schematic line drawings) across subject matter domains as well as across different topics within the same domain; and (e) domain parsing: the need to understand how a particular domain of knowledge should be "parsed" for optimal presentation to learners of a given level of expertise. The "parse" should include a characterization of the type(s) of knowledge that are to be conveyed as well as suggestions for the type(s) of representations that would best convey them.

I also concluded that the role played by graphics in learning is in principle no different than the role played by any other information conveyance method, to the extent that all of the characteristics, constraints, limitations, and so on imposed by the information processing system itself will be imposed on all new information indiscriminately. That is, the processing of all representations would be constrained by the relevant parts of the system architecture. Nevertheless, the goal is to develop a principled means of choosing one or another portrayal method as being better suited to a particular application, and to incorporate these principles into an automated instructional design system. To achieve the first goal will require shifting the research emphasis from how a graphic portrays something (e.g., in color or monochrome; in detail or schematically) to what needs to be conveyed in the portrayal (e.g., information about structures, functions, processes and procedures, rules, etc.). Only then might a comparison across media types prove fruitful. That is, although I do not underestimate the importance of finding aptitude treatment interactions and understanding their etiology, it might do to recognize that there are other interactions—such as that between the type of information to be learned and the type of information best afforded by a given type of graphic representation—which might be more fundamental to this enterprise.

In the present section, I outline an approach toward the role of graphics in learning and memory that tries to accommodate the factors, such as domain specificity and graphical conventions, that were identified as likely to be important in assessing the effectiveness of different methods of presenting information. I first discuss three different methods of categorizing graphics. Two—media of presentation and amount of realism—have been used almost exclusively (if implicitly) in past research, and the third—type of information afforded—is being advocated within the current approach. I then outline a conceptual framework and discuss each of its components. I argue that knowledge domains should be characterized according to the type of information needed to acquire expertise and that these characterizations should be formulated in terms of representational needs. Finally, I take the reader through a detailed example, to illustrate the most important concepts in the framework.

Categorizing graphics media differences and the dimension of realism. Previous efforts to construct a theoretical framework to describe the role of graphics in education have typically emphasized either physical differences between visual media or differences between types of graphic representations along the dimension of realism. In addition, as mentioned earlier, a great deal of research in education combines these two methods of categorization to investigate the relative efficiency of learning from aural or visual prose by itself versus learning when the prose is augmented by relatively realistic graphic representations. Or, learning from prose is compared with learning from some other sort of representation, such as a flowchart. With a few specific exceptions, this approach has not been a useful way to proceed.

Media differences refer to actual distinctions that exist between different physical methods of conveying visual information, such as film, TV, CRT pages, filmstrips, slides, posters, photographs, drawings, etc. Standard textbooks about using audiovisual media in teaching often discuss the media according to such physical characteristics (e.g., projected versus nonprojected media; Erickson & Curl, 1972), or else, according to pragmatic issues such as availability.

From the present perspective, it is generally inappropriate to compare different physical media unless they afford the conveyance of the same type of information or else, the stimulus equivalence issues are at least known.

For instance, film and video both afford movement information directly, in real time. In contrast, line drawings afford movement information indirectly, through the use of conventions like action lines that require prior experience to interpret. Moreover, since a single drawing does not have temporality, a sequence of such drawings is necessary to convey a given movement from beginning to end, and thus, not only must information be inferred between drawings, but each drawing must be explicitly recognized as part of the previous temporal sequence and integrated within it. Thus, to the extent that information about movement is an important part of the knowledge to be conveyed within a domain, media comparisons between film or TV and more static representations like drawings may be most informative. However, this particular example is almost an exception. For the most part, different physical media can convey the same semantic information (e.g., in the simplest case, one could present a text in almost any media, including film). Thus, although media do differ on physical dimensions like size and resolution, for the most part such physical differences are probably unimportant. This is not to ignore the fact that some media may have characteristics that make them more desirable than others. For example, a child may be able to control a filmstrip by him or herself, or a large format presentation may be more "attention-getting" than a small format presentation, or it might be less expensive or difficult to make materials in one media than another. However, these considerations are irrelevant when considering the ability of a particular medium to convey a particular type of information, which is the perspective of the present report.

On the other hand, differences in the extent to which a visual representation maintains fidelity to its referent are at least an intuitively plausible means by which some types of graphic representations might be better than others for portraying information within particular learning environments. Table 10.1 shows several different kinds of graphic representations and where they seem to be ordered along a realistic-abstract dimension.

It can be seen that, generally speaking, pictorial or depictive representations resemble their referents more closely than schematic or iconic representations, in which relations are normally correct but the objects represented are usually more abstract than their referents. It should be noted, however, that even relatively abstract representations such as flowcharts and wiring diagrams often maintain at least functional and sometimes structural fidelity to their referents. More important, much like physical media differences, the amount of fidelity that is maintained by a representation is likely to be irrelevant unless considered within the context of the purpose for which the representation is likely to be used. Thus, for example, in one of the most comprehensive investigations of the use of graphics in science education, Dwyer (1972) found that "small amounts" of realistic details added to line drawings of the heart were more effective for learning heart

Type of Fidelity	Examples
REALISTIC	
Depictive/Pictorial	3D Models, color photographs, and shaded, detailed drawings
Schematic	Maps, monochrome line drawings, and caricatures
Iconic	International signs and hieroglyphics
Structural/Functional	Flowcharts, writing diagrams, blueprints, and graphs
Symbolic	Traffic signs, logos, and symbols (e.g., sheriff's badge or skull and crossbones)
Arbitrary	Tables, charts, and text
ABSTRACT	

Table 10.1. Categorization of Graphics.

structures than were colored photographs of an actual heart that were presumably more realistic. In this instance, the line drawings emphasized the structures to be learned, whereas the photographs were mostly homogeneous.

Neither the medium of presentation nor the extent to which a representation is realistic can be used exclusively as a meaningful basis for categorizing graphic representations. This is because neither of these factors by itself takes account of differences in the information conveyance requirements that might be imposed by a particular subject-matter domain. That is, just as encoding specificity needs to be taken into account when evaluating whether a given test is sensitive to a particular method of acquisition, researchers in graphic instruction need to be more aware of the potential influence of the subject matter per se.

Information affordances and knowledge requirements. One potentially productive way to categorize different types of graphic representations is in terms of the type(s) of information they each afford (e.g., Gibson, 1966). Having done so, it would then make sense to compare different representations against each other in terms of, for example, the directness or explicitness or efficiency with which they represent and convey particular types of information.

If graphics are to be categorized in terms of the information they afford, it is necessary to identify and possibly also categorize types of information per se. Table 10.2 shows a partial classification of particular types of information that different representations might convey more or less well. The types listed are principally visual in nature. Thus, for example, characteristics such as weight, smell, hardness, and the like, are not considered.

It should be emphasized that the categories in Table 10.2 are based on intuition, and that other classifications are certainly plausible, such as one that distinguishes between static information (e.g., objects and states) and dynamic information (e.g., processes and stages). Ultimately, the classification that is most useful in terms of describing information conveyance needs and affordances will have to be determined empirically.

The table defines three broad classes of information, and two subcategories within each. The three classes are information about visual appearance, information about static spatial relations, and information about events and sequences of events. All three classes of information can convey a concept or part of a concept either directly or via analogy or metaphor. For example, if we know that an important structural characteristic of the solar system is that its planets revolve around the sun, then by asserting that

Type of Information	Primary Characteristics	Secondary Characteristics
Appearances	shape, color size, and texture	identity, category membership, and visual similarity
Static Relations	orientation, spatial location, and internal structure	distance, spatial proximity, structural similarity, and functional similarity
Events/Sequences	collections of objects, associative relationships, cause-effect relationships, temporal relationships, and action sequences	temporal proximity, rate of change, amount of change, duration of states, and duration of change

Table 10.2. Categorization of Information Types.

an atom is like the solar system we are predicating that same structural characteristic to the structure of an atom (Gentner, 1983). Thus, in principle, the same representation could be used for each domain.

The distinction between primary and secondary characteristics has been made because it might be important or useful to distinguish the information or data that are directly represented from the inferences or conclusions that such data can support. So, for example, the primary characteristics listed under appearance information can, singly or in combination, support conclusions about object identity or category membership, but the latter information is not directly given by the appearance of an object. Similarly, primary information about location supports computations of distance, and information about temporal relationships supports conclusions about rate and duration of change.

In general, once different information types have been distinguished and appropriately categorized, it should be possible to compare graphic representations to determine how well they convey each type. It is only at this juncture that different graphical conveyance methods can be categorized in terms of information affordances.

Bobrow (1975) pointed out that representations differ in the explicitness with which they afford information. Thus, there is an important difference between primary and secondary information types and the relative explicitness with which they are represented. For example, the fact that a square is an equilateral polygon is only implicit in its appearance and must therefore be derived from a pictorial representation (though it may be a trivial operation to do so).

In contrast, a propositional (or text) representation of the concept "square" could have explicit arguments stating that squares have four equal sides and angles, but then the appearance of the square would have to be derived. Similarly, a photograph, a line drawing, a film, and a text could all explicitly represent the primary appearance information that canaries are yellow, whereas, excluding the possibility that pictures can be labeled, only a text can explicitly represent the information that a canary is a songbird. Conversely, the shape of a canary is explicit in a drawing, film, or photo, whereas shape is generally only implicit in text representations. Either a text or a graphic representation may be more appropriate, according to whether one wants to convey the information that a canary is a songbird or that it has a particular shape.

Thus, even after the type of knowledge that is to be conveyed is known, it is still necessary to choose an appropriate method of conveying it, given the overall educational goal. In this view, then, an ideal communication is one in which the conveyance needs dictated by a given subject-matter domain are well-matched to the affordances of the representations used to communicate them.

Sketch of a Framework

Figure 10.1 is a diagram of a theoretical framework that attempts to relate the influences of the domain knowledge itself, the human system architecture, the specific educational objectives at hand, known and new representational conventions, and world knowledge. The framework takes as an assumption the idea that, in general, the information necessary to achieve a criterion level of expertise in a given knowledge domain eventually needs to be characterized in terms of representational needs and specific conveyance methods. There are presently no principled or empirically-based guidelines from which to do this.

Among other things, expertise in a domain entails knowing its vocabulary, terminology, facts, associative and causal relationships, laws, problem-solving methods, pattern recognition heuristics and algorithms, and so on. However, referring to domain knowledge in this (conventional) way does not necessarily address specific conveyance needs. Hence, assuming that a knowledge domain has been broken down into coherent units that are to be presented in logical sequence, there still needs to be a *domain parser* that analyzes each unit (or lesson) in terms of conveyance needs.

The conveyance needs then need to be reformulated by an *information parser* in terms of the information categories in Table 10.2 (or some other set of empirically-justifiable categories), and recommendations made regarding the type(s) of representations best suited to each need. Thus, the *representation packages* that are the result of this analysis delineate the type(s) of information to be conveyed, along with suggestions about the best methods to use to do so. Several representations may be suggested for each topic.

Ideally, the suggested methods of presenting information should be implemented and analyzed according to the notion that each representation acts like an information transfer function. That is, each representation will emphasize, pass, de-emphasize, and omit various aspects of the original information. Thus, the *representation analyzer* should be able to determine, for each representation, exactly what information it will convey. Different representations of the ''same'' information can then be compared with each other along dimensions such as ease of acquisition, interpretability, memorability, original educational goals, etc.

It should be obvious that the main work of the model is done by the two parsers. The domain parser has the task of analyzing domains or topics according to the information needed to acquire expertise, while taking account of the constraints imposed by the human system architecture as well as by specific educational objectives that must be considered. Included in educational objectives is information about the presupposed level of expertise of the targeted student population, since this is the yardstick against which criterion performance is measured.

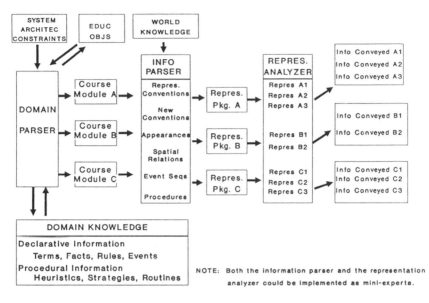

Figure 10.1. Theoretical Framework.

The domain parser performs its task with a specific view towards suggesting aspects of the knowledge domain that might lend themselves to particular conveyance needs or methods. Under normal circumstances, domain knowledge is not characterized according to this perspective. Indeed, at best, domain knowledge is characterized according to the conclusions, or secondary characteristics, that need to be acquired. For example, domain knowledge is often broken down into that which is declarative (e.g., facts; rules; laws) and that which is procedural (e.g., motor skills; problem-solving heuristics or algorithms), yet this particular breakdown is normally neutral with respect to representational issues. Thus, the domain parser has to parse any "conclusion needs" into packages that are appropriate for specific conveyance methods and hence, for specific types of representations.

It should be noted that the domain parser should be able to request more knowledge about the domain under consideration, including knowledge about the relative importance of various pieces of information. In addition, it should be able to request modifications of educational objectives, if current objectives are perceived as difficult or impossible to implement.

The information parser categorizes each piece of knowledge from the domain parser according to its probable information type. Sometimes, two or more types of representations might be suggested for a given piece of knowledge. For example, suppose the information that a water molecule is composed of two hydrogen atoms and one oxygen atom is to be conveyed. The formula $2H^+ + O^- = H_2O$ represents this information as a quantitative relationship; there is an equality between the valences of the three ions on the left and the molecule on the right. Underlying this quantitative relationship, however, is a structural one involving the numbers of electrons that are permitted to be in orbitals at different mean distances from a nucleus. It is not clear, a priori, whether the formula representation or a graphic representation of the atomic structure is more appropriate here, so both might be suggested.

The information parser should also have a category for new graphical conventions that might need to be learned. To be able to discern such new conventions, and to facilitate suggestions for representations, the information parser must have access to information regarding representational conventions in general. It also must have world knowledge (at a level appropriate to the targeted student population), to be able to determine what structural and functional analogies might be appropriately used in the representations it suggests.

The information conveyed by each representation can ultimately be compared to the original domain knowledge, to the educational goals, to the criterion performance of some target population, etc. As more is learned about the success with which various representations convey different types of information, this knowledge can be input back into the system as further constraints on both parsers.

It should be obvious that the necessary empirical information to create a working implementation of either the domain parser or the information parser is missing from the literature. However, it is hoped that the current framework can provide a guideline for identifying the type of data that would be useful to acquire in the service of such an implementation.

An Example from Biology

Suppose that one lesson in a typical university introductory biology class is centered around the structure of DNA and how it replicates, and that the following information, which has been distilled from an introductory biology textbook (Alberts, Bray, Lewis, Raff, Roberts, & Watson, 1983), is the input to the domain parser.

The DNA molecule is a two-stranded polymer composed of four different nucleotide bases: adenine (A), cytocine (C), guanine (G), and thymine (T). Specific hydrogen bonding between G and C and between A and T causes complementary base pairing in which each member of a base pair is located on opposite sides of the two-stranded helix which is the DNA structure. The nucleotide bases are located on the inside of the helix.

DNA replication entails a separation of the double helix, with each strand acting as a template for the formation of a new molecule. Nucleotides are added to the parent template sequentially by a process that requires them to form complementary base pairs. Daughter strands are complementary in sequence to their parent template strand, so that each replication duplicates the genetic information entirely.

This particular set of facts is declarative in nature, and the domain parser might choose to represent them using a propositional format. The job of the domain parser is to break this information up into units that have coherence and yet that are amenable to being described in terms of conveyance needs, or, better yet, information types. For example, if the information above were passed through the parser, it might be broken up into smaller parcels, such as:

(a) The DNA molecule is a two-stranded polymer that is shaped like a double helix.

(b) The molecule is composed of four different subunits: adenine (A), cytocine (C), guanine (G), and thymine (T).

(c) There is specific hydrogen bonding between G and C and between A and T (i.e., the members of a pair "fit together" molecularly). This is called "complementary base pairing."

(d) The nucleotide bases are located on the inside of the helix, with each member of a base pair on opposite sides.

(e) To replicate, the double helix must separate into two strands.

(f) Each parent strand acts as a template for the formation of a new DNA molecule.

(g) Nucleotides are added to the parent templates one at a time by a process that forms complementary base pairs.

(h) Daughter strands have a nucleotide sequence that is the complement of their parent's, so that each replication duplicates the genetic information entirely.

We shall further suppose that, much as the original information is presented in two paragraphs, the parsed information will be output in two information packages, one containing points [a] through [d], and the other, points [e] through [h]). There will be suggestions within each information package regarding conveyance needs. For example, in the unit consisting of facts [a] - [d], there is an obvious need to convey information about an event. The facts, together with the suggested conveyance needs, are passed on to the information parser.

Given such strong hints, the information parser would corroborate the suggestions of the domain parser, and identify several additional primary information types within each of the two information packages. In the current example, there may be information to be conveyed about new representational conventions (e.g., the chemical notation for molecular bonding), as well as appearance and identity information (the shape of the double helix; the molecular structure of the bases), spatial relation information (the location of the nucleotides on the strands; complementary base pairing), and event information (separation of the parent strand; sequential addition of complementary nucleotides to the daughters).

The information parser might also identify and include in its output an analogy or metaphor for one or more of the information types, based on its world knowledge. For example, it might suggest that a spiral staircase could serve as an appearance analogy for the shape information, a "lock and key" metaphor could serve as a functional analogy for the complementary base pairing idea, and a zipper could serve as a process analogy for the beginning step of the DNA replication process.

Finally, the information parser will make suggestions about how to best represent the information it has parsed. In this case, for example, it might recommend that both structural and relational information about complementary base pairing (point [c]) be combined in a single diagrammatic representation, partly because the base pairing idea is somewhat complex and partly because it will involve relatively unfamiliar notation. The remaining appearance and spatial relation information (points [a], [b], and [d]) might then be combined into a second representation.

Once the information parser has made its suggestions, they must be implemented in actual representations. The parser might suggest several alternatives for implementing each of the representations it has suggested. Until there is more knowledge about the information affordances of different types of representations, it will probably be useful to implement more than one instance of each suggestion, and to make a choice based on the output of the representation analyzer. The representation analyzer should allow selections of which representatives to use to be based on the specific information that is conveyed by each.

To illustrate how graphic representations of the same subject matter portrayed in the same physical media with the same relative level of realism can nevertheless afford quite different information, I would like to end this section with some examples of figures that are meant to convey some or all of the information stated in points [a]-[d] above. Though all of the figures share a lot of "surface" similarities, they nevertheless do not afford the same data.

Figures 10.2-10.5 show four different ways to represent some of the ideas inherent in the concept of complementary base pairing, and Figures 10.5–10.7 show different representations of the structure of DNA. All of the figures are black and white schematic line drawings with at most two additional colors used for highlighting. I wish to make no judgments about the relative merits of these figures; indeed, that is an empirical issue to be decided in the context of information about particular educational goals, student aptitudes, other simultaneously available representations (e.g., text), etc.

In terms of information conveyed, Figure 10.2 depicts only the two base pairs, but uses chemical bonding notation and is thus specific with respect to the molecular structure and the location and type of hydrogen bonding between bases. In contrast, Figure 10.3 omits these details by representing the bonding schematically, while at the same time, it places the base pairs in the context of a portion of the DNA molecule as a whole. Thus, although the specifics of the hydrogen bonding are omitted in Figure

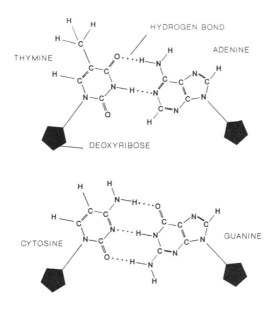

(Adapted from Felsenfeld, G. 1985. DNA.
Scientific American, Volume 253, pages 58-67.)

Figure 10.2. DNA - Hydrogen Bond.

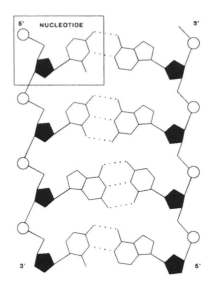

Figure 10.3. DNA - Nucleotide.

10.3, some additional structural information is conveyed. Figure 10.4, on the other hand, conveys a combination of the information from Figures 10.2 and 10.3, insofar as the specifics of the molecular bonding are included along with contextual information about the structure of DNA.

Figure 10.5, like Figure 10.3, conveys the bonding between base pairs schematically, yet it also conveys information about the shape of a double helix (point [a]), and about the location and identity of the nucleotide bases (points [b] and [d]). In addition, it conveys information about the specificity of the bonding via a visual analogy that somewhat poorly instantiates the lock and key analogy, since it appears as though A is as likely to bond with G as it is with T.

Figures 10.6 and 10.7, like Figure 10.5, are also representations of the structure of the DNA molecule. Whereas both 10.6 and 10.7 convey some information to the effect that the molecule is three-dimensional, Figure 10.6 emphasizes the arrangement of the atoms that comprise the DNA molecule, whereas Figure 10.7 again emphasizes that pairwise structure of the bases that make up the double helix.

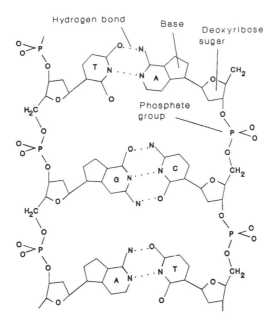

(Adapted from Purves, W.K., & Orians, G.H. 1983.
Life: The Science of Biology . Boston, MA: Willard Grant Press.)

Figure 10.4. DNA - Molecular Bonding.

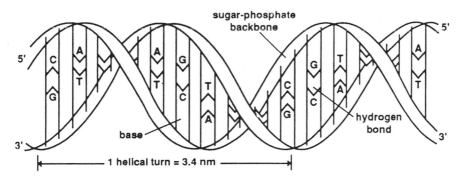

Adapted from Alberts, B., Bray, D., Lewis, J., Raff, M., Roberts,
K., & Watson, J.D. (1983). Molecular Biology of the Cell. NY: Garland Publishing Co.

Figure 10.5. Double Helix Structure.

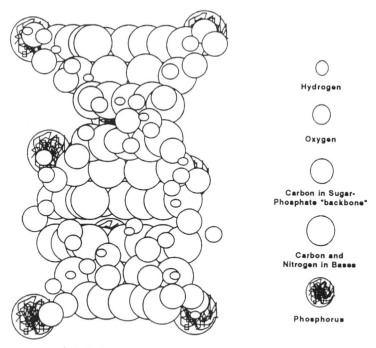

Hydrogen

Oxygen

Carbon in Sugar-
Phosphate "backbone"

Carbon and
Nitrogen in Bases

Phosphorus

(Adapted from Purves, W.K., & Orians, G.H. 1983.
Life: The Science of Biology . Boston, MA: Willard Grant Press.)

Figure 10.6. DNA - Atomic Structure.

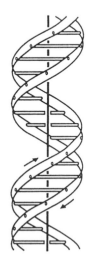

Figure 10.7. Pairwise Double Helix.

It should be clear, from just these few examples, that relatively subtle differences between representations (e.g., compare Figures 10.3 and 10.4, and Figures 10.5 and 10.7) can nevertheless result in the conveyance of different information, both in the quantitative and qualitative sense. We are quite a long way from implementing an information or domain parser. Most previous research has implicitly concentrated on questions about the representation analyzer and the transfer functions; that is, most research has compared the educational results of learning from different types of representations. What is needed at this juncture is research that is focused toward discovering the principles underlying the construction of representations that achieve particular information affordances. In addition, research is needed which can give us guidelines for reformulating domain knowledge in terms of conveyance needs.

Conclusion

The effective use of graphics in education requires good models of the domains to be learned as well as good models of the learners. In particular, we need to know what information should be conveyed from a domain to achieve specific educational goals, what constraints are imposed by the system architecture on the learner, what conventional and world knowledge can be assumed and what must be explicitly taught, what role individual differences might be expected to play in the process, and what type of information is best conveyed by different graphic representations. At present, we have only partial knowledge about any of these factors, and in some cases, none at all.

The proposed framework is an attempt to clarify the interaction that can be expected to occur between conveyance needs that may be domain-specific, representational methods that differ widely in terms of what they are capable of conveying, and a receiver environment that will change as a function of prior knowledge and current and desired level of expertise.

It should be clear that much research is still required to understand the role of graphics in education. In addition, research is needed to validate the general and specific assumptions of the framework. It should be noted that the framework itself stands as a set of guidelines for this research. It also stands as an exhortation about attacking old problems in new ways that incorporate more about what are known to be psychologically relevant factors.

It seems fair to say that the commonly held belief regarding the utility of graphic representations under almost any circumstance needs to be questioned. Indeed, it will be useful to identify those domains for which graphic representations are not necessary for the effective conveyance of information. Similarly, it seems fair to say that complexity is not always a necessary feature of an informative representation, and that the conditions which warrant simpler displays need to be identified.

References

Alesandrini, K. L., & Rigney, J. W. (1981). Pictorial presentation and review strategies in science learning. *Journal of Research in Science Teaching, 18,* 465–474.

Allen, W. H., & Weintraub, R. (1968). *The motion variables in film presentation.* OE Final Report (Project No. 5–1125). Los Angeles, CA: University of Southern California, Department of Cinema.

Anderson, J. R. (1983). *The architecture of cognition.* Cambridge, MA: Harvard University Press.

Atkinson, R., & Shriffrin, R. (1971). The control of short-term memory. *Scientific American, 225*(2), 89–90.

Badre, A. N. (1982). Designing chunks for sequentially displayed information. In A. N. Badre & B. Shneiderman (Eds.), *Human/computer interaction.* Norwood, NJ: Ablex.

Baggett, P. (1979). Structurally equivalent stories in movie and text and the effect of the medium on recall. *Journal of Verbal Learning and Verbal Behavior, 18,* 333–356.

Baggett, P. (1986). Understanding visual and verbal messages. In S. Chipman & R. Wu (Eds.), *Learning by eye.* Hillsdale, NJ: Lawrence Erlbaum Associates.

Baggett, P., & Ehrenfeucht, A. (1982). Information in content equivalent movie and text stories. *Discourse Processes, 5,* 73–99.

Baker, E. L. (1989). *Technology assessment: Policy and methodological issues.* Proceedings of the 2nd Intelligent Tutoring Systems Research Forum (pp. 151–157). San Antonio, TX: Air Force Human Resources Laboratory.

Biederman, I., Glass, A. L. & Stacy, Jr., E. W. (1973). Searching for objects in real-word scenes. *Journal of Experimental Psychology, 97,* 22–27.

Bobrow, D. (1975). Dimensions of representation. In D. Bobrow & D. Collins (Eds.), *Representation and understanding.* New York: Academic Press.

Borg, W. R., & Schuller, C. F. (1979). Detail and background in audiovisual lessons and their effects on learners. *Educational Communications and Technology Journal, 27,* 31–38.

Bower, G. H., & Springston, F. (1970). Pauses as recoding points in letter series. *Journal of Experimental Psychology, 83,* 421–430.

Bransford, J. D., & Johnson, M. (1973). Considerations of some problems of comprehension. In W. G. Chase (Ed.), *Visual information processing.* New York: Academic Press.

Brooks, P. H. (1977). The role of action lines in children's memory for pictures. *Journal of Experimental Child Psychology, 23,* 98–107.

Burton, R. R. (1988). The environment module of intelligent tutoring systems. In M. C. Polson & J. Richardson (Eds.), *Foundations of intelligent tutoring systems* (pp. 109–142). Hillsdale, NJ: Lawrence Erlbaum Associates.

Butler, T. W. (1983). Computer response time and user performance. In A. Janda (Ed.), *CHI 83 Conference Proceedings.* Boston, MA: ACM SIGCHI, pp. 58–62.

Carmody, D. P. (1985). Free search, restricted search, and the need for context in radiologic image perception. In R. Groner, G. W. McConkie, & C. Menz

(Eds.), *Eye movements and human information processing.* New York: Elsevier Science Publishing Co.

Chase, W. G., & Chi, M. T. H. (1981). Cognitive skill: Implications for spatial skill in large-scale environments. In J. H. Harvey (Ed.), *Cognition, social behavior, and the environment* (pp. 111–136). Hillsdale, NJ: Lawrence Erlbaum Associates.

Chase, W. G., & Simon, H. A. (1973). The mind's eye in chess. In W. G. Chase (Ed.), *Visual information processing.* New York: Academic Press.

Dwyer, F. M. (1972). *A guide for improving visualized instruction.* State College, PA: Learning Services.

Dwyer, F. M. (1975). On visualized instruction effect on student's entering behavior. *The Journal of Experimental Education, 43,* 79–83.

Edyburn, D. L. (1982). The effects of two levels of microcomputer graphics on reading comprehension. *ERIC Education Document, 218,* 593.

Egan, D., & Schwartz, B. J. (1979). Chunking in recall of symbolic drawings. *Memory & cognition, 7,* 149–158.

El-Gazzar, A. L. I. (1984). A signal detection analysis of digitized and photographic image modes and color realism in a pictorial recognition memory task. *ERIC Education Document, 243,* 419.

Ericsson, K. A., & Chase, W. G. (1982). Exceptional memory. *American Scientist, 70,* 607–614.

Erickson, C. W. H., & Curl, D. H. (1972). *Fundamentals of teaching with audiovisual technology, Second Edition.* New York: Macmillan.

Friedman, A. (1979). Framing pictures: The role of knowledge in automatized encoding and memory for gist. *Journal of Experimental Psychology: General, 108,* 316–355.

Friedman, A., & Bourne, L. E. (1976). Encoding the levels of information in pictures and words. *Journal of Experimental Psychology: General, 105*(2), 169–190.

Friedman, A., & Liebelt, L. S. (1981). On the time course of viewing pictures with a view towards remembering. In D. F. Fisher, R. A. Monty, & J. W. Senders (Eds.), *Eye movements: Cognition and visual perception* (pp. 137–155). Hillsdale, NJ: Lawrence Erlbaum Associates.

Friedman, A., & Polson, M. C. (1980). Hemispheres as independent resource systems: Limited-capacity processing and cerebral specialization. *Journal of Experimental Psychology: Human Perception and Performance, 7*(5), 1031–1058.

Gentner, D. (1983). Structure-mapping: A theoretical framework for analogy, *Cognitive Science, 7,* 155–170.

Gentner, D., & Gentner, D. R. (1983). Flowing waters or teaming crowds: Mental models of electricity. In D. Gentner & A. L. Stevens (Eds.), *Mental models* (pp. 99–129). Hillsdale, NJ: Lawrence Erlbaum Associates.

Gibson, J. J. (1966). *The senses considered as perceptual systems.* New York: Houghton Mifflin Company.

Glaser, R., & Bassok, M. (1989). Learning theory and the study of instruction. In M. R. Rosenzweig & L. W. Porter (Eds.), *Annual Review of Psychology* (Vol. 40, pp. 631–666). Palo Alto, CA: Annual Reviews, Inc.

Greeno. J. G. (1983). Conceptual entities. In D. Gentner & A. L. Stevens (Eds.), *Mental models* (pp. 227–252). Hillsdale, NJ: Lawrence Erlbaum Associates.

Halff, H. M. (1988). Curriculum and instruction in automated tutors. In M. C. Polson & J. Richardson (Eds.), *Foundations of intelligent tutoring systems* (pp. 79–108). Hillsdale, NJ: Lawrence Erlbaum Associates.

Haring, M. J., & Fry, M. A. (1979). Effects of pictures on children's comprehension of written text. *Educational Communications and Technology Journal, 27*, 185–190.

Haviland, S. E., & Clark, H. H. (1974). What's new? Acquiring information as a process in comprehension. *Journal of Verbal Learning and Verbal Behavior, 13*, 512–521.

Hegarty, M., Just, M. A., & Morrison, I. R. (1988). Mental models of mechanical systems: Individual differences in qualitative and quantitative reasoning. *Cognitive Psychology, 20*, 191–236.

Holliday, W. G. (1973). Critical analysis of pictorial research related to science education. *Science Education, 57*, 210–214.

Holliday, W. G. (1975). The effects of verbal and adjunct pictorial-verbal information in science instruction. *Journal of Research in Science Teaching, 12*, 77–83.

Holliday, W. G., Brunner, L. L., & Donais, E. L. (1973). Differential cognitive and affective responses to flow diagrams in science. *Journal of Research in Science Teaching, 14*, 129–138.

Jeon, U. H., & Branson, R. K. (1981). Performance and simulated performance test results as a function of instruction by still and motion visuals. *Journal of Educational Technology Systems, 10*, 33–44.

Kahneman, D. (1973). *Attention and effort.* Englewood Cliffs, NJ: Prentice-Hall.

King, W. A. (1975). A comparison of three combinations of text and graphics of concept learning. *ERIC Education Document, 112*, 936.

Kintsch, W. (1989, September). A theory of discourse comprehension: Implications for a tutor of word algebra problems. Paper presented at meetings of the European Association for Research in Learning and Instruction, Madrid, Spain.

Knapp, B. G., Moses, F. L., & Gellman, L. H. (1982). Information highlighting on complex displays. In A. Badre & B. Shneiderman (Eds.), *Directions in human/computer interactions* (pp. 195–215). Norwood, NJ: Ablex.

Lamberski, R. J., & Dwyer, F. M. (1983). The instructional effect of coding (color and black and white) on information acquisition and retrieval. *Educational Communications and Technology Journal, 31*, 9–21.

Lang, R., & Soloman, R. (1979). Effects of pictures on learning to read common nouns. *British Journal of Educational Psychology, 49*, 138–149.

Larkin, J. H., McDermott, J., Simon, D. P., & Simon, H. A. (1980). Models of competence in solving physics problems. *Cognitive Science, 4*, 317–345.

Lesgold, A. M., Levin, J. R., Shimron, J., & Guttman, J. (1975). Pictures and young children's learning from oral prose. *Journal of Educational Psychology, 67*, 636–642.

Loftus, G. R. (1972). Eye fixations and recognition memory for pictures. *Cognitive Psychology, 3*, 525–551.

Luder, C. B., & Barber, P. J. (1984). Redundant color coding on airborne CRT displays. *Human Factors, 26*, 19–32.

Mandler, J. M., & Johnson, N. S. (1976). Some of the thousand words a picture is worth. *Journal of Experimental Psychology: Human Learning and Memory, 5*, 529–540.

Mandler, J. M., & Johnson, N. S. (1977). Remembrance of things parsed: Story structure and recall. *Cognitive Psychology, 9*, 111–151.

Marcel, T., & Barnard, P. (1979). Paragraphs of pictographs: The use of non-verbal instructions for equipment. In P. A. Kolers, M. E. Wrolstad, & H. Bouma (Eds.), *Processing of visible language, Volume 1* (pp. 501–518). New York: Plenum Press.

Mayer, R. E. (1979). Twenty years of research on advance organizers: Assimilation theory is still the best predictor of results. *Instructional Science, 8*, 133–167.

Mayer, R. E., & Bayman, P. (1981). Psychology of calculator languages: A framework for describing differences in user's knowledge. *Communications of the ACM, 24*, 511–520.

McDaniel, M. A., Friedman, A., & Bourne, Jr., L. E. (1978). Remembering the levels of information in words. *Memory & Cognition, 6*, 156–164.

Miller, J. R. (1988). The role of human-computer interaction in intelligent tutoring systems. In M. C. Polson & J. Richardson (Eds.), *Foundations of intelligent tutoring systems* (pp. 143–190). Hillsdale, NJ: Lawrence Erlbaum Associates.

Moore, M. V., & Nawrocki, L. H. (1978). The educational effectiveness of graphic displays for computer assisted instruction. *ERIC Education Document, 169*, 917.

Moore, M. V., Nawrocki, L. H., & Simutis, Z. M. (1979). The instructional effectiveness of three levels of graphics displays for computer-assisted instruction. *ERIC Education Document, 178*, 057.

Moyer, R. S., & Bayer, R. H. (1976). Mental comparison and the symbolic distance effect. *Cognitive Psychology, 8*, 228–246.

Nathan, M. (1989). *Empowering the student: Prospects for an unintelligent tutoring system.* (ICS Technical Report #89–11). Boulder, CO: Institute of Cognitive Science, University of Colorado.

Navon, D., & Gopher, D. (1979). On the economy of the human-processing system. *Psychological Review, 86*, 214–255.

Norman, D. A. (1983). Design principles for human-computer interfaces. In A. Janda, (Ed.), *CHI 83 Conference Proceedings* (pp. 1–10). Boston, MA: ACM SIGGCHI.

Norman, D. A., & Bobrow, D. (1975). On data-limited and resource-limited processes. *Cognitive Psychology, 7*, 44–64.

Nugent, G. C. (1982). Pictures, audio, and print: Symbolic representation and effect on learning. *Educational Communications & Technology Journal, 30*, 163–174.

Oldfield, R. C., & Wingfield, A. (1965). Response latencies in naming objects. *Quarterly Journal of Experimental Psychology, 17*, 273–281.

Palmer, S. E. (1975). Visual perception and world knowledge: Notes on a model of sensory-cognitive interaction. In D. A. Norman & D. E. Rumelhart (Eds.), *Explorations in cognition.* San Francisco: Freeman.

Perkins, D. N. (1980). Pictures are the real thing. In P. A. Kolers, M. E. Wrolstad, & H. Bouma (Eds.), *Processing of visible language 2* (pp. 259–278). New York: Plenum Press.

Pick, A. D., & Pick, H. L. (1978). Culture and perception. In E. C. Carterette & M. P. Friedman (Eds.), *Handbook of perception, Volume X* (pp. 19–39). New York: Academic Press.

Potash, L. M. (1977). Design of maps and map related research. *Human Factors, 19*, 139–150.

Potter, M. C., & Falconer, B. A. (1975). Time to understand pictures and words. *Nature, 253*, 437–438.

Pressley, M., Levin, J. R., Pigott, S., LeComte, M., & Hope, D. J. (1983). Mismatched pictures and children's prose learning. *Educational Communications and Technology Journal, 31*, 131–143.

Reid, D. J., & Miller, G. J. A. (1980). Pupils' perception of biological pictures and its implications for readability studies of biology textbooks. *Journal of Biological Education, 14,* 59–69.

Reitman, J. S. (1976). Skilled perception in Go: Deducing memory structures from interresponse times. *Cognitive Psychology, 8,* 336–356.

Rigney, J. W., & Lutz, K. A. (1976). Effects of graphic analogies of concepts in chemistry on learning and attitude. *Journal of Educational Psychology, 68,* 305–311.

Rohwer, Jr., W. D., & Harris, W. J. (1975). Media effects on prose learning in two populations of children. *Journal of Educational Psychology, 68,* 205–209.

Royer, J. M., & Cable, G. W. (1976). Illustrations, analogies, and facilitative transfer in prose learning. *Journal of Educational Psychology, 68,* 205–209.

Ruch, M. D., & Levin, J. R. (1977). Pictorial organization versus verbal repetition of children's prose: Evidence for processing differences. *Audio Visual Communication Review, 25,* 269–279.

Ryan, T., & Schwartz, C. (1956). Speed of perception as a function of mode or representation. *American Journal of Psychology, 69,* 60–69.

Schwartz, S. H., & Fattaleh, D. L. (1972). Representation in deductive problem solving: The matrix. *Journal of Experimental Psychology, 95,* 343–348.

Shepard, R. N. (1967). Recognition memory for words, sentences, and pictures. *Journal of Verbal Learning and Verbal Behavior, 6,* 156–163.

Snodgrass, J. G. (1980). Towards a model for picture and words. In P. A. Kolers, M. E. Wrolstad, & H. Bouma (Eds.), *Processing of visible language 2* (pp. 565–584). New York: Plenum Press.

Spector, J. M. (1990). *Designing and developing an advanced instructional design advisor.* Brooks AFB, TX: AFHRL Technical Paper AFHRL-TP-90-52.

Stein, B. S., Morris, C. D., & Bransford, J. D. (1978). Constraints on effective elaboration. *Journal of Verbal Learning & Verbal Behavior, 17,* 707–714.

Stone, V. L. (1983). Effects of color in filmed behavior sequences on description and elaboration by Liberian schoolboys. *Educational Communications and Technology Journal, 31,* 33–45.

VanLehn, K. (1988). Student modeling. In M. C. Polson & J. Richardson (Eds.), *Foundations of intelligent tutoring systems* (pp. 55–78). Hillsdale, NJ: Lawrence Erlbaum Associates.

Way, D. S. (1973). *Terrain analysis: A guide to site selection using aerial photographic interpretation.* Stroudsberg, PA: Dowden, Hutchinsohn, & Ross, Inc.

Wickens, C. D. (1984). Processing resources in attention. In R. Parasuraman & R. Davies (Eds.), *Varieties of attention.* New York: Academic Press.

Winn, W. (1981). Effects of attribute highlighting and diagrammatic organization on identification and classification. *Journal of Research in Science Teaching, 18,* 23–32.

Winn, W. (1982). The role of diagrammatic representation in learning sequences, identification, and classification as a function of verbal and spatial ability. *Journal of Research in Science Teaching, 19,* 78–89.

Young, R. M. (1983). Surrogates and mapping: Two kinds of conceptual models for interactive devices. In D. Gentner & A. L. Stevens (Eds.), *Mental models* (pp. 35–52). Hillsdale, NJ: Lawrence Erlbaum Associates.

Chapter Eleven

Evaluation

Daniel J. Muraida, J. Michael Spector, Harold F. O'Neil Jr., and Mary R. Marlino

Introduction

In this chapter, we address the critical issues associated with the evaluation of instructional design in general and with the development of an Advanced Instructional Design Advisor (AIDA) in particular. Our reason for including remarks about the evaluation of progress on AIDA is twofold: (1) to illustrate the evaluation principles we introduce, and (2) to emphasize just how important we believe that evaluation is to the successful creation of instructional materials.

As we discuss critical evaluation issues, we shall review how the AIDA project has been evaluated, how a core technology to be elaborated in XAIDA (transaction shells) has been evaluated, and how these evaluations have led to the conception of a model to guide future evaluations. This chapter will be quite different from the others in that it will incorporate reports from actual AIDA review meetings.

First, we need to establish what we mean by evaluation. As Halff has remarked in Part II, there are three aspects of evaluation to be considered: quality control, formative evaluation, and summative evaluation. Quality control is concerned primarily with the quality of a product. Before performing formative and summative evaluations, it is worth verifying that the product (a course or a courseware design advisor) meets pre-established quality standards. Relevant quality criteria, for example, might include the frequency of student interactions with the instructional software, the consistency of screen designs, and the integrity of files maintained by the system. One way to determine what constitutes quality control is to view it as an attempt to answer this question: Is this product ready (good enough) for subsequent evaluation? We regard quality control as a kind of alpha test performed internally within an organization.

Formative evaluation is a serious attempt to examine how the product could be improved. If it is a course that is being evaluated, then perhaps different versions might be considered. If the product being evaluated is AIDA, then the default instructional parameters (see Merrill's chapter in Part II) are worth careful consideration. Formative evaluation could be likened to beta testing in which independent evaluators are recruited to make a prescriptive analysis of a product.

Summative evaluation is an attempt to describe how a product has performed. The assumption is that the course or product has been placed in field settings. Relevant considerations for summative evaluation of a course include student outcomes (e.g., training performances, job performances, skill/knowledge retention, and course completion times). Relevant considerations for AIDA might include average development time for a lesson module as well as student outcomes.

What sets the stage for any of these aspects of evaluation, of course, is a plan with definite goals. The plan itself should be subject to some of these aspects of evaluation. In essence, this illustrates one of Tennyson's principles (see Part II): evaluation should be integrated into each phase of Instructional Systems Development (ISD). We concur with Tennyson's principle of integrating evaluation throughout the process of developing instruction, including the development of an instructional advisor such as AIDA. Furthermore, we acknowledge that there are often not clear boundaries separating these three aspects of evaluation. At the highest level is the desire for quality and for successful instruction. We want to build the right product (quality control and formative evaluation), and we want to build the product right (quality control and summative evaluation that feeds back into design and development). But first, we must decide what the right product to build is. Essentially, what we are proposing is a technology assessment (TA) (Ahmad, 1989). This means identifying the social goals that a technology might serve, identifying feasible technologies, assessing technological alternatives, and conducting a posthoc impact analysis. Obviously this concept overlaps considerably with the process of program evaluation (Rossi, Freeman, & Wright, 1979). TA, however, places more emphasis on front-end analysis, employing Delphi and scenario construction, among other techniques. TA is an attempt to determine technology choices and to evaluate the consequences early in the R&D process.

In the following sections we will present a synopsis of the processes followed in the evaluation of AIDA's specifications. These processes included a Delphi-like method for soliciting expert opinion and consensus, proof of concept studies, scenario construction, and instructional design modeling. Our goal is to give the reader an idea of how a TA for evaluation of specifications might be carried out in instructional design R&D. The obvious problem is that TA methods have yet to be formalized enough to provide evaluators with a set of algorithms. What follows can be considered as an initial effort to derive some of the principles for technology evaluation. As Robert Mager indicates in the preface to *Preparing Instructional Objectives* (1975), "The moral of this fable is that if you're not sure where you're going, you're liable to end up someplace else."

Evaluating the Design of AIDA

Where should AIDA be headed? How should this be decided? Much of the interesting progress on the AIDA project has involved the numerous academic and military advisors. In our attempts to establish an optimal technological profile for AIDA we have solicited the input of an interdisciplinary team of civilian and military consultants who have no vested interest in a particular technology. In accordance with Ahmad's (1989) description of TA, we brought them together in a Delphi-like process to generate and prioritize technology selections. We include here some of their evaluative remarks concerning the shape that AIDA should take. Friedman's chapter in Part III on designing graphics is a detailed example of how the evaluation of AIDA specifications has affected the initial AIDA prototype. That AIDA is conforming more to Merrill's conception (Part II) is an outcome of the process reflected below.

AIDA Features (The Plan)

It is possible and desirable to perform formative evaluation of specifications, as Tennyson argued in Part II. These evaluations were carried out in a series of review meetings. Among those who participated in these meetings were Mr. Michael Brown-Beasley (Mei Technology's AI consultant), Lt. Col. Larry Clemons (retired) (an Air Training Command R&D representative), Mr. Brian Dallman (Technical Applications Officer at an Air Force Technical Training Center), Dr. John Ellis (a Navy advisor to the project), Dr. Albert Hickey (Mei Technology's Principal Investigator), Maj. Bob Mongillo (an Air Training Command R&D representative), Dr. Scott Newcomb (Chief of the Instructional Design Branch), Dr. Robert Seidel (an Army advisor to the project), and the authors of this volume. O'Neil's evaluation matrices and the conceptions of AIDA presented in Part II of this volume were the primary subject of the discussions reported below.

In one AIDA review meeting, Halff posed these seven questions to consider in evaluating courseware needs (Hickey, Spector, & Muraida, 1991):

1. What is/ought to be taught?

2. How should it be taught?

3. What is the development context? What is the corporate knowledge? What are the individual competencies?

4. What was actually developed?

5. What accounts for the differences in 1 through 4?

6. How do we implement fixes to the system?

7. If one had to build AIDA for all instructional settings under consideration, then what would it be like? How would AIDA work?

Halff's last question led to a discussion of all the things that we wanted to accomplish with AIDA. There was clearly more to be done than could be accomplished with a single project or product. O'Neil had administered a planning study to aid the group in deciding what to include in AIDA and what might be postponed or left for other projects. The complete tabulation of O'Neil's evaluation matrix is included below.

Respondents used LOW, MEDIUM, and HIGH to indicate the relative merit of 22 potential AIDA features with respect to 11 areas. Respondents were grouped with regard to their role in the training process: Managers, Instructional Designers, and Researchers. In an attempt to identify areas of consensus, results were averaged using a value of 2 for LOW, 6 for MEDIUM, and 10 for HIGH.

The 22 potential features are lettered A through V and represent the following:

A — instructional templates
B — automated ISD paperwork
C — cognitive science augmentation
D — instructor aids
E — computerized measurement
F — type of media (multi-media)
G — formative evaluation tools

H — updated ISD mode
I — updated learning theory
J — author management system
K — cost-effectiveness tool
L — task database tool
M — catalog of courseware
N — catalog of author aids
O — research justification (explanation feature)
P — ITS (intelligent tutoring system) for ISD
Q — intelligent job aid
R — intelligent template interfaces
S — intelligent help
T — hyper-media
U — on-line documentation
V — portability

The 11 areas are numbered 1 through 11 as follows:

1 — technical merit
2 — value to the SME (subject-matter expert)
3 — value to the instructional designer
4 — state-of-the-art technology
5 — R & D costs
6 — implementation costs
7 — risk
8 — Air Force gain/impact
9 — contribution to science and technology
10 — joint service utility
11 — feasibility to complete as resource

The following matrices tabulate the results of O'Neil's evaluation. This data was collected as part of our effort to achieve consensus on major features and functionality of AIDA. No attempt has been made to make statistical inferences and no implications beyond group consensus are offered here.

An initial review of this data suggests the following:

1. Column 11 (feasibility to complete AIDA as resourced) should not be regarded as reliable due to insufficient responses.

2. If columns 2 & 3 (value to SME and Instructional Designer, respectively) are regarded as a measure of expected utility to AIDA users, then there is some agreement (and some disagreement) about what

O'NEIL'S EVALUATION RESULTS (6 INSTRUCTIONAL DESIGNERS)

	1	2	3	4	5	6	7	8	9	10	11
A	7.3	9.3	8.7	4.7	6.0	3.0	3.6	9.3	3.6	10.0	10.0
B	6.3	8.0	6.7	2.8	3.6	3.0	3.6	9.3	4.4	10.0	10.0
C	8.7	8.0	8.4	10.0	9.0	8.0	10.0	6.0	10.0	6.0	2.0
D	6.0	6.0	7.3	4.0	4.0	2.0	3.6	8.0	5.2	8.0	10.0
E	6.0	3.6	6.0	6.0	6.0	3.3	6.0	7.3	6.0	8.0	2.0
F	6.7	6.0	8.0	5.3	5.0	6.0	4.4	7.3	4.4	7.3	6.0
G	7.3	8.0	9.3	6.7	7.0	7.3	5.2	8.7	6.8	8.7	6.0
H	6.7	4.7	6.7	6.7	6.0	2.0	2.0	6.7	7.3	7.3	10.0
I	8.7	5.3	8.0	10.0	8.7	3.3	6.8	6.7	10.0	6.0	6.0
J	7.3	8.0	9.3	4.0	3.3	3.3	2.8	7.6	3.6	8.7	10.0
K	5.3	4.0	5.3	5.7	6.0	5.0	6.0	7.3	5.2	6.7	10.0
L	7.3	8.7	7.3	5.3	4.7	4.7	2.8	8.0	4.0	8.0	6.0
M	5.3	7.3	8.7	3.3	3.0	3.3	2.0	6.0	6.0	6.7	10.0
N	7.3	6.0	7.3	4.4	3.6	3.0	2.0	5.3	2.8	5.0	10.0
O	6.0	2.0	5.0	5.0	4.7	2.0	6.0	5.2	5.2	4.7	2.0
P	6.7	6.7	6.0	8.7	10.0	7.3	10.0	5.7	6.8	6.7	2.0
Q	9.3	7.3	9.3	10.0	10.0	8.0	9.2	8.0	7.6	8.0	2.0
R	8.7	8.0	8.7	9.3	8.7	4.7	9.2	8.7	7.6	8.7	2.0
S	10.0	8.0	9.2	10.0	10.0	4.0	8.4	8.0	6.8	8.0	2.0
T	6.7	6.0	7.3	8.7	6.0	4.0	2.8	6.7	3.6	8.0	10.0
U	9.3	9.3	9.3	6.0	3.3	3.3	2.0	6.7	3.6	8.0	10.0
V	7.6	5.3	6.7	8.4	10.0	4.0	8.4	8.7	7.3	9.3	2.0

Figure 11.1. O'Neil's Evaluation Matrices.

would be useful. Managers regarded most features as useful; a cost-effectiveness tool was ranked of medium value; automated ISD paperwork ranked of highest value. Instructional designers also ranked a cost-effectiveness tool of medium value, but they ranked an explanation feature even lower; on-line documentation was ranked of highest value. Researchers ranked a cost-effectiveness tool relatively low and ranked intelligent help relatively high.

3. The use of instructional templates was generally ranked of high value to the SME and of low risk. An ITS for ISD and an intelligent job aid were generally ranked of high risk.

The next two sections are re-creations of the April 1990 critique of AIDA. They are based primarily on Spector's notes of that meeting (Hickey, Spector, & Muraida, 1991). They represent a sampling of the type

O'NEIL'S EVALUATION RESULTS (3 MANAGERS)

	1	2	3	4	5	6	7	8	9	10	11
A	8.7	10.0	8.7	3.3	3.3	3.3	2.0	6.0	6.0	10.0	10.0
B	10.0	10.0	10.0	6.0	4.7	4.7	3.3	10.0	7.3	8.7	10.0
C	8.7	7.3	7.3	10.0	7.3	6.0	2.7	7.3	7.3	10.0	4.0
D	10.0	7.3	6.0	6.0	4.7	4.7	3.3	10.0	4.7	7.3	6.0
E	8.7	6.0	8.7	4.7	4.7	4.7	6.0	8.7	8.7	10.0	6.0
F	7.3	8.7	8.7	8.7	7.3	7.3	7.3	6.0	6.0	8.7	6.0
G	8.7	7.3	7.3	7.3	4.7	4.7	4.7	7.3	7.3	10.0	8.0
H	8.7	7.3	8.7	6.0	4.7	4.7	4.7	7.3	7.3	6.0	8.0
I	8.7	7.3	8.7	6.0	3.3	3.3	6.0	7.3	7.3	10.0	10.0
J	8.7	8.7	8.7	7.3	6.0	6.0	4.7	7.3	6.0	10.0	6.0
K	10.0	6.0	6.0	7.3	6.0	6.0	6.0	8.7	8.7	10.0	8.0
L	10.0	8.7	10.0	7.3	6.0	6.0	4.7	8.7	6.0	4.7	6.0
M	8.7	7.3	7.3	4.7	4.7	4.7	2.0	7.3	3.3	6.0	8.0
N	8.7	8.7	8.7	4.7	4.7	3.3	2.0	7.3	4.7	8.0	8.0
O	10.0	10.0	7.3	6.0	4.7	4.7	3.3	6.0	4.7	6.0	6.0
P	8.7	10.0	8.7	10.0	10.0	8.7	10.0	10.0	10.0	10.0	2.0
Q	10.0	8.7	8.7	8.7	6.0	7.3	10.0	10.0	10.0	10.0	5.0
R	8.7	7.3	7.3	7.3	6.0	6.0	10.0	7.3	8.7	10.0	2.0
S	10.0	8.7	10.0	8.7	8.7	8.7	8.7	10.0	8.7	8.7	6.0
T	7.3	7.3	7.3	8.7	6.0	4.7	4.7	8.7	8.7	10.0	8.0
U	10.0	10.0	10.0	6.0	3.3	3.3	2.0	8.7	4.7	10.0	8.0
V	8.7	8.7	8.7	10.0	7.3	7.3	10.0	10.0	10.0	10.0	4.0

Figure 11.1. O'Neil's Evaluation Matrices (continued).

of discussion that preceded and followed the ranking exercise as the group moved toward consensus on a number of AIDA specifications.

O'Neil's Critique of Possible AIDAs

Following the initial ranking and discussion of functional specifications for AIDA, O'Neil presented a critical summary of the discussion up to that point. O'Neil argued that there was more on the AIDA plate than could be funded. Maintaining some diversity in the functional specifications would be a challenge. He viewed the context as one of conceptualizing and prototyping a strawman system and then testing and fixing that system. O'Neil thought the inclusion of default values (Merrill, Part II) in the first-cut system was a good idea. He thought an explanation facility should be added to Merrill's transaction shells. A reference library has yet to be established to support that facility, and that could be the focus of a basic research ef-

O'NEIL'S EVALUATION RESULTS (8 RESEARCHERS)

	1	2	3	4	5	6	7	8	9	10	11
A	6.6	9.5	7.7	5.4	5.3	2.7	3.0	8.9	5.0	8.3	5.3
B	6.0	8.9	8.0	3.4	4.7	4.7	2.6	7.7	2.5	6.6	5.3
C	9.0	5.0	6.6	9.5	9.4	6.6	9.4	7.0	9.0	5.1	6.0
D	6.0	4.5	6.0	4.9	5.4	6.0	4.0	7.5	5.0	7.3	6.0
E	9.5	6.0	8.3	8.0	8.5	4.8	5.8	7.5	7.5	6.6	4.0
F	7.5	6.5	8.9	7.5	7.7	6.6	5.5	8.0	5.3	6.0	6.0
G	7.0	7.5	9.4	6.0	7.7	7.1	6.5	8.5	9.0	7.0	6.0
H	8.0	6.6	9.3	7.5	6.6	4.0	5.5	7.0	6.5	7.1	6.0
I	9.0	6.6	8.7	8.5	10.0	4.0	7.0	6.5	9.5	7.1	4.0
J	7.0	7.0	7.7	7.0	7.1	6.6	5.5	7.5	4.5	7.7	6.0
K	6.5	4.3	6.0	6.0	6.7	5.3	7.3	8.5	5.0	8.9	8.0
L	8.5	6.5	8.3	8.5	7.7	7.3	5.5	8.0	5.0	8.9	6.0
M	4.3	9.5	8.9	2.5	3.1	3.7	2.0	6.5	2.5	7.7	8.0
N	4.0	7.0	6.5	2.6	2.0	3.3	2.0	6.0	2.0	6.6	10.0
O	10.0	4.5	7.1	8.0	8.4	5.2	5.5	6.0	9.5	6.0	4.7
P	8.3	6.0	8.0	10.0	10.0	9.3	8.5	6.5	8.5	6.0	3.3
Q	7.5	7.5	8.3	9.5	8.7	6.0	8.5	7.5	9.0	7.5	6.0
R	7.5	7.5	9.4	9.0	8.0	6.0	9.0	8.0	9.0	6.0	4.7
S	8.3	9.0	9.4	9.5	8.7	6.0	8.3	8.0	8.5	6.6	4.7
T	7.7	6.6	10.0	7.7	6.0	5.2	8.7	8.3	8.9	6.7	6.0
U	5.0	8.3	8.7	4.3	4.7	4.0	3.0	8.5	3.5	6.0	7.3
V	7.7	8.3	7.3	6.7	7.3	6.0	6.0	9.4	3.7	8.3	6.0

Figure 11.1. O'Neil's Evaluation Matrices (continued).

fort. O'Neil viewed Merrill's AIDA (see Part II) as full of diversity and relatively expensive. A first cut (XAIDA) would have to be more restricted than Merrill envisioned.

O'Neil said that Halff's contrast of CAI 'R' Us and the TTC System (see Halff's chapter in Part II) was quite to the point and helped to clarify a critical choice. One way to focus AIDA would be to aim the effort at tools to improve the contracting effort. He also thought Tennyson's proposal (Part II) was an excellent conception of the next generation of ISD. The next generation needed to consider the level of users and adjust the ISD model to the user's level—hereafter dubbed AISD for adaptive ISD.

O'Neil identified two primary viewpoints with regard to AIDA conceptualizations: 1) development view (Gagné, Merrill, and Tennyson), and 2) research view (Halff, Polson, Friedman). As a consequence, O'Neil stated a need to reach closure on several of these issues: 1) Whether to include alternative configurations of AIDA, 2) Whether to use an incremental development model, 3) how to prioritize features, and 4) whether to embed AIDA in another instructional environment.

O'Neil made it a point to separate development and delivery issues, in contrast to Merrill. He reiterated the need for an explanation facility. If the focus continued to be on procedural learning, then it would be necessary to consolidate relevant research findings in one place. O'Neil indicated that it would be desirable to include some emphasis on metacognitive learning in an AIDA.

Brown-Beasley claimed that what was needed was a rapidly prototyped version of Merrill's transactions coupled with an expert system using an expert system shell such as CLIPS. He estimated that such a task would require a year. Everyone seemed to agree that we did need annual products and prototypes in times of tight money. The accepted fact was that procurement would end up determining where AIDA would actually head.

O'Neil maintained that AIDA needed an author management system and a course management system. Without computer-managed instruction there would be no benchmarks to determine progress and there would be weak Air Force support.

The AIDA project could also provide sets of lessons learned to transition to the field. Answering these questions would go a long way in that direction: 1) Why is traditional ISD dead in the DoD? 2) Why didn't the Air Force adopt ISS (Instructional Support System—an authoring language developed by the Air Force)? 3) What success stories for authoring systems exist? and 4) What are the cost drivers and trade-offs pertinent to authoring systems?

O'Neil cited the need to address procedural learning and metacognitive skills, the need to automate existing paperwork, the need to integrate an AI based simulation authoring tool, and the need to include an evaluation tool kit in AIDA. O'Neil believes that CBT authoring will be team-based, yet he did not see how AIDA would handle team authoring; this underlined his interest in an author management system, similar to that recommended by Tennyson (Part II).

O'Neil maintained that AIDA should be able to handle existing media and be able to accommodate new media. He also claimed that it was not too early to give thought to what the user interface should look like. In addition, evaluations of Merrill's transaction shells should provide further input data to user interface decisions. Results of these evaluations are reported later in this chapter.

O'Neil thought that if the near term AIDA were to be a research tool, then measurement and evaluation issues needed to be confronted directly and soon. More data gathering would have to be put into the system to allow it to function as a research tool. This capability was added to the transaction shells evaluated at the Air Force Academy and the Lowry Technical Training Center. Basically, the system recorded the time each menu item was selected, making it possible to track how much time was spent on a particular authoring activity and in what order authoring tasks were accomplished. This data has proved essential to the creation of a preliminary model of courseware authoring with transaction shells, which we shall discuss in more detail later in this chapter.

O'Neil addressed two issues raised in Tennyson's proposal (Part II): 1) a centralized facility for sharing courseware, and 2) a database of representative users. The Air Training Command advisors reacted in a positive manner to these suggestions, although they are most likely expensive options. O'Neil also recommended targeting a particular Air Force system to use in developing instruction with an experimental AIDA.

O'Neil concluded with a list of eight critical issues that needed to be addressed in an AIDA system:

1. An investment strategy.

2. Benchmarks.

3. An explanation system.

4. Prototype tryouts with users.

5. An R & D agenda.

6. A CMI (computer-managed instruction) system.

7. Focus on procedural and metacognitive skills.

8. State-of-the-art assessments.

Most of O'Neil's suggestions have already been accepted (#3 and #6 are not being implemented in the initial XAIDA prototype).

Reigeluth's Critique of Possible AIDAs

Charles Reigeluth provided a much different perspective on how to proceed with implementing an AIDA based on his model of instructional development. He believed that a first-cut AIDA system should epitomize the long range AIDA (see Reigeluth's chapter in Part I). As a consequence, he argued, it becomes more important to articulate the grand view of AIDA as much as possible. Reigeluth argued that developing an epitome system using simplifying conditions to enhance success and investment in all parts would simplify the long range plan and provide a rational development model. The long range areas of interest were: 1) Determine the status and structure of the instructional design knowledge base, 2) Specify functional requirements for instructional design guidelines, 3) Conduct empirical studies of instructional guidelines delivery, and 4) Conduct empirical tests of instructional design guidance methodologies.

Reigeluth agreed with the focus on intermediate users in the first-cut system. He would further restrict the subject matter domain from electronics maintenance to something like avionics maintenance. He agreed with the decision to emphasize an instructional design advising system first and worry about automated development and delivery later.

Reigeluth disagreed with the tentative plan to have the starting input to a first-cut AIDA be well-formulated learning capabilities. He preferred to start with the epitome of input, which in this case is a cognitive task analysis or possibly an enterprise analysis.

Reigeluth argued that Merrill's conception of AIDA (Part II) could be simplified in a number of ways (e.g., restrict the audience, restrict the environment, restrict the task, restrict the transactions involved, restrict user control, etc.).

Reigeluth found the AIDA functional diagram (Introduction to Part II) provocative and offered the extension depicted in Figure 11.2.

While his line of reasoning is similar to Halff's, Reigeluth did point out some differences. With regard to Halff's three dichotomies (general vs. domain specific, black box transactions vs. primitives, and general vs. detailed specifications), Reigeluth denied the inescapable nature of the dichotomies and recommended a compromise combination in each case.

Reigeluth warned against confusing the operationalization of strategies with the automation and instantiation of strategies. The former apply to particular content domains; the latter apply to particular delivery systems. In general, Reigeluth liked Halff's focus and viewed it as a version of epitomizing.

Reigeluth questioned whether tutoring (Tennyson, Part II) should be a primary feature of AIDA. Reigeluth indicated that it was not clear who Tennyson's users were. Reigeluth saw AIDA as replacing, not retraining, instructional designers. The idea of AIDA was to help SMEs develop effective courseware without resorting to the expense of human expert instructional designers. Reigeluth would omit the content knowledge base from the first-cut system. He also warned against attempting to break new ground in all areas. For example, AIDA is not trying to break new ground in the areas of expert system methodologies.

Dallman contended that if AIDA was aimed at training development branch personnel, then some tutoring in instructional design of courseware would be helpful. In general, Dallman claimed that what was needed was a

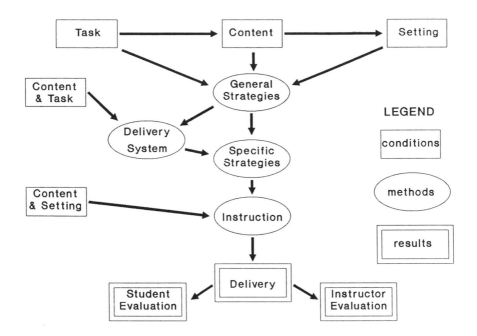

Figure 11.2. AIDA Functions.

cooperative system with humans still in the design and decision-making loop.

Brown-Beasley said that we needed to optimize the SME's and the instructional designer's time. Reigeluth was in favor of retaining user overrides with an explanation or rationale capability.

Ellis wanted to know if AIDA would accommodate remediation in secondary training settings? The emphasis on electronics maintenance and CBT indicated that it might support remediation in CBT developed for field training detachments, for example. Newcomb indicated that the focus was on CBT in primary instructional settings at the TTCs. Seidel and Ellis noted that the Army and the Navy did not support CBT in primary instructional settings.

Seidel added that we should clearly separate development from delivery. The need was to help training developers. To accomplish this end, we should concentrate on front-end analysis. A multi-level system with much flexibility would be required. Users should be involved in the development of AIDA.

It should be noted that Armstrong Laboratory has made a serious attempt to involve users from the very beginning of the AIDA effort. A needs assessment for CBT planning and implementation was conducted at Lowry AFB (Spector, 1990). Representatives from the Air Training Command have also been actively involved as have representatives from a Technical Training Wing, a Technical Training Squadron, the ATS (Advanced Training System) System Program Office, the Air University, the Air Force Reserve, the Air Force Academy, and the other military services. In addition, Muraida and Spector have conducted a series of transaction shell studies which involved instructional designers and developers at the Air Force Academy and the 3400th Technical Training Wing at Lowry AFB (Spector & Muraida, 1991a).

Responses to the Critiques

Tennyson defended a system usable by both novices and experts (see Part II). Complete novices will be "coached" through the system by the ISD Expert, which will make most of the decisions. More advanced users will be "advised" through the system with users able to pre-empt system defaults and decisions. An advanced instructional design system should be adaptive, just as an ITS adapts its instruction to the student.

Tennyson dropped the requirement for a mainframe and restated that requirement in the form of a need for an open architecture and a centralized, large capacity database with remote access via personal computers or workstations. He estimated that it would take about five years and $10 million to construct such a system. As a consequence, he agreed with Reigeluth and Halff that it would be necessary to establish simplifying conditions in the beginning so that within one year a minimal system prototype could be built. In subsequent years, that initial system would need to be field tested and elaborated. Tennyson stressed that his overall aim was to build a total ISD environment and deliver yearly growth products along the way to that goal.

Merrill offered a variety of comments. He first distinguished two separate issues: 1) What to include in an AIDA system, and 2) How to implement what is selected. Merrill saw Armstrong Laboratory as having sole responsibility for #2; the consultants and advisors ought to provide insights for #1. In order to make decisions about epitomizing and rapid prototyping, Merrill offered eight activities in a possible development plan:

1. Choose the environment, users, and content.

2. Identify a number of transaction shells to handle most of the instruction.

3. Identify initial parameters for those shells.

4. Build the initial shells.

5. Test, tryout, and modify as necessary—loop #1.

6. Add intelligence and mini-experts—loop #2.

7. Add management system—loop #3.

8. Add integrating shells—loop #4.

Merrill then warned of several hazards with such a plan. First, avoid the temptation to produce specifications all the way down to level #8. Second avoid the temptation to make specifications for multiple iterations at the looping levels. Third, make sure that there is a firm commitment to go through level five and one loop in the first attempt.

Reigeluth asked about expanding the number of shells. Merrill replied that iterations through the loops provided a mechanism to accomplish this. Reigeluth indicated that an alternative elaboration strategy would be to begin the second loop after a single trip through Merrill's first loop.

Halff indicated three concerns: 1) Would AIDA(n) be a smaller version of AIDA(n + 1)? 2) Would AIDA(n) collect data to help with AIDA(n + 1)? and 3) How would users be kept in the loop throughout the AIDA development? Halff liked Merrill's cyclic approach to the development and O'Neil's idea to collect data for the next version.

Ellis was worried that Merrill's first-cut system still leaves users not knowing what they don't know. This may not be an unacceptable situation if what they don't know are specific principles and practices of instructional design, and the primary users will continue to be SMEs with little experience in instructional design.

Merrill indicated that his tryout loops involved users. He took the occasion to add a fifth loop to his cyclic development involving automated learning systems. Such systems might be based on artificial neural networks and are clearly futuristic in an instructional design setting; however, they are not unimaginable or impossible.

Halff stressed that the context in which AIDA is used would be the major factor in determining what it should be like. Seidel said that academics did not have an exclusive hold on instructional knowledge; rather, there was a great deal of such knowledge in the intuitions and practices of users. As a consequence, users needed to be kept in the AIDA development loop in order to insure that their knowledge was imparted to AIDA.

Polson wondered how users would react to a system that helped a lot with naming but none with using rules. Merrill and Polson agreed that one hazard of making a nomenclature transaction available would be that its ease of use and power might tempt users into using it in inappropriate situations. In Dallman's terminology, Merrill's Wrong-Objective-Syndrome could become Merrill's Wrong-Transaction-Syndrome (the acronym WTS being appropriately unpronounceable).

Seidel said that we needed to distinguish developers from students. A corollary is that user requirements should be separated from learning requirements. With regard to tools and interfaces, the emphasis should be on the developers point of view. With regard to the instructional design knowledge contained in the transactions, learning requirements need to be embodied in some form somewhere in AIDA.

Reigeluth and Halff had a discussion about the extent to which user needs should be accommodated. Reigeluth thought that we should not attempt to implement a user need that was too difficult to operationalize. Halff thought that we should give the user authority over our investment strategy.

O'Neil stressed the need to build an evaluation system into the development plan and into the system. If the system collected data to be used for evaluation, then users could turn in that data which would prove important in refining AIDA.

Polson's response stressed a need to prioritize functions and features proposed for AIDA. She said that we should not view AIDA as a complete authoring system. We don't need CMI in the first-cut, nor do we need to worry about automating paperwork. In fact, part of the specification of the ATS is to automate the ISD documentation. She agreed with Reigeluth's notion of epitomizing. She saw a need to have a system capable of handling a problem complex enough to show that AIDA was doing some good, yet the system should be simple enough to remain manageable. She agreed with O'Neil's need to prioritize, but disagreed with him about including metacognitive skills in a first-cut system.

Muraida pointed out that one way of keeping users in the loop was to insure that AIDA communicated with them in their everyday language— don't allow AIDA to intimidate or alienate them.

Tennyson and Mongillo pointed out that aircraft designers did not consult pilots in designing planes until the design was fairly well along. Seidel countered that the instructional design domain was not so well formed as aerodynamics. Halff added that Merrill's strategy was designed to wash out useless ideas in the iterations through the loops.

Ellis and Merrill claimed that AIDA could act as a cognitive extender. Halff indicated that for an explanation users want examples and lessons learned, not academic references to articles in journals. Merrill indicated several levels of explanation that could be included. For example, one level might be a trace of the rules used in reaching a particular decision; a second level might be informal data in the user's terms. Merrill did not see an immediate use for O'Neil's citations of formal studies and experiments.

Gagné thought that 'performance' needed to be well defined in the manual. Merrill thought that enterprises should replace objectives in planning instruction. Several individuals have already expressed the belief that any ISD material should be incorporated into AIDA in a way that is largely transparent to users.

It was further agreed that enterprises should be added to the AIDA consensus list, although the role of an enterprise in integrating transaction shells might take a while to clarify. The short term AIDA should provide for integratable transactions. The longer term AIDA should provide mechanisms for actually integrating transactions.

Merrill agreed with most of Gagné's remarks about the need to include enterprises and the possibility of building transaction shells for enterprises. However, only an enterprise scenario would have a relatively simple transaction shell. Merrill's notion of an extended enterprise transaction involves all the knowledge pertaining to an enterprise and would be a relatively complex elaborated frame network.

Halff thought there were still unresolved issues concerning what AIDA should do. He did think that we had agreed to focus on CBT development and design and that we had identified the Technical Training Center CBT developers as a target user audience. It was noted that Reigeluth wanted the first-cut AIDA system to address the analysis phase of ISD and that Merrill wanted the first-cut system to automate the production of usable instructional materials.

Ellis indicated that the first-cut AIDA system need only incorporate nomenclature and checklist procedure transactions. Dallman agreed that these two transaction types mapped nicely onto the avionics maintenance area.

Reigeluth said that the first-cut AIDA should focus on easier procedural tasks. The Knowledge Analysis and Acquisition System (KAAS—see Merrill, Part II) need not be a massive component. Merrill countered that we needed the capability to teach all the knowledge pertaining to an entity. If there are only a few transaction shells, then the KAAS can be quite small.

Gagné liked the focus on maintenance training, but wondered about the user interface and how information about students, tasks, and the environment would be collected. There was considerable discussion about what kind of explanations a first-cut AIDA should include, if any. This led to a list of items that had obviously not been resolved:

1. What would be the entry point/input into the system?

2. What computer platform would be used?

3. Would AIDA provide tutoring/training?

4. Would AIDA allow user overrides?

Merrill distinguished two kinds of rules currently in his transaction shells: 1) those which were parameterized, and 2) those which were not parameterized. Parameterized rules could easily be overridden by users, if/when that was deemed appropriate. Merrill added a few items to the consensus list:

1. Rapid prototyping (Armstrong Laboratory is calling this incremental development).

2. Built-in data collection on both instructors and students.

3. No content semantics in the first-cut AIDA.

4. Use of Merrill-like transactions.

The long-term AIDA could then address such items as an intelligent advisor, integrated instructional strategies, an instructional model, etc.

Merrill provided a sketch of how transactions might be made integratable. First, use an object-oriented programming paradigm, so that transactions could pass messages back and forth. Second, develop a hierarchy of transactions, so that transactions could inherit parameter values and attributes from elsewhere in the hierarchy. The Knowledge Analysis and Acquisition System would have to indicate what to ask SMEs, and how to represent the information elicited. That representational scheme would provide a way to write objectives, classify objectives, and to classify outcomes. Transactions would have access to all the information in the representation system.

The Consensus Conception

Spector indicated that there was substantial agreement on the following:

1. Focus on CBT development and design.

2. Focus on maintenance training at a Technical Training Center.

3. Target current Air Force CBT developers.

4. Provide a help facility.

5. Provide some kind of explanation facility.

6. Allow limited user overrides of defaults.

7. Provide for the collection of information about students, tasks, and the environment.

8. Use the rapid incremental development approach.

9. Provide built-in data collection on students and users.

10. Do not attempt to provide content semantics.

11. Build on Merrill's transaction shell concept.

12. Adopt situated development.

13. Initially target intermediate users.

14. Involve users in the development process.

Disagreement remained with regard to the following:

1. The number and type of shells required.

2. Whether or not to include the analysis phase.

3. Whether or not to include non-maintenance areas.

4. What the starting input to AIDA should be.

5. What computer platform/architecture to use.

6. Whether to provide tutoring and embedded training.

Following Spector's summary of the points of agreement and disagreement further discussion occurred which demonstrated that a number of issues still remained unresolved despite the formal exercise of prioritizing specifications and characteristics. Among the issues which generated further discussion and debate were:

1. Need for "Benchmarking" or a system for establishing standard evaluation criteria for AIDA.

2. Role of the knowledge acquisition component.

3. The need for simulations in a prototype AIDA

4. Whether or not the prototype AIDA should be able to address instructional research questions that transcend its system characteristics.

Summary

We have attempted to give the reader a glimpse of the level and type of critique that led to the functional specifications of AIDA. We have undertaken this enterprise in order to illustrate one of the principles already introduced: evaluation belongs in every phase of instructional planning and development. The discussion reviewed above was somewhat lengthy, but it was much shorter than the two in-depth critiques that AIDA underwent. What follows is a discussion of the formative evaluation of one of the core technologies proposed for AIDA: transaction shells.

Proof of Concept

Professor Merrill allowed the Air Force Armstrong Laboratory to evaluate two transaction shells. The purpose of these evaluations was to determine the usability of Merrill's transaction shell approach for the AIDA project (Muraida & Spector, in press). A needs assessment had already indicated that military technical training developers were seeking some kind of authoring guidance (Spector, 1990; Muraida, Spector, & Dallman, 1990).

Evaluation Methodology

Data were collected on two separate occasions. The first study involved a single subject matter expert who had no previous computer experience. He was an instructor at the Air Force Academy responsible for navigation instruction. His task was to develop a CBI module on the T-37 instrument panel for use in a navigation course. Merrill's Naming Transaction Shell was the only instructional design software used in the initial study (Canfield & Spector, 1991).

A second study was conducted with eight subject matter experts at the Lowry AFB Technical Training Center and the same instructor at the Air Force Academy. Two transaction shells were used in the follow-on study: 1) Naming the parts, and 2) Checklist procedures. These two shells were the most completely developed shells from Utah State University, and they clearly represented instructional transactions likely to occur in technical training settings.

In each study, subjects had approximately 30 hours to design and produce a lesson module requiring at least one hour of student instruction. In the first study, the time was spaced out over a two week period. In the second study, the time was contained in a one week period. In both cases, total time (approximately 30 hours) included time to learn how to use the software effectively.

In the first study, the subject did not create any of his own graphics, although his total time includes time to plan graphics—what to put in each graphic, how to group parts, etc. In the second study, all but one subject also created some or all of their graphics using a simple MS-DOS based draw program, Dr. Halo.™ None of the subjects were acquainted with this program prior to the study.

Subjects were given an initial profile sheet, which was used to gather biographical data. They were given approximately six hours of instruction on the software. Subjects in the second study received approximately two hours of instruction on the draw program. Subjects then went about the task of planning, designing, and creating their lessons. They kept a log of observations about the software. The software itself kept track of the time on each task selectable from a Transaction Shell menu.

In addition, their questions and verbal observations were logged by the authors. At the end of the study, the lessons underwent a peer review procedure and subjects were debriefed and given an exit interview. Remarks were again recorded in the log.

The total development time was not allowed to exceed 30 hours because one objective of these studies was to determine if Merrill's Transaction Shells held any promise of providing a truly cost-effective courseware authoring environment. Various studies suggest that anywhere from 200 to 600 hours of total development time are required for an hour's worth of CBI (Carter, 1990). These studies would not have been possible with a full-featured authoring environment such as TenCore™ or Quest™. Learning to use such complex software would have required far in excess of the 30 hours available.

Results

One significant finding of these studies is that Merrill's Transaction Shells do provide a highly cost-effective authoring environment that is indeed accessible to novice CBI designers. All subjects who were able to complete the study (two of the Lowry AFB subjects were assigned other military duties in the middle of the study) did in fact create lessons which were nearly complete enough to deliver to students. One Lowry AFB subject has already field tested his courseware with four students in order to uncover any deficiencies in the lessons before incorporating the material into the regular course, which is expected to take place in July, 1991.

Some specific observations are in order, as they reflect unexpected findings. One of the Lowry subjects had some CBI experience, extensive experience in the subject area, and some experience with computers. Another subject had no CBI experience but recent experience with the computers used in this study (Zenith Z-248s) and a computer at home. The individual with recent Z-248 experience was able to create two lesson modules, whereas all others completed the equivalent of a single lesson module. Lesson modules represented between one and three hours of instruction for a student. This suggests that recent computer experience might be more relevant to CBI design success using Merrill's Transaction Shells than CBI design experience in another environment.

Another observation is that the pattern of revisions was not at all constant, yet all subjects produced roughly equivalent results. For example, some subjects preferred to postpone all revisions until a complete version of the lesson had been created. Others revised each part of the lesson as they proceeded through the process. Peer review of these lessons revealed no significant differences in quality. As yet there is no emergent pattern between input profiles and revision profiles.

Of the nine subjects involved in these studies, only one had any significant CBI experience—about a year's experience authoring in the Quest™ environment. This individual gave the lowest estimate of the time that would have been required to achieve a comparable lesson in a full-featured CBI authoring environment. All but one had extensive experience as subject-matter experts (SMEs). Even the relatively inexperienced SME was able to complete a lesson module, although he spent more off-line time planning the lesson than the others. Only two of the nine had extensive experience as instructors. One of these indicated on the first day of the study that he thought that stand-up, lecture-based instruction was the only effective way to teach. At the end of the week, he had become an outspoken advocate of CBI.

Five of the seven subjects who completed the study indicated a desire to deliver their lessons to students and a willingness to continue to use this form of CBI. All five of those who tried to use the Checklist Procedure authoring software found it problematic—generally less understandable than the Naming software. All found some faults with the software—lack of integrated functionalities, limited word processing and graphics capabilities, too much student control allowed, etc. However, all indicated that this software was effective and contributed to their productivity. It should be noted that these versions of Merrill's transaction shells were originally intended to be demonstrations of a concept, and not commercial grade authoring instruments.

One last observation is that none of the subjects ever expressed a fear of being replaced by the computer. This question was posed directly only to the Air Force Academy subject. His response was that he viewed the software as yet another resource or support tool. This opinion was expressed indirectly by all of the Lowry AFB subjects. See Spector and Muraida (1991b) for a more complete evaluation of transaction shells.

Scenario Construction

Another element of the effort to establish the functional specifications of AIDA was the construction of a paper-based scenario of an automated instructional design advisor which instantiated the major functional characteristics of the near-term AIDA: pull-down menus, knowledge analysis, development tools, and a set of instructional transactions. Mei Technology produced the scenario with the intention of providing the consultants with a tangible example of what kind of functionality they were proposing. The demonstration of this paper-based model enabled the consultant group to observe the human-computer interface conventions they had incorporated by virtue of their consensus development exercises. The scenario enabled the group to critique and revise their initial proposals in view of the operational characteristics of their "strawman" AIDA. Examples of the scenario screens are provided in Hickey, Spector, & Muraida (1992).

Developing a Cognitive Model for Courseware Development

If automated tools are to realize their potential to augment the designer's problem solving capacity, it will be necessary to create models of the instructional design process at a level of granularity that permits researchers to relate the cognitive complexity of the design task, scope of the design effort, design experience, and authoring system flexibility to various indices of courseware quality (e.g., level of interactivity). An obvious requirement is the necessity to develop models which accurately reflect the instructional design process from the user's perspective.

Models of Instructional Design

Models of instructional design and models of design in other domains undeniably exist. The most prevalent instructional models are based on an engineering approach to curriculum development called Instructional Systems Development (ISD). There are a number of these models in use today (Andrews & Goodson, 1980; Tennyson, 1989). They typically divide the process of developing instruction into five stages and prescribe more or less detailed procedures for each stage. As indicated earlier, we consider instructional *development* to refer to all five stages, while instructional *design* refers to a particular and important phase within the larger process of developing instruction. A partial ISD model is depicted in Table 11.1.

Both Tennyson and Van Merriënboer describe versions of such an instructional development model and then elaborate ways to refine the analysis and design phases so as to integrate those phases with cognitive science (Tennyson, 1990; Van Merriënboer *et al.*, 1991). The development and validation of user models for automated instructional design will result in an evaluation tool. This tool could enable developers to determine optimum fit between instructional design task, the available instructional design system configuration, and the system's level/ease of use.

Models of Courseware Authoring

In arguing for an updated ISD model appropriate to CBI settings, Tennyson observed that there is a need to attend to the specific authoring activities in each phase (Part II). In the course of describing specific courseware authoring activities, Tennyson has built a potentially more useful model of the instructional design process. The usefulness of Tennyson's model results from its emphasis on human activities (what instructional designers do) as opposed to the idealized results of those human activities. We contend that the human activities of automated instructional design need to be

ISD PHASE	TYPICAL GOALS
ANALYSIS	Define training requirements. Analyze target population. Establish performance levels.
DESIGN	Specify instructional objectives. Group and sequence objectives. Design instructional treatments. Specify evaluation system.
PRODUCTION	Develop learning activities. Develop test items. Perform formative evaluation.
IMPLEMENTATION	Implement learning activities. Administer test items. Assess student results.
MAINTENANCE	Revise content materials. Revise test items. Assess course effectiveness.

Table 11.1. Typical ISD Model.

analyzed in terms of the cognitive demands of an illstructured task that includes the complexities of authoring and instructional planning.

Making the instructional designer a primary unit of analysis in the model immediately introduces an additional complicating factor: levels of experience. What the experienced designer does may differ radically (in both order and substance) from what the novice designer may do, yet they may both produce effective (or ineffective) courseware designs. It is a commonplace in cognitive psychology that experts perform differently than novices (e.g., Glaser, 1989). Novices are characterized as attending to the superficial and perceptible aspects of a problem. Experts, by contrast, can focus immediately on the relevant aspects. Moreover, the expert is usually capable of marshalling his/her procedural and declarative knowledge for use at the right time and place. Experts achieve levels of automaticity with regard to common procedures. Evidence also indicates that experts chunk problems much differently than novices. We hypothesize that instructional design expertise runs along the same sort of continuum.

In addition to the need to account for relevant instructional design experiences, a complete model of the computer-based instructional design process will need to take into account how and whether various activities are supported within a particular automated instructional design system. The degree of support and its level of success will have a direct impact on the complexity of the instructional design process. For example, if the instructional design model identifies as a critical authoring activity the specification of an instructional strategy, then relevant questions to ask of a candidate courseware authoring tool are the following:

1. Does the system allow users to input strategies?

2. If so, is strategy input optional or required?

3. If optional, how is a default strategy determined?

4. What does the system do with the user's input strategy?

5. Are strategies implemented implicitly or explicitly?

6. Can users get advice about strategies?

7. Are selected strategies critiqued by the system?

8. If so, are they critiqued before or after sequencing?

This list of questions is not meant to be complete. It is only meant to suggest that in a computer-based authoring setting, the critical factors of an instructional design model that are expected to correlate with quality and cost effectiveness of courseware produced are those which take into account what users of various levels of experience can and actually manage to do with a particular system.

One implication of our view is that particular courseware authoring environments will produce instructional design models (when such models are fully elaborated) that are fitted to a restricted set of related authoring situations. The criteria for points of demarcation among those sets require empirical identification. Van Merriënboer's distinction between recurrent and nonrecurrent procedures can be used to illustrate this point (1991). What is a recurrent procedure in one authoring environment may not be a recurrent procedure and may not even occur in another environment.

Likewise, Tennyson's analysis of complexity can also be used to make the same point (1991). Different authoring environments differ in levels of complexity. One environment may require users to use an operating system to find files or to be familiar with a particular instructional theory or vocabulary; another may not place such demands on the user.

One way to build such models is to include data gathering features into test versions of an authoring tool. Data to be gathered should include sequence of items selected, time spent on a task, number and type of revisions, and the like. As will be shown below, such data provides a rich source of both qualitative and quantitative data for the instructional design modeling process.

Method

The general approach proposed here is based on the studies of Nelson, Magliaro, & Sherman (1988) in the area of cognitive processes in instructional design work, and the research of Hammond, Hamm, Grassia, & Pearson (1987) in the field of problem solving. Nelson *et al.* (1988) have portrayed instructional design as a predominately ill-structured problem-solving process. They contend that instructional design problems and models lie on a continuum from ill-structured to well-structured. Furthermore, they assert that instructional designers vary along the same dimension from novices to experts with corresponding cognitive differences in the way they approach their tasks. Nelson (1987) substantiated this in a study of novice and expert instructional designers' thought processes. What Nelson *et al.* (1988) have done to the domain of instructional design is to subject it the cognitive analysis of its most current instructional strategies. This implies that instructional designers may use the same type of problem-solving techniques and tools (e.g., schemata, metacognitive processes) to accomplish their work. Furthermore, this implies that communicating with the designer, as in communicating with the learner, requires a message tailored to his/her level of expertise. Tennyson's (1990) view of instructional design as inherently iterative ties in closely with Nelson's (1987) assertion that designers often go from level to level of a design problem rather than working in a "top-down" fashion. The work of Hammond *et al.* (1987) and Hamm (1988a) appear to provide a close analogue instructional design problem solving. Hammond *et al.* (1987) and Hamm (1988a) have presented evidence to support the notion that complex problem solving often requires a shift between analytic and intuitive thinking. Analytical thinking, according to Hamm, is characterized as slow and deliberate, and usually highly accurate and consistent. Intuitive thinking is, by contrast, rapid, unconscious data processing, characterized by moderate levels of accuracy. Hamm's (1988a) efforts to study the effects of task characteristics on a moment by moment basis appear to provide a molecular level of analysis which would enable observers to pinpoint the components of the instructional design task which require differing levels of intuitive or analytical thinking.

Using two observational instruments, which focus respectively, on observer assessments and task performer perceptions, Hamm (1988a) has attempted to capture the continuum of cognitive modes between intuition and analysis by scaling general features of cognitive modes common to a broad range of problem solving activities. Data are collected using protocols obtained as subjects "think aloud" (Rowe, 1985). Hamm's methodology has demonstrated the capacity to identify intuitive and analytical components of complex task performance in content areas where a fair amount of agreement exists on the manner in which cognitive modes are distributed (e.g, clinical diagnosis, Hamm, 1988b; and engineering, Hammond *et al.*, 1987, and Hamm, 1988a).

The cognitive continuum dimension appears to be useful in that it provides an abstract, meta-language to describe the real-time process of instructional design that is not tied to the peculiarities of a particular authoring environment. By relating the cognitive mode of the designer to activities at a particular juncture in an instructional design task it should be possible to determine which aspects of a design task could benefit from algorithms, and, conversely, which should be left to individual ingenuity.

At a more molar level, the use of the cognitive continuum approach incorporates the variable types alluded to above: designer experience and ability, and the design environment, in conjunction with the nature of the design task. It is expected that these variables will be related to the type of cognitive mode a designer applies to a design task, as well as the ensuing product.

This approach is an attempt to combine variables related to the designer, the instructional design tasks, and the instructional design environment into a model which is representative of most automated design and development situations. This can be accomplished by identifying the most representative variables in the above categories, rather than attempting to create an overspecified (in the regression sense) model. This approach could provide an evaluator with the means to pinpoint problems in instructional design guidance. It is intended to provide the evaluator with a source of systematic formative evalution data.

Another way of expressing our methodology is to think of high level variables or facets of instructional design in three layers: inputs, processes, and outputs. The initial model proposed for analysis is encapsulated in Table 11.2.

Such a model as the one depicted above can be used as the basis of both a formative and a summative evaluation. In addition, if the data is collected and analyzed dynamically as a course is being developed, the system could potentially predict how successful the course would be. This kind of information would be essential to Tennyson's ITS for ISD and for Duchastel's critiquing system (1990).

Our main contention here, however, is that making effective use of an authoring environment is an exercise in optimization. Further, what needs to be optimized will vary with the authoring environment and instructional development task. As a consequence, in order to make the most of a particular automated environment it will become increasingly important to develop and validate courseware development models similar to that suggested above. It is our belief that one of the primary research issues concerning automated instructional designs concerns the modeling process (see Muraida's conclusion to Part III).

Conclusion

In this chapter we have attempted to indicate the importance of evaluation to successful instructional design and development. We have introduced several principles (e.g., evaluate all phases of ISD, perform quality control before evaluation, and build data collection into automated systems). We have shared some of the evaluation process applied to the AIDA project with the reader to illustrate these points. In addition, we have ar-

INPUTS	PROCESSES	OUTPUTS
ID experience.	Times on each authoring	Overall dev. time.
CBI experience.	activity.	Peer review.
Subject matter experience.	Number of revisions.	Development cost.
Computer experience.	Purpose of revisions.	Student results.
Instructor experience.	Sequence of activities.	Student time under
Personal data—age, rank,		instruction.
sex, educ.		

Table 11.2. Initial CBI Instructional Design Model.

gued that a long range goal should be to develop an automated instructional design system with built-in data collection that could be used to model and predict the outcomes of a particular development effort. The future of automated instructional design systems may include dynamic formative evaluation of the design process, which could be viewed as the analog of dynamic student modeling in an ITS.

References

Ahmad, A. (1989). Evaluating appropriate technology for development: Before and after. *Evaluation Review, 13*(3), 310–319.

Andrews, D. H., & Goodson, L. A. (1980). A comparative analysis of models of instructional design. *Journal of Instructional Development, 3*(4), 2–16.

Carter, J. (1990). *The interactive courseware decision handbook.* Randolph AFB, TX: HQ ATC Technical Report.

Canfield, A. M., & Spector, J. M. (1991). *A pilot study of the naming transaction shell* (AL-TP-1991-0009). Brooks AFB, TX: Technical paper for the Training Systems Division of the Air Force Armstrong Laboratory (Human Resources Directorate).

Dick, W., & Carey, L. (1985). *The systematic design of instruction.* Glenview, IL: Scott Foresman.

Duchastel, P. C. (1990). Cognitive designs for instructional design. *Instructional Science, 19*(6), 437–444.

Gagné, R. M., & Merrill, M. D. (1990). Integrative goals for instructional design. *ETR&D, 38*(1), 23–30.

Gagné, R. M., Briggs, L. J., & Wager, W. W. (1988). *Principles of instructional design* (3rd edition). New York: Holt, Rinehart, & Winston.

Geol, V., & Pirolli, P. (1989). Motivating the notion of generic design within information processing: The design space problem. *AI Magazine, 10*(1), 18–35.

Glaser, R. (1989). Expertise and learning: How do we think about instructional processes now that we have discovered knowledge structures? In D. Klahr & K. Kotovsky (Eds.), *Complex information processing: The impact of Herbert Simon.* Hillsdale, NJ: Lawrence Erlbaum Associates.

Hamm, R. M. (1988a). Moment by moment variation in expert analytic and intuitive cognitive activity. *IEEE Transactions on Systems, Man, and Cybernetics, 18*, 5.

Hamm, R. M. (1988b). Clinical intuition and clinical analysis: Expertise and the cognitive continuum. In J. Dowie & A. Elstein (Eds.), *Professional judgment: A reader in clinical decision-making.* Cambridge, UK: Cambridge University Press.

Hammond, K. R., Hamm, R. M., Grassia, J., & Pearson, T. (1987). Direct comparison of the efficacy of intuitive and analytical cognition in expert judgment. *IEEE Transactions on Systems, Man, and Cybernetics,* Vol. SMC-17.

Hickey, A. E., Spector, J. M., & Muraida, D. J. (1991). *Specifications for an advanced instructional design advisor (AIDA) for computer-based training* (ALTP19910014). Brooks AFB, TX: Technical Paper for the Air Force Armstrong Laboratory, Human Resources Directorate.

Hickey, A. E., Spector, J. M., & Muraida, D. J. (1992). *Design specifications for the advanced instructinal design advisor (AIDA)* (Vols 1 & 2) (AL-TR-1991-0085).

Brooks AFB, TX: Technical Report for the Air Force Armstrong Laboratory, Human Resources Directorate.

Mager, R. F. (1975). *Preparing instructional objectives*. Belmont, CA: Fearon-Pitman Publishers.

Muraida, D. J., & Spector, J. M. (in press). Advanced instructional design advisor. *Instructional Science*.

Muraida, D. J., Spector, J. M., & Dallman, B. E. (1990). Establishing instructional strategies for advanced interactive technologies. *Proceedings of the psychology in the DoD symposium*, USAFA, CO, April, 1990.

Nelson, W. A. (1987). Procedural differences and knowledge organization in expert and novice instructional designers. Paper presented at meeting of American Educational Research Association, Washington, DC.

Nelson, W. A., Magliaro, S., & Sherman, T. M. (1988). The intellectual content of instructional design. *Journal of Instructional Development, 11*(1).

Pirolli, P. (1989). On the art of building: Putting a new instructional design into practice. In H. Burns & J. Parlette (Eds.), *Proceedings of the 2nd intelligent tutoring systems research forum*, San Antonio, TX, April, 1989.

Rossi, P. H., Freeman, H. E., & Wright, S. R. (1979). *Evaluation: A systematic approach*. Beverly Hills, CA: Sage Publications.

Rowe, H. A. H. (1985) *Problem solving and intelligence*. Hillsdale NJ: Lawrence Erlbaum Associates.

Spector, J. M. (1990). *Designing and developing an advanced instructional design advisor* (AFHRL-TP-90-52). Brooks AFB, TX: Technical Paper for the Training Systems Division of the Air Force Human Resources Laboratory.

Spector, J. M., & Muraida, D. J. (1991a). Automating the design and delivery of computer-based instruction. *Journal of Interactive Instruction, 4*(2), 25–30.

Spector, J. M., & Muraida, D. J. (1991b). Evaluating transaction theory. *Educational Technology, 31*(10), 29–35.

Tennyson, R. D. (1989). Cognitive science update of instructional systems design models. Brooks AFB, TX: Technical presentation for the AIDA project at the Air Force Armstrong Laboratory (AL/HRTC, formerly AFHRL/IDC).

Tennyson, R. D. (1990). Framework specifications document for an instructional systems development expert system. Brooks AFB, TX: Technical presentation for the AIDA project at the Air Force Armstrong Laboratory (AL/HRTC, formerly AFHRL/IDC).

Tennyson, R. D., Elmore, R. L., & Snyder, L. (1991). Advancements in instructional design theory: Contextual module analysis and integrated instructional strategies. Paper presented at the Annual Meeting of the American Educational Research Association, April, 1991, Chicago, IL.

Van Merriënboer, J. J. G., Jelsma, O., & Paas, F. G. W. C. (1991). Training for reflective expertise: A four-component instructional design model for complex cognitive skills. Paper presented at the Annual Meeting of the American Educational Research Association, April, 1991, Chicago, IL.

Implications for R & D

Daniel J. Muraida

As this section clearly demonstrates, the automation of instructional design sorely needs answers to the problems of how to provide useful instructional principles as well as how to make them cognitively accessible and ergonomically appropriate for nonexpert users.

The work on task analysis described in this section is absolutely critical to the success of an automated instructional design system. Without accurate data on the cognitive complexity of tasks that can be readily transformed into user friendly terms, subsequent design and development work will most likely produce ineffective courseware. The major obstacle for researchers in this area will be how to affect the translation between the results of an analysis and the user's frame of reference.

It has become increasingly apparent that visualization techniques will play a major role in the way computers interact with humans in the workplace and in instructional settings (Ripley, 1990). Halff and Friedman point out the highly complex issues that must be resolved if we are to make intelligent use of graphics and scenarios for creating the desired mental models. Both papers cite the need for researchers to couple instructional objectives with the complexity of the associated content and desirable cognitive models. Moreover, they emphasize that domains will often require their own specific cognitive models. This implies the existence of families of domain-based cognitive models for problem solving and troubleshooting (see Halff's chapter in Part II). As yet researchers have not explored the limits of cognitive models across related domains on an extensive basis.

Evaluation is finally becoming recognized for the critical and pervasive role that it plays throughout the lifetime of an instructional system. It is becoming apparent that the development of automated tools for an enterprise as complex as instructional design requires a program of evaluation, beginning with the development of functional specifications, and carrying through to the production and revision of the full-scale system. This program of evaluation may be known by various names (e.g., technology assessment), but its common characteristic is the varied nature of the evaluation processes that it encompasses, from structured judgments (e.g., Delphi), to scenario building, and decision-oriented research (e.g., proof of concept studies; modeling instructional design processes). This arsenal of evaluation processes is tailored to the nature of the problems that characterize each stage of the development process. It remains for the developers of AIDA and similar systems to document the impact of an expanded evaluation role on the quality of the ensuing instructional development systems.

Reference

Ripley, G. D. (1990). DVI—A digital multimedia technology. *Journal of Computing in Higher Education, 1*(2), 74–103.

Conclusion

J. Michael Spector

We have covered a great deal of the labyrinth of automated instructional design issues in this volume. The ostensible motivation for our journey was the Air Force AIDA project. AIDA is aimed at providing automated and intelligent instructional design assistance to subject-matter experts who are responsible for developing computer-based instructional materials but who have had very little formal training in instructional technology or educational psychology. In the course of developing an intelligent aid for these novice instructional designers, we believe that we have encountered the major issues involved in automating instructional design.

The issues that emerged from Part I involved the need to take into account principles of cognitive learning theory in planning computer-based instruction (CBI). Polson has indicated that there is a great deal of overlap in these principles, especially when they are viewed at a very high level. For example, there is general agreement concerning the importance of timely and informative feedback. Polson also indicated that there were some differences, most especially with regard to emphasis. Gagné and Reigeluth were more directly concerned with the instructional designer, while Kintsch and constructivists in general were more directly concerned with the learner. Emphasizing the designer is aimed at improving the sophistication and quality of computer-based instructional materials. Emphasizing the learner is aimed at improving the sophistication and quality of the learner in a computer-based environment. Clearly both concerns are legitimate.

A similar point is made by Wilson & Cole (1992) in their evaluation of nine cognitive teaching programs. They found no common specific design strategies, although they did find general agreement at a high level represented by these six guidelines (Larkin & Chabay, 1989):

1. Make a detailed description of the processes to be acquired.

2. Address all of the knowledge involved in those processes.

3. Provide most of the instruction by way of active work on specific tasks.

4. Provide time and informative feedback.

5. Repeat each knowledge unit several times.

6. Limit attention demands placed on the learner.

Wilson & Cole (1992) accounted for the differences they encountered in terms of the following considerations:

1. Orientation of the material (problem solving vs. skill acquisition).

2. Level of cognitive task analysis (detailed vs. broad).

3. Control over the delivery (learner vs. system).

4. Feedback usage (error-restricted vs. error-driven).

These differences are legitimate in the sense that each has an appropriate use or place in the design and delivery of computer-based instruction. Wilson & Cole (1992) conclude with a plea for a continuation of the dialogue between instructional designers and cognitive psychologists. It should be obvious that the first part of this book makes an important step in that direction. Polson is right to notice the differences in emphases in the learning principles covered in Part I, and she is right in arguing for the legitimacy of both the constructivist and the instructivist views.

In Part II we elaborated several different approaches to the automation of instructional design and noted that other approaches were possible. As indicated in the introduction, there is a range of possibilities concerning the automation of instructional design which includes the following:

A powerful set of multimedia authoring tools;

An on-line help system with implementation examples;

Automated but restricted design frameworks (templates);

Automated and intelligent design frameworks (transactions);

An expert instructional design advisor;

An expert instructional design critic; and

An intelligent tutoring system for instructional design.

We did not present an example of automation at the top end of this scale. The powerful toolset approach is probably best represented by IDE (Pirolli & Russell , 1991) and is not generally targeted for novice instructional designers. As a result, the more interesting issues concerning support for cognitive learning principles are not addressed explicitly by such a system. It should be clear from Part III that we do not believe that enough is known about the details and variability of human learning in computer-based environments to construct an intelligent tutoring system (ITS) for the domain of instructional design. However, the development of an ITS for instructional design as described by Tennyson in Part II remains a worthwhile long-range goal.

In closing, I think it is worth emphasizing the research benefits to be gained by attempts to automate instructional design. The design of effective computer-based instructional materials is a complex process involving interactions between individual learner characteristics, instructional delivery media, the nature of the subject area, the type of specific knowledges and skills being taught, and the strategies and methods used to teach the material. Using computers to enhance education and training can be cost-effective. It can also be quite costly. Examples of highly effective CBI are abundant. However, there are also abundant examples of poorly designed and ineffective CBI. What is needed is a systematic methodology to determine how to optimize new technologies in support of training and education.

Instructional design is part art and part science. There will continue to be a need for creativity in instructional design just as there remains a need for creativity in graphical design in spite of highly automated graphical design settings. Well chosen examples of effective CBI can serve to inspire other creative designs, and advanced multimedia tools and automated libraries of CBI materials can be useful in support of the art of instructional design.

However, the science of instructional design can also be improved by some of the methods presented in Part II. The automated instructional design systems described there can be used to rapidly prototype CBI materials which can then be delivered to students and tested for effectivness. Carefully altering individual aspects of these materials can result in a systematic exploration of the interactions between learner characteristics, media, subject area, knowledge type, and methodology. That exploration is well worth pursuing because it might result in significant improvements in the use of computers in education and training.

This point about the usefulness of computer-based instructional proto-types is made by Glaser & Bassok (1989):

> Progress in an area is often made on the basis of instrumentation that facilitates scientific work, and, at the present time, a significant tool is the design of instructional interventions that operationalize theory in the form of environments, techniques, materials, and equipment that can be carefully studied. These investigations can be testing ground for new theories of learning and instruction that will benefit both the prac-tice of education and the advance of science (p. 662).

Kozma (1991) makes a similar point when he argues that there is much about the mechanisms of learning with media that we do not know, and that "computers provide a unique opportunity to examine learning processes and how these interact with the capabilities of a medium." Going forward with this research and development in automated instructional design will eventually result in much improved learning environments and may teach us a great deal about human learning in general.

References

Glaser, R., & Bassok, M. (1989). Learning theory and the study of instruction. In M. R. Rosenzweig & L. W. Porter (Eds.), *Annual Review of Psychology, 40,* 631–666.

Kozma, R. B. (1991). Learning with media. *Review of Educational Research, 61*(2), 179–212.

Larkin, J. H., & Chabay, R. W. (1989). Research on teaching scientific thinking: Implications for computer-based instruction. In L. B. Resnick & L. E. Klopfer (Eds.), *Toward the thinking curriculum: Current cognitive research.* Chicago, IL: University of Chicago Press.

Pirolli, P., & Russell, D. M. (1991). Instructional design environment: Technology to support design problem solving. *Instructional Science, 19*(2), 121–144.

Wilson, B. W., & Cole, P. (1992). A review of cognitive teaching models. *Educa-tional Technology Research and Development, 39*(4), 47–64.

Appendix

Instructional Design Models & Authoring Activities

Robert D. Tennyson

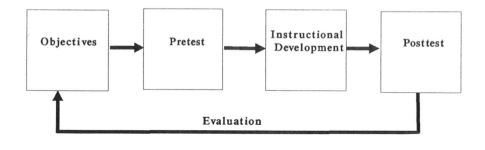

Figure A.1. 1st Generation ISD Model (1960s).

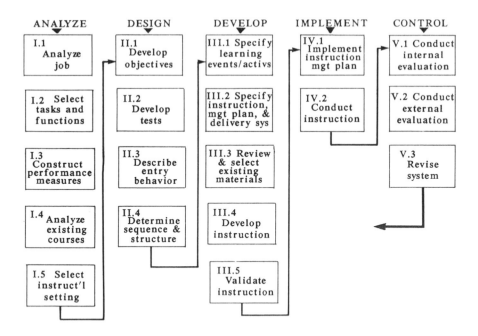

Figure A.2. 2nd Generation ISD Model (1970s).

ASSESSMENT PHASE	DESIGN PHASE	PRODUCTION PHASE	IMPLEMENT'N PHASE
Specifications	Analysis	Produce	Implement
a. Instructional problem b. Learner apt/attitude c. Situational variables d. Instructional objectives	a. Content/beh b. Lrn'r assess't c. Mgt design deliv'y strategies Prototype Development a. Develop't strategy b. Materials preparation	a. Materials & system b. Document'n c. Dissemination	a. Management system b. Instructional system
Feasibility Evaluation: a. Document'n b. Decision - adapt/modify/dev	Formative Evaluation: a. Content review b. Test/seq val c. 1 to 1 tryout d. Sim'd tryout	Summative Evaluation: a. Group compar b. Lrn'r attitude c. Cost effectiveness	Maintenance Evaluation a. Cost-benefits b. Perf/attitude c. Content/behav d. Media review

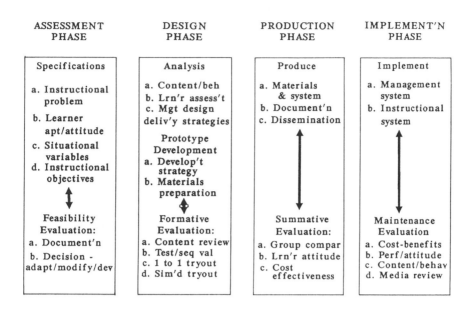

Figure A.3. 3rd Generation ISD Model (1980s).

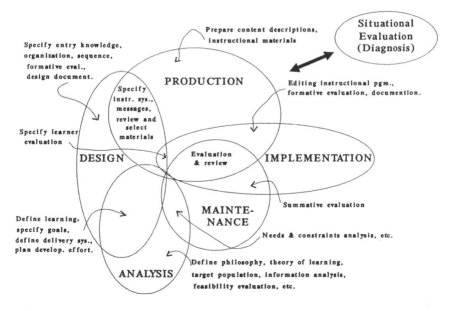

Figure A.4. 4th Generation ISD Model (1990s).

Authoring activities knowledge base for 4th generation ISD Model and ISD expert tutor

Analysis	Authoring Activities
Define philosophy and theory of learning conditions	These conditions influence each step in the ID process. Thus, the generic steps are adjusted to account for the defined
Analyze target population	Determine learner characteristics: geographic location, age, ability, need for motivation, present skill levels, number of students. Determine learner differences: cognitive style, aptitude learning style, personality factors, motivation, perception
Feasibility evaluation	Validate the analysis process

Analysis-Design

Identify specific information to be learned	Define learning variables
Define the learning environment	Establish scope and constraints of the ID process
Specify goals	State abstract descriptions of what knowledge is to be acquired (levels of knowledge—declarative, conceptual, and procedural)
Specify learning objectives	State objectives for learning program, specifying: desired conditions of learning (e.g., verbal information, intellectual skills, cognitive strategies, motor skill, attitudes)

Analysis-Design (continued)	**Authoring Activities**
Define management and delivery system	Establish role of computer in management of the learning environment. Identify basic goals for computer delivery of instruction (and identify other alternative systems; e.g., interactive video)
Define specifications of instruction	Document conditions and specifications of program: length, structure, proportion presented by allowable media, target population description, definition of constraints, goals and information to be covered, levels of program intelligence within management, and instructional system
Plan design and development effort	Consider whether to: buy and use existing materials, modify an existing course, develop a new course, or discontinue development effort. Estimate costs and resource requirements for each alternative
Analysis information (micro)	Knowledge engineering activities: Identify organization of information. Establish knowledge base. Determine schematic structure from knowledge base (referenced to conditions of learning). Determine schematic structure from semantic structure. Determine semantic structure for content attribute characteristics

Analysis-Maintenance	**Authoring Activities**
Analyze learning needs and/or problem	Identify discrepancies between desired and actual learning and performance. Determine consequence of learning and performance discrepancies
Define constraints restricting resolution of learning and performance discrepancies.	Identify the scope of the need/problem (i.e., curriculum, course, module and/or lesson)
Maintenance Evaluation	

Design

Define entry knowledge	Identify and determine learner entry knowledge and behaviors. Determine learner (student) model: Background knowledge, associative knowledge, prerequisite knowledge, prior knowledge
Define organization and sequence of information	Determine sequence of information through: a) course, b) module, c) lesson
Specify formative evaluation system	Outline strategy for validating learning materials
Prepare design document	Document all design decisions to guide development of prototype learning materials

Design-Development

Specify instructional system	State meta-instructional strategy
Specify meta-instructional strategies	Specify use of meta-instructional strategy variables: drill variables, placement of items, display time, label

Design-Development (continued)	Authoring Activities
	definition, context, best examples, expository examples, interrogatory examples, strategy operation, attribute elaboration
Specify mode of interaction	State level of system interaction: program initiative, mixed initiative
Specify screen management	Determine screen layout, positioning, sizing, etc.
Specify presentation modes	select input/output modes: keyboard, positional, speech
Specify computer-based enhancements	Select computer-based enhancements: worked examples, display time, format of examples, amount of information, sequence, embedded refreshment & remediation
Specify methods of management	Design method of management per selected level of intelligence: flowchart, algorithmic, heuristic
Specify message design	Select display characteristics (e.g., graphics, text, color). Design screen layout
Specify human factors	Design: menus, function key prompts, special helps glossaries. Identify hardware configurations
Review/select existing materials	Select portions of existing materials appropriate for inclusion

Design-Development (continued)	**Authoring Activities**
Define situational variables	Identify existing materials, compare them with needs/problem Identify source manuals, subject matter experts, and resource people

Design-Development-Implement

Define conditions of learner assessment/evaluation	Determine the method(s) for assessing and evaluating learner knowledge acquisition (e.g., methods of diagnosis, error detection, error analysis)
Specify learner evaluation system	Determine ontask learning assessment and level of diagnosis (e.g., preventive, overlay, reactive, advisement, coaching) determine use to be made of pretests, progress checks, and posttests. Determine how assessments are to be administered (i.e., by computer or by paper)

Development

Prepare content narratives	Acquire and document subject matter content (i.e., knowledge base and schematic structure)
Prepare learning activity design	Review learning activity designs and associated content for adherence to design and for accuracy and completeness
Develop learning activities	Employ strengths of medium. Implement instructional strategies

Development-Implement	Authoring Activities
Editing of learning program	Establish format and composition requirements. Review all materials for grammar, style and consistency
Formative evaluation	Conduct one-on-one tryout of prototype materials. Revise on the basis of one-on-one result. Conduct simulation tryout. Refine on the basis of simulation test Edit and produce. Perform technical and mechanical review
Documentation	

Design-Implement-Maintenance

Develop assessment instrument	Develop items appropriate for each objective and learning activity. Develop items consistent with designed assessment system
Reviews	Subject matter experts review material for accuracy and completeness. Designers review material to determine whether it meets requirements established in analysis and development phases

Implement

	Reproduce materials. Establish/modify support services. Distribute materials. Deliver instruction. Collect data on learner performance and learner attitude

Implement-Maintenance	Authoring Activities
Summative Evaluation	Analyze data. Distribute report and recommendations. Determine whether to make major revision (go to Analysis) or minor maintenance (go to Maintenance)
Maintenance	
	Perform maintenance on learning activities and test items

Author Index

Subject Index

A

Abstraction attributes, 177

Abstraction sequence for transactions, 182

Abstraction transactions, 47, 184-185

Active learning principle, 171

ACT* Theory: Acquisition of proceduralized skills, 18-19
intelligent tutoring systems based on, 18-19

Advance organizers in learning, 260

Advisement and coaching, need to distinguish, 195

Advisory approaches to automating instructional design
advantages of, 77-78
assumptions of, 78-79
compared with generative approaches, 79-80

Advisory systems
problems with, 78-79
and views of instruction, 79

Affective learning, 51-52
dimensions of, 51

AIDA
See also Automating instructional design
AIDA Executive. *See* AIDA Executive
aims of, 327

analyzing and representing instruction for integrated goals, 154-155

approach used in elaboration, 172-173

automating, 125-128. *See also* Automating instructional design

at CAI 'R' Us, 124-125, 127-128

cognitive learning principles important in development of, 327

content component. *See* Content component of AIDA

content information required by, 135-137

critical issues for, 102-103

design goals, 126, 127

design related to design goals, 126, 127-128

elaboration of, 172-188

evaluating design of, 297-313

evaluation at CAI 'R' Us, 124-125

evaluation component, 98-102, 103, 113, 187-188

evaluation of transaction shells, 313-316

First Generation Instructional Design (ID$_1$). *See* First Generation Instructional Design (ID$_1$)

information component, 174-175.

345